◇　**The African American Heritage of Florida**

◇ *The* **African**

University Press of Florida
Gainesville Tallahassee Tampa Boca Raton Pensacola Orlando Miami Jacksonville

◈

edited by

David R. Colburn

and

Jane L. Landers

American

Heritage of Florida

A Florida Sesquicentennial Book

Copyright 1995 by the Board of Regents of the State of Florida
Printed in the United States of America on acid-free paper

00 99 98 97 96 95 C 6 5 4 3 2 1

00 99 98 97 96 95 P 6 5 4 3 2 1

Library of Congress Cataloging-in-Publication Data
Colburn, David R.
The African American heritage of Florida / David R. Colburn, Jane L.
Landers.
p.   cm.
Includes bibliographical references and index.
ISBN 0-8130-1332-1 (alk. paper)
ISBN 0-8130-1412-3 (pbk.)
1. Afro-Americans — Florida — History.   2. Florida — History.
I. Landers, Jane.   II. Title.
E185.93.F5C65   1995
975.9'00496073 — dc20   94-40977

An earlier version of chapter 3, "African Religious Retentions in Florida," by
Robert L. Hall, was published in *Africanisms in American Culture*, ed. Joseph E.
Holloway (Bloomington: Indiana University Press, 1990); reprinted courtesy of
Indiana University Press. An earlier version of chapter 6, "Blacks and the
Seminole Removal Debate, 1821–1835," by George Klos, was published in
Florida Historical Quarterly 68 (July 1989), 55–78; reprinted by permission. An
earlier version of chapter 12, "Groveland: Florida's Little Scottsboro," by
Steven F. Lawson, David R. Colburn, and Darryl Paulson, was published in
Florida Historical Quarterly 65 (July 1986): 1–26; reprinted by permission.

The University Press of Florida is the scholarly publishing agency for the State
University System of Florida, comprised of Florida A & M University, Florida
Atlantic University, Florida International University, Florida State University,
University of Central Florida, University of Florida, University of North
Florida, University of South Florida, and University of West Florida.

University Press of Florida
15 Northwest 15th Street
Gainesville, FL 32611

For George E. Pozzetta, colleague and friend
1942–1994

◇ Contents

◇ **Acknowledgments**

THE ENJOYABLE PART of completing any book manuscript is the chance to say thank you to the many people who made the experience worthwhile and even enjoyable at times. We owe a special debt of gratitude to Addie Elder, our secretary, who communicated with all the contributors on a regular basis, talked to the special collections managers about photographs, and handled much of the correspondence with the publisher. Throughout she remained her usual personable, optimistic, and cheerful self, never letting us doubt for a moment that the project would be completed on time. When we tired of dealing with this or that aspect of the manuscript, we could count on her to take over the details while we tried to recapture our own commitment to the project.

Our colleagues Jimmie Franklin, George Pozzetta, Bob McMahon, Darrett Rutman, Bert Wyatt-Brown, Kimberly Hanger, and Bob Zieger remained supportive throughout, despite the pressures of their own work. Each seemed to understand the importance of this work and continued to remind us of it as we labored through various stages. We also acknowledge the work done by other scholars and friends in the field of African American history, which helped shape and define our own work, especially Peter Wood, John TePaske, Steven Lawson, William Chafe, Kathleen Deagan, Gwendolyn Hall, Eugene Genovese, Frank Tannebaum, Jacqueline Jones, Joel Williamson, Dan Carter, John Hope Franklin, Colin Palmer, and Daniel Usner.

We were aided throughout this process by the fine staffs at the P. K. Yonge Library of Florida History, especially Elizabeth Alexander and Bruce Chappell; at the Florida State Archives, especially David Coles; and at the St. Augustine Historical Society, especially

Page Jacobsen, Ken Barrett, and Cindy Bears. We received a great deal of help in gathering and reproducing photographs and illustrations from Patrick Payne of the Office of Instructional Resources at the University of Florida, Darcie MacMahon and Max Nickerson at the Florida Museum of Natural History, Robin Lauriault at the Special Collections Office, Library West, University of Florida, and Joan Morris and Jody Norman at the Florida State Photographic Archives. We thank each of them for their considerable assistance.

The University Press of Florida and its very able and talented staff offered us much advice and guidance throughout the process. We particularly thank Director George Bedell, Editor-in-Chief Walda Metcalf, and the editorial staff, especially Deidre Bryan, Alexandra Leader, and Larry Leshan.

Whatever strengths this book has and whatever contributions it makes to enhancing our understanding of the African American past, we owe to all these good people. Any mistakes or problems are probably our fault, although we would be happy to share them with others.

To our families, we thank Jim and Vance and Marion, David Jr., Katherine, and Margaret, who provided encouragement and occasional diversion from the project—which probably delayed the book's final publication but which made the whole process and life generally more worthwhile.

We also owe a special debt of gratitude to our colleagues who contributed essays to this volume. They all have their own book-length projects underway but believed that this project was sufficiently important for them to put those projects on the shelf for the moment. We thank them for their personal commitment to this effort and for their ongoing study of Florida's African American heritage.

We have dedicated this book to our colleague and friend George Pozzetta, who died much too early in life. As editor of *The Florida Historical Quarterly* and through his own work, George encouraged and inspired the study of all aspects of Florida's past and especially the study of the state's racial and ethnic minorities. He would have been delighted to witness the completion of this book and would have been the first to congratulate all its authors. We thank him for his wonderful support and very much miss his congratulations.

David R. Colburn and Jane L. Landers

◇ **1**

Introduction

David Colburn

EW READERS are likely to realize that Africans were among the first nonnative peoples to set foot in Florida. The free black conquistador Juan Garrido arrived with Juan Ponce de León's expedition in 1513, after having served with other Africans in the earlier explorations and the conquest of Hispaniola and Puerto Rico. Africans were, in fact, part of all the Spanish expeditions in Florida, and they helped assure the success of the Spanish settlement established at St. Augustine in 1565. Almost two hundred years later Africans and African Americans developed the first free black town within the present boundaries of the United States, Gracia Real de Santa Teresa de Mose, which stood two miles north of St. Augustine and was for some time the northernmost outpost of the Spanish empire.

African American history in Florida continued to be a rich and diverse one in the post-Spanish era. With the advent of a United States territorial government, and later statehood, and with the growth of plantation agriculture, African Americans experienced a decline in their living conditions and had fewer opportunities for freedom. But they struggled, nonetheless, to negotiate the terms of their labor and the ways in which they conducted their lives. During the Civil War, for example, enslaved Floridians fled bondage and joined Union forces in order to secure freedom of those still enslaved. Despite the restrictions imposed by postwar segregation, black Floridians shaped their own lives and helped develop communities in the new urban centers of Tampa, Jacksonville, and Miami during the late nineteenth and twentieth centuries. While continuing to constitute the main source of labor for the citrus, agricultural, and timber industries, they also entered the new urban service industries in growing numbers. During the 1940s they joined the statewide and national struggle for civil rights against extraordinary obstacles.

For centuries the African American heritage in Florida has been ignored by a white population unwilling to acknowledge that people of color had been instrumental in the creation of this state, that they governed themselves responsibly as free and independent people, and that they contributed in a variety of meaningful ways to the development of Florida and the United States as a whole.

In fact, the history of the African American experience in Florida has only recently begun to be examined, and it will take at least another generation of historical research and writing to bring citizens of the state and students of Florida history to a reasonably full understanding of the African American contribution. The standard textbook on Florida for over twenty years, for example, contains almost no reference to the role played by African American peoples in the development of the state. In the nearly five hundred pages of text in Charlton Tebeau's *History of Florida*, black Floridians appear only occasionally, as slaves and as people whose lives were shaped by white Floridians. Tebeau's recounting offers very little understanding of Florida's African American heritage. In fairness to Tebeau, it should be noted that he depended upon the scholarship of others. As he himself said in the preface, "This book is a synthesis of what we know about Florida's past." Few historians, however, had written about the state's African American heritage or its African American people prior to the revised 1980 edition of Tebeau's study. Indeed, Florida's history as it appeared in earlier textbooks has been a white man's story, portraying black Floridians as little more than a mass of humanity that stood somewhere in the background, contributing principally their physical presence and physical labor.

It was first ethnohistorians and anthropologists, and later historians in the 1960s, who began to recognize African American agency in shaping the history of the Americas and the American South. Still, research on the African American history of Florida has lagged. Scholars of the colonial era and of slavery, like John TePaske and

Peter Wood, have long recognized the importance of Florida and its African American history, and more than twenty years ago they called for studies of the state's early Spanish and British periods. Historians, however, have been slow to undertake this research. Part of their reluctance has been due to the obstacles in consulting the early documents on the African American story and on Florida, which are in Spanish and are held in the Spanish Archives. The other difficulty is that any study of early Florida has to come to terms with its connection to the Spanish Caribbean world and to the colonial South. Florida's early history and especially its African American heritage is closely linked to both. This is at once the appeal and the challenge of Florida's early history.

In fact, throughout its history, Florida's African American heritage has typically differed from that of its southern neighbors, and it is these differences that make the state's past an important area for historical research. The political scientist V. O. Key, Jr., observed in 1949 that Florida was a unique state in his classic study *Southern Politics in State and Nation*, but Florida's differences long preceded the twentieth century. Its linkages to the Spanish and Caribbean worlds as well as to the British and the American South gave it a unique character in the colonial era. In addition, from its earliest years Florida has been a multiracial society of Native Americans, Hispanics, and Africans. The Spanish settlement in St. Augustine incorporated various Native American groups as well as free and enslaved people from several African nations. This multiethnic heritage has attracted the contributors to this volume, who see the opportunity to revisit the arguments of such historians as Frank Tannenbaum, Eugene Genovese, and Peter Wood and to examine the recent work of historians Gwendolyn Hall, Michael Mullin, and Daniel Unser, whose comparative and interdisciplinary scholarship has reshaped our understanding of the early Americas.[1]

In addition to its multiracial cast, Florida offers historians another attraction. Unlike most other sections of the South during the eighteenth and the first half of the nineteenth centuries, Florida had a number of free black communities, including the Mose site and African, African American, and maroon villages in and around present-day Gainesville, Tallahassee, Apalachicola, and Sarasota. Florida served as a haven for African American and African slaves from the

British areas to the north who desperately sought freedom in Spanish Florida and fled there in substantial numbers, despite enormous obstacles. The role of Spanish Florida as a sanctuary for slaves was extraordinarily important for African Americans, but it also greatly concerned the British and Americans, who saw Florida as a major threat to their plantation economies. Even after Florida was ceded to Britain, the Seminoles who offered African Americans a refuge from slavery threatened the aims of white southerners in the United States.

The history of Florida and especially of the African American experience is thus one of considerable complexity and importance. Throughout the two Spanish periods, the British period, and finally the American era, Africans and African Americans adjusted to many political and cultural transitions. In the process, they were both agents of and respondents to change. Despite the dramatic changes experienced by African Americans during this period, there was a surprising amount of continuity in race relations as Florida went from Spanish hands to British hands in 1763, back to the Spanish in 1784, and then to the United States in 1821. As a number of the contributors to this volume note, Spanish racial traditions continued to influence race relations in Florida, in obvious and not so obvious ways, long after the Spaniards departed for the Caribbean and Spain.

For these reasons, Florida provides an important environment in which to examine the policies and cultural practices of different nations and different peoples with respect to race. It raises important questions as scholars try to understand the nature of race relations of the respective nations that occupied and governed the region. To what extent, for example, did Spain's multiracial tolerance differ from that of the British and the Americans? In what ways did African Americans adjust to and restructure their lives and their environment as the governments of Florida changed? How did the Spanish racial policies influence those of the British and the Americans in Florida? In what ways were British and American policies toward their slaves influenced by the presence of Spain and Native American nations on their southern borders?

The uniqueness of Florida's racial traditions continued well beyond its early history, as V. O. Key has argued. During the postbellum period and into the twentieth century, Florida became much more a part of the American South and its racial patterns, but even during the Reconstruction and Jim Crow periods, some Florida cities had a multiracial cast that made their race relations distinct from those of their southern neighbors. Moreover, since World War II, Florida, besides remaining part of the South, has reestablished its ties to the Caribbean world and developed characteristics similar to those of the Sunbelt states that stretch from California to the Florida coast. It is this difference in perspective that has encouraged the contributors to this volume to reexamine the historiographical arguments about urbanization, race, and crime made by such scholars as Edward Ayers, Dan Carter, Arnold Hirsch, Roger Lane, Jacqueline Jones, Howard Rabinowitz, and Joel Williamson.[2]

The Florida story is a record of what might have been in American race relations. It is also the story of human failing, of shifting international and national struggles, of African American agency, of multiracial linkages, and of a series of decisions to oppress a people principally because of their color, even though the historical record demonstrated their capacity for self-government and their desire for freedom for themselves and their children. Florida's racial heritage belongs not only to the past; indeed, it continues to influence our views of one another and to place race and color at the forefront of today's social and political agenda.

The twelve essays in this volume examine the African and African American experience in Florida, from the earliest period of Spanish settlement and the establishment of the free African settlement at Fort Mose to the late twentieth century's racial and multiracial developments in Miami and their impact on African American residents. Along the way, the essays examine the African American heritage and experience through the colonial, revolutionary, antebellum, Reconstruction, post-Reconstruction, and segregation eras. As in all collections of this kind, this volume is not intended to tell the entire story of the African American experience in Florida, nor is it capable of doing so, given the limited scholarly research in several areas. Instead, it is meant to be an introduction, to chart the terrain rather than explore specific themes, and to suggest lines of inquiry that other scholars might pursue in search of further insight into Florida's past and into the African American experience.

Jane Landers begins this collection by examining "Traditions of African American Freedom and Community in Spanish Colonial

Florida." Noting the importance of Frank Tannenbaum's book, *Slave and Citizen, The Negro in the Americas*, in initiating a comparative analysis of slavery, Landers contends that "Spanish Florida allows an alternative test of Tannenbaum's thesis since both Spanish and Anglo planters held slaves in the colony and competing concepts of slavery coexisted."

Relying on records in the Archivo General de Indias in Seville, in Cuba, and in the East Florida Papers, Landers traces black activism from the establishment of the free black town of Gracia Real de Santa Teresa de Mose through the second Spanish period. In the process, she finds that Spanish Florida offered Africans and African Americans greater opportunities for freedom and participation in society, the economy, government, and military service than they enjoyed under the British. The Spaniards, for example, recognized that slaves had a moral and juridical personality as well as certain rights and protections that were not found in other slave systems. She also notes the key role played by "personalism" in Spanish Florida, which linked slave masters to slaves as godparents and which engendered a greater sense of responsibility and accountability for the existence of slaves by owners. The British, by contrast, "restricted free blacks, adopted a slave code based on that of South Carolina, and often subjected slaves to brutal punishments." They also made it difficult for free blacks to obtain any but unskilled work, while the Spanish allowed free black men and women to compete for jobs with whites.

Landers notes that, under the Spanish system, Africans participated in many arenas of economic, political, and military life. Along the way they built extended family networks and a strong community linked by church, economic, and military ties. These social institutions were valued by Spaniards and thus, while they served to enhance African American lives, they also facilitated incorporation into the Spanish community.

Robert Hall's focus in "African Religious Retentions in Florida" centers on two issues: the degree to which African culture survived the slave experience and the question of whether slave religion was, essentially, a docile one or rebellious in nature. Hall, like Melville Herskovits, believes that these issues were not dichotomous but complementary.

Hall argues that it was through the church, in particular, that

Africans became African Americans and that it was the church that enabled them to do so without surrendering their African heritage. Examining the work of historians and anthropologists from Herskovits, Ira Berlin, and Mechal Sobel to Peter Wood, J. Leitch Wright, and William Bascom, Hall carefully documents the persistence of distinctive cultural patterns among Florida's black population up to the late nineteenth century.

Hall characterizes the church as both a sanctuary and a portal for African Americans. It offered an institutional mechanism that sheltered them from the oppression of race and also enabled them to become Americans without losing their cultural identity.

In " 'Yellow Silk Ferret Tied Round Their Wrists,' " Dan Schafer examines the experiences of African Americans in British East Florida in the period from 1764 to 1785. Utilizing the British records on East Florida and the papers of British Governor James Grant, Schafer reassesses Bernard Bailyn's contention that the region's economic development efforts were a failure.

Schafer demonstrates that the British established a successful plantation system in Florida involving rice and indigo, and he examines the lives of African American slaves in this British economic and social enterprise. In his description of relations between whites and slaves and of relations between slaves, he offers new evidence about work experiences, plantation management, ethnic origins of slaves, and the slave trade between Africa and Florida. In finding examples of interethnic jealousies between African-born and American-born slaves, Schafer builds upon the work of Gwendolyn Hall and David Geggus. These tensions among slaves, Schafer believes, help to explain why there was not more violence against plantation owners and their property when only one overseer supervised the activities of many slaves. He also notes, however, that when provoked, slaves resorted to violence on occasion, as when they drowned an overseer for his capricious and heavy-handed mistreatment.

Despite sporadic violence and the loss of many runaway slaves who fled to lands occupied by the Indians, the plantation system in Florida, Schafer argues, was not only large and complex but also functioned very profitably for its British owners. He notes that in only seven years' time, several major plantations had started operating in East Florida. Profitable though it was for the British, the plantation system took a tragic toll on Africans and African Americans, Schafer writes. After enduring enslavement in Africa and the harshness of the British plantation system, their lives were once again uprooted by the vagaries of international politics. As their masters prepared to retrocede Florida to the Spaniards in 1784, some slaves found themselves on a long and convoluted journey from British East Florida to the Caribbean and, in some cases, back to South Carolina.

George Klos assesses the relationships among Seminoles, blacks, and whites in Florida in "Blacks and the Seminole Removal Debate, 1821–1835." According to Klos, the status of blacks among whites and Indians played a crucial role in the efforts of the United States to remove the Seminoles from Florida. As he notes, blacks moved much more freely in the Seminole world than they did elsewhere in the white South, and it was this relationship that concerned whites. They feared, in particular, that blacks who lived with the Seminoles were aiding slaves to flee to the Seminole tribes. Klos states that this was, in fact, happening.

Not all blacks enjoyed equality and freedom in the Seminole community, but even the lowliest of blacks, according to Klos, felt they were better off with the Seminoles than as chattel slaves in plantation Florida. Klos finds that white efforts to remove the Seminoles became quite complicated because blacks often acted as interpreters in negotiations between Seminoles and representatives of the United States, and blacks were anxious to maintain the Seminole presence in Florida as a buffer against the oppression of plantation slavery.

Southern whites, however, were determined to eliminate any variance in slave patterns in the region, and they demanded that military officials force the sale or seizure of black Seminoles and remove the Seminoles from the region. Klos points out that such negotiations were doomed because the Seminoles refused to surrender the black members of their tribe. The demand for racial conformity by southern whites led to one of the longest and costliest Indian wars in American history and one of the most ironic for the United States. Blacks and their Seminole allies opted for war to secure their freedom; white Americans chose war to secure the bonds of slavery.

Larry Rivers's essay, "Troublesome Property: Master-Slave Relations in Florida," examines racial developments during Florida's territorial and early statehood period, from 1821 to 1865. Rivers finds, as Landers and Schafer do in their essays, that the master-slave relationship in Florida was both complicated and steadily evolving. He notes that American planters moved quickly into the north-central area of the region, which extended from north of Gainesville to south of Tallahassee, after it was acquired from Spain in 1821, and they established through their territorial council severe slave codes to secure control over the slaves in the region.

But Rivers observes that these codes provide only a limited, occasionally distorted picture of the master-slave relations that subsequently emerged. By examining the records of the plantations, Rivers finds that there was great flexibility in these relationships. Even when slave owners were inclined to exercise a heavy hand, for example, slaves resisted through feigned illness, work slowdowns, poor performance, violence, and escape.

In analyzing the practices of plantation owners, Rivers finds that they did not necessarily adhere to the slave codes. Many found it wise and profitable to permit slave marriages, to allow for some mobility on weekends, to agree to town visitations and religious services on Sundays, and generally to treat their slaves in a humane fashion. In some cases, the actions of masters were motivated by their own decency, in others by their interest in improving the productivity of their slaves. Whatever the policies of plantation owners, they often found that even those slaves they considered most loyal or those who were closest to the family opted to run away to secure their freedom—to the utter shock and dismay of the owners.

Making extensive use of the records of the Union and Confederate armies as well as personal correspondence, diaries, and newspapers, Dan Schafer reconstructs the experiences of African Americans in the Jacksonville area during the Civil War in "Freedom Was as Close as the River: African Americans and the Civil War in Northeast Florida." Schafer finds that most slaves hesitated to flee slavery in the first year of the war because of the personal risks. But when Union troops arrived in Jacksonville and it was reasonably safe to cross their lines to freedom, slaves abandoned their masters in droves. Plantation owners commented that it was "impossible to keep negroes" on the plantation. Most of the departing slaves, according to Schafer, took their families with them.

Initially, Union forces were not sure how to handle the slaves,

Schafer writes, even returning some to their former owners. But as the war continued, with no end in sight, Union officers saw the wisdom of recruiting African Americans and assigning them to specific military actions. Building on the work of Ira Berlin and James McPherson, Schafer points out that the former slaves responded enthusiastically to the opportunity to participate in military action and to help free others.

Schafer also provides a brief synopsis of the readjustment of the African American soldiers after the war. Supplementing the work of Leon Litwack in *Been in the Storm So Long*, Schafer finds that those who returned to the Jacksonville area "made diverse and individual adjustments to postwar life," ranging from economic pursuits to efforts to enhance family and community life.

Patricia Kenney's essay is an important local study of the establishment and development of a free African American community in LaVilla, Florida, during the post–Civil War period that builds on Schafer's study of Jacksonville during the war years. Entitled "LaVilla, Florida, 1866–1887: Reconstruction Dreams and the Formation of a Black Community," her essay describes the efforts of blacks who had relocated in the Jacksonville area to secure freedom, autonomy, land, and opportunity.

Kenney's study adds to the writings of historians Howard Rabinowitz, Robert Engs, and John Blassingame and their analyses of broad social, economic, and political trends among blacks in the urban South. But it also goes beyond their work by offering a particular examination of the process of black community formation, self-government, job creation, and social organization. Kenney's study also examines the African American experience as it took place in relative isolation from white interference during the immediate post–Civil War period.

Even though they were geographically separated in their own community, and perhaps because of it, black Floridians from LaVilla, Kenney notes, still could not escape the pressures of racism and segregation that mounted in Florida and the rest of the South in the latter part of the nineteenth century. The residents of LaVilla struggled to hold onto their community but found that their economic and financial needs brought them increasingly under the influence of white Jacksonville. With the intrusion of the predominantly white community into their lives, they gradually lost control of their local government and with it their own destiny. Indeed, in many ways, LaVilla was too dangerous an example for whites to allow during the age of segregation, for it demonstrated that blacks had the ability to govern themselves and to shape their own futures.

In "Black Violence in the New South: Patterns of Conflict in Late-Nineteenth-Century Tampa," Jeffrey Adler explores the rising tide of black violence in a southern city and tests the validity there of Roger Lane's hypothesis about northern black violence. Adler points out that Tampa and the South as a whole were generally more violent than northern communities at this time, with rates of violence averaging more than three times those found in the North. He notes significantly that whites in the South used allegations of "mounting black violence" to justify acts of retribution and lynching against blacks.

Were white contentions about black violence, in fact, remotely accurate? In a sophisticated answer that explores the nuances of this question, Adler finds high levels of black violence in Tampa. But he adds that black violence arose out of an environment in which the legal system functioned for whites only, leaving blacks to look elsewhere for equity. To protect themselves against the lawlessness and social conflicts that authorities allowed to take place within their community, blacks bore arms to defend themselves and also occasionally to seek retribution. The results contributed to a significant level of violence in their lives.

In "No Longer Denied: Black Women in Florida, 1920–1950," Maxine Jones brings to light the history of African American women in Florida. Relying on census data and a variety of primary and secondary accounts, Jones reconstructs the daily life of these women, from leaders like Mary McLeod Bethune to those who toiled in virtual anonymity. Until Jones's research, the story of African American women in Florida had been a record buried within the poorly told history of the African American experience. Her essay recounts the activities of these women, their investment in their families, and their role in the development of Florida.

As Jones's study reveals, African American women were central providers in their homes and took jobs in nearly every sector of the Florida economy: from schools to medical care to farming to industry, and to domestic work. Despite the pervasive racism in Florida during this period, they found employment in a variety of unskilled and skilled areas, and they struggled to balance work and family life.

Jones also reveals that a few prominent black women in Florida participated in the emerging civil rights effort to change the racial culture that suppressed opportunities for black men and women. They constituted an important, and generally ignored, element in the black community that took up the banner for freedom and opportunity in the post–World War II era.

In "Under a Double Burden: Florida's Black Feeble-Minded, 1920–1957," Steven Noll examines the impact of the color line on Florida's invisible minority. Throughout most of this period, racism and segregation shaped the state's approach to addressing the needs of the black feeble-minded. Adding to the burden on African American families was the general poverty of Florida for much of the early twentieth century, which made it difficult for state officials to provide for even the most basic needs of its white population. Under such circumstances, Florida policy makers simply refused to provide any facilities or treatment for the black feeble-minded.

Noll utilizes regional, state, and local records to examine both southern area and Florida state policies toward the black feeble-minded and the role of the federal government in care and treatment. He finds that the care provided by southern states for much of this period can be described at best as primitive. Noll observes that the federal government gradually became involved in the supervision of the feeble-minded in the 1930s and slowly expanded its role, until by the 1950s it was establishing minimum standards of care for both races in all southern states. In the process, federal authorities took steps to eliminate segregation in public facilities for the mentally handicapped. When Florida finally constructed facilities for the black feeble-minded in 1953, it did so not to meet the needs of these residents but to avoid being forced to provide integrated facilities for them. Without a facility of any kind for blacks, state officials worried that the federal courts would require them to provide one facility for all.

In "Florida's Little Scottsboro: The Groveland Story," Steven F. Lawson, David Colburn, and Darryl Paulson examine race relations during the period from the end of World War II to the *Brown* decision in 1954, through the prism of an alleged rape of a white woman by four black men. Encouraged by their involvement in the war, black residents in central Florida fought for the removal of segregation barriers in the South. From a voter registration campaign to resistance to resuming low-wage jobs in the citrus groves, black Floridians demonstrated their opposition to the racial customs of the past during this postwar era.

Building upon Dan Carter's work on racial violence in the prewar era, the authors note that whites in the central region of Florida had no intention of allowing the segregation barriers to be removed, and the Groveland rape charge against four black men revealed how far whites were willing to go to keep blacks in their place. The authors write, "With racial barriers under attack throughout the South, whites felt extremely anxious and . . . inclined to preserve their supremacy through violent means if necessary."

Groveland involved the intersection of race and gender in which both traditional racial customs and gender roles were called into question. In contrast to the lynch law of the prewar era, the authors find that the community turned increasingly to the sheriff's department and the courts in the 1940s and 1950s to maintain these artificial standards of the past.

In the Groveland story, the NAACP and the Workers Defense League, a Socialist organization, were involved in the struggle to represent the needs of the black community. In the end, however, no amount of representation could save the accused defendants. Two were killed, one during the course of arrest and the other while being transported by the sheriff to trial. The extraordinary efforts of some whites to suppress the rights of the accused and to prevent a fair trial revealed the extent of their commitment to the region's racial barriers.

Raymond Mohl concludes this series of essays by examining the rise of multiculturalism in the state and its impact on black Floridians in "The Pattern of Race Relations in Miami since the 1920s." Mohl focuses particularly on the relationships among blacks, whites, and Hispanics in Miami from the perspective of its black residents. Despite the city's prominence as an area of settlement for people of color from the Caribbean and Latin America, Mohl finds that multiculturalism has done little to ease the plight of Miami's black population.

At the same time that the community began to accept the civil rights reforms of the 1960s, it became a refugee center for Cubans fleeing Castro. As Cubans settled into the city and sought employment, economic opportunities that would otherwise have gone to black Miamians in the aftermath of the civil rights reforms quickly evaporated as employers showed a preference for Cuban workers. Moreover, as the Cuban immigrants established their own businesses to meet the special needs of their ethnic group, blacks found themselves frozen out of these jobs.

Mohl tells a devastating story of blatant and subtle discrimination that has left the promises of the Civil Rights Act of 1964 unfulfilled in Miami and has raised serious questions about such matters as fairness and equity for black residents of the community. These findings for Miami parallel those of Arnold Hirsch in his study of Chicago. Like Hirsch, Mohl notes that Miami's political leaders often acted in concert with real estate developers to isolate local blacks and to deny them the opportunity to obtain more than menial work.

The Miami experience underscores concerns of black Americans more generally about their continuing place in American society. Despite being one of the first groups to settle in Florida and despite their contribution to the state's development at every stage in its evolution, blacks remain at the bottom of the economic ladder. Bypassed by one of the state's more recent immigrant groups, African Americans understandably see race and color as the sources of their continuing deprivation.

These essays suggest that African Americans are historically correct in their assessment and that Florida has yet to come to terms with its racial heritage, in part because the public remains so ignorant of it. Perhaps these essays will help to inform Floridians more fully about their multiracial past and contribute in a small way to a new age for the state's African American citizens.

Historians often end their books and articles with the words "much research still remains to be done on this subject." This is a subtle way of establishing the importance of their study, justifying their ongoing work on the topic, and encouraging others to join them in enhancing the significance of the topic. Jane Landers and I and the other contributors to this volume believe this statement has particular relevance (and we don't want to be subtle about it) for the study of African American history in Florida. As noted earlier, Florida and its African American story are at once part of the South and part of a larger world. In the seventeenth, eighteenth, and nineteenth centuries, the region stood within the Spanish empire, the antebellum South, and the Caribbean world. In the twentieth century, it stands as part of the South, the Sunbelt, and the sphere of the Caribbean and Central America. The opportunity for comparative study of the African American experience can only be suggested by this volume. As for the complex multiracial aspects of the African American story, remarkably little has been written about the interconnection between blacks and other racial and ethnic groups. And finally, every stage in the African American record in Florida needs further elucidation. Such studies will not only help us understand the African American experience in Florida; indeed, they will also contribute to our knowledge of the larger world of which Florida and its African American population are a significant part.

Notes

1. See Frank Tannenbaum, *Slave and Citizen: The Negro in the Americas* (New York: Vintage Books, 1947); Eugene Genovese, *Roll Jordan Roll: The World the Slaves Made* (New York: Vintage Books, 1976); Peter Wood, *Black Majority: Negroes in Colonial South Carolina from 1670 through the Stono Rebellion* (New York: Norton Press, 1974); Gwendolyn Hall, *Africans in Colonial Louisiana: The Development of Afro-Creole Culture in the Eighteenth Century* (Baton Rouge: Louisiana State University Press, 1992); Michael Mullin, *Africa in America: Slave Acculturation and Resistance in the American South and the British Caribbean, 1736–1831* (Urbana: University of Illinois Press, 1992); and Daniel Unser, *Indians, Settlers, and Slaves in a Frontier Exchange Economy: The Lower Mississippi Valley Before 1783* (Chapel Hill: University of North Carolina Press, 1992).

2. See Edward Ayers, *Vengeance and Justice: Crime and Punishment in the Nineteenth-Century South* (New York: Oxford University Press, 1984); Dan Carter, *Scottsboro: A Tragedy of the American South* (Baton Rouge: Louisiana State University Press, 1969); Jacqueline Jones, *Labor of Love, Labor of Sorrow: Black Women, Work, and the Family from Slavery to the Present* (New York: Basic Books, 1985); Arnold Hirsch, *Making the Second Ghetto: Race and Housing in Chicago, 1940–1960* (Cambridge, England: Cambridge University Press, 1983); Roger Lane, *Roots of Violence in Black Philadelphia,*

1860–1900 (Cambridge, Mass.: Harvard University Press, 1979); Howard N. Rabinowitz, *Race Relations in the Urban South, 1865–1890* (New York: Oxford University Press, 1978); and Joel Williamson, *The Crucible of Race: Black-White Relations in the American South since Emancipation* (New York: Oxford University Press, 1984).

◇ **2**

Traditions of African American Freedom and Community in Spanish Colonial Florida

Jane L. Landers

RANK TANNENBAUM'S important book *Slave and Citizen: The Negro in the Americas* initiated a long historiographic debate about the relative severity of slave systems and the transition from slavery to freedom in the Americas. Many subsequent studies examined these themes in plantation areas, where rapid development of export economies meant deterioration in slave life and reduced opportunities for freedom, and these works clearly demonstrated the flaws in Tannenbaum's analysis.[1] However, to examine the origins of the significant free black class that intrigued Tannenbaum, and to focus on the agency of African Americans in the emancipation process, one must look beyond the plantation. Spanish Florida provides a perfect laboratory to test Tannenbaum's thesis, since both Spanish and Anglo planters held slaves in the colony and competing concepts of slavery coexisted.

Tannenbaum's critics correctly noted that the institutions that he claimed made Spanish slavery less severe — the church and the law — were not commonly accessible to field hands in remote agricultural settlements; this restriction, however, does not mean that his argument was equally flawed for an urban setting or for a plantation system where slaves were able to connect to the economy and institutions of a city such as St. Augustine. Michael Mullin's recent study of slavery in the contemporary British Caribbean demonstrates how geographic context and the organization of labor and the slave market also shaped the institution of slavery. Slavery in Florida exhibited a number of the features that Mullin contends mitigated the oppressive nature of slavery: it was generally organized by the task system, and slaves had free time to engage in their own social and economic activities; slaves were able to utilize the resources of both frontier and coast to advantage; the trade in slaves was never massive, and the paternal model of plantation management prevailed, even on Florida's largest commercial plantation.[2] In addition, the geopolitical pressures exerted by Spain's southeastern and Caribbean rivals gave slaves additional leverage and made the Spanish more dependent upon free people of color. Tannenbaum's contention that a lenient attitude toward manumission was crucial in a slave society, and that it foreshadowed the former slave's role in freedom, is also borne out in Spanish Florida.[3]

As Tannenbaum documented, Spanish law and custom granted the enslaved a moral and juridical personality, as well as certain rights and protections not found in other slave systems. Slaves had a right to personal security, and there were legal mechanisms by which to escape a cruel master. A slave could legally own and transfer property and initiate lawsuits—a significant provision that in the Caribbean evolved into the right of self-purchase. Social and religious values in Spanish society promoted honor, charity, and paternalism toward "miserable classes," a category that included the enslaved. Although legal and social ideals did not always obtain, slaves in Spanish Florida made good on the institutional promises of freedom through creative and persistent individual efforts, aided by community support. The exceptionally rich documentary evidence on African Americans in Florida, demonstrates how, given the proper conditions, the enslaved could actually "work" the system. This is not to suggest that Spain and its colonies were free of racial prejudice; however, acknowledgment of a slave's humanity and rights and a liberal manumission policy made it possible for a significant free black class to exist throughout the Spanish world.[4]

It is not surprising, then, that African-born people, free and slave, played important roles in Florida's Spanish history. Indeed, their history dates to the earliest Spanish explorations of the colony. Several free Africans, including Juan Garrido, accompanied Juan Ponce de León when he "discovered" Florida, and by then they were already veterans of the Spanish conquest of Hispaniola, Puerto Rico, and

African-born explorer Juan Garrido, ca. 1519. The free African Juan Garrido participated in the Indian wars in Hispaniola and Juan Ponce de León's "discovery" of Florida and is shown here accompanying Hernando Cortés on his campaign in Mexico. (Reprinted from Fray Diego Duran's, *Historia de las Indias de Nueva España y yslas de tierra firme.* Courtesy of the Florida State Museum of Natural History.)

Cuba. Other Africans, free and slave, took part in the expeditions of Lucas Vásquez de Ayllón, Pánfilo de Narváez, and Hernando de Soto, and slaves helped Pedro Menéndez de Avilés establish St. Augustine, the oldest European city in what is today the United States.[5]

Florida's race relations and the patterns of African American society in Florida evolved during Spain's first tenure in the province (1565–1763). They were both shaped by complex interethnic relations and international political factors. Like other areas in the Spanish Caribbean, Florida suffered from early and dramatic Indian depopulation and a shortage of European manpower, and this demographic imperative created a demand for black labor, artisan, and military skills. Florida's first slaves came from Spain, but thereafter royal officials and private owners imported slaves from nearby regions of the Caribbean, primarily Cuba. The Crown considered slave labor indispensable in Florida, noting that the work of cutting and sawing wood for fortifications and ships was unceasing, and the entire government subsidy would not have been sufficient had wages to be paid.

The government found many other uses for its royal slaves, such as quarrying coquina from Anastasia Island, making lime, loading and unloading government ships, and rowing government galleys. Private owners of slaves employed them in domestic occupations, as cattlemen and overseers on Florida's vast cattle ranches, and in a myriad of plantation jobs. In times of crisis slaves were also incorporated into militia units and expected to help defend the colony.[6]

The hard and dangerous work demanded of them and various "pests and contagions" kept the slave and free black populations of Florida low through the sixteenth and seventeenth centuries. Population figures are scarce for the early years, but a census of 1600 counted only twenty-seven royal slaves in a non-Indian population of 491 people.[7] By the end of the seventeenth century, however, numbers were up—augmented by imports from Cuba and incoming runaways from Carolina. By 1683 the free black militia boasted a complement of forty-eight men, and numbers of both free and enslaved blacks rose slowly through the early eighteenth century.[8]

During Great Britain's interregnum in Florida (1763–84) the colony's black/white ratio increased dramatically; however, many of the slaves introduced by the English departed with their masters.[9] Hoping to encourage immigration and settlement of its vacant frontier, in 1790 Spain instituted a head rights system. Within a few months three hundred whites had moved into the province bringing with them almost a thousand slaves.[10] Florida censuses from 1784 to 1814 show that the black population was never less than 27 percent of the total throughout these years, and by 1814, blacks represented 57 percent of the total population of Spanish Florida. Free blacks averaged 10 percent of the black population and sometimes approached 20 percent of that population.[11]

By the late eighteenth century, entrepreneurs in Spanish Florida had developed significant plantations with sizeable slave labor forces of fifty to one hundred slaves. These were often diversified operations managed by the task system, sometimes employing black overseers. Some plantations, such as those of Francisco Xavier Sánchez, were devoted to cattle, which required a mobile and fairly autonomous workforce, as did the timbering operations Sánchez and others managed in Spanish Florida.[12] By 1815 a workforce of 250 slaves labored

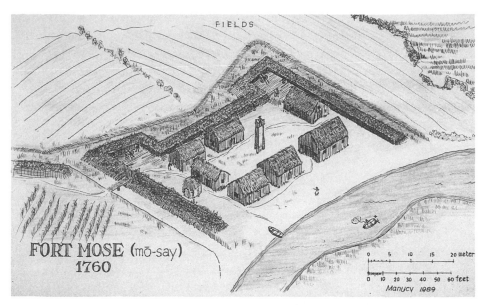

FORT MOSE (mō-say)
1760

Manucy 1989

A modern rendering of Gracia Real de Santa Teresa de Mose in 1760, by Albert Manucy. This village, located about two miles north of St. Augustine, was built by Africans in 1752. Courtesy of the Florida State Museum of Natural History.

in the various Panton Leslie establishments, which included trading stores, agricultural plantations, and cattle ranches.[13]

In most cases, several generations of slave families lived and worked together, and the paternal model of slave management was reinforced by religion, law, and community norms. Slave masters were often linked to their slaves as godparents, further underscoring paternal obligations. Urban slaves also could benefit from the strength of "personalism" and popular understandings of justice and honor in the Spanish community. Slaves used these intangible, but very real, assets to improve their conditions, petitioning the courts when they were ill-treated, not materially provided for as required, or when they wanted to change owners. They also employed these assets to achieve freedom.[14]

Slaves of Spanish masters in Florida became free through a variety of mechanisms including manumission by their owners, *coartación*, or gradual self-purchase, and judicial process.[15] Other enslaved people

St. Christopher's medal discovered at Gracia Real de Santa Teresa de Mose. One of the Africans living at Gracia Real de Santa Teresa de Mose in the eighteenth century made this pewter medallion, which was probably worn on a thong around the neck. St. Christopher is the patron saint of travelers and of Havana, Cuba. Courtesy of the Florida State Museum of Natural History.

adeptly exploited Anglo-Spanish rivalry in the Southeast to achieve freedom. In 1670 English planters challenged Spanish territorial claims to the entire Atlantic seaboard and established a settlement at Charles Town. Shortly thereafter, their slaves began escaping to St. Augustine, claiming they desired baptism in the "True Faith." Rather than return the runaways as English owners demanded, the Spaniards offered them religious sanctuary. A royal decree of 1693 granted "liberty to all . . . the men as well as the women . . . so that by their example and by my liberality . . . others will do the same."[16]

During the next decades more fugitives from Carolina straggled into St. Augustine, and in 1738 the Spanish governor established the runaways in the free black settlement of Gracia Real de Santa Teresa de Mose, about two miles north of St. Augustine. While conditions were harsh on this frontier, the black homesteaders were at least free to farm their own lands, build their own homes and live in them with their families—in short, free to begin the process of community formation. Spaniards commonly administered subject populations through indigenous leaders, as they did at Mose. Florida's governor recognized the group's spokesman and the captain of their militia, Francisco Menéndez, as the "chief" of Mose and referred to the others living at the village as his "subjects."[17] This degree of autonomy and Mose's distance from the Spanish city also served to develop black community identity. The residents of Mose established complex family and fictive kin networks over several generations, and successfully incorporated into the founding group incoming fugitives, Indians from nearby villages, and slaves from St. Augustine. Community and familial ties were further reinforced by a tradition of militia service at Mose.[18]

The freedmen and freedwomen in Spanish Florida represented many different cultures and experiences, but over time they formed a fairly cohesive community. This process was assisted by a variety of mechanisms. Some ex-slaves shared previous work experiences and geographic origins. Others were related by blood or had formed affinal bonds prior to entering Florida. In St. Augustine these bonds were consecrated in the church, and families were also joined in ritual kinship through *compadrazgo*, or godparentage networks. Such networks not only linked families horizontally, but in many cases *compadrazgo* also functioned to link clients vertically to important patrons in the Spanish community. In both cases the fictive kin were linked by mutual obligations, and they shared a pool of resources and talents greater than that enjoyed by individuals in the community.[19] Free blacks testified in each other's behalf, working collectively to seek legal remedies in the courts and to obtain the freedom of their enslaved kin and friends. They also fought together in the free black

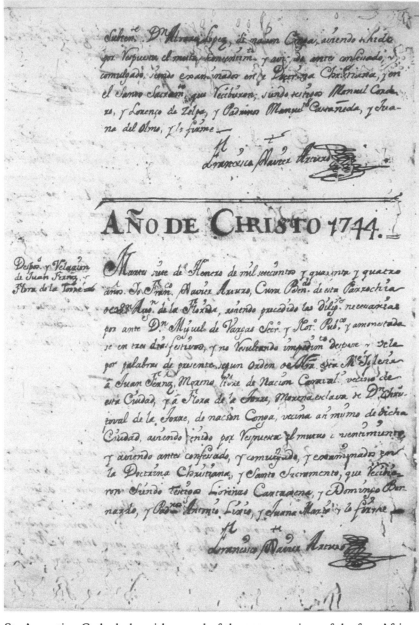

St. Augustine Cathedral parish record of the 1744 marriage of the free African Juan Fernández, of the Carabalí nation, and the enslaved Flora de la Torre, of the Congo nation. Fernández was a resident of Gracia Real de Santa Teresa de Mose, while Flora lived in the home of her owner in St. Augustine. On microfilm at the P.K. Yonge Library of Florida History, University of Florida, Gainesville, Florida. Courtesy of the Florida State Museum of Natural History.

militias and enjoyed certain privileges associated with military corporatism, including exemption from tribute and civil prosecution. The loyalty and effective service of Florida's black militia in defending St. Augustine against British invasions in 1728 and 1740 and against later British-inspired Indian attacks earned them the gratitude of the governors and, perhaps, the Spanish citizenry.[20] However, even their valor was not sufficient to prevent Spain's loss of Florida, for in 1763 the Treaty of Paris awarded Florida to Britain and required Spain to evacuate the province. Spaniards, slaves, free blacks, and allied Indians all boarded ships for Cuba, where the Spanish government resettled the multiracial Floridians.[21]

Under British rule (1763–84), black freedom in Florida became only a remote possibility. Anglo planters established vast indigo, rice, sugar, and sea-island cotton plantations modeled after those in South Carolina and Georgia, and wealthier planters, such as Richard Oswald, imported large numbers of African slaves to work them.[22] Soon blacks were the most numerous element of Florida's population. The American Revolution accelerated that trend, for after the Patriots took Charleston and Savannah, planters shifted whole workforces into East Florida, the last Loyalist haven in North America. The colony's population grew by about 12,000 persons, over half of whom were black, and the black/white ratio was approximately three to one. Although a small number of the blacks were free, for example those who had performed military service for George III, most were not. British Floridians restricted free blacks, adopted a slave code based on that of South Carolina, and often subjected slaves to brutal punishments.

At the conclusion of the American Revolution, Florida was retroceded to Spain, and many slaves took advantage of the chaos of war and the subsequent colonial transfer to escape British control. Untold numbers found sanctuary among the Seminole nation, which had established flourishing villages in the central plains of North Florida. Others, however, claimed a refuge among the incoming Spaniards, and although the Spanish governor doubted the religious motivation of the latter-day supplicants, he was forced to honor the sanctuary policy, which was still in effect. After appearing before notaries to be documented and to show proof of work, at least 251 individuals were manumitted under the sanctuary provisions. Their declarations identify family relationships as well as other linkages that existed when apparently unrelated slaves ran away from the same owner. Some had been on the run together for several years. Some were searching for family members from whom they had been separated. Many reported bad treatment by former owners. These individuals formed the nucleus of the free black community in the second Spanish administration of Florida (1784–1821), and it is possible that having experienced a much more restrictive form of slavery, they were all the more motivated to test the limits of freedom among the Spaniards.[23] By this time the Spaniards had abandoned the peripheral mission-village system that had given rise to the free black settlement at Mose, but despite a more dispersed residential pattern, the free black community in Florida still demonstrated vitality and cohesion, absorbing refugees from the American and Haitian revolutions and adapting to changing economic, social, and political pressures as needed over time.

Prince Witten, his wife, Judy, and their children, Polly and Glasgow, were among those presenting themselves to be manumitted, and their lives demonstrate how exceptional and ambitious persons were able to maximize the benefits of free status in Spanish Florida. Notices from Georgia reported that Prince had run away to Florida "to avoid a separation from his family to which he is much attached."[24] Once Witten and his family were granted sanctuary in Florida, they adapted to the civil, religious, and military expectations of successive Spanish governments and prospered. The family's freedom was dependent upon religious conversion, and the children were baptized within a year of entering the province. Adult baptism required prior religious instruction and usually took somewhat longer to accomplish, but in 1792 Prince and Judy were also baptized. Later Prince and Judy had their marriage of twenty-one years legitimated by the Catholic church and became choice godparents for the black community, free and slave. Prince served as godfather to twenty-three children, and Judy was godmother to thirty-one children, including the child of her slave. When Polly and Glasgow grew older, they, too, were popular godparents.

Witten was a skilled carpenter and hired himself out to a variety of employers. He also earned money by working on government construction projects, and by 1793 he and his family were living between

Petition of the free African, Prince Witten (a.k.a. Juan Bautista Wiet), 1795.
Although unable to write, Witten asked the Spanish governor in St. Augustine
to grant him and other blacks land on the basis of their citizenship. Governor
Quesada granted the request. Courtesy of the Florida State Archives.

prominent white neighbors in the city. In the following year, Judy, a laundress and cook, acquired a female slave. Prince joined the free black militia, defended St. Augustine from attacks by the State of Muskogee from 1800 to 1803, and eventually attained the rank of lieutenant and heroic status during the so-called Patriot rebellion of 1812.[25]

Treasury accounts, census returns, notarized instruments, and civil petitions provide insights into the lives of less notable members of the free black community as well. Antonio Coleman was a skilled tailor who also supported himself by playing the fiddle at dances. Manuel Alzendorf fished for turtles when he was not barbering, and several other free blacks reported that they worked at "whatever presents itself."[26] A variety of economic opportunities existed in this Atlantic port city, and as they had in the first Spanish period, many free black males worked for the government: on fortifications projects, in the royal armory, unloading ships at the wharf, delivering the mails, cutting timber, and as pilots and oarsmen on government boats. Although in some major cities blacks were forbidden to compete with whites in the marketplace, no such restrictions operated in St. Augustine. Free blacks were cartwrights, jewelers, shoemakers, tanners, butchers, and innkeepers, to name but a few of their varied occupations. One entrepreneur, Juan Bautista Collins, had mercantile links to South Carolina, Havana, New Orleans, Pensacola, and the Seminole nation in the heart of Florida. He bought and sold everything from butter to large herds of cattle, acquired property, and like other ambitious free men of color in St. Augustine, observed the Catholic faith and joined the black militia.[27]

Although the lives of women are more difficult to document, records show that free black women in St. Augustine were laundresses or cooks or had small businesses, selling crafts or foodstuffs.[28] Others advanced themselves through unions with, and sometimes marriages to, white men of property. They managed homesteads and even sizable plantations, bought and sold property, including slaves, and entered into business agreements with both black and white townspeople.[29] Miscegenation was a common and accepted feature of life in St. Augustine, and although most white men did not marry the black mothers of their children, they routinely acknowledged their children at baptism and in their wills. Children of interracial unions in St. Augustine often received education, training, or property from their white fathers.[30] Free black parents also left properties, more modest, to their children. They tried to arrange good marriages for their daughters and sought to advance their sons by enrolling them in St. Augustine's parochial school or by apprenticing them to tradesmen.[31]

While their former slaves went about creating new lives for themselves, Georgian slaveowners complained bitterly about the provocation inherent in Florida's sanctuary policy. Finally in 1790, Spain bowed to the protestations of the new U.S. government, delivered forcefully through Secretary of State Thomas Jefferson, and abrogated the policy, but all who had already claimed freedom in Florida remained free.[32]

Enslaved people could no longer utilize Florida's religious sanctuary provision to achieve freedom, but they still had the possibility of purchased or granted freedom. Access to work opportunities and a cash economy were requisites for achieving purchased freedom. Equally important, however, was access to the Spanish legal system, located in St. Augustine. Slaves had to be able to visit St. Augustine to approach the court. Slaves resident on outlying plantations were sometimes brought into the city for baptism or sent on plantation business. Others were assigned to work for certain periods in their owners' town houses. If they could not get to town any other way, some slaves ran away from the plantation to seek legal recourse in St. Augustine. There, the administration of justice was the responsibility of the governor, assisted by a counsel and a notary. The governor's tribunal heard the slaves' memorials when they reported abusive behavior, petitioned to change masters, objected to the terms of their sale, complained about manumissions promised but denied, or when they challenged the price an owner asked for self-purchase or purchase of family members. Specialists assessed the fair market value of slaves petitioning for self-purchase or resale, and in cases involving the manumission of a minor child, a special advocate was assigned to protect the child's interests. Slaves commonly complained to the court that they were denied adequate food, clothing, or access to church, all of which, by Spanish law, the master owed them. Usually these charges preceded a request for the court to establish their value and to permit them to seek new owners. Owners were required to answer the charges before the tribunal, and usually, if the price was satisfactory, they agreed that the slave could, in effect, sell himself or herself to a new owner or buy personal freedom.[33]

Purchased emancipation was not common in St. Augustine, where most of the studied cases involved self-purchase. In five cases, however, husbands bought the freedom of their wives, and five parents bought the freedom of their children. In some cases, persons not acknowledged as relatives paid for a slave's freedom. Average prices for adult slaves were between 200 and 300 pesos and children were usually freed for less than 100 pesos. The average day's pay for a man was a half peso and women commonly earned about half that, if they were lucky enough to have access to the city and paid employment. It would have been an arduous process to save a few hundred pesos, much less what it would have required to free several family members. From 1784 to 1800 only thirty-four requests to purchase freedom were considered by the governor's tribunal, although some cases included more than one individual. However, of the cases reaching the court, in only one case was freedom denied, and slaves were not reluctant to pursue legal avenues, even given the occasional opposition from powerful masters.[34]

The lengthy coartación case of Francisco Phelipe Sánchez, also known as Edimboro, illustrates this point and provides unique insights into the black community of St. Augustine. Edimboro, and his wife, Filis, who were (like Prince) Guinea-born, were the slaves of Francisco Xavier Sánchez, East Florida's wealthiest rancher and the government's meat and timber contractor (and creditor). Edimboro was a valuable asset to the Sánchez operations, for he butchered cattle, harvested timber for sale, and acted as an overseer on the ranch when Sánchez made periodic trips to Havana. At certain times of the year, Sánchez sent Edimboro to St. Augustine, where he was hired out as a butcher and lived unsupervised. Filis was also sent into the city to serve as a laundress at the Sánchez town house. This access to the St. Augustine economy allowed the couple to earn money and begin the process of freeing their family. Edimboro and Filis served Sánchez for almost twenty years before Edimboro petitioned to secure their manumission gratis, in return for saving Sánchez's life.

Although Spanish courts sometimes freed slaves for such acts, Sánchez wanted 250 pesos apiece for the couple. Edimboro found the sum exorbitant, especially after he had just paid forty pesos to purchase the freedom of his infant daughter, and he then argued that, since Sánchez had received all his services for more than twenty years, he had been more than sufficiently reimbursed. In this argument Edimboro employed the concepts of contract, just price, and moral economy in seeking his freedom without paying. His master, however, then exercised his legal right to ask how much money the couple had and how they had obtained it. Edimboro had saved 312 pesos earned since childhood through hunting, fishing, butchering, and doing other odd jobs. Later Filis added to this nest egg by washing clothes and selling baked goods and hand-crafted toys. The couple had also rented the top floor of a home on the main street of St. Augustine to put on dances for the black community, for which Filis provided refreshments, and the party-goers paid admission. Sánchez depicted the dances Edimboro hosted as depraved affairs where "throughout the night the Blacks loudly toasted the courtesy of Don Francisco Sánchez's slave, Edimboro."

Despite Sánchez's wealth and standing in the community, his attempts to defame Edimboro with racial stereotypes and to impede his emancipation were unsuccessful. Edimboro was well known to the people of St. Augustine as a hard and honest worker, and since Sánchez himself had so often entrusted him with responsibility and had never before lodged any complaints against him, Sánchez's last-minute charges did not convince the court. Meanwhile, Edimboro and Filis took steps to improve their position by being baptized in the Catholic church, and shortly thereafter they married. When the court met again, one assessor noted of Edimboro that "his conduct, abilities, love of work and presence recommend him," and although Sánchez argued that Edimboro was worth much more than the quoted 500 pesos, and that he himself had rejected offers of 800 pesos for the slave, the rancher seemed to understand that continued resistance was useless and finally accepted the price. With the down payment of 312 pesos, Edimboro became a *coartado*, and within four months after initiating his suit, he made his final payment to the court. The notary then gave Edimboro a certificate of freedom, "in virtue of which he shall be free, and reputed as free, and can enter into contracts, appear as a witness, and engage in all legal acts which the laws permit free persons." [35]

Like the Wittens, Edimboro and Filis became reputable citizens of the community. They acquired property (and debts), baptized their twelve children in the church, and served repeatedly as godparents and marriage witnesses for other members of the free and slave communities, including slaves who belonged to their former owner, as well as Prince and Judy Witten. One of the couple's sons attended the free school taught by the town priest, and Edimboro and his sons joined the militia. Edimboro reached the rank of sergeant, commanding a unit of fourteen men, including his sons. They were often posted among the Seminoles (perhaps because of the Seminole connections to cattle), and over the years Edimboro and his sons served honorably against a variety of Spain's North American and Native American enemies.[36]

Service against Spain's enemies constituted another avenue to freedom. During the slave revolt in Saint Domingue, thousands of the rebels allied themselves to the Spanish Crown and were organized into a force known as the Black Auxiliaries of Carlos IV. Among its leaders was Jorge Biassou, who commanded an army of 40,000 men and who outranked the famous Toussaint Louverture. When Spain concluded a peace treaty with the Directory of the French Republic, the Black Auxiliaries were disbanded and dispersed to various locations in the Caribbean and Spain.[37] The decorated and well-pensioned Biassou, and his "family" of kin and dependent troops, chose relocation in St. Augustine, where they were absorbed into the polyglot black community.[38]

The Spanish governors were not pleased by the "proud and vain character" and "high temper" Biassou displayed, and they worried about the bad example he and his band might set. Still, they had no choice but to receive him. Biassou and his men were quick to remind Florida's governors and the captain general of Cuba of their service in various campaigns in Hispaniola, of the promises made them by the king, and of their status as his loyal and free vassals.[39] Biassou retained the title of *Caudillo* in St. Augustine, and the governors employed him and his battle-hardened men in guerrilla operations against hostile Indian groups terrorizing the colony from 1800 to 1803.[40]

Despite major differences in language and culture, Biassou's "family" quickly blended into the free black community. Within three months of their arrival in St. Augustine, Biassou's brother-in-law and heir apparent, Jorge Jacobo, married Prince Witten's daughter, María Rafaela (aka Polly), effectively linking the leading families among the North American and Haitian refugee communities. Witnesses at the church ceremony and at the later baptisms of the couple's children included members of both families, along with other members of the black militia.[41]

When Biassou died, his friends and extended family arranged a wake, an elaborate mass, and a church burial with full honors. The governor and other persons of distinction accompanied the cortege to the church graveyard, as did drummers and an honor guard of the black militia.[42] This ceremony was a dramatic display of the military corporatism and the many family and social linkages uniting the disparate free blacks in Spanish St. Augustine. These ties were also evident at other communal events, such as masked balls and parties, militia reviews, parades and commemorative processions, feast day celebrations, church ceremonies such as baptisms and weddings, and even court appearances.

Toward the end of the second regime, Spain's costly European wars and efforts to contain independence movements throughout Spanish America left it financially unable to support Florida adequately. Deteriorating economic conditions in St. Augustine, and the rising prices of slaves, meant that fewer owners were willing to manumit slaves without payment.[43] Nevertheless, the judicial process was effective and might even be regarded as sympathetic to the goal of liberty, and slaves continued to pursue coartación. And despite reduced circumstances, some owners still freed their slaves for good services or reasons of affection until the Spanish left Florida.

When Spain turned over the province to the officials of the U.S. territorial government, it did not abandon its free black citizens. As in Louisiana, cession treaties required that the legal status and property rights of free blacks be respected by the incoming government. Some free blacks, like Edimboro and Prince, who had acquired property and invested years of hard work in improving it, decided to stay in Florida and risk trusting the newcomers to honor their treaty promises. But Prince's daughter, María, joined her husband and most of the free black community in a second exodus to Cuba. Like their predecessors from the 1763 exile, they received government assistance as they remade their lives in Cuba. Finding the racial climate in Florida increasingly restrictive, other free blacks left for Cuba in the following years, and in 1857 another community of free blacks living in Pensacola departed for Mexico.[44]

African Americans who had made their free lives among the Seminoles, rather than among the Spanish, were also at risk from the incoming Americans, who brought with them chattel slavery and a firm conviction of their racial superiority. These new homesteaders had long objected to the free blacks living in Florida, fearing their militancy, their alliance with Native Americans, and the dangerous example they set for plantation slaves. Georgia's governor, David Mitchell, had warned President Monroe that the Spaniards "have armed every able-bodied negro within their power . . . our southern country will soon be in a state of insurrection." Patriot leader John McIntosh echoed these sentiments in his own letter to Monroe, complaining that Florida was a refuge for fugitive slaves and that its emissaries "will be detached to bring about the revolt of the black population of the United States."[45]

In response, Monroe's government had covertly supported a number of hostile actions in direct violation of Spain's territorial sovereignty, including the Patriot War of 1812, a naval attack on the black and Indian fort and settlement at Prospect Bluff on the Apalachicola River in 1815, and Andrew Jackson's devastating raids against Seminole villages along the Suwannee in 1818. The same hostility toward free blacks living among the Seminoles, and the Seminoles' refusal to return their allies and family members to slavery, lay at the heart of the three Seminole wars that took place from 1818 to 1859.[46] As they had since the sixteenth century, Florida's free black communities continued to shape international geopolitics in the Southeast, yet their existence and their impact has been obscured by traditional historiography.

This brief review of the possibilities for freedom and community life for blacks in Spanish Florida demonstrates that African Americans created viable and vibrant free communities when circumstances permitted. The institutional framework in place was sufficient for determined slaves to pursue freedom through legal channels, and Spanish Florida's particular geographic, demographic, economic, and political factors enabled them to do so. Enslaved Africans adeptly manipulated a variety of political contests, as well as the demographic exigencies of the Spaniards in Florida, to secure their freedom in ways not anticipated by older Spanish law or by Tannenbaum. Through their own initiative, Africans expanded the emancipatory potential of Spanish law and reshaped their lives. In effect, they judged Anglo slavery by "voting with their feet" and by risking their lives repeatedly to forestall its advance into Florida, and their political actions seem to confirm at least the basic tenets of Tannenbaum's comparative analysis.

Contemporary ethnohistorical studies such as those of Daniel Usner, Gwendolyn Hall, Kimberly Hanger, and Peter Wood show that Florida is not an anomaly, and that African Americans, free and slave, made pragmatic and astute political decisions based on their understanding of a variety of European and Native American political, economic, and social systems. These works also confirm that African Americans exercised more important and varied roles in the colonial history of the Spanish frontiers of the United States than has previously been appreciated.[47] New archaeological studies such as those of Kathleen Deagan, Theresa Singleton, and Leland Ferguson are also unearthing the lost cultural and material past of African Americans in Florida and the rest of the Southeast, although many of the sites discussed in this essay have yet to be investigated.[48] Together these new, more sensitive inquiries and methodologies tell us that the history of the United States and its race relations is seriously distorted by neglecting the complex and sometimes more empowered past that Africans experienced in Florida and in the colonial Americas.

Notes

1. Frank Tannenbaum, *Slave and Citizen, the Negro in the Americas* (New York: Knopf, 1946; reprint, Boston: Beacon Press, 1992). Eugene D. Genovese, "The Treatment of Slaves in Different Countries: Problems in the Application of the Comparative Method," in *Slavery in the New World: A Reader in Comparative History*, ed. Laura Foner and Eugene D. Genovese, (Englewood Cliffs, N.J.: Prentice-Hall, 1969), 202–10. Rebecca J. Scott, *Slave Emancipation in Cuba: The Transition to Free Labor, 1860–1890* (Princeton: Princeton University Press, 1985).

2. Michael Mullin, *Africa in America: Slave Acculturation and Resistance in*

the American South and the British Caribbean, 1736–1831 (Urbana: University of Illinois Press, 1992). Jane Landers, *African Society in Spanish St. Augustine* (Urbana: University of Illinois Press, forthcoming).

3. Landers, ibid. Gwendolyn Hall finds the same dependence in Spanish Louisiana in her *Africans in Colonial Louisiana, The Development of Afro-Creole Culture in the Eighteenth Century* (Baton Rouge: Louisiana State University Press, 1992), 242.

4. In addition to Hall's work (n. 3), other works that discuss free blacks in the Hispanic world include Kimberly Hanger, *Personas de varias clases y colores: Free People of Color in Spanish New Orleans, 1769–1803* (Durham: Duke University Press, forthcoming), and David W. Cohen and Jack P. Greene, *Neither Slave Nor Free: The Freedmen of African Descent in the Slave Societies of the New World* (Baltimore: Johns Hopkins University Press, 1972).

5. Jane Landers, "Africans in the Land of Ayllón: The Exploration and Settlement of the Southeast," in *Columbus and the Land of Ayllón*, ed. Jeannine Cook (Darien, Ga.: Lower Altamaha Historical Society, 1992), 105–23.

6. The king to Captain General Sancho de Alquía, April 9, 1618, Santo Domingo 225 (hereinafter cited as SD), Archivo General de Indias, Seville (hereinafter cited as AGI); Fernando Miranda to the king, August 20, 1583, cited in Verne E. Chatelain, *The Defenses of Spanish Florida, 1565–1763* (Washington, D.C.: Carnegie Institute, 1941), 138; Landers, *African Society*. A free black militia operated in Spanish Florida as early as 1683, and individual blacks were incorporated into primarily white units even before that time. Roster of Free Black and Mulatto Militia for St. Augustine, September 20, 1683, SD 266, AGI. Both Hall and Hanger find that blacks filled similar military roles in Spanish Louisiana.

7. In 1581 the royal treasurer noted the arrival from Havana of twenty-three men and seven women slaves, destined for work on St. Augustine's great stone fort, the Castillo de San Marcos. Report of Juan de Cevadilla, Jan. 22, 1581. SD 229, AGI. Census of July 1600, SD 231, AGI. The number of privately owned slaves is not given, nor is a figure for free persons of African descent.

8. Roster of the Free Pardo and Moreno Militia of St. Augustine, September 20, 1683. SD 226, AGI. For a comprehensive look at the demographics of the triracial South, see Peter H. Wood, "The Changing Population of the Eighteenth-Century South: An Overview, by Race and Subregion, from 1685–1790," in *Powhatan's Mantle: Indians in the Colonial Southeast*, ed. Peter H. Wood and Gregory A. Waselkov (Lincoln: University of Nebraska Press, 1988).

9. J. Leitch Wright, "Blacks in British East Florida," in *Florida Historical Quarterly* 54 (April 1976): 427–41.

10. Carlos Howard to Luis de Las Casas, July 1, 1791, Cuba 1439, AGI.

11. For 1784, the figures are 574 blacks, with no figures being given for free persons, and 1,418 whites. Report of Vicente Manuel de Zéspedes, October 20, 1784, SD 2587, AGI. For 1814, the figures are 1,302 whites and 1,773 blacks, of whom 122 were free. Report of Sebastian Kindelan, October 5, 1814, microfilm reel 76, East Florida Papers (hereinafter cited as EFP), P. K. Yonge Library of Florida History, University of Florida, Gainesville, (hereinafter cited as PKY). In 1797 there were 1007 whites, 483 slaves, and 102 free blacks counted in St. Augustine. For remaining years see Census Returns 1784–1814, on microfilm reel 148, EFP, PKY, and Jane Landers, *African Society* (forthcoming).

12. Jane Landers, "Francisco Xavier Sánchez, Floridano Planter," in *Spanish Pathways in Florida, 1492–1992*, ed. Ann L. Henderson and Gary R. Mormino (Sarasota: Pineapple Press, 1991), 168–87.

13. Census Returns 1784–1814, microfilm reel 148, EFP, PKY; List of Property at the San Pablo Plantation, Feb. 8, 1815, Cuba 417, AGI.

14. Amy Bushnell, *The King's Coffer: Proprietors of the Spanish Florida Treasury, 1565–1702* (Gainesville: University Presses of Florida, 1981), 21–23. Jane Landers, *African Society*.

15. Hubert H. S. Aimes, "Coartación: A Spanish Institution for the Advancement of Slaves into Freedmen," *Yale Review* (February 1909): 412–31.

16. Royal Edict, November 7, 1693, SD 58-1-2/74 in the John B. Stetson Collection, PKY.

17. The establishment of Mose and the various petitions of the Carolina fugitives gathered for review by Governor Manuel de Montiano are described in SD 844, fols. 521–46, microfilm reel 15, PKY.

18. Jane Landers, "Gracia Real de Santa Teresa de Mose: A Free Black Town in Spanish Colonial Florida," *American Historical Review* 95 (February 1990): 9–30.

19. Stephanie Blank, "Patrons, Clients, and Kin in Seventeenth-Century Caracas: A Methodological Essay in Colonial Spanish American Social History," *Hispanic American Historical Review*, 54 (May 1974): 260–82; George M. Foster, "*Cofradía* and *Compadrazgo* in Spain and Spanish America," *Southwestern Journal of Anthropology* 9 (1953): 1–28; Sidney W. Mintz and Eric Wolf, "An Analysis of Ritual Co Parenthood (Compadrazgo)," *Southwestern Journal of Anthropology* 6 (1950): 341–367

20. John Jay TePaske, *The Governorship of Spanish Florida, 1700–1763* (Durham: Duke University Press, 1964), 130–58.

21. Evacuation Report of Juan Joseph Elixio de la Puente, January 22 1764, SD 2595, AGI. For a full account of the diplomatic history see Robert L. Gold, *Borderland Empires in Transition: The Triple-Nation Transfer of Florida* (Carbondale: Southern Illinois University Press, 1969).

22. Richard Oswald and his partner, Henry Laurens, imported hundreds

of Africans from their operation on Bance Island, a major slave shipping center in the middle of the Sierra Leone River. See Daniel L. Schafer, " 'Yellow Silk Ferret Tied Round Their Wrists': African Americans in British East Florida, 1763-1784," this volume.

23. Census Returns, 1784-1821, on microfilm reel 148, EFP, PKY. Jane Landers, "Spanish Sanctuary: Fugitive Slaves in Florida, 1687-1790," *Florida Historical Quarterly* 62 (September 1984): 296-313.

24. Letter of Alexander Semple, December 16, 1786, "To and From the United States, 1784-1821," microfilm reel 41, EFP, PKY. According to this letter, Prince had attempted to escape twice before.

25. For information on Prince's escape and occupational contracts, see Census Returns, 1784-1821, on microfilm reel 148, EFP, PKY. For the baptisms of Polly and Glasgow, see Cathedral Parish Records (hereafter CPR), Diocese of St. Augustine Center, Jacksonville, Florida, microfilm reel 284J, fol. 41, PKY. For the baptisms of Prince and Judy, see CPR, microfilm reel 284J, fol. 118. The multiple baptisms at which the Witten family members served as godparents are also in CPR, on microfilm reel 284J, PKY. The household appears in the city census of 1793 on microfilm reel 148, EFP, PKY. Prince's various military appointments appear in Cuba 357, AGI. In 1812 he commanded a guerrilla ambush of U.S. Marines and lifted the siege of St. Augustine. J. H. Alexander, "The Ambush of Captain John Williams, U.S.M.C.: Failure of the East Florida Invasion," *Florida Historical Quarterly* 56 (July 1977): 286-96.

26. Civil Proceedings, 1785-1821, Petition of Antonio Coleman, January 9, 1794, on microfilm reel 152, EFP, PKY; Papers on Negro Titles and Runaways, Testimonies of Manuel Alzendorf and Juan Baptista, August 8, 1799, on microfilm reel 167, EFP, PKY.

27. Notarized Instruments, Suits brought by Juan Bautista Collins against Job Wiggins, March 22, 1798; Margarita Ryan, May 9, 1799; and Don José Antonio Yguiniz, January 16, 1810, on microfilm reels 166-167, EFP, PKY. Memorials of Juan Bautista Collins, December 11, 1792, and November 29, 1793, microfilm reel 78, EFP, PKY. "The Panton Leslie Papers, Letters of Edmund Doyle to John Innerarity," *Florida Historical Quarterly* 17 (1938): 54.

28. Census Returns, 1784-1814, microfilm reel 148, EFP, PKY.

29. Black Marriages, microfilm reel 284L, CPR, PKY. Nansi Wiggins inherited hundreds of acres of land and a plantation from Job Wiggins, the white planter who was her common-law husband. She appears frequently in court cases and contested property deals, including a case in which she opposed her slave's attempts at self-purchase. *Jorge Sanco vs. Nansi Wiggins*, Civil Proceedings, June 4, 1810, microfilm reel 160, EFP, PKY.

30. For instance, Don Thomas Tunno freed his slave Cecilia, and her

young daughters, Cecilia Francisca, age three, and Catalina Joaquina, age one, without acknowledging that he was the father of the children; however, he is stated to be their father in their baptismal records. Baptisms of Cecilia Francisca Tunno and Catalina Joaquina Tunno, August 2, 1786, Black Baptisms, CPR, microfilm reel 284J, PKY. Job Wiggins did the same for the children of Nansi Wiggins. Although their father died intestate, the legitimate white heirs of Francisco Xavier Sánchez upheld the inheritance of their mulatto half-sisters and -brothers. Testamentary Proceedings, F. X. Sánchez, 1807, no. 1, fols. 169–71, EFP, PKY. Both Hanger and Hall document the same patterns for Spanish Louisiana; Hanger, *Personas de varias clases*, and Hall, *Africans in Colonial Louisiana*, 256–57.

31. Rules and Instructions to be Observed for the Governance and Direction of Schools, 1786, SD 2588, AGI; Roster of School Boys, March 25, 1796, SD 2531, AGI; Notarized Instruments, vol. 2, Apprenticeship of Nicolás Mañe, microfilm reel 168, EFP, PKY; Apprenticeship of Andres Bacus, May 8, 1801, microfilm reel 167, EFP, PKY.

32. Governor Juan Nepomuceno de Quesada to Leonard Marbury, August 23, 1790, To and From the United States, microfilm reel 41, EFP, PKY. Thomas Jefferson to Quesada, March 10, 1791, ibid.

33. Notarized Instruments 1785–1800, microfilm reels 169–70, and Civil Proceedings, microfilm reels 152–69, EFP, PKY.

34. Rebecca J. Scott has shown that by the late nineteenth century, the utility of coartación in Cuba was limited both by distance from the courts and by rising slave prices, and that coartados represented only a small proportion of slaves. Nevertheless, she agrees that the institution was important in developing Cuba's large free black population. Scott, *Slave Emancipation in Cuba*, 13–14; Notarized Instruments, 1785–1800, microfilm reels 169–70, EFP, PKY. Gwendolyn Hall's findings on the nature and number of emancipations in a contemporary frontier region of Spanish Louisiana are remarkably similar. Despite spotty records, she finds that a minimum of seventy-eight slaves were freed from 1763 to 1803. That rate is slightly surpassed in Florida. Hall, *Africans in Colonial Louisiana*, 266–67.

35. Civil Proceedings, petition of Felipe Edimboro, July 6, 1794, microfilm reel 152, EFP, PKY. Baptisms of Joseph Phelipe Sánchez, aka Edimboro, and of Maria Felicia Sánchez, aka Filis, July 15, 1794, CPR, microfilm reel 284J, PKY; Marriage of Edimboro and Filis, July 29, 1794, CPR, microfilm reel 284L, PKY.

36. Report of Fernando de la Puente, August 19, 1809, microfilm reel 68, EFP, PKY; Review lists for the Free Black Militia of St. Augustine, 1802 and 1812, Cuba 357, AGI; Reviews of Garrison, 1807 and 1809, microfilm reel 68, EFP, PKY.

37. C. L. R. James, *The Black Jacobins—Toussaint L'Ouverture and the San Domingo Revolution*, 2d ed., rev. (London: Allison and Busby, 1992), 93, 106; Captain General Joaquin García to the Duque de la Alcudia, February 18, 1794, Estado 14, doc. 85, AGI; Captain General Luis de las Casas to the Duque de la Alcudia, January 18, 1796, Estado V-A, doc. 24, AGI. Jane Landers, "The French Revolution on Spain's Northern Colonial Frontier: Rebellion and Royalism in Spanish Florida," in *The French Revolution and the Greater Caribbean*, ed. David Barry Gaspar and David Geggus (Bloomington: Indiana University Press, forthcoming.)

38. Jane Landers, "An Examination of Racial Conflict and Cooperation in Spanish St. Augustine: The Career of Jorge Biassou, Black Caudillo," *El Escribano* 25 (December 1988): 85–100.

39. Governor Juan Nepomuceno de Quesada to Captain General Luis de las Casas, January 25, 1796, and March 5, 1796, Cuba 1439, AGI.

40. Council of War, June 30, 1800, and Orders for General Biassou, 1801, microfilm reel 55, EFP, PKY; Council of War, January 29, 1802, Cuba 357, AGI.

41. Marriage of Jorge Jacobo and María Rafaela Kenty (aka Polly), April 12, 1796, CPR, microfilm reel 284L, PKY. Witnesses at the marriage included Biassou's wife and Jorge Jacobo's sister, Romana, and María Rafaela's brother, Francisco (aka Glasgow). Black Baptisms, CPR, microfilm reel 284L, PKY.

42. Black Deaths, Burial of Jorge Biassou, July 4, 1801, microfilm reel 284L, CPR, PKY; Testamentary Proceedings of Jorge Biassou, microfilm reel 138, EFP, PKY.

43. Jane Landers, *African Society*, forthcoming.

44. Relation of the Florida Exiles, August 22, 1821, Cuba 357, AGI. Ruth B. Barr and Modeste Hargis, "The Voluntary Exile of Free Negroes of Pensacola," *Florida Historical Quarterly* 17 (July 1938): 3–14.

45. Kenneth Wiggins Porter, *The Negro on the American Frontier* (New York: Arno Press, 1971), 186–94. J. H. Alexander, "The Ambush of Captain John Williams, U.S.M.C.: Failure of the East Florida Invasion," *Florida Historical Quarterly* 56 (July 1977): 286.

46. Rembert W. Patrick, *Florida Fiasco: Rampant Rebels on the Georgia-Florida Border, 1810–1815* (Athens: University of Georgia Press, 1954); James Covington, "The Negro Fort," *Gulf Coast Historical Review* 5 (Spring 1990): 72–91; Canter Brown, "The 'Sarrazota, or Runaway Negro Plantations': Tampa Bay's First Black Community, 1812-1821," *Tampa Bay History* 12 (Fall/Winter 1990): 5–19; Virginia Bergman Peters, *The Florida Wars* (Hamden, Conn.: Archon Books, 1979).

47. Hall, *Africans in Colonial Louisiana*; Daniel H. Usner, Jr., *Indians,*

Settlers, and Slaves in a Frontier Exchange Economy: The Lower Mississippi Valley Before 1783 (Chapel Hill: University of North Carolina Press, 1992); Peter W. Wood, *Black Majority: Negroes in Colonial South Carolina from 1670 through the Stono Rebellion* (New York: Norton Press, 1974); Hanger, *Personas de varias clases*, forthcoming.

48. Kathleen A. Deagan and Jane Landers, "Excavating Fort Mose: A Free Black Town in Spanish Florida," in *"I, Too, Am America": Studies in African American Archaeology*, ed. Theresa A. Singleton (Charlottesville: University Press of Virginia, forthcoming); Leland Ferguson, *Uncommon Ground: Archaeology and Early African America, 1650–1800* (Washington, D.C.: Smithsonian Institution Press, 1992).

3

African Religious Retentions in Florida

Robert L. Hall

KNOTTY ISSUES in African American culture and religion are raised by an examination of the religious experiences of blacks living in Florida from the founding of St. Augustine in 1565 through the early twentieth century. This essay addresses the cultural distinctiveness of African Americans by placing spirit possession and ritual ecstatic dance at the heart of the controversy over African cultural survivals in the United States.

Because the cultural transformation of African Americans is best viewed as a dynamic process that occurred over a long period, a consideration of the eighteenth century is critical to an understanding of the relevance of African cultures to American culture. The bulk of the essay, however, describes African survivals in nineteenth-century Florida. Although ritual scarification, naming practices, magical beliefs, and material culture are mentioned, emphasis is on religion as the matrix of nineteenth-century African American life and the centerpiece of African cultural influences in Florida.

Revisiting a Controversy

In discussions of African American religious life, two troublesome and interlocking concerns usually emerge. First is the question of the degree to which African culture survived in slave communities. Second, and closely linked, is the question of whether slave religion was essentially docile or basically rebellious. Too often, as David E. Stannard observed, historians have confronted these issues with a "sharply dichotomous approach": a given element of antebellum or postbellum black American culture either is or is not considered African.[1] Such an approach creates several problems. The assumption that a particular aspect of black culture can be neatly pigeonholed as either African or European in origin obscures a fundamental similarity in the general pattern of the cultures of Africa and Europe that anthropologist William Bascom believed "justifies the concept of an Old World Area which includes both Europe and Africa."[2] This approach also obscures the cultural blending process that Melville J. Herskovits illuminated.[3]

One unconquered problem of the African survivals theory advanced by Herskovits is identifying, as precisely as possible, the cultural and geographical core areas in Africa that are relevant to the particular local New World black populations being studied. That is where earlier theorists went astray or were stymied by the truncated state of African historical studies in the United States at the time they were working. A significant part of the problem derives from imprecise or shifting labeling of the coastal and geographical areas from which the African ancestors of U.S. blacks came. Some writers and speakers who say that the African ancestors of black Americans came from "West Africa" mean the entire Atlantic coast, from the Senegal River to Angola. Others use the same term but then proceed to cite ethnographic examples only from the area between the Senegal River and the Cameroons, omitting Kongo-Angola almost entirely, as did George P. Rawick.[4] But recent research has shown that Angola and the Kongo are relevant to studying retentions, not only in the Caribbean and Brazil but also in the southern United States. Robert Farris Thompson, citing linguistic and artistic evidence, raised serious questions about the primacy of Dahomean and Yoruba groups in the New World and suggested that the Kongolese and Angolan influences were scarcely less important in either South America or the United States.[5] As Bennetta Jules-Rosette suggested, "Many of the ambiguities concerning African musical retentions may be clarified when the Central African cultural complex [as distinguished from the narrowest definition of West Africa] is viewed as a source for Black American expressive form."[6] Linguistic evidence and data summarizing the origins of African newcomers to the lower South during the middle of the eighteenth century suggest that Central

African Bantu influences were more prominent in the coastal zones of Florida, Georgia, and South Carolina than heretofore recognized.[7]

The study of African American religious practices and magical beliefs is central to the controversy over African cultural retentions. In *The Myth of the Negro Past,* Herskovits wrote that "African religious practices and magical beliefs are everywhere to be found in some measure as recognizable survivals, and are in every region more numerous than survivals in other realms of culture," such as material aspects of life or political orientation.[8] In Herskovits's scheme of things, then, if one cannot find African survivals or influences in African American religious practices and magical beliefs, one cannot find them anywhere. Although subsequent research by historical archaeologists has forced reconsideration of Herskovits's statement that "Africanisms in material aspects of culture are almost lacking," it remains accurate to say that religion constitutes the centerpiece of his tapestry of African survivals.

The Eighteenth Century

As Mechal Sobel indicated, "It seems likely that during the eighteenth century large enclaves of several tribal peoples existed from Maryland south, although among each group many languages were spoken."[9] Eighteenth-century planters in the lower South had clear ethnic preferences among African groups and appear to have attached greater importance to origins than did their counterparts in the Chesapeake area.[10] Ira Berlin argued persuasively that during the seventeenth and eighteenth centuries three distinctive slave systems evolved in North America: the northern nonplantation system, the Chesapeake Bay system, and the Carolina and Georgia lowcountry plantation system. According to Berlin, "The mass of black people, however, remained physically separated and psychologically estranged from the Anglo-American world and culturally closer to Africa than any other blacks on continental North America." Lowcountry blacks, Berlin argued,

> incorporated more of West African culture—as reflected in their language, religion, work patterns, and much else—into their new lives than did other black Americans. Throughout the eighteenth century and into the nineteenth century, low country

blacks continued to work the land, name their children, and communicate through word and song in a manner that openly combined African traditions with the circumstances of plantation life.[11]

The experience of blacks in Florida during the colonial period was closer to Berlin's Carolina and Georgia low-country slave system than to the two other systems. Indeed, well into the nineteenth century several Florida slaveholders perceived a particular style of speech among slaves as "low country." It was said that Primus, a runaway from Conecuh County, Alabama, "speaks after the manner peculiar to most negroes raised in the low country."[12] Jacob, who escaped from E. T. Jankes in Florida in 1841, spoke "thick like an African negro."[13] And John, a stout, dark-complexioned man who ran away from Gadsden County, Florida, in 1852, was described as "slow and low country spoken, having been raised in East Florida."[14]

The evidence provided by language and naming practices strongly supports Sobel's notion that "several African languages may well have survived the initial slave trade into the Americas."[15] The "Nine New Negro Men" from the Gold Coast who were advertised for sale near Savannah in 1764 surely spoke their mother tongues.[16] Over one-fourth of the advertisements for runaways printed in the *Georgia Gazette* during 1765 indicated that the fugitives in question spoke no English.[17] Since more than 40 percent of the African slaves who arrived in the British colonies of North America between 1770 and 1775 arrived in South Carolina, the Carolina experience has direct relevance to the history of blacks living in Florida during the eighteenth century. Black fugitives from South Carolina and later Georgia established a maroon tradition in Florida that persisted well into the nineteenth century.[18] Other fugitives from colonial South Carolina sought and received asylum, nominal freedom, and Catholic religious instruction near St. Augustine during the first period of Spanish rule.[19] Fugitive blacks from the Carolinas and Georgia had been finding refuge in Florida since the late 1600s because, as John D. Milligan pointed out, the area's semitropical climate, sparse white settlement, and chronic political instability made it an ideal haven for runaway slaves.[20] Asserting the particularly aggressive character of the Florida maroon, Milligan concluded: "Quite clearly, if in the first place newly imported Africans had been encouraged by a propitious environment to found the maroon and to mold its activist character, once they had established the tradition, American-born fugitives took advantage of that same environment to continue the maroon." [21]

The peak of the colonial import trade in slaves was probably reached between 1764 and 1773, a period that overlaps nine of the twenty-one years of British occupation of Florida. More narrowly, more than 8,000 black newcomers were landed in Charleston alone between November 1, 1772, and September 27, 1773.[22] Thus the most recently purchased among the slaves brought to Florida by refugee Loyalists during the American Revolution were likely to have come directly from Africa. By 1767 Richard Oswald had more than one hundred blacks on his East Florida plantation, many of them shipped directly from Africa. Probably most of the Africans were secured through Charleston slave traders such as Henry Laurens.[23] It was in 1767 that the first cargo of seventy slaves arrived from Africa in British East Florida.[24] In the same year Governor James Grant estimated that six hundred slaves were working in the province.[25] Thus, even in the unlikely event that none of the remaining 530 slaves was born in Africa, no fewer than 11.7 percent of the blacks in East Florida in 1767 were shipped directly from Africa. Between 1764 and 1772 two ships from Africa arrived at St. Augustine (one in 1769 and the other in 1770).[26] Then on the night of November 18, 1773, the *Dover*, with one hundred Africans aboard, wrecked near New Smyrna, losing two mariners and about eighty of the Africans.[27] We also know that at least a few slaves residing in Pensacola in the 1760s and 1770s spoke African languages. A fugitive escaping Pensacola early in 1770 was described by his master as speaking African and Indian languages but no English.[28]

The persistence of African naming practices during the era of British control of East Florida (1763–84) underscores the probability that African religious patterns exerted continuing influence among St. Augustine's black population. J. Leitch Wright, Jr., discovered the names of fifty East Florida blacks from the British era, roughly half of whom were clearly of African origin, including Qua, who was publicly executed for robbery in St. Augustine in 1777. Qua was a popular West African day-name (Akan group), meaning male child born on Thursday.[29] Even as late as 1840 an occasional Ashanti day-name appears in advertisements for runaway slaves, including another Qua, who had "one front tooth a little shorter than the others."[30]

When the government of East Florida was transferred back to the Spanish in 1784, 450 whites shifted their allegiance to the new Spanish government and remained in the colony. Remaining with them were two hundred blacks, the surviving nucleus of an East Florida black population that may have numbered more than 9,000 at the peak of the Loyalist refugee period. The immediate geographical and cultural roots for most of them were in the English-speaking colonies of Georgia and South Carolina, especially the coastal region stretching from Cape Fear to Cumberland Sound. They partook of the Creole cultures developed during the eighteenth century in those regions.

Evidence of the persistence of African naming practices during the second Spanish period is contained in a 1792 inventory of the estate of Dona Maria Evans, an Anglo-American who had migrated to Florida from South Carolina in 1763. The inventory lists a total of twenty blacks, organized into three nuclear family units of four, six, and two members, respectively, and eight unattached individuals. Some had African-sounding names: Zambo, Pender, Sisa, Fibi, Ebron, Congo.[31]

The eighteenth century, then, was not only the century in which the United States was launched politically; it was also the incubation period for what some historical linguists have called the creolization of African American culture.[32] Religiously and intellectually, the question of whether to convert the African and African American slaves to Christianity was a focal point of debate among white clergy and slaveowners. Peter H. Wood suggested that the controversy over African American conversion was also a topic of heated debate among African Americans themselves and hence constituted "a forgotten chapter in eighteenth-century southern intellectual history."[33]

The Nineteenth Century

In 1804 about fifty Africans, almost evenly divided between men and women, arrived in Florida and were settled on the St. Johns River, where their importer and owner, Zephaniah Kingsley, consciously eschewed the imposition of Christianity and other aspects of European culture. Kingsley, who generally purchased slaves directly from the African coast, adopted a policy of nonintervention in all areas of slave culture except manual training: "I never interfered with their connubial concerns, nor domestic affairs, but let them regulate these after their own manner." [34] If these Africans continued their native dances for a number of years after their arrival, as Kingsley asserted, the likelihood is great that they also continued African styles of worship. In fact, most of the "native dances" that they perpetuated were probably part of their indigenous religious patterns.

Although "salt water Negroes" from Africa became less numerous following the official close of the overseas slave trade by the U.S. Congress in 1807, illegal imports from Africa continued. Some of the Africans entered the United States through Florida, which remained under Spanish control until 1821. In October 1812 Richard Drake, an Irish-American and a U.S. citizen, made a slaving voyage from Rio Basso on the Windward Coast to Pensacola Bay.[35] During the waning years of Spanish jurisdiction over Florida, a considerable stir arose over slaving activities from Amelia Island. Toward the middle of January 1818, two privateers, carrying a combined total of 120 slaves, arrived at Amelia Island. A week later a committee of the U.S. House of Representatives issued a report on the illicit introduction of slaves into the United States from the island.[36]

Besides the black populations concentrated around St. Augustine and, to a lesser extent, Pensacola, there were maroons who had managed both to escape their owners in South Carolina and Georgia and to avoid the areas of Florida that were effectively controlled by the Spaniards. Large, quasipermanent maroon communities thrived in border areas that generated international rivalry. Close relations that had developed between blacks and American Indians in Florida when it was a Spanish territory continued into the American period. These black fugitives frequently settled among the Indians of northern Florida, usually living in "Negro towns" associated with Indian villages. Although sources describing their religious behavior are scarce, provocative linguistic clues to their cultural status exist in the form of Florida place names conventionally described as being of unknown origin. The river and town of Aucilla are near the site of the old Negro Fort (now known as Fort Gadsden). Variant spellings include Assile, Agile, Axille, Aguil, Ochule, Ocilla, and Asile. Winifred Vass, for twelve years editor of one of the largest and oldest vernacular periodicals in Central Africa, suggested that Aucilla might derive from the Bantu verb *ashila*, which means "to build or construct a house for someone else."[37] Vass also suggested that the name of the Suwannee River might derive from the Bantu word *nsub-wanyi*, which means "my house, my home." A large black settlement along this river was destroyed in 1818 during the Seminole Wars. Perhaps as many as twelve hundred African American maroons were living in the Seminole towns by 1836. Because the black fugitives were better acquainted with the language, religion, and other ways of whites than were their Indian hosts and nominal masters, the blacks served as cultural go-betweens for Native Americans and whites. That this was the case in matters of religion is strongly suggested by the Reverend Isaac Boring's stratagem of preaching to the blacks of an "Indian town" as a way of gaining missionary access to the Indians themselves, the principal aim of his visits.[38]

Even after Florida became a part of the United States in 1821, it was not unusual to find Africans bearing tribal marks. In 1835, for instance, Charles, aged forty, who ran away from Henry W. Maxey near Jacksonville, bore "the African marks on his face of his country."[39] While some "illegal aliens" from Africa may have been shipped directly, others probably arrived in Florida in the clandestine Cuba-to-Florida trade. Despite wildly clashing estimates of the extent and significance of the trade, there is no doubt that some Africans bound for Cuba ended up in Florida. Milo, one of eight slaves transported to Florida on the schooner *Emperor* in 1838, said not only that he was from Africa but "that he was brought here from Havana."[40] There is also the example of the *lucumi* slave encountered by the Swedish novelist Fredrika Bremer during her visit to Florida in the 1850s. When Bremer asked the middle-aged African whether he had "come hither from Africa," he replied yes, "that he had been smuggled hither from Cuba many years ago."[41] Illegal slave trading persisted in South Carolina as late as 1858, when the slave yacht *Wanderer* arrived and small parcels of its cargo of four hundred Africans were sold into Florida.[42]

The African roots of modern African American culture in Florida had weakened considerably even as early as the Reconstruction era, especially in terms of the presence of individuals who had actually been born in Africa. By the middle of this era, we clearly are dealing primarily with a U.S.-born black population in Florida, as elsewhere in the South. Only eighty-eight African-born persons were enumerated in Florida in the 1870 U.S. census. Among the more elderly of these Africans was Jeff Martin, aged 102, who had been born around 1768 in an unidentifiable region of Africa. Martin, who resided in Jefferson County at the time of the census, was the sole black Floridian who listed his occupation as "root doctor." He was one of twelve African-born persons residing in Jefferson County in 1870. Of seventeen other Florida counties having African-born residents, only Leon had as many as twelve. Of the 9,645 blacks counted in the entire 1870 census who were born outside the United States, 1,984 (20.6 percent) were born in Africa. Eighty-eight (4.4 percent) of all the African-born residents of the United States in 1870 lived in Florida.[43] If Martin reached American shores at age ten, he would have arrived legally in 1778, the year Virginia outlawed the overseas slave trade. If he arrived legally between the ages of ten and twenty, he may have entered a port in Pennsylvania, Maryland, South Carolina, or Georgia, which abolished the slave trade after Virginia did.

Martin was by no means the only practitioner of herbalism or the occult. Both before and after the Civil War, black and white Christians were embedded in a cultural milieu in which "conjur" and other rural folk beliefs exercised considerable power. In her memoirs, Ellen Call Long mentioned Delia, a slave who "began to droop at about age 18" and soon died.

> After death the nurse (a character on every plantation), brought to my mother a small package of dingy cloth, in which was wrapped two or three rusty nails, a dog's tooth, a little lamb's wool, and a ball of clay. Trembling with awe, she said: "This is what killed Delia, ole Miss, I most knowed it was jest so. I most knowed as how she was conjured, and jest found dis under her matrass where she die."
>
> On inquiry we found that she was the cause of jealousy to a companion negro girl, who had made threats towards her; and moreover, we learned, that every negro on the plantation had known all the time what power was at work upon Delia, but dared not, as they expressed it, "break the spell," for the evil spirit would have turned on the one that told it.[44]

The slaves on this Leon County plantation obviously believed in the potency of the medicine man who had cast the spell on Delia. If all others in this slave community knew of the spell, it is very likely that the victim also knew. The combination of knowledge that a root doctor was working magic against her and the belief in the power of such magic may have caused her literally to lie down and die. Such appears to be the case in voodoo death as described by anthropologist W. B. Cannon.[45]

Folk belief in sympathetic magic did not disappear overnight after the end of legal slavery. In an account set down in 1892, Ellen Call Long noted that "negro witchcraft" was thriving in Leon County during the early 1870s. The occasion for her observation was the tragic death of five black children between the ages of four and six.

> Thus it was that near the end of the first decade of freedom to the negro, I saw one of the most remarkable exhibitions of superstition ever beheld by intelligence—the more so, that what I shall relate occurred in what was considered the purlieu of those most cultured and educated of the middle Florida country.[46]

During and after Reconstruction, black ministers contended with the power of both Divine Providence and folk beliefs. When in 1880 the horse of a black drayman died after the fellow had "cussed out" his preacher, the minister interpreted the man's misfortune as "a visitation of Divine Providence for his cussedness." [47] Equally powerful was belief in the abilities of special individuals to cast spells on people who had wronged them. A man in Tallahassee, assisted by an elderly woman, astounded onlookers by appearing to vomit nails, moss, and other debris. "His friends believe strongly in the reality of it all," noted the *Floridian*, "and insist that he had had 'a spell' put upon him by a woman to whom he was engaged but whom he jilted and who now protests that she intends to pay him off for his base desertion." [48]

Most blacks living in Florida during the last half of the nineteenth century had been born neither in Africa nor in the Caribbean but in six southeastern states: Florida, Georgia, South Carolina, Virginia, Alabama, and North Carolina. In 1890, 122,170 individuals, making up 76.3 percent of Florida's total black population, were native Floridians. Only 5.7 percent (7,411) of all Florida-born blacks lived outside the state of their birth in 1890, whereas between 11.1 percent and 25.9 percent of the blacks born in North Carolina, South Carolina, Georgia, Alabama, and Virginia did so. Between 1880 and 1890 Florida experienced a net gain of 30,528 black inhabitants through interstate migration. During the same decade Georgia, South Carolina, Alabama, North Carolina, and Virginia experienced net losses in the black population. Put another way, a hefty 23.7 percent of the blacks living in Florida in 1890 had been born in other states, compared with percentages of 1.7 in South Carolina, 2.8 in North Carolina, 2.9 in Virginia, 6.6 in Georgia, and 10.0 in Alabama.[49]

If distinctive cultural patterns bearing traceable African origins are found in postbellum Florida, they cannot be explained simply by the presence of large numbers of African-born individuals in the state's black population. Other explanations must be found for the persistence of such culturally distinctive and widely acknowledged African-influenced elements of culture as basket-making styles, grave markers, mortuary customs, and shouting (spirit possession) in African American religious rituals in the latter half of the nineteenth century. These Africanisms had become Americanisms and persisted in Florida and elsewhere in the Deep South as integral parts of an interconnected circum-Caribbean Creole culture that had been forged in Florida, Georgia, and South Carolina during the previous century and had alternately influenced and been influenced by the customs and lifeways of southern whites and Indians.

Although native Africans still alive during the 1870s and 1880s lacked any significant influence because of their minuscule numbers and proportions, indirect and even direct African influence was possible. Some of Florida's older American-born black adults, such as the Reverend Eli Boyd, remembered deceased African-born parents and grandparents. A self-designated "Geechee" interviewed in Miami during the 1930s, Boyd recalled, "My grandfather was brought directly from Africa to Port Royal, South Carolina." [50]

The possibility of vivid memories of African-born parents and grandparents was underscored strikingly in a conversation I had with Richard McKinney, son of a black Baptist minister who figures prominently in the history of Live Oak's African Baptist Church. The McKinney family oral tradition posits links of kinship stretching from Jacob, an Ashanti African born around 1820, to the present.[51] And while the proportion of Florida's black population born in Africa had diminished to statistical insignificance by 1870, personal memories of African family ancestors had not disappeared even as late as the 1930s, when Shack Thomas, born a slave in Florida in 1834, recalled that his father had come from the Congo: "Pappy was a African. I knows dat. He come from Congo, over in Africa, and I heard him say a big storm drove de ship somewhere on de Ca'lina coast. I 'member he mighty 'spectful to Massa and missy, but he proud, too, and walk straighter'n anybody I ever seen. He had scars on de right side he head and cheek what he say am tribe marks, but what dey means I don't know."[52]

From these and other African ancestors, no longer alive when the census takers made their rounds in 1870, some older country-born black Floridians like Mrs. Lucreaty Clark of Lamont (Jefferson County) may have learned African basket-weaving techniques handed down across several generations, as did George Brown in South Carolina.[53] Although South Carolina's African American basket-weaving tradition, which Peter H. Wood said "undoubtedly represents an early fusion of Negro and Indian skills,"[54] is widely known and highly visible to tourists along the roadsides of the low country, less attention has been focused on the traditions of basket weaving still practiced by some African American craftspeople in Florida today. In describing the white oak baskets made by Lucreaty Clark, James Dickerson wrote: "Within her fingertips is carried the memory of an ancient African craft fast disappearing from the face of the Florida Panhandle. African slaves, once brought to the Panhandle to work on plantations, made baskets to hold cotton picked from the fields."[55]

The tendency once was to assume that in those instances when Africans did not bring African-made artifacts with them in the slave ships, there was no possibility of reproducing the ancestral material culture. That conception of how diffusion, even of material culture, works is entirely too physicalistic. The specific materials from which the artifacts are made is one thing; the form and design concepts are another matter altogether. The artifact might be most appropriately viewed as the analogue of a phenotype and the ideal traditional form as the genotype. What we see is not necessarily what the craftsworker has in his or her head. It is, rather, the end product of an interaction among the craftsperson's image of the cultural tradition or ideal; the materials available to work with; and the craftsperson's skill, practice, and ability to shape the materials in conformity with the ideal image. The ideal image is carried, not in the hands or on the backs of the African bondsmen, but in their heads. The reappearance of artifacts conforming reasonably well with African cultural ideas for pot, basket, chair, or door is therefore a mental feat before it becomes a physical reality. One archaeologist called the idea of proper form, which exists in the mind of the craftsperson who is fashioning an artifact, "the mental template," an apt phrase.[56]

Spirit Possession and Ritual Ecstatic Dance

A high degree of emotionalism has often been considered characteristic of black religious life.[57] The frequency, long duration, and emotional nature of black church services in Florida have drawn comment from a number of observers. The image of black religionists as vocally demonstrative in their worship was so widespread that finding a group of black worshipers during Reconstruction that was "not noisy" was cause for comment.[58] While traveling in Florida in 1870 G. W. Nichols visited St. Augustine and Jacksonville, where he witnessed "shocking mummeries, which belonged to the fetich worship of savage Central Africa and not of Christian America." [59] If we substitute "traditional African religion" for the ethnocentrically loaded "fetich worship" and bracket the obviously biased adjective *savage*, an important kernel of historical truth may remain in this jaundiced account. What did Nichols mean by Central Africa in geographical terms? Was he making a distinction between West Africa and Central Africa or was this simply his verbal shorthand for "primitive Africa" in general? In 1871 the Jacksonville *Courier* reported the complaints of local whites about the duration of demonstrative services in a revival that continued several weeks.[60] The same year Miss E. B. Eveleth, an American Missionary Society instructor at Gainesville, wrote that "many of those old church goers, still cling to their heathenish habits, such as shouting and thinking the more noise and motion they have the better Christians they are." [61] Eveleth and a colleague attended a service at which a woman jumped up in the middle of a sermon, clapped her hands, screamed, danced up to the pulpit, and whirled around like a top before throwing herself back into her seat. She was followed by another woman with similar motions.

In an 1879 article entitled "Begin Worship Earlier," the Tallahassee *Weekly Floridian* reported that white citizens residing in "the neighborhood of the colored people's churches" had complained about "the singing and exhorting at a late hour." Ever helpful, the *Floridian* suggested that "the colored people begin services earlier and preach short sermons." [62]

In 1873 Jonathan Gibbs, a Dartmouth-educated Presbyterian minister who became Florida's first black secretary of state, was apologetic about the ecstatic religious behavior of blacks. They "still preach and pray, sing and shout all night long," said Gibbs, "in defiance of health, sound sense, or other considerations supposed to influence a reasonable being." [63] One seeming example of how some black worshipers shouted in defiance of health was described by James Weldon Johnson. A woman known as Aunt Venie, out of respect for her age, was "the champion of all 'ring shouters'" at St. Paul's Church in Jacksonville, Johnson recalled:

> We were a little bit afraid of Aunt Venie, too, for she was said to have fits. (In a former age she would have been classed among those "possessed with devils.") When there was a "ring shout" the weird music and the sound of thudding feet not the silence of the night vibrating and throbbing with a vague terror. Many a time I woke suddenly and lay a long while strangely troubled by these sounds, the like of which my great-grandmother Sarah had heard as a child. The shouters, formed in a ring, men and women alternating, their bodies close together, moved round and round on shuffling feet that never left the floor. With the heel of the right foot they pounded out the fundamental beat of the dance and with their hands clapped out the varying rhythmical accents of the chant; for the music was, in fact, an African chant and the shout an African dance, whole pagan rite transplanted and adapted to Christian worship. Round and round the ring would go. One, two, three, four, five hours, the very monotony of sound and motion inducing an ecstatic frenzy. Aunt Venie, it seems, never, even after the hardest day of washing and ironing, missed a "ring shout." [64]

Johnson's speculation that the sounds of the ring shout resembled the sounds his great-grandmother had heard in childhood is noteworthy because his maternal great-grandmother, Sarah, was born and raised in Africa. She was aboard a slave ship headed for Brazil when the ship was captured by a British man-of-war and taken to Nassau.

It is fairly well known that African Methodist Episcopal Bishop Daniel Alexander Payne opposed the ring shout and tried to eliminate all forms of religious dance. One shocking spectacle that Payne observed at St. Paul's A.M.E. Church in Jacksonville (where Aunt Venie shouted) left such an impression upon him that he recorded his frustrations in his personal journal in 1892. His frustrations were intensified by the realization that even the parishioners of a Wilberforce-educated pastor (who should know better) danced at an A.M.E. "Love Feast." [65]

Another eyewitness account may serve as a definitive example of this persistent, ritually induced and culturally patterned behavior known as shouting. Charles Edwardes, a white traveler, observed the event on a freezing January day some time in the early 1880s in an unspecified black church in Jacksonville. The building was filled with three to four hundred adults who initiated a "bread-and-water forgiveness festival" with the singing of this verse, repeated again and again:

> While Heaven's in my view,
> My journey I'll pursue;
> I never will turn back,
> While Heaven's in my view.

Then the spirit possession began:

One woman—she was almost a girl—cried herself into what might have been a fit. But if a fit, it was of a kind well known to the other women, her neighbors, for two of these stood up by her side, and taking, each of them, an arm of her, they guided or supported her through all her contortions, with faces showing their amusement rather than concern. Even when she wrenched herself away from them, and threw herself backward, so that her head and the upper part of her body hung over into the next pew, they pulled her back and tightened their hold, while a third lady tried to put order into the dress and hair of the girl—and not one of the three was so absorbed by her task that she would devote her eyes and ears to it exclusively.[66]

The foregoing descriptions have in common the depiction of religious hysteria or possession-like behavior, popularly known as "shouting," "getting happy," or "getting the spirit." Observed in certain black churches, it has been variously attributed to innate primitive emotionalism, residues of African culture, or just the simple emotionalism of the unwashed and uneducated masses. In 1930 Herskovits raised the question of the relation of "religious hysteria" among peoples of African origin in the United States, Haiti, the Guianas, and the West Indies to similar African phenomena. But, as Herskovits pointed out, few answers were forthcoming in 1930 because little systematic study of the religious practices of blacks in the United States had been conducted from the point of view of the ethnologist.[67]

Certainly not all black churchgoers exhibit the same degree or type of demonstrativeness in religious ceremonies. The amount of heat and emotional ecstasy generated seems to be closely related to social position. "It is of no little significance," wrote Louis Lomax, "that these mulatto Negroes of the 'genteel tradition' were Episcopalians, Presbyterians and Congregationalists while the black masses were members of the 'common' churches, such as the Baptist and Methodist congregations." The difference between the "genteel tradition" and the "common" tradition was to be found in the nature of the services. Those who claimed to be of the "genteel" group considered their services to be of a "higher order," which, according to Lomax, made their services "a good deal less exciting." The association of the black masses with denominations having the more exciting brand of services led the Reverend Thomas Lomax, a black Georgia Baptist firebrand of the late nineteenth and early twentieth centuries and grandfather of Louis, to crack: "If you see a Negro who is not a Baptist or a Methodist, some white man has been tampering with his religion." [68]

Some writers viewed the ritual known as the ring shout, or simply the shout, as a phenomenon found only among the Gullah-speaking blacks of the Sea Islands off Georgia and South Carolina.[69] It is true

Pastor George Morgan calls on parishioners to be baptized in the San Sebastian River, near St. Augustine, in the summer of 1944. The staff he holds bears a resemblance to Yoruba staffs from West Africa. Photograph by J. Carver Harris. Courtesy of the St. Augustine Historical Society.

that some of the most vivid eyewitness accounts of shouts originated in that region. Laura M. Towne, for example, described the shout as a religious ceremony representing possibly a modification of "the negro's regular dances; which may have had its origin in some native African dance."[70] Bernard Katz wrote that the antebellum and Civil War era shout usually came after the praise meeting was over, and no one but church members were expected to join.[71] The musicologist Eileen Southern considered the shout, held after the regularly scheduled service, to be "purely African in form and tradition," arguing that "it simply represented the survival of African tradition in the New World."[72] If this argument is accepted, there can be little doubt that the religious-musical-dance-drama form called the shout

Members of the Shiloh Baptist Church on King Street in St. Augustine gather at Fiddler's Flat, on the banks of the San Sebastian River, to watch a baptism in 1944. Photograph by J. Carver Harris. Courtesy of the St. Augustine Historical Society.

exhibited a remarkable stability over time. The ring shout described by James Weldon Johnson probably happened in the late 1870s or early 1880s. In antebellum times, when most of the furnishings of the praise houses in which the shouts occurred were movable, the physical form of the shout was rather literally a ring. Wooden chairs or benches that were not nailed to the floor of the cabins were easily moved to the side, leaving empty floor space in the center of the building. After the Civil War the circular form of the shout probably persisted longest in churches with movable seats. With the appearance of heavy wooden pews, which were usually permanently riveted to the floor, the circular form of the shout had to be either modified or abandoned altogether.

Spirit possession pushes us toward direct confrontation with what has been called the Frazier-Herskovits debate over the extent and impact of African cultural influences in various parts of the Western Hemisphere. Two kinds of altered states of consciousness are pertinent here—drug trance and possession trance, both of which are widespread. In a survey of altered states in 488 societies, Erika Bourguignon found possession trance to be prevalent in (but of course not limited to) continental Africa. Bourguignon and others influenced by Herskovits argued, "It is clear that possession trance in Haiti is historically related to what is essentially the same phenomenon in West Africa and in other West African–derived societies in the Americas."[73] If so, there is every reason to expect that similar behaviors exhibited by Western and Central African–derived black populations in the United States are historically related to those parts of Africa. Possession behaviors are learned in both formal and informal ways, along with beliefs and associated ritual action. In human communities that view possession as a peak religious experience, the behavior is widely interpreted as a communal event, an act that helps cement a spiritual and social community.

One universal aspect of spirit possession is the accompaniment of drumbeats or drumlike rhythms. Although little systematic research has been conducted, Andrew Neher offered a tentative physiological explanation of the behavior found in ceremonies involving drums. "This behavior," he wrote, "is often described as a trance in which the individual experiences unusual perceptions or hallucinations. In the extreme case, twitching of the body and generalized convulsion are reported." Neher found support for the notion that "the behavior is the result primarily of the effects of rhythmic drumming on the central nervous system." Drumbeats are made up of many frequencies that are transmitted along different nerve pathways in the brain. Since low-frequency receptors of the ear are more resistant to damage than high-frequency receptors, "It would be possible to transmit more energy to the brain with a drum than with a stimulus of a higher frequency." In a second part of his study, Neher obtained responses to drumming that were similar to responses observed with rhythmic light stimulation of the brain. He argued that possession takes place when drum, or drumlike, pulses are used deliberately in rituals to bring about a state of dissociation, or trance. Analyses of the drum rhythms of the beer dance of the Lala of Northern Rhodesia, the Sogo dance of the Ewe of Ghana, the beer dance of the Nsenga of Central Africa, and of Vodoun, Ifo, and Juba dances in recorded Haitian music found that the agitated possession behavior occurred at beats between seven and nine cycles per second. Polyrhythmic percussive techniques, such as the ones described for the Jacksonville ring shout by James Weldon Johnson, tend to heighten the intensity of the response.[74]

Death, Burial, and Funeral Rites

Numerous ethnographic accounts underscore the assertion of Fortes and Dieterlen that in many traditional African systems, "death alone is not a sufficient condition for becoming an ancestor entitled to receive worship." A proper burial, they said, is "the sine qua non for becoming an ancestor deserving of veneration." [75] While the precise number of African-born individuals who arrived illegally in Florida after 1821 is not known, we do know from specific descriptions of "salt water" Negroes who arrived in antebellum Florida that they were not hit with cultural amnesia the moment they stepped off the slavers. Accounts of the arrival of cargoes of Africans confiscated in midpassage on the seas and of their behavior upon landing in the United States clearly establish the carrying over of such cultural items as burial ceremonies. In May 1860, for example, the illegal slavers *Wildfire* and *Williams* were captured on the seas by two U.S. gunboats, the *Mohawk* and the *Wyandotte,* and taken to the port of Key West. Shortly after the arrival of the three hundred Africans aboard these two ships, one of the children died. Jefferson B. Browne described the burial ceremony:

> The interment took place some distance from the barracoon, and the Africans were allowed to be present at the services, where they performed their native ceremony. Weird chants were sung, mingled with wails of grief and mournful moanings from a hundred throats, until the coffin was lowered into the grave, when at once the chanting stopped and perfect silence reigned, and the Africans marched back to the barracoons without a sound.[76]

Some slaves in the lower South made a semantic distinction between "burying" and "preaching the funeral." James Bolton, a former slave in Oglethorpe County, Georgia, said: "When folkses on our plantation died, Marster always let many of us as wanted to go lay off work 'til after the burying. Sometimes it were two or three months after the burying before the funeral sermon was preached." [77] Among the African societies that traditionally practiced "second burial" was the Igbo:

> Greater complications arose when many children of many family heads became Christians, and were forbidden by the teaching of the missionaries to perform the second burial of their fathers. The Igbo practice was to bury an elderly person soon after death, with preliminary ceremonies. Then after a year or less, sometimes more, the second burial would take place with a lot more elaborate ceremonies than the first. It was believed that this second burial was the one that helped the spirit of such departed elderly persons to rest comfortably with the ancestors in the land of ancestral bliss, from where they plead effectively with the gods for the well-being of their children on earth.[78]

In the traditional Igbo setting, the matter of the inheritance of the father's property could not be properly settled until after the second burial. Being slaves, the community was not likely to have found this consideration significant. One real-world element that reinforced the practice of second burial in its traditional Old World cultural setting was thus stripped away from the Igbos who were imported into the American colonies. A second consideration in the traditional context was the belief that without a proper second burial, the extended family would be harassed and victimized by the hovering restless spirit of the dead person. This notion probably lost little weight in the transition from Africa to North America, and there is considerable evidence among late antebellum slaves, as recounted in WPA narratives and published narratives and autobiographies, that belief in roaming, restless spirits was still something to contend with long after the majority of the slaves were American-born.[79]

The distinction between burial and "second burial" or "preaching the funeral," a concept in many African societies from which slaves were extracted, is important to an understanding of how Africans adapted to the restrictions on funeral attendance in the Old South. The deceased might be buried at night during the work week (so as not to disrupt farm work), leaving days or even weeks or months to pass before the public funeral was performed. The funeral ritual, then, as distinguished from the physical act of burying the body, is a public phenomenon. Funeral rites in traditional African societies were often occasions for celebration, creating an intensely renewed sense of family and communal unit among the survivors. It was perhaps an analogous sense of celebration that, during the Reconstruction era, gave Ambrose B. Hart the mistaken impression that services among blacks were held more for recreation than for religion. Among the events reinforcing Hart's impression was an incident that bears a striking resemblance to the Igbo "second burial." Hart observed a group of Florida freed slaves gather to "repreach a funeral service for a child that had been 'buried prayed for and preached over two months ago.' " [80] It is conceivable that immediate interment of the corpse was necessitated by the limitations of embalming techniques at the time. Both blacks and whites in the antebellum period buried rather soon after death. If burial waited until the nearest Sunday, it would not preempt a scheduled day of work, and the maximum number of people in the neighborhood would be able to attend. But after slavery the patterns began to diverge between blacks and whites to the point where one Leon County resident in the 1970s perceived that "white people don't have no respect for their dead . . . they bury them so quick." With the advent of improved methods of embalming, the physical necessity of nearly immediate burial declined, but the possibility of delay was perhaps even the preference, among rural blacks. It is not unusual for more traditionally oriented and rural-based families to delay "preaching the funeral" for weeks, even now.

Richard Wright recognized in the 1930s that there was "a culture of the Negro which has been addressed to him and to him alone, a culture which has, for good or ill, helped to clarify his consciousness and create emotional attitudes which are conducive to action. This culture stemmed mainly from two sources: (1) the Negro church; and (2) the fluid folklore of the Negro people." According to Wright:

It was through the portals of the church that the American Negro first entered the shrine of Western culture. Living under slave conditions of life, bereft of his African heritage, the Negro found that his struggle for religion on the plantation between

1820–60 was nothing short of a struggle for human rights. It remained a relatively progressive struggle until religion began to ameliorate and assuage suffering and denial. Even today there are millions of Negroes whose only sense of a whole universe, whose only relation to society and man, and whose only guide to personal dignity comes through the archaic morphology of Christian salvation.[81]

By focusing on blacks living within the confines of present-day Florida, this essay has depicted the entrance of African Americans "through the portals of the church" into what Wright called "the shrine of Western culture." By this entry, they not only transformed themselves into African Americans without totally losing their African past but also helped transform and enrich Western culture itself.

Notes

1. David E. Stannard, "Time and the Millennium: On the Religious Experience of the American Slave," in *Prospects: An Annual of American Cultural Studies*, ed. Jack Salzman (New York: Burt Franklin, 1976), 2: 349.

2. William R. Bascom, "Acculturation among the Gullah Negroes," *American Anthropologist* 43 (1941): 43–50; reprinted in *The Making of Black America*, ed. August Meicr and Elliott Rudwick (New York: Atheneum, 1969), 1: 34–41.

3. Anthropologists and folklorists often call this blending process *syncretism*. Two folklorists defined the term: "The merging of two or more concepts, beliefs, rituals, etc. so that apparent conflicts are rationalized away. Old beliefs and associated actions are not necessarily replaced or destroyed by new ones; they are, rather, reinterpreted and absorbed. Syncretism may be seen in elements of early pagan rites modified to survive in later Christian rituals. Symbolism in Christmas (trees, etc.) and Easter (egg, etc.) celebrations are examples." Kenneth Clarke and Mary Clarke, *A Concise Dictionary of Folklore*, Kentucky Folklore Series no. 1 (June 1965), 32.

4. George P. Rawick, *From Sundown to Sunup: The Making of the Black Community* (Westport, Conn.: Greenwood, 1972), 14–29.

5. Robert Farris Thompson, "Black Ideographic Writing: Calabar to Cuba," *Yale Alumni Magazine*, November 1978, 29. Also see Thompson's "Kongo Influences on African American Artistic Culture," in *Africanisms in American Culture*, ed. Joseph E. Holloway (Bloomington: Indiana University Press, 1990), 148–84.

6. Bennetta Jules-Rosette, "Creative Spirituality from Africa to America:

Cross-Cultural Influences in Contemporary Religious Forms," *Western Journal of Black Studies* 4 (Winter 1980): 275.

7. See, for example, Winifred Vass, *The Bantu Speaking Heritage of the United States* (Los Angeles: UCLA, Center for Afro-American Studies, 1979).

8. Melville J. Herskovits, *The Myth of the Negro Past* (Boston: Beacon Press, 1958), 111.

9. Mechal Sobel, *Trabelin' On: The Slave Journey to an Afro-Baptist Faith* (Westport, Conn.: Greenwood, 1979), 59.

10. Darold D. Wax, "Preferences for Slaves in Colonial America," *Journal of Negro History* 58 (October 1973): 371–401; Daniel C. Littlefield, *Rice and Slaves: Ethnicity and the Slave Trade in Colonial South Carolina* (Baton Rouge: Louisiana State University Press, 1981).

11. Ira Berlin, "Time, Space, and the Evolution of Afro-American Society on British Mainland North America," *American Historical Review* 85 (February 1980): 67. See also a recent treatment of the evolution of slave-naming practices: Cheryll Ann Cody, "There Was No 'Absolom' on the Ball Plantations: Slave-Naming Practices in the South Carolina Low Country, 1720–1865," *American Historical Review* 92 (June 1987): 563–96.

12. Pensacola *Gazette*, January 9, 1836.

13. *Florida Herald and Southern Democrat*, May 28, 1841.

14. *Florida Sentinel*, April 17, 1852.

15. Sobel, *Trabelin' On*, 29–30.

16. *Georgia Gazette*, April 2, 1764; quoted in Sobel, *Trabelin' On*, 26.

17. Sobel, *Trabelin' On*, 36.

18. Roderick Brambaugh, "Black Maroons in Florida, 1800–1830," paper read at the Annual Meeting of the Organization of American Historians, Boston, 1975.

19. Larry W. Kruger and Robert L. Hall, "Fort Mose: A Black Fort in Spanish Florida," *Griot* 6 (Spring 1987): 39–48.

20. John D. Milligan, "Slave Rebelliousness and the Florida Maroons," *Prologue* 6 (Spring 1974): 4–18.

21. Ibid., 9.

22. Robert W. Higgins, "South Carolina Merchants and Factors Dealing in the External Negro Trade, 1735-1775," *South Carolina Historical Magazine* 65 (1964): 205–17.

23. Peter H. Wood, *Black Majority: Negroes in Colonial South Carolina from 1670 through the Stono Rebellion* (New York: Knopf, 1974), xiv.

24. Charles Loch Mowat, *East Florida as a British Province, 1763–1784* (1943; reprint, Gainesville: University Press of Florida, 1964), 157.

25. James Grant to Lord Shelburne, December 25, 1767, and March 12, 1768, Colonial Office 5/549, 45–46.

26. Mowat, *East Florida*, 157.

27. *South Carolina and American General Gazette*, December 24, 1773.

28. *Georgia Gazette*, January 10, 1770; cited in *Journal of Negro History* 24 (July 1939): 252.

29. The state reimbursed Qua's owner for the loss of a laborer resulting from this execution, General Account of Contingent Expenses, East Florida, June 25, 1777-June 24, 1778, Colonial Office 5/559; cited in J. Leitch Wright, Jr., "Blacks in British East Florida," *Florida Historical Quarterly* 54 (April 1976): 431. On specific traditional African language and naming practices, see David Dalby, "Ashanti Survivals in the Language and Traditions of the Windward Maroons of Jamaica," *African Language Studies* 12 (1971): 31–51; Roger W. Westcott, "Bini Names in Nigeria and Georgia," *Linguistics: An International Review* 124 (1974): 22–32; and Frederick W. H. Megeod, "Personal Names amongst Some West African Tribes," *Journal of the African Society* (1917): 117. Other relevant articles and studies include F. Gaither, "Fanciful Are Negro Names," *New York Times Magazine*, February 10, 1929, 19; U. T. Holmes, "A Study in Negro Onomastics," *American Speech* 5 (1930): 463–67; Hennig Cohen, "Slave Names in Colonial South Carolina," *American Speech* 28 (1952): 102–7; N.C. Chappell, "Negro Names," *American Speech* 4 (1929): 2772–75; Newbell N. Puckett, "Names of American Negro Slaves," in *Studies in the Science of Society*, ed. G. P. Murdock (New Haven: Yale University Press, 1937), 471–94; Puckett, *Black Names in America: Origins and Usage* (Boston: G. K. Hall, 1975); and John C. Inscoe, "Carolina Slave Names: An Index to Acculturation," *Journal of Southern History* 49 (November 1983): 527–54.

30. Pensacola *Gazette*, December 12, 1840.

31. Patricia C. Griffin, "Mary Evans: Woman of Substance," *El Escribano* 14 (1978): 71.

32. For a discussion of the concept of creolization by a linguist, see Robert A. Hall, Jr., *Pidgin and Creole Languages* (Ithaca, N.Y.: Cornell University Press, 1966), esp. xi–xv. Mechal Sobel suggests that the pidginization-creolization language process parallels, chronologically, analogous developments in the evolution of African Christianity, *Trabelin' On*, 36.

33. Peter H. Wood, "Jesus Christ Has Got Thee at Last," *Bulletin*, Center for the Study of Southern Culture and Religion 3 (November 1979): 1–7.

34. Zephaniah Kingsley, *A Treatise on the Patriarchal, or Co-Operative System of Society as it Exists in Some Governments under the Name of Slavery* (n.p., 1829), 14.

35. James Pope-Hennessy, *Sins of the Fathers: A Study of the Atlantic Slave Traders (1441–1807)* (New York: Knopf, 1968), 3.

36. *Niles Weekly Register*, December 27, 1817, 296; January 10, 1818, 324;

and January 17, 1818, 336–37. Cited in T. Frederick Davis, *Digest of the Florida Material in Niles' Register* (N.p., 1939), 27, 29.

37. Vass, *Bantu Speaking Heritage*, 48.

38. Isaac Boring's diary, entry dated May 27, 1828, excerpted in John C. Ley, *Fifty-Two Years in Florida* (Nashville: Publishing House of the Methodist Episcopal Church, South, 1899), 42.

39. Jacksonville *Courier*, April 16, 1835.

40. Dorothy Dodd, "The Schooner Emperor: An Incident of the Illegal Trade in Florida," *Florida Historical Quarterly* 13 (January 1935): 117–28.

41. Fredrika Bremer, *The Homes of the New World: Impressions of America*, trans. Mary Howitt (London: Arthur Hall, Virtle, 1853), 289–90.

42. Charles J. Montgomery, "Survivors from the Cargo of the Negro Slave Yacht Wanderer," *American Anthropologist* 10 (October 1908): 611–23.

43. *The Ninth Census of the United States (1870)*, Washington, D.C., 1872; see table 6, "Selected Nativity by Counties," 349.

44. Ellen Call Long, *Florida Breezes; or, Florida New and Old* (Gainesville: University of Florida Press, 1962; reprint of 1883 edition), 181.

45. W. B. Cannon, "Voodoo Death," *American Anthropologist* 44 (1942): 169–81.

46. Ellen Call Long, "Negro Witchcraft," typed manuscript fragment dated 1892, P. K. Yonge Library of Florida History, University of Florida, Gainesville, 1–3.

47. *Tallahassee Semi-Weekly Floridian*, September 17, 1880.

48. *Tallahassee Weekly Floridian*, February 12, 1878.

49. U.S. Department of Commerce, Bureau of the Census, *Thirteenth Census of the United States, vol. 1, Population, 1910* (Washington, D.C., 1913), 151.

50. Eli Boyd interview, WPA Slave Narratives; reprinted in *The American Slave: A Composite Autobiography, 17, Florida Narratives*, ed. George P. Rawick (Westport, Conn.: Greenwood, 1972), 39–41; hereinafter cited as Rawick, *Florida Narratives*.

51. Richard I. McKinney, interview with the author, July 9, 1981. The link was consolidated and immolized by George Patterson McKinney, a prominent Baptist minister during the late nineteenth and early twentieth centuries. George, the son of Ishmael (born into slavery around 1837), was the grandson of an Ashanti African known as Jacob. Jacob, born in West Africa around 1820 and illegally imported into the United States, repeatedly told all eight of his children, "You are Ashanti."

52. Shack Thomas interview, WPA Slave Narratives; quoted in Lawrence W. Levine, *Black Culture and Black Consciousness: Afro-American Folk Thought from Slavery to Freedom* (New York: Oxford University Press, 1977),

87. Several African-born slaves who ran away between 1820 and 1850 had tribal marks or scars. Maria, "African by birth . . . face tattooed," ran away from her owner, Henry De Grandpre, in 1829, Pensacola *Gazette*, December 16, 1829. In 1842 Abraham, who had "worked in the employ of a corporation in the city of Tallahassee for two years," ran away bearing a "mark over the eyes on the forehead, as Africans are frequently marked"; *Florida Sentinel*, October 14, 1842.

53. Edith M. Dabbs, *Face of an Island* (Columbia, S.C.: R. L. Bryan, 1970), contains a photograph taken in 1909 of Alfred Graham, a former slave, who learned to weave baskets from his great-uncle, who brought the trade of basketry from Africa. Graham later taught George Brown, who became instructor of basketry at the Penn School on St. Helena Island. Joseph E. Holloway elicited this path of transmission in an unpublished interview with Leroy E. Brown, George's son.

54. Wood, *Black Majority*, 122.

55. James Dickerson, "Basket Weaving, Down-Home Style," Tallahassee *Democrat*, November 23, 1978. For further discussion of African-inspired material culture in the low country, see Robert E. Purdue, Jr., "African Baskets in South Carolina," *Economic Botany* 22 (1968): 289–92.

56. James Deetz, *Invitation to Anthropology* (Garden City, N.Y.: Anchor, 1967), 45.

57. Some writers have suggested that much of the emotionalism of southern evangelical religion derives from the contagious influence of blacks on revivalistic frontier religion. At least one prominent black scholar, however, argued that, instead, the emotionalism of the early evangelical faith of the whites influenced the nature of black religious worship. As Harry V. Richardson, "The Negro in American Religious Life," in *The American Negro Reference Book*, ed. John P. Davis (Englewood Cliffs, N.J.: Prentice-Hall, 1966), 400, wrote: "But if the simplicity of the evangelical faith did much to determine the number of Negroes who became Christian, the emotionalism of the early evangelical faith did much to determine the nature of Negro worship. The religion that the Negro masses first received was characterized by such phenomena as laughing, weeping, shouting, dancing, barking, jerking, prostration and speaking in tongues. These were regarded as evidence of the Spirit at work in the heart of man, and they were also taken as evidence of the depth and sincerity of the conversion. It was inevitable, therefore, that early Negro worship should be filled with these emotional elements. Although there is some tendency to regard high emotionalism as a phenomenon peculiar to the Negro church, in reality it is a hangover from the days of frontier religion."

58. Mrs. E. W. Warner to E. P. Smith, September 3, 1866, American Missionary Association Papers, Amistad Research Center, Tulane University.

59. G. W. Nichols, "Six Weeks in Florida," *Harper's New Monthly*, October 1870: 663.

60. *Jacksonville Courier* as quoted in the *Tallahassee Weekly Floridian*, October 3, 1871.

61. E. P. Eveleth to E. M. Cravath, February 25, 1871, American Missionary Association Papers.

62. *Weekly Floridian*, August 12, 1879.

63. Jonathan Gibbs, *Florida Agriculturist*, January 17, 1874, p. 23.

64. James Weldon Johnson, *Along This Way: The Autobiography of James Weldon Johnson* (1933; reprint, New York: Da Capo Press, 1973), 22.

65. Journal of Daniel Alexander Payne for 1891–93, entry of December 12, 1892; cited in David W. Wills, "Womanhood and Domesticity in the A.M.E. Tradition: The Influence of Daniel Alexander Payne," in *Black Apostles at Home and Abroad*, ed. David W. Wills and Richard Newman (Boston: G. K. Hall, 1982), 144.

66. Charles Edwardes, "A Scene from Florida Life," *Living Age*, September 13, 1884, 685.

67. Melville J. Herskovits, "The Negro in the New World: The Statement of a Problem," *American Anthropologist* (1930); reprinted in Herskovits, *The New World Negro: Selected Papers in Afroamerican Studies* (Bloomington: Indiana University Press, 1966), 10. One of the few studies published before 1966 was that of Alexander Alland, Jr., " 'Possession' in a Revivalist Negro Church," *Journal of the Scientific Study of Religion* 1 (April 1962): 204–13.

68. Louis Lomax, *The Negro Revolt* (New York: Harper, 1962), 58.

69. Wood, *Black Majority*, 172.

70. *Letters and Diary of Laura M. Towne, Written from the Sea Islands of South Carolina, 1862–1884*, ed. Rupert Sargent Holland (New York: Negro Universities Press, 1969 reprint), 67.

71. Bernard Katz, *The Social Implications of Early Negro Music in the United States* (New York: Arno, 1969), 4–5.

72. Eileen Southern, *The Music of Black America* (New York: Norton, 1971), 162.

73. Erika Bourguignon, *Dance Perspectives* 35 (Autumn 1968): 33–35. This special issue, written entirely by Bourguignon, was devoted to possession trance and ritual ecstatic dance.

74. Andrew Neher, "A Physiological Explanation of Unusual Behavior in Ceremonies Involving Drums," *Human Biology* 34 (May 1962): 151–60.

75. *African Systems of Thought*, ed. M. Fortes and G. Dieterlen (London: Oxford University Press, 1965), 16.

76. Jefferson B. Browne, *Key West: The Old and the New* (Gainesville: University of Florida Press, 1973; facsimile reprint of 1912 edition), 16–17.

77. *Slavery Times (When I Was Chillun Down on Marster's Plantation)*, ed.

Ronald Killion and Charles Waller (Savannah, Ga.: Beehive Press, 1975), 58.

78. Edmond Ilogu, *Christianity and Ibo Culture* (Leiden: E. J. Brill, 1974), 109. For another description of Igbo second burial, see Lorna McDaniel, "An Igbo Second Burial," *Black Perspective in Music* 6 (Spring 1978): 49–55. McDaniel indicates that the ceremony might take place from one month to a year after death and might last several weeks.

79. Elliott J. Gorn, "Black Spirits: The Ghostlore of Afro-American Slaves," *American Quarterly* 36 (Fall 1984): 549–65. See, as an example, *Florida Narratives*, 196–97.

80. Letter from Ambrose B. Hart to father, June 15, 1869; quoted in Joe M. Richardson, *The Negro in the Reconstruction of Florida* (Tallahassee: Florida State University Press, 1965), 89.

81. Richard Wright, "Blueprint for Negro Literature," in *Amistad 2*, ed. John A. Williams and Charles F. Harris (New York: Vintage, 1971), 6. A shorter version of Wright's paper was published in the fall 1937 issue of *New Challenge*.

4

"Yellow Silk Ferret Tied Round Their Wrists"

African Americans in British East Florida, 1763–1784

Daniel L. Schafer

GOVERNOR JAMES GRANT arrived in St. Augustine on August 29, 1764, determined to transform Britain's new East Florida colony into a plantation province through the labor of African slaves. Earlier experiences in South Carolina had convinced Grant that plantations could only be developed in warm-climate colonies by black workers. White migrants from Europe could be utilized later, the governor reasoned, but only after the enormous burdens of initial development had been completed.[1]

Historian Bernard Bailyn has recently concluded that the inability of James Grant and his successors to recruit adequate numbers of white settlers was the major reason why British East Florida was an expensive and exotic two-decade failure. Bailyn believes a significant reason for the success of the northern British American colonies, which was not replicated in East Florida, was a labor system based on family farms. But there is little evidence that the governing establishment in Florida intended to follow that pattern, nor that they would have agreed with Bailyn that the dominant labor system that emerged, "plantations, large and small, worked by gangs of black slaves," was necessarily a sign of failure. Bailyn's contention that "this outcome had not been predicted and had not been expected" is at odds with both the plans and actions of James Grant, the principal architect of East Florida's plantation society.[2]

Governor Grant's model was South Carolina, the only British

mainland colony with a black majority. Historian Peter Wood has shown that during South Carolina's first three decades, 1670–1700, its laborers were primarily white migrants from Barbados engaged in small-scale agriculture and exports of corn, livestock, and lumber. After discovering that rice could be a profitable export crop, and that Africans were generally experienced rice farmers and cattle drovers and were less susceptible than white settlers to malaria and yellow fever, the Carolina planters turned increasingly to black slaves. By 1735 a Charles Town (later Charleston) resident expressed what had already become a common belief: "[Rice] can't (in any great quantity's) be produced by white people. Because the Work is too laborious, the heat very intent, and the Whites can't work in the wett at that Season of the year." [3]

Historian David Galenson's comparison of colonial servitude and slavery established that all the southern British American provinces depended on white indentures during the initial decades of development, but that Africans predominated after a staple crop was established. The changeover in South Carolina came in the first decades of the eighteenth century, when rice became the staple export crop. Servants that arrived in the colonies after staple crops prevailed tended to be skilled tradesmen. When the expense of white skilled labor continued to climb, however, planters began training their slaves, especially those born in America. [4]

Decades before East Florida became a British colony, therefore, black slaves had become the laborers of choice in the rice and indigo fields of British America and had replaced whites as carpenters and coopers and in the other artisan trades. "By 1740," Charles Joyner has written, "two-thirds of South Carolina's settlers were Africans, nearly 40,000 people. On the Waccamaw [a coastal rice region] the proportions were even more lopsided." [5] When James Grant arrived in South Carolina in 1760, he found a long-established, distinctive racial demography that prompted one man to say that the colony "looks more like a negro country than like a country settled by white people." [6]

Grant encountered a dramatically different settlement pattern in East Florida in 1764. St. Augustine was an empty town with a garrison force of fewer than two hundred men, and outside the town walls, the new governor found only "a State of Nature when I landed . . . , not an acre of land planted in the Country and nobody to work or at work."[7] The exchange of flags between Spain and Britain had precipitated the evacuation of approximately 3,000 St. Augustine residents in January 1764, leaving only three families as transition settlers. After touring the province in September 1764, Grant complained that he had not found "ten acres of corn in the country," although "some straggling woodsmen already [were] upon [the St. Johns River]."[8] It was vital that land be cleared and crops planted immediately and that roads and other public improvements be attended to soon, and these tasks could only be accomplished if large numbers of workers moved into the province. But Grant was determined that workers would not be American frontiersmen, or "crackers," as he contemptuously referred to them.

Grant turned immediately to South Carolina, recruiting among the leading planters for men who could fill government offices and, not coincidentally, also bring into the province large numbers of Carolina-born slaves. John Moultrie was lured with promises of the lieutenant governorship and grants of free land. Moultrie, a graduate in medicine from Edinburgh University in Scotland, had written his thesis on the South Carolina yellow fever epidemic of 1745, finding that Africans were the least likely group to contract the disease. Calling Moultrie "a very well informed planter who makes the best Indigo in Carolina," the governor predicted that he would become an "oracle" in Florida, a man who would be consulted by other planters and who would recruit "some of [his] friends to come and live amongst us."[9] The bonus would be Moultrie's 180 slaves, who were already familiar both with the slash-and-burn techniques necessary to clear virgin lands and with the cultivation of rice, indigo, and other provisions projected for Florida. Some of his friends had even larger slave forces. His brother James Moultrie and William Drayton, Duke Bell, and Francis Kinloch were among many Carolinians who established Florida plantations through the labors of their slaves.

"only . . . by the labor of slaves"

Some of the first plantations attempted in East Florida by British absentee owners employed white indentures, but the results were so unsuccessful that James Grant warned others against using them. Even German immigrants, so prized in the northern colonies, "won't do here" Grant told one absentee in 1766. He conceded that they were "industrious" when self-employed, but he warned that when contracted to work for others, they routinely absconded: "Upon their landing they are immediately seized with the pride which every man is possessed of who wears a white face in America and they say they won't be slaves and so they make their escape." [10]

Grant elaborated on this theme in the many letters he sent to the absentee landowners. He alerted Thomas Thoroton that transporting white workers to Florida would be costly: daily wages of at least four shillings per day for common laborers and six for tradesmen were customary. Even at these wages, Grant observed, Germans in Florida were likely to conclude that "it is below the dignity of a White Man to be a slave to anybody, and that Negroes are the proper people to do the work." [11] He told the Earl of Cassillis, "No produce will answer the expense of white labor"; artisans sent from estates in Scotland, especially those accustomed to living in towns, became in Florida "generally drunk and idle." [12]

Grant's letters also contained encouraging news: Although white workers were prohibitively expensive, there was a moderately priced alternative in Carolina-born slaves, common field hands who could be purchased for between £40 and £50 sterling each and provided with food, clothing, and tools at an annual cost seldom as high as thirty shillings each. At these prices, and given that black slaves generally increased in number and value, it seemed only logical to the governor that "work in this new world and indeed in every warm climate must be carried on by Negroes." [13]

In June 1768 Grant visited an estate being prepared for John Perceval, the second Earl of Egmont, at Mount Royal on the St. Johns River and witnessed the work of white craftsmen sent from Egmont's estates in Britain. They appeared to be skilled and willing to work, Grant thought, but they tired so quickly in the heat that the governor concluded: "Settlements in this warm climate must be formed by Negroes. Our indented white people can hardly be prevailed upon to work for their own subsistence"—much less for the well-being of a master. Only after plantations were established and profitable could white laborers and small planters be introduced, "but such a plan my Lord is not to be thought of till this new world has in some means been created . . . [and] this country can only be brought to that rich and plentiful state by the labor of slaves."[14] Grant urged Egmont to discharge his expensive white tradesmen and replace them with skilled slaves trained in South Carolina.

"Country born" or "new Negroes"?

Grant advised the absentee owners to start plantations with "country born" Negroes available in South Carolina who were familiar with the planting practices and the language of their owners. "Seasoned" Africans—residents of South Carolina for several years and familiar with the crops and the language—could also be included among the slaves designated to start a new plantation. After these experienced workers had cleared the land, planted provisions, and constructed shelters, "new Negroes" direct from the coast of Africa could be merged into the labor force, at savings of one-third or more in purchase costs.

Grant brought ten domestic servants to St. Augustine, including Francois, a butler; Baptiste, a cook; Ragout, an assistant cook; and Alexander, a baker.[15] Over the following years he and his agent purchased many more slaves. In 1764 Grant bought eight slaves from Henry Laurens to start a 350-acre farm immediately adjacent to the northern boundary of the town. The five men and three women, purchased at an average price of £62, were "country born."[16] Included were Will and his son Charles, who had been the property of William Simpson. In 1767 Simpson wrote from South Carolina asking the governor to purchase Will's wife and four other children: "The fellow writes his wife frequently . . . in great distress for want of her; he disobliged me, otherwise I would not have parted with him; but he is now sufficiently punished. . . . A separating of those unhappy people is adding distress to their unfortunate condition."[17] It is not possible to tell from the records if the family was reunited, but Will stayed with Grant for two decades. He was occasionally hired out to other planters as a plowman, and he became manager of all planting activities at one of Grant's estates.

Grant continued to purchase country-born slaves when he found bargains at probate and other sales and when he was in need of laborers with special skills. Among the "seasoned" Africans he bought were Jimmy Lowe, Harford, and Adam, who were described by Henry Laurens as "used to water works" and "good hands. The first two speak and understand English pretty well." [18] The three men were put to work on the provincial schooner.

"New Negroes" were sent to the farm in April 1765 when Laurens shipped five "Angola boys" for £30 each, considerably less expensive than the Carolina-born men and women they joined. Apparently men in their late teens, they became field laborers under the tutelage of Will and the established crew. Within six months, one of these Africans was added to Grant's staff of domestics.[19] Dick must have learned the craft quickly, since he was sold as a cook in 1769 for £70. Robin, another "Angola boy," also joined Grant's domestic staff as a worker in "marsh grasses," probably a basket maker.[20]

In 1768 Grant opened an indigo plantation a few miles north of St. Augustine. Intended to "put a spur" to absentee grantees to speed up development, "Grant's Villa" became a training school for the province's inexperienced overseers. "New Negroes" made up 66 percent of the fifty-one laborers who initiated the villa.[21] Grant boasted that his first indigo crop brought a modest profit, and that he expected his second crop to "clear a good 15 percent for all the money I have laid out. . . . All my expense was upon Negroes who are walking about, no white face belonging to the plantation but an overseer." [22] He told Lord Egmont: "My Negroes, about 40 working hands, live in Palmetto huts for the time in the course of winter without putting me to any expense but the first cost of the boards and a few nails. The Negroes after doing their tasks will find scantling and shingles or clapboards and will build their houses themselves without any assistance." [23]

"Ebo's . . . don't go off well"

Sales of slaves to East Florida were arranged primarily by two colonial merchants, Henry Laurens of Charles Town and John Graham of Savannah. Little has been written about Graham, who shipped hundreds of slaves to Florida, including Africans he purchased in Savannah and Charles Town from African traders, "refuse" Africans bought in the West Indies and sent to Savannah, and seasoned and country-born Negroes from plantation sales and probate sales in

Georgia, South Carolina, and Antigua and other West Indies locations. In the latter category were field laborers, sawyers, artisans, domestics, and even black drivers and plantation managers.

In January 1766 Graham warned Grant to be wary of the Africans being sold in St. Augustine by a Mr. Rogers, whose low price (£34) disguised his "lack of orthodox principles."[24] Grant ignored the advice and purchased from Rogers "an able fellow and a very handsome wench," but he also placed an order with Graham for "a few men boys for my farm. I should like them well lookt."[25] Graham was selective when purchasing Africans, looking at their health, age, and appearance. When a shipment of ninety-six Africans sold for only £16 on average, Graham refused to buy "such wretches as I never saw before."[26] He also rejected a shipment of healthy and attractive Africans, "nearly all boys and girls, only 27 grown men in all," but too expensive at £48 each.[27]

In December of 1767, Grant placed an order with Graham for 100 to 115 Africans, to be delivered "the sooner the better for they are much wanted."[28] He said he would trust the merchant to set a fair price, but "since it is our first purchase [Grant was ordering on behalf of seven other planters] you will bring that as low as you can." The only other condition of sale set by the sociable governor was that "the business must be finally concluded in my house over a bottle of Madeira."

Three days later Graham sent thirty-five slaves he had purchased from merchants "in the islands." He also sent a "young lad in sailor's jacket, eight months on vessel, speaks good deal English and clever. You may want him on the Province schooner, . . . if he fails a tryal, put him in the field."[29] Grant named the young sailor Adam and placed him in charge of the boats at his indigo plantation.[30]

Two vessels arrived in Savannah in July of 1768 with cargoes of slaves from the Windward Coast of West Africa. Nearly ninety were sent to East Florida, including six males for Governor Grant at a price of £43 each. Graham said, "I think I never saw finer people."[31] One month later the merchant shipped thirty-five men from the Gold Coast for Lord Egmont and six for James Moncrief.[32]

Late in January of 1769, Graham sent Grant four "black ladies . . . [including] two very strong and able wenches, and will do as much work as any man, and are also young . . . [and] a very likely, young smart girl goes by her country name Sulundie. Your Tom speaks her language." [33] Look for the ship, Graham told Grant, and for "your four wenches . . . [marked] with yellow silk ferret [ribbon] tied round their wrists." He also advised Grant that few African ships were arriving at that time of the year. There had been some imports from the West Indies, but they had been mainly "Ebo's, who don't go off well." [34] Charles Town would probably draw the first of the shipments in spring and summer, when prices would be £50 for adult men and £39 for women. Graham predicted prices would fall to about £37 for "choice" men in August and October, when "the fiery edge of the Carolina planters will be off and in general all of them pretty well supplied."

Graham described the "fiery edge" after returning from a Charles Town sale of Africans from the Grain Coast and Windward Coast. With great difficulty, and even with the assistance of seven men, Graham had been able to claim only fifty-three Africans (including five men for James Grant and eighteen for a new St. Johns River plantation). The problem at the sale had been that "people were pulling, hawling and pushing one another down as if they had been to gott for nothing." [35]

"exceeding good Carpenter and Boatbuilder"

The enterprising merchant also searched the countryside for country-born slaves with the special skills Florida buyers requested. He sent two "excellent Sawyers and Squarers, absolutely a bargain" at £54 each, to a Halifax River planter in March of 1769. [36] When a Georgia man sold five hundred head of cattle to a Florida planter in 1767, Graham arranged the sale of his slave drover for £105. He described the man as a "Cowpen Keeper Negro" who was "bred up from his infance in this business . . . [and] is remarkably clever and can manage any stock." [37]

Several families of skilled slaves were sent to Florida in 1768 from the plantation of Jonathan Bryan, a prominent planter in Georgia who had fallen on hard times. Four of the men were skilled sawyers who had each earned Bryan £18 a year in rental income; they sold for £61 each. All the men were "good on rice and every kind of plantation work and are capable of the management of a plantation themselves." [38] Graham thought the best bargain was a "a remarkable choice family" of husband and wife and two "fine grown boys and a girl." He described the man as an "exceeding good Carpenter and Boatbuilder, also a good planter, having for two years past managed Mr. Bryan's plantation himself without any overseer, and is perhaps one of the most valuable Negroes in the two provinces." Graham said he did not want "to buy the family but I could not get him [the husband and father] without them. The wench likewise very valuable, is a good washer and ironer, has for years past cut out and made herself all the Negroe cloaks for Mr. Bryan's people and is otherwise a good House Wench." The entire family, including sons who worked as house servants, waited on their master, and cared for the horses, sold for £290.

The correspondence of Graham and Laurens provides evidence that skilled slaves, drivers, and plantation managers from Georgia and Carolina plantations were available to Florida planters. When a Florida planter placed a standing order in 1768 for a black driver capable of "managing Rice & Indigo," Laurens attended auctions until he found a satisfactory person. Laurens wrote in February of 1768 that he had "purchas'd at a Publick Sale a Negro of a good Character & who was said to have been a driver for the last five Years Constantly which I thought much In his favor but he has a Wife tack'd to him; however I believe you will think the Couple cheap at £710 [Carolina currency; approximately £101 sterling]." [39]

Laurens also supplied the laborers for Mount Oswald, a 20,000-acre plantation on the Tomoka and Halifax rivers that was to be established for wealthy Scotsman Richard Oswald. Oswald was part owner of Bance Island, a slaving fortification in the Sierra Leone River, and he had previously shipped consignments of African slaves to Laurens in Charles Town.[40] Grant advised Oswald that thirty Carolina-born slaves with at least one year's experience in indigo fields would be needed to start Mount Oswald. Work was to begin in 1765 during fall season and continue through the winter; shelters were to be built and land cleared and prepared for spring planting of provisions. Oswald's black pioneers would also be expected to clear ground for indigo planting and to build houses for thirty additional Carolina-born slaves who would arrive in the second year at the site. During the third year Oswald would send sixty "new" Africans, for a total of 120 laborers. The goal was to become self-sufficient in foodstuffs during the first year and to establish four separate plantations by the end of the third, devoted respectively to indigo, cotton, sugar, and rice.[41]

Grant selected and surveyed a promising 20,000-acre site on the Tomoka River while Henry Laurens assembled a labor force for Oswald's new estate.[42] Laurens advertised in the *South Carolina Gazette* for "two Negro Carpenters, two Coopers, three pair of Sawyers, forty Field Negroes, young men and women, some acquainted with indigo making, and all with the ordinary course of Plantation work in this country."[43] In 1765 Laurens shipped twenty-four men, seven women, and three children to work on Oswald's new plantation. Nine of the men were "new" Africans, billed at an average price of £29. Of the seven women, four were described as capable of a variety of domestic skills, including Silvia, a "wench highly recommended as a quick and willing slave" for housework and gardening; Lucy, the mother of two young children, who could "wash very well, iron and cook tolerably"; and Maggy, who could wash, iron, and cook, "but loves Rum." Mary, the least expensive at £20, was a "stout, able new Negro, middle-aged, bought when low in flesh, would sell for 50 percent more now." Chloe was born in Carolina and bought "of a transient person" for about two-thirds of her value. The most costly was Jenny, "a young woman used to drudgery about house and garden," bought for £48.[44]

The last of the seven women, Nanny, is of particular interest. Governor Grant transferred her to another planter because he judged her too valuable for plantation work. Laurens described Nanny as eighteen or nineteen years old, able to wash and iron "exceeding well, is very orderly and can do any house work."[45] She carried with her to St. Augustine a "pretty child named Minto in arms." Nanny and the child were billed at £64. Laurens said about Grant:

> The Governor does not understand Plantation affairs so well as some of us Southern folks. I have not less than ten Negro Women upon 3 Plantations that would sell for more than Nanny but I do not think them too valuable. Such Negroes for their ability in making Negro Cloths, attending sick people, & a hundred things which new or Ship's Negroes cannot perform are invaluable. Nanny is a breeding Woman & in ten Years time

may have double her worth in her own Children. Mrs. Laurens had a great covetousness for her [as a house servant] when I first bought her but knowing her value I would not convert the property. I shall take the Liberty to hint this to His Excellency.[46]

"be discreet & carry a steady command"

The twenty-four male slaves Laurens bought for Oswald were primarily field hands, but several had additional skills like sawing, attending horses, butchering, and driving carts. Caesar was a "very stout well made young man, orderly, country born, about 19," a cooper who had served four years as an apprentice. Caesar was evaluated at £65. Harry, with five years' experience as a carpenter, was the most costly, at £71.

Laurens found it difficult to fill Grant's order for the second round of laborers for Oswald. With Carolina-born slaves hard to find, he advised that Grant accept "fine young Gambians or Gold Coast [imports]. They are fit to work immediately and the next year will be as good hands as any and less inclined to wander."[47] In November he sent, as replacement for Nanny, a "truly promising New Negro" named Liberty.[48]

The workers Laurens selected were healthy and well behaved, "fine specimens" according to Grant. Since they arrived too early in the year to begin the Mount Oswald settlement, Grant put them to work at his own farm near St. Augustine, clearing brush, planting corn, and digging a ditch around the entire three hundred acres.[49]

Despite Oswald's fears of high mortality rates in the Tomoka area, and his concerns that Carolina-born slaves were then relatively expensive, Grant was able to persuade him to accelerate development and to augment the workforce with "new" Africans. He also approved the purchase of thirty additional Carolina-born workers, and began speculating on acquiring from Antigua or St. Christopher a "few old Negroes who know how to raise and clean cotton."[50]

The arrival of Oswald's new overseer, identified only as Mr. Hewie, was delayed until mid-1766, prompting Grant to postpone sending the "Negroes alone into the Wilderness." When Hewie arrived from South Carolina in June, the governor "immediately" ordered him to Tomoka with twelve male slaves. The women and younger slaves stayed behind at Grant's farm.[51]

Henry Laurens had sent Hewie to Florida after receiving strong recommendations of his managerial abilities. Yet Laurens remained concerned about the isolated location of Mount Oswald, fearing that if provoked by "the arbitrary power of an Overseer," the slaves might become "tempted to knock him in the head & file off in a Body." [52] His fears were heightened by reports of Hewie's quarrels with the governor and his difficulties in controlling the slaves.

The governor objected to Hewie's episodes of drunkenness, his excessive and abusive labor demands, and his unreasonably severe punishments, which led some slaves to run away. Still, Grant could report at the end of August that work was progressing as expected and that none of the laborers had died. [53]

Before the year ended, however, the slaves rebelled and drowned Hewie. Laurens was moved to lament:

> The catastrophe of the wretched [Hewie] & the poor Negroes is affecting. He might have been, according to his credentials a good Servant, but I see clearly that he was unfit for the sole management of a Plantation. His successor the Indian Johnson must behave above the rank of common Carolinian Fugitives, to save his Scalp a whole year. He must be discreet & carry a steady command otherwise the Blacks will drown him too, for of all Overseers they love those of their own colour least. [54]

There is no surviving record of Oswald's reaction to the death of his overseer, beyond his decision to send additional whites to Mount Oswald for security. [55] The success of "Indian Johnson," the overseer who replaced Hewie, may also have convinced Oswald to accelerate the pace of development. Laurens implied that Johnson was a black man, or of mixed Indian and African ancestry; others have concluded from Laurens's remarks about Johnson that he was Indian. But whether African American or African Indian, Johnson was one of several nonwhite managers that capably discharged their duties in East Florida. [56]

"sending such a number of Africans"

Oswald planned to use John Graham, of Savannah, to broker a regular slave trade from Bance Island and reduce the cost of slaves for his

Florida plantation. He also anticipated occasional trips to "Barbados to buy Refuse Slaves at half the money, which with a little care would be as good as any we could get on ye coast."[57] In 1767 Oswald notified Grant that Captain Richard Savery was sailing for Bance Island to secure approximately one hundred Africans for Mount Oswald and would anchor the *St. Augustine Packet* off St. Augustine in September. Worried that "it might be of bad consequence if the men slaves now on the Plantation remained longer unprovided with wives," Oswald had "ordered 30 young women to be shipped and 30 more lads and large girls of such as they may be fit for field labor in about two years." He also directed his agents in Africa "to send a few full grown men, not exceeding ten in number, . . . [who were] used to the Trades of their country believing they will become soon useful and handy in a new plantation."[58]

Savery delivered seventy Africans for Mount Oswald, but only twenty were old enough to be considered working hands. The other fifty were excellent-quality boys and girls not yet mature enough for field work, but Oswald predicted that if raised at Tomoka they would eventually be "worth two imported at full age." With approximately 120 men, women, and children to feed, however, Oswald worried that stores of provisions might be inadequate. He advised Grant to consider selling the "smallest [children] for good bills or cash," but if the food supply was satisfactory, he wanted the governor to "sell none."[59]

Oswald soon organized a trade involving the Florida plantations, the Caribbean, Africa, and Britain.[60] His vessel, the *Charlotte Cape*, sailed from St. Augustine to St. Croix to pick up rum for sale in Africa before "returning to St. Christophers with about 100 Negroes." Oswald promised that if a satisfactory trade plan could be "settled among the Florida gentlemen" the *Charlotte* would "be at their service in any shape they please."[61]

Despite the threat of late season storms Captain Savery brought another "cargo of very fine Slaves . . . from the coast of Africa" to St. Augustine in December.[62] The entire cargo was sold by early January at prices lower than Savannah merchants were then charging. Between 1767 and 1770 Oswald delivered at least four shipments of Africans to St. Augustine, providing much-needed laborers for the East Florida plantations.[63] Let other grantees grumble about "money laid out and nothing returned but accounts of inundations, cater-pillars, etc.," Oswald wrote to Grant. "I hope you will allow I have done my part for getting things forward by sending such a number of Africans, with whom I hope everybody is pleased." [64]

Oswald's ships continued to carry slaves to East Florida in 1771 and 1772, probably the peak years for the trade. Thomas Taylor believes that in 1771 at least a thousand slaves were imported.[65] In July 1772 David Yeats rejoiced that "Mr. Oswald's vessel . . . is expected next month from the Coast of Guinea, tis to be hoped she will dispose of her cargoe here as Negroes are much wanted at the present." [66] Three planters had orders for ninety Africans, but Yeats hoped there would be at least 120 aboard.

The number of slaves at Mount Oswald grew from more than 100 in 1767 to 240 in 1780.[67] Most of the thirty workers who initiated the plantation had been country-born in South Carolina; the remainder were shipped from Oswald's trading establishment at Bance Island. In 1774 Laurens announced that Oswald planned to send to East Florida "about one hundred of the Grametas or Island Slaves" em-ployed at Bance Island. Oswald had promised "not to expose them to public Sale in the manner of African Cargoes, but if possible & with their liking & good behaviour to keep them together to work on his plantation." Fearing "the Neighbouring King & his people would immediately Seize & Sell them to the next Trading Vessel" if discharged from their duties in Africa, Oswald decided to send the "Island Slaves" to East Florida. Laurens stated: "Mr. Oswald is de-sirous of keeping them all together or in plantations near each other, & objects to hiring any of them out." [68]

By 1776 there were fifteen other major plantations in the general vicinity of Oswald's estate, in what came to be called the Mosquito District. It can be assumed that a significant percentage of the Afri-cans in the district were transported by Oswald's ships, but there was also an East Florida–based slaving firm that began business as early as 1767. In November 1767 Laurens wrote two letters of credit for Penman and Co. for £2,000 each to the leading African merchants in St. Christopher and Barbados. Laurens commented on January 15, 1768, that the firm had sold ninety "new" Africans in East Florida the previous November and December. James Penman became a rice planter on the St. Johns River and a leading merchant in St. Augustine; his partners in the slaving firm, William Mackdougall and Robert Bissett also became prominent planters. Few records survive to document their involvement in the slave trade to East Florida.[69]

James Grant returned to London in 1771 for treatment of a painful gout condition, leaving behind a thriving core of East Florida plantations. The new governor, Colonel Patrick Tonyn, who arrived in 1774, found estate owners still eager to buy Africans. Even in 1776, after the American Revolution had begun and Georgia rebels and privateers had destroyed plantations, disrupted indigo exports, and raided for slaves, Tonyn could report that optimistic planters were "purchasing new Negroes." Moreover, shipments to the West Indies of naval stores and lumber for shipbuilding led to a new boom and expansion in the province that lasted until the British evacuation in 1784.[70]

"as happy as the nature of their servitude will admit"

British Florida's slave population was quite diverse. Carolina- and Georgia-born blacks were in the majority in the 1760s, but Africans took the lead in the 1770s. Specific ethnic origins are seldom identifiable, but it is safe to generalize that most "new" Africans came from homelands in interior Senegal, Mali, Gambia, Guinea, and Sierra Leone, with additional numbers from Nigeria and Angola.[71]

Their labor proved to be as diverse as their origins. Slaves engaged in indigo, rice, and provisions production, and later in lumbering, naval stores, and turpentine extraction. They were also domestics, drovers, sailors, hunters, basket makers, carpenters, coopers, wheelwrights, sawyers, indigo makers, dairymaids, weavers, washerwomen, drivers, and plantation managers. Some worked for wages in town and on plantations.[72]

As slaves created indigo, rice, cotton, and sugar plantations from virgin soils in wilderness woodlands and swamps, they constructed their own shelters, at minimal cost to their owners. Moreover, unless drought intervened, the produce of their provisions fields typically exceeded household demands, and the surplus was sold in St. Augustine. John Moultrie's slaves harvested two crops from his rice fields at Tomoka River in 1775, with "the second cutting . . . very little in-

Slave labor on a rice plantation. This illustration from *Frank Leslie's Illustrated Newspaper*, October 20, 1806, shows the variety of skills required to grow rice. Richard Oswald's African-born slaves performed the grueling labor of establishing new rice plantations at several northeast Florida locations.

ferior to the first." They also constructed his "handsome stone house at Bella Vista" on the Matanzas River. Moultrie planned to retire there, thinking the house "will last forever, a good country house with ten rooms, plows & carts going in the fields . . . , more rice than I can beat out . . . fine stock of cattle & hogs & plenty of . . . fish, butter & cream, cheese, everything." Everything that Moultrie thought he would need in life was entirely the result of the hard work and remarkable productivity of his black slaves.[73]

What cannot be defined with certainty are the specific conditions of life and labor imposed by Moultrie and the other Florida planters. The daily lives of East Florida slaves are seldom mentioned in the primary sources, beyond obscure hints and references filtered through the perceptions of white male slaveowners. There are rare comments like one overseer's description of bondsmen "obliged to be upon foot night and day in order to save as much of the indigo

The main house at the Kingsley Plantation, Fort George Island. Zephaniah Kingsley settled in East Florida in 1803. He moved to this home in 1814 with his African-born wife, Anna Madgigine Jai. From here they supervised Kingsley's numerous plantations. Courtesy of the Florida State Archives.

from the worms as possible," but the implication elsewhere in the letter is that this was atypical.[74] In general, there are insufficient data to generalize on hours of labor, daily food rations, incidence of illness, medical care, and treatment of slaves by their owners.

Information on rebellions or other types of large-scale disorders is almost nonexistent in the records, which, given the paucity of whites in the plantation regions, is puzzling. With only a single white man supervising the slaves at James Grant's indigo plantation, why did the blacks not replicate the fate of poor Mr. Hewie at Mount Oswald. But such did not happen again at Oswald's estate, nor at Grant's Villa and the other plantations in the province. Oswald raised the number of white overseers as a deterrent to uprisings, but other planters used slaves as drivers to direct field work and even to manage all plantation activities. Perhaps the skills of these black drivers as mediators and leaders explains the minimal incidence of recorded violence. Another factor worth consideration is the practice of setting up plantations with Carolina-born slaves before adding "new"

Africans to the workforces, which may have served as a social control mechanism while at the same time providing an acculturative transition for the newcomers.

On the latter point, however, there are hints of conflicts among the slaves, perhaps prompted by interethnic jealousies and by something resembling class antagonisms. The poisoning of two of James Grant's slaves, for instance, may have been the work of "new" Africans brought to his indigo plantation. Grant's agent, Dr. David Yeats, informed him June 5, 1780, of

> a most shocking affair that has lately happened at your plantation. Leander, one of your best Negroes, and Jack his brother, old Carolina's sons, have been poisoned and are both dead. They died suddenly within two days of one another in great agony and all the symptoms of poison. What makes this matter still worse, three of your own Negroes have been accused of it. Two fellows and a wench and one of the fellows (Walley), has since shot himself. . . . I should be happy to have this fellow punished as he deserves for so atrocious a deed and to deter others from the like, if we can fix it upon him, but [it is] a difficult matter to come at the truth where none but Negroes are concerned.[75]

Leander and his brother and mother had been in Grant's employ since 1765. During that time the workforce had changed from majority-born in Carolina to majority-born in Africa. Leander, the plantation carpenter, and the other Carolina-born men had become the elite of the slave quarters; they were the skilled tradesmen, plowmen, drivers, and managers. It is possible their lengthy tenure also gave them the privilege of spouses, which could have sparked further envy and resentment.[76]

The planters believed that balancing sex ratios was an effective way to control the behavior of their male slaves. In 1771, Yeats wrote to Grant: "The plantation negroes are all healthy and behave well except Jack, who has got such a liking to this town that there is no keeping him out of it unless he is constantly chained."[77] Ten years later, with a larger workforce and a higher percentage of Africans, Yeats encountered this problem again, with added intensity. He urged Grant to purchase "young wenches for the plantation which suffers so much by having so few, for you not only lose by your Negroes not

Slave cabins built in the 1820s at the Kingsley Plantation. The two-room tabby structures with brick fireplaces were still inhabited by African American families at the time this photograph was taken (ca. 1870). Courtesy of the Florida State Archives.

increasing, but frequently the labour of the young fellows, who are either absenting themselves after the wenches in Town, or inducing them to run away and concealing them in the woods in the neighborhood of the plantation. I have frequent complaints on this head, and their guise is what must they do for wife?"[78]

Security had been Richard Oswald's reason for sending African women to his Tomoka plantation in 1767. Social control was also on John Tucker's mind when he decided to "make all my black servants as happy as the nature of their servitude will admit. I have added ten women more to the twenty mentioned [previously] to provide each of the men slaves with a wife as a means of keeping them at home and to do their work cheerfully."[79]

In 1769 the Earl of Egmont ordered young African women for his male laborers in Florida, hoping to render the Negroes I now have happy and contented, which I know they cannot be without having each a Wife. This will greatly tend to keep them at home and to make them Regular and tho the Women will not work all together so well as ye Men, Yet Amends will be sufficiently made in a very few years by the Great Encrease of Children who may easily [be trained] and become faithfully attached to the Glebe and to their Master.[80]

Some owners offered incentives to labor that may also have served as control mechanisms. One owner gave Sundays off, then paid for cutting wood, making indigo boxes, and other work performed on that day. Governor Grant paid wages to slaves who did extra work like carting and cutting stones for his garden wall and making seed baskets, as well as to "Dick the fisherman" and "Black Sandy the hunter."[81]

Others believed that the way they treated their slaves made a difference in how they behaved and worked. James Grant, for example, described the work routine at his estate as "very strict" and regular as "clockwork." Looking back on his slaves in 1784, he judged that "the Negroes . . . served me well and faithfully. . . . I dare say there are no better slaves anywhere, they have always been well fed and cloathed."[82]

John Moultrie considered himself "a patron and protector as well as master to my Negroes" and pledged to make them "happy" as they aged "and wore out," as long as they "continued faithful, diligent, industrious and well behaved, attentive to my wishes."

> Quamino has never behaved amiss, always sweet, has never had a blow and . . . he never may, he will I think never deserve it. I desire to make him independent of the overseers. He must be allowed to go about among my people giving them good advice and seeing that they do not do amiss. He is an old planter and may be of service in directing the Negroes, but he must not be struck by any manager or overseer. He is trusty and so is old Frank, and may keep the keys of any stores, etc.[83]

There is, of course, a clear implication that some Moultrie slaves were believed by authorities to have behaved amiss and that whippings were not unheard of.

After hearing in 1783 that East Florida would be returned to Spain,

Moultrie became concerned about "a number of faithful servants brought up for several generations in our family," and he contemplated freeing them, burning his houses, and becoming "a real philosopher." Instead, he sent them to the Bahamas, from where Quamino wrote in 1795, long after Moultrie had settled in England.

"My Dear Master

This will be delivered you by Doctor Bailey who was on your plantation since we left St. Augustine. I have had pretty good health but now am growing very old and weak and if you had not placed us in the care of such good men as Mr. Moss's are I don't know what would have became of us. When we are sick we are attended by a Doctor and everything we can in reason expect. I had the misfortune about three months ago to lose my wife Margaret which I feel a great deal at a loss for. We have long been looking for some of our young masters who you said should come and be amongst us but am sorry to hear of their only coming about half way, and I have now given up hopes of ever seeing you or any of your family. But please to give my kind love to my old mistress, Miss Sally, Bella and Martha, Master Tacky, George and Timmy, and I will wish God may bless you and give you your health. Brother Andrew also joins me in love too. I remain dear master,

your ever faithful Servt,
Quamino"[84]

"mismanagement and a capricious cruelty"

While Moultrie was seen by his peers as a paternalistic slave manager concerned about the welfare of his bondsmen, there was at least one prominent East Florida official whom contemporaries condemned for cruelty to his black servants: the second governor of East Florida, Colonel Patrick Tonyn.

Multiple informants—including Frederick George Mulcaster, surveyor general of the province, a member of the Royal Engineers, and reputedly an illegitimate half-brother of King George III; the Reverend John Forbes, Episcopal cleric; Dr. David Yeats, secretary of the province; and Alexander Skinner, an overseer and government agent to the Indians—all accused the governor and his wife of brutal treatment of Alexander, Peg, and Sue, three of Grant's slaves whom Tonyn had hired. Yeats informed Grant that the three were "greatly complaining about bad usage, which indeed is no fault of his but the WOMAN'S, who appears to be of a hard-headed disposition, at least to the servants." [85] Reverend Forbes heard similar complaints and investigated. He told Grant: "They plead hard and the town says [they] have Iron Caps. . . . Alexander complains that Madam is the devil, he told me the governor was well enough, but since I saw him he has had the cap above mentioned and been flogged." [86] Within two days, Forbes had investigated further and sent an urgent appeal: "Your Negroes, from the mismanagement and a capricious cruelty of a fine lady, are considered as being in a state of the most abject slavery. Alexander has got an iron cap with which he walks the streets." [87]

James Grant was in Halifax, Nova Scotia, at the time, having traded his place in Parliament for service in the British army. When he heard of the floggings and the cruel imposition of an iron mask clamped about the head of Alexander—a punishment that caused great pain and prevented slaves from feeding themselves through its iron bars—he reacted decisively. He scolded Dr. Yeats for permitting Tonyn to subject the "poor creatures" to a "degree of severity which they had never been accustomed to meet with in my house," and for acquiescing when Tonyn sent Sue to work as a field slave at his St. Johns River plantation. Bring Sue home immediately, Grant told Yeats, and added, "If Alexander and Peg are still in the woods [runaways], which I wish them to be, you are publickly to make it known that Governor Tonyn has nothing to do with them, that they have nothing to fear, and are to live in the future at Grant's Villa." [88] He also notified his overseer, Alexander Skinner: "I will neither sell or hire Alexander, Peg and Sue to Governor Tonyn, and have directed him . . . to send them to the Villa within twenty-four hours after he receives my letter . . . where they are to live in future in peace and quiet." He promised to disguise Skinner's involvement: "Tis a cross talk if the Governor sees it, but I care not a farthing about him." [89]

Four eyewitnesses, all important and credible people with more to lose than gain by reporting the incidents, sent the former governor corroborating accounts of Tonyn's cruel treatment. That Grant believed them, and denounced Governor Tonyn in public view, prompts questions about the daily lives and treatment of the other slaves working at Tonyn's St. Johns River plantation.

"in the woods some time"

Florida slaves, like slaves elsewhere, ran away to escape mistreatment, and some found refuge among the Indians.[90] Grant wrote that four slave runaways crossed the St. Johns River and joined a band of Indian hunters, "who were very fond of them, and employed them as Servants, but immediately gave them up when they were applied for."[91]

Another Indian hunting party assisted a "stout Negro fellow of . . . the Ebo country named Boatswain" to escape from James Penman's estate.[92] Boatswain had been seen stealing corn and ran away to escape punishment. Penman went looking for him, and for Peter, a runaway from another plantation who had been "in the woods some time." Penman was unable to find Peter, but he returned with Boatswain and three other runaways. Ten days later Penman scoured the wilderness five miles south of Mount Oswald until he found a runaway who had "constantly lived without fire, or any nourishment but the Palmetto Berry" for several months.[93]

The continuing tendency of the Indians to shelter runaways prompted a bounty of £2 for every escapee returned to British authorities. When Indians turned in seven runaways in June 1771, Moultrie said: "It has been a practice for negroes to run away from their Masters and to get into the Indian towns, from whence it proved very difficult and troublesome to get them back."[94] Although the Indians denied it, Moultrie insisted they often "sequestered or rescued" slaves who escaped to their villages. The return of seven escapees would hopefully send a strong message to Florida slaves that refuge among the Indians had ended and would "soon put a stop to runaway Slaves flying into their towns." Moultrie gladly paid the £14 in bounties, and also compensated a Georgia man for returning eight other runaways captured near the boundary of Indian lands. Slaves absconding to the Florida Indians would be a familiar theme for decades, whether Britain, Spain, or the United States controlled the province.[95]

The closing years of the province's brief history must have been traumatic for the black slaves of East Florida. Georgia privateers and border marauders frequently raided for cattle and slaves. Andrew Turnbull was so fearful of Georgia raids in 1776 that he made plans to "sneak" his slaves down the Indian River and into hiding spots in the woods. Turnbull's estate was indeed raided, on November 29, 1779; eighteen slaves were carried off by privateers, believed at the time to be Spaniards.[96] London merchant John Wilkinson's plantation west of the St. Johns River was destroyed in July 1777, and the raiders abducted more than thirty of his slaves. Next they proceeded to sack a neighboring estate and steal a slave family.[97]

The military threat from Georgia resulted in a degree of freedom for some East Florida black men. In 1776 Governor Patrick Tonyn created four black militia companies to join in defense of the province. The governor, anticipating rebelliousness, appointed "double or treble white officers" for each company. Even so, it seems improbable that armed black slaves could have been controlled so easily under frontier military conditions, or that they would have fought with enthusiasm unless freedom was the incentive. But fight they did, as members of the St. Johns Rangers, a mixed regiment of whites, Indians, and blacks who ranged widely within the province and participated in attacks on enemy fortifications in Georgia. They also became adept border marauders who brought thousands of cattle to St. Augustine. John Moultrie summarized these guerrilla raids in October 1776: "Georgia began to plunder us, we retaliated, the common frontier quite abandoned on both sides, horses and crops destroyed, people and cattle moved away." [98]

For other slaves the war meant only an exchange of overseers and a switch from field work to construction of fortifications. The General Assembly passed a labor draft law in 1781 requiring each planter to send one in ten of his slaves to work under the direction of military engineers. Recompense for owners was one shilling per day, which Tonyn estimated at one-fourth or one-fifth the true value. Six months later, the General Assembly drafted one in every five slaves. Tonyn acknowledged that slaveowners were making major sacrifices through loss of labor at a time of great profitability in agriculture and naval stores. He also commented on the "immense labor" demanded of drafted slaves.[99]

Some planters resorted to drafting measures of their own in futile efforts to protect their property. The exposed location of Jeremyn Wright's estate led him to arm fifty slaves. In 1771 Wright had purchased a rice plantation established in the previous decade by South Carolina planter Andrew Way on a "tide river swamp, on St. Mary's River."[100] Wright accumulated more than 1,000 acres and eventually imported 170 black slaves. After constructing dwellings and barns, clearing and planting extensive fields of corn and peas, as well as a four-hundred-acre rice field, Wright found himself the target of rebel attacks. His company of armed slaves was used by provincial troops to help repel attacks on Amelia Island in August 1776, but the following July they were overwhelmed by vengeful Georgians, who abducted twenty slaves and destroyed the plantation. Survivors escaped into the woods and made their way to St. Augustine.[101]

"till this new world has in some means been created"

Visitors to the Amelia Island plantation of Lord Egmont in 1773 and 1774 recorded large fields of potatoes, 140 acres of corn and peas, over 200 acres of indigo, and a herd of "fat and well" cattle pastured on the island. The estate was self-sufficient in foodstuffs and sent 1,000 bushels of corn to market in 1773. Wandering naturalist William Bartram, whose own plantation at Picolata on the St. Johns River had failed, also admired the excellent indigo fields and the "cotton, corn, batatas, and almost every esculent vegetable" that he saw at the Amelia Island plantation.[102]

To defend the Egmont estate from attack, plantation manager Stephen Egan armed twelve slave men to join provincial troops patrolling the St. Marys River, but in 1777 raiders destroyed the estate, sending the Egan family and more than one hundred slaves in flight to an undeveloped tract east of the St. Johns River, two miles south of the cow ford (today's Jacksonville). For the third time in a decade the Egmont slaves would begin carving a new plantation from the East Florida wilderness. Starting in 1768 as a force of thirty-five Africans from the Gold Coast, they had built shelters, cleared land, and planted corn, rice, and indigo at Mount Royal on the St. Johns River. They later established the 10,000-acre tract at the north end of Amelia Island, abandoned after the 1777 raids. At the third site, named Cecilton, the well-seasoned laborers began anew the exhausting and dangerous burdens of creating a Florida plantation. As productive and versatile as before, they drew from the forests a bountiful harvest of timber, tar, pitch, and turpentine.[103]

Prior to the British evacuation, Governor Tonyn inventoried Cecilton plantation. Living at the estate were Egan and his wife and three sons, along with twenty-two of Egan's slaves and seventy-eight slaves belonging to the Egmonts. Three men had died at Cecilton: Peter of old age, Nero of "dropsy," and Robin of drowning. Juba, Joe, Nestor, Hannibal, and Pan had escaped to the Indians, and others had been abducted by the Georgia rebels, but there were still fourteen slave families, totaling fifty-nine men, women and children, and nineteen single males working under Egan's supervision. The women's occupations included field slave, washer, needleworker, cotton spinner, and midwife. The men were described as sawyers, squarers, makers of turpentine and pitch and tar and adept at all lumber and naval stores, carpenters, coopers, drivers, and cattle-keepers. Charles was listed as: "sawyer, squarer, hunter, field slave, understands management of horses and cattle." After the Treaty of Paris returned East Florida to Spain in 1783, the Egmont slaves were evacuated in 1785 to start new lives yet again at coffee plantations in Dominica.

"realising something out of the wreck"

Evacuation forced John Moultrie to make some disposition of his slaves, and the choices he faced were troubling. "I cannot think," Moultrie wrote, "of selling a number of faithful servants brought up for several generations in our family. . . . I sometimes think I had better turn a real philosopher; burn my house, give freedom to my Negroes and get rid of all encumbrances which I find property really to be at this period." Moultrie may have become a philosopher after settling in Shropshire, England, at an estate inherited by his wife, but he did not emancipate his slaves. Instead, he sent them to cotton fields in the Bahama Islands.

One absentee planter feared he would suffer great losses during the evacuation. Henry Strachey realized that his 10,000-acre estate would not sell during a time of mass exodus, but slaves represented his most valuable property, and since they could be moved to markets where prices might be better, he instructed Governor Tonyn: "My object is to get rid of them at the most advantage consistent with Humanity; If Georgia or Carolina would take them and pay for them on delivery, I hold that to be the most advisable mode—if not you must do the best you can, but, in all Events secure the payment that I may be sure of realising something out of the wreck." [104]

"safe in harbour"

There would be many "wrecks" during these turbulent and traumatic times, none more dramatic than the experiences of the inhabitants of Mount Oswald. Prompted by the violence and economic uncertainty of the American Revolution, Oswald transferred 240 slaves and other movable property to Savannah in 1781. En route, privateers attacked the transport and abducted seventy slaves. Those not taken stayed only briefly in Georgia before being sent back to Oswald's Tomoka River estate in July 1782. Within two years the slaves were evacuated to Charles Town, where Henry Laurens witnessed their arrival and informed Oswald: "The poor Negroes are safe in harbour." [105]Destined to work rice fields at Santee River, South Carolina, 170 survivors of a tragic intercontinental migratory odyssey, a mixture of country-born and "new Negroes" who had carved an important plantation from the New World wilderness of British East Florida, were temporarily "safe in harbour."

James Grant's slaves went briefly to the Bahamas and were later sold to a consortium of Santee River rice planters—at prices almost double their cost to Grant in the 1760s. For Robin, a driver, Cain, a jobbing carpenter, and George, an indigo maker, the journey to Santee River would pass through Charles Town Harbor, their second arrival in these waters. The first time, they had been victims of the African slave trade, "new Negroes" about to be purchased and reshipped to St. Augustine. The second time they were veterans of nearly two decades of plantation development in East Florida. Not until eight decades later would their descendants be emancipated under the Thirteenth Amendment to the Constitution, free to start their own estates.

Notes

1. For Grant's life prior to 1764, see Alastair Macpherson Grant, *General James Grant of Ballindalloch, 1720–1806* (London: privately published by A. M. Grant, 1930).

2. Bernard Bailyn, "Failure in Xanadu," chapter 12 of *Voyagers to the West: A Passage in the Peopling of America on the Eve of the Revolution* (New York: Alfred A. Knopf, 1986).

3. Samuel Eveleigh, quoted in Peter H. Wood, *Black Majority: Negroes in Colonial South Carolina, from 1670 through the Stono Rebellion* (New York: Alfred A. Knopf, 1974), 84.

4. Planters in Barbados relied on white indentures until sugar was introduced in the 1640s, and whites worked tobacco fields in the Chesapeake until the 1680s; Africans predominated in the fields thereafter. David W. Galenson, *White Servitude in Colonial America: An Economic Analysis* (Cambridge: Cambridge University Press, 1981), 153–68, 177–78; *Markets in History: Economic Studies of the Past* (Cambridge, 1989), 52–96; and *Traders, Planters, and Slaves: Market Behavior in Early English America* (Cambridge, 1986).

5. Charles Joyner, *Down by the Riverside: A South Carolina Slave Community* (Urbana: University of Illinois Press, 1984), 15.

6. Samuel Dyssli, December 3, 1737, quoted in Wood, *Black Majority*, 132.

7. Grant to the Earl of Egmont, June 16, 1768, in the governor's letterbook, a series of bound ledgers identified as bundle 659, for Ballindalloch Castle Muniments; hereafter BCM 659. The papers of James Grant of Ballindalloch are in possession of Sir Ewan Macpherson-Grant, Bart. Access permission must come from The Secretary, National Register of Archives (Scotland), P.O. Box 36, Edinburgh.

8. Grant to Richard Oswald, September 20, 1764, BCM 659. Evacuation is discussed in Jean Parker Waterbury, *The Oldest City: St. Augustine, Saga of Survival* (St. Augustine Historical Society, 1983), chapters 3 and 4. Also in Major Francis Ogilvie to Board of Trade, St. Augustine, January 26, 1764, Great Britain, Public Record Office, Colonial Office, series 5, volume 540 (hereafter CO 5/540).

9. Grant to Oswald, November 21, 1764, BCM 659. For evidence of Moultrie's efforts to recruit settlers and to send seeds, tools, and advice see his 1764 and 1765 letters to Grant in BCM 261. Daniel Littlefield also found that Grant based his plans on South Carolina; see his *Rice and Slaves: Ethnicity and the Slave Trade in Colonial South Carolina* (Baton Rouge: Louisiana State University Press, 1981), 63. See also Grant to Lords of Trade, August 29 and September 2, 1764, CO 5/540. For Moultrie's medical degree and thesis, see Wood, *Black Majority*, 82.

10. Grant to Richard Oswald, August 31, 1766, BCM 659. For responses

of seventeenth-century English colonists to heat in the tropical colonies, see Karen Ordahl Kupperman, "Fear of Hot Climates in the Anglo-American Colonial Experience," *William and Mary Quarterly* (3d series), 41 (April 1984): 213–40.

11. September 1, 1766, BCM 659.

12. February 9, 1768, BCM 659.

13. Ibid.; a similar letter to Lord Moira, June 20, 1768, BCM 659.

14. June 16, 1768, BCM 659. Egmont had only recently resigned as First Lord of the Admiralty. See Daniel L. Schafer, "Plantation Development in British East Florida: A Case Study of the Earl of Egmont," *Florida Historical Quarterly* 43 (October 1984): 172–83.

15. Eight who arrived with Grant in 1764 were highly trained and expensive "French Negroes" purchased in London. Grant to Henry Laurens, November 18, 1764, BCM 659; Grant to Egmont, March 6, 1765, BCM 399.

16. Grant to Egmont, March 6, 1765, BCM 399.

17. June 15, 1767, BCM 243.

18. Laurens to Grant, June 21, 1765, BCM 359. The cost for these men was £45, or "bare cost" to Laurens.

19. Grant to Laurens, August 17, 1765, BCM 659.

20. Schedule of Grant's affairs by computation, June and September 1769; May and June 1770 (all in BCM 305).

21. Grant to Lords of Trade, January 6, 1770, CO 5/551.

22. Grant to Michael Herries, October 1, 1770, BCM 659.

23. For the next decade Grant's indigo plantation brought him high returns. September 11, 1769, BCM 659.

24. January 18, 1766, BCM 401. All Graham correspondence cited here is in bundle 401.

25. April 23, 1766, BCM 659. Price was £63.

26. Graham to Grant, October 29, 1767.

27. September 16, 1767.

28. December 14, 1767.

29. December 17, 1767.

30. Plantation Inventory, May 13, 1770, BCM 305.

31. Graham to Grant, June 25, 30, 1768. For place names on the African coast, see Littlefield, *Rice and Slaves*, 38.

32. August 22, 1768. The Gold Coast is today's Ghana.

33. January 25, 1769.

34. The Ibo homeland is southeast Nigeria.

35. September 11, 1769.

36. March 19, 1769.

37. June 2, 1767.

38. March 10, 1768.

39. Laurens to James Penman, Charles Town, February 9, 1768, in George C. Rogers, Jr., ed., *The Papers of Henry Laurens*, vol. 5, *September 1, 1765–July 31, 1768* (Columbia: University of South Carolina Press, 1976), 592, 573–4. The new owner was pleased with the man but complained that "unfortunately he had a Wife Tack'd to him, a good stout wench." See Penman to Grant, February 16, 1768, BCM 491.

40. On Oswald and Bance Island, see A. P. Kup, *A History of Sierra Leone, 1400–1787* (Cambridge: Cambridge University Press, 1961), 190–91. See also *Public Ledger*, Edinburgh, September 11, 1784, an advertisement for the sale of Bance Island (copy in National Library of Scotland, Edinburgh).

41. November 21, 1764, BCM 659.

42. Engineer James Moncrief found the land low, but concluded that if drainage ditches were dug it would produce excellent crops of indigo. Ibid., February 12, 1765.

43. February 23, 1765. See Rogers, *The Papers of Henry Laurens* 4:585.

44. Laurens to Grant, April 20, 1765, BCM 359.

45. Ibid. John Graham was also aware of value that could accrue from natural increase, recommending to Grant that young women always be included in purchases: "The young ones will even do more than keep up the number. A few likely young Wenches must be in the parcell, & should their Husbands fail in their duty, I dare say my friend Sweetinham & other publick Spirited Young Men, will be ready to render such an essential service to the Province as to give them some help." July 19, 1765, BCM 401, quoted in Littlefield, *Rice and Slaves*, 64.

46. Laurens to Oswald, October 16, 1767, in Rogers, *Papers of Henry Laurens* 5:370.

47. April 20, 1765, BCM 359.

48. November 1, 1765, BCM 359.

49. Grant to Oswald, October 12, 1765, BCM 659.

50. Oswald to Grant, February 24, 1766, BCM 295; also May 17, 1765 and February 12, 1766. Grant to Oswald, October 12, 1765, BCM 359.

51. Grant to Oswald, August 31, 1766, BCM 659.

52. Laurens to Oswald, August 12, 1766, Rogers, *Papers of Henry Laurens* 5:156.

53. Grant to Shelburne, November 27, 1766, CO 5/548.

54. Laurens to Grant, January 30, 1767, in Rogers, *Papers of Henry Laurens* 5:227. For information on Hewie, see Thomas W. Taylor, " 'Settling a Colony over a Bottle of Claret': Richard Oswald and the British Settlement of Florida" (master's thesis, University of North Carolina at Greensboro, 1984), 34–36.

55. Oswald to Grant, March 15, 1767, BCM 295.

56. Taylor, "Settling a Colony," 269.

57. Oswald to Grant, February 12, April 28, June 9 and 14, 1766, BCM 295.

58. Ibid., May 20 and 29, 1767. To obtain slaves of the "best quality" Oswald authorized Savery to spend up to £22 per person, a price he implied was high for the time. Oswald sent a white carpenter, Philip Herries, who would train slaves to replace him. If all went well he would add a "Smith and Smith's Shop at Timoka—a Wheeler or two, a Cooper or two & a few other white people, who shall be obliged to teach the Negros."

59. Ibid., February 19, 1768; Grant to Hillsborough, March, 1768, CO 5/5439; Grant to Oswald, February 9, 1769, BCM 659.

60. Grant to Oswald, January 22, 1769, BCM 659.

61. Ibid.

62. Grant to Hillsborough, January 16, 1770, CO 5/551.

63. Oswald to Grant, February 1, 1769, BCM 295. See also June 8, 1770, for evidence of delivery. Oswald gave thirteen of the Africans to Grant for assistance at Mount Oswald. Oswald's cost had been "£22 per head." The *Charlotte Cape* delivered another eighty to one hundred slaves from Bance Island to St. Augustine in September 1770.

64. Oswald to Grant, April 4, 1770, BCM 295.

65. Taylor, "Settling a Colony," 55.

66. Yeats to Grant, July 2, 1772, BCM 250.

67. Wilbur Henry Siebert, *Loyalists in East Florida, 1774-1785: The Most Important Documents Pertaining Thereto, Edited With An Accompanying Narrative*, 2 vols. (DeLand, Fla., 1929) 2:58; Taylor, "Settling a Colony," 56.

68. Oswald to John Lewis Gervais, Westminster, April 9 and 13, 1774, in Rogers, *Papers of Henry Laurens* 9:395-98, 445-47.

69. Laurens to Grant, May 1, 1767, in Rogers, *Papers of Henry Laurens* 5:245.

70. Tonyn to George Germain, October 30, 1776, CO 5/557; also January 15, 1777, and December 30, 1775, 5/556.

71. Graham, Laurens, and Oswald frequently mentioned departure points of the African ships, but supply routes led from coastal forts hundreds of miles into the interior. For internal routes of trade and ethnicity, see Philip D. Curtin, *Economic Change in Precolonial Africa: Senegambia in the Era of the Slave Trade*, 2 vols. (Madison: University of Wisconsin Press, 1975); Richard L. Roberts, *Warriors, Merchants, and Slaves. The State and the Economy in the Middle Niger Valley, 1700-1914* (Stanford, Calif.: Stanford University Press, 1987); David Geggus, "Sex Ratio, Age, and Ethnicity in the Atlantic Slave Trade: Data From French Shipping and Plantation Records," *Journal of African History* 30 (1989); and Patrick Manning, *Slavery and African Life: Occidental, Oriental, and African Slave Trades* (Cambridge: Cambridge University Press, 1990).

72. Moultrie to Grant, October 2, 1775, BCM 242. On rice elsewhere in

East Florida, see May 7, 1772, Nov. 3, 1773, Dec. 23, 1774, Oct. 2, 1776, and March 12, 1780, BCM 242.

73. Moultrie to Grant, March 3, 1778, BCM 242.

74. Alexander Skinner to James Grant, September 21, 1775, in Peter Force, *American Archives*, 4th series, *Containing a Documentary History of the English Colonies in North America, from the King's message to Parliament, of March 7, 1774, to the Declaration of Independence by the United States* (Washington, D.C.: 1843), 4:329.

75. June 5, 1780, BCM 250.

76. Yeats describes the robbery of a St. Augustine store by two of Grant's slaves in August 31, 1771, BCM 250.

77. July 2, 1771.

78. February 3, 1781.

79. Tucker to Grant, London, December 12, 1769, BCM 412.

80. Egmont to Grant, May 4, 1769, BCM 264.

81. Record of plantation expenses, May 9 to December 31, 1771, BCM 517; Grant to Alexander Skinner, April 27, 1771, BCM 659.

82. "Proceeds of sale of Negroes," July, 1797, BCM 619.

83. "Thoughts that may be of use to my people and plantation in the Bahamas," May 16, 1784. Copy in the author's possession, courtesy of Robert H. Pratt, of Milwaukee, Wis.

84. Nassau, New Providence, June 22, 1795, from the Pratt copies.

85. October 23, 1775, BCM 250.

86. November 1, 1775, BCM 483.

87. November 3, 1775.

88. April 26, 1776, BCM 772.

89. April 24, 1776, BCM 772.

90. Robert Grant to James Grant, August 14, 1764, BCM 305.

91. Grant to Lords of Trade, April 26, 1766, CO 5/541.

92. Penman to Grant, Orange Grove, October 9, 1769, BCM 491.

93. Ibid., October 19, 1769.

94. Moultrie to Lord Hillsborough, June 29, 1771, CO 5/551, and April 23, 1770, for four runaways from John Tucker's plantation. See Tonyn to Germain, February 1, 1779, Co 5/559, for ten runaways returned from a Creek village.

95. Owner claims for reimbursement for runaways can be found in Siebert, *Loyalists in East Florida*, vols. 1 and 2. For quantification and case studies, see Jane Landers, "Black Society in Spanish St. Augustine, 1784–1821" (Ph.D. diss., University of Florida, 1988), 164–70; and "Spanish Sanctuary: Fugitives in Florida, 1687–1790," *Florida Historical Quarterly* 62 (January 1984): 296–313.

96. Turnbull to Arthur Gordon, Smyrna, September 1, 1776, CO 5/556; Tonyn to Germain, November 29, 1779, CO 5/559.

97. Tonyn to Germain, July 18, 1777, CO 5/557.

98. Creation of the militia companies is in Tonyn to Germain, August 21, 1776, CO 5/556.

99. Tonyn to Germain, July 30, 1781, CO 5/560; for planter confirmation of the sacrifices, see Yeats to Grant, March 20, 1781, BCM 250.

100. Siebert, *Loyalists in East Florida* 1:26, 39; 2:168–71.

101. Tonyn to Secretary of State, August 15, 1776, and July 18, 1777, in CO 5/556, 557. The nearby William Chapman plantation was also destroyed.

102. Francis Harper, ed., *The Travels of William Bartram: Naturalist's Edition* (New Haven, 1958), 42–43. Visitor reports can be seen in Moultrie to Grant, June 3, 1773, BCM 370, and Mulcaster to Grant, August 9, 1774, BCM 369. For Bartram's plantation, see Bailyn, *Voyagers*, 469–74.

103. On Cecilton and evacuation to Dominica, see Egmont Papers, Additional Manuscripts 47054 A, British Museum, London, folios 39–84; and Schafer, "Plantation Development . . . A Case Study of the Earl of Egmont."

104. London, March 31, 1783, CO, 5/560.

105. Taylor, " 'Settling a Colony over a Bottle of Claret,' " 86–87.

◇ **5**

A Troublesome Property
Master-Slave Relations in Florida, 1821–1865

Larry E. Rivers

HE PROFUSION of historical studies on antebellum southern slavery eloquently testifies to the long, continuing interest that the subject commands. The literature ranges from early-twentieth-century "happy-slave-on-the-old-plantation" portraits to quantitative analyses of the size and numbers of slave revolts, to psychological reflections on "social death" and the results of the exercise of absolute power by one human being over others. One particularly important body of research has addressed the dynamics of the master-slave relationship, which scholars such as John W. Blassingame and Eugene D. Genovese, among others, have argued was the defining feature of the southern slave system.[1] Despite the proliferation of these studies, scant attention has been given to the subject as it relates to antebellum Florida.

Florida differed in several respects from other states in the Old South. As a Spanish colony, it represented a haven for runaway slaves from the southern United States. Fugitives, free blacks, and Seminole Indians formed alliances and lived together in East Florida as well as in remote sections of the peninsula. Among these groups, the tradition of resistance flourished.[2] Regarded from 1821 as a lawless territorial outpost and after 1845 as a frontier state, Florida remained sparsely settled through the Civil War. In 1860, for example, only three of its towns claimed a population of more than 2,000 inhabitants.[3] However, the region lying between the Apalachicola and Suwannee rivers developed early a slave-based plantation economy similar to that of other southern states. The area—which consisted of present-day Jackson, Gadsden, Leon, Jefferson, and Madison counties—was called Middle Florida. There, well-heeled planter families from Maryland, Virginia, North and South Carolina, and Georgia established substantial plantation operations.

Planters from other states began moving into Middle Florida with high expectations shortly after the territory was acquired in 1821, but they clearly understood the potential for troubled relations with their slaves in the new locale. To maintain and shore up their power, territorial planters soon enacted severe slave codes and other race-related statutes designed to ensure physical and psychological dominance over their laborers. Slaves, however, resisted the absolute power of their masters, leading many owners to view their slaves as, indeed, "a troublesome property."[4]

This essay examines three arenas in which the tensions between masters and slaves were manifested: religious behavior, interpersonal relations, and work. Planters and managers varied in their attitudes toward religious expression. Some believed it represented autonomy and, therefore, threatened the domination of slaves, while others felt religion should be used as an instrument of control. Zephaniah Kingsley, one of Florida's most flamboyant slaveholders, was skeptical about allowing any type of religious worship on his Duval County plantation. "All the late insurrections of slaves," he claimed, "are to be traced to influential preachers of the gospel." However, when Kingsley attempted to eliminate black religious activity on his plantation, he was largely unsuccessful. The slaves resisted efforts to disband their church and continued to hold "private nightly meetings" once or twice a week. In fact, Kingsley noted that one slave, "calling himself a minister," had completely taken "all authority over the negroes" from the overseer and himself. Kingsley may have exaggerated this point, but he continued to complain that slaves were harder to manage, disobeyed his orders more frequently, and stole more of his food after the minister's arrival.[5]

In Madison County, Judge Wilkerson would not permit slave gatherings of any sort. Despite their owner's noted cruelty and their own awareness of the consequences of their actions, some of Wilkerson's slaves continued to meet and conduct religious services in secret. Wilkerson's ex-slave Charlotte Martin reported that her brother had paid the ultimate price for such defiance, being "whipped to death for taking part in one of the religious ceremonies." Thereafter the secret religious meetings ceased. Unlike Kingsley, Wilkerson was willing to use brutal force to assert hegemony over the slaves in this regard.[6]

Slave religion also proved a source of conflict on one of two Jefferson County plantations owned by George Noble Jones, an absentee landlord. The overseer of the El Destino plantation believed that the slave church was at the root of his disciplinary problems, which included acts of insubordination, flight, and low productivity. In a letter to Jones, overseer D. N. Moxley stated, "I have heard since I came to town that Jim Page [El Destino's free-black minister] and his crew has bin the cass of all the fuss."[7] A month later Moxley announced that he had "stopped Page from coming to the plantation." During the remainder of the overseer's three-year tenure he made no further mention of the plantation church. Since El Destino slaves had Sundays off, however, some bondsmen may have continued their "religious activities" without James Page's assistance.[8]

Some planters actively encouraged religiosity in their slaves, believing it facilitated slave control. Leon County planter Thomas Randall allowed bondsmen to build a church before they built their own cabins. He then generously offered a "helpful" hand in selecting their preacher.[9] Susan Bradford Eppes recalled that on her father's Leon County plantation, the "negroes were preached to every Sunday," although by a white preacher.[10] A former bondsman on the Bradford plantation, Claude Augusta Wilson, remembered that the slaves were allowed to gather at "a poorly constructed frame building which was known as the Meeting House," to give praise to "their" God.[11] Similarly, Bolden Hall, who grew up on a Jefferson County plantation, noted that his master "did not interfere with [slaves'] religious quest" and that he and many other bondsmen "were permitted to attend church with their masters to hear the white preacher and occasionally . . . an itinerant colored minister preached to the slaves instructing them to obey their master and mistress at all times."[12]

Planters like Jackson County's James Carr often sought to gain the confidence and loyalty of their slaves by allowing or requiring them to worship with plantation whites. However, Carr's ex-slave Margaret Nickerson recalled that "de white preachers . . . tole us to mind our masters and missus and we would be saved; if not, dey said we wouldn'. Dey never tole us nothin 'bout Jesus." Carr's wife, Jane, served as the plantation church's Sunday school teacher, but was careful not to allow the slaves to touch her books for fear that some might learn to read and write. Despite her precautions, however, the slave Uncle George Bull did learn to read and write from the weekly lessons and was subsequently beaten for his impudence.[13]

Former slave Douglas Dorsey echoed Nickerson's skepticism concerning the type of religious instruction delivered by whites. He reminisced that "slaves were order[ed] to church to hear a white minister, . . . [and he would tell] them to honor their masters and mistresses, and to have no other God but them, as 'we cannot see the other God, but you can see your master and mistress.' " The ex-slave also stated that the slave driver's wife, who could read and write a little, would tell the slaves that what the minister had just said was "all lies." [14]

Even black preachers who were paid by planters encountered skepticism from slaves. James Page, who had been "freed by the Parker Family" of Tallahassee and selected by planters to preach to bondsmen and -women on various Middle Florida plantations, found that some slaves rejected his ministry and did not "accept Christ" at his behest. At least, ex-slave Louis Napoleon insisted that such was the case.[15] However, such resistance did not deter masters from continued attempts to direct the religious expression of their slaves.

Slaveholders even sought posthumously to exert religious control over their slaves. In their wills, William Bailey and John Bellamy stipulated that their slaves be instructed in religion at least "once or twice a month on the Sabbath day." [16]

Another private arena of slave life that masters sought to control was the interpersonal relations of their slaves. Although neither federal nor state laws sanctioned slave marriages, masters usually allowed slaves to marry and maintain families, believing that the practice led to good behavior and higher productivity. Zephaniah Kingsley noted that slaves were attached to their homes, wives and children, and domestic life and that "they were less troublesome, more productive and a growing property" when they could live in their own "cabins as married couples." [17] Thomas Randall, the overseer of Wirtland plantation, also believed that family ties were criti-

The Reverend James Page. Page was a traveling slave preacher who was freed by his owner in 1851. He became the first black ordained minister in Florida and was the first pastor of the Bethel Missionary Baptist Church in Tallahassee, Florida, in the late nineteenth century.

cal to happiness and productivity. He feared that one of his bonds-men, David, "would infect the whole body of the black community with his despondence" if his children and wife were not purchased and brought to Wirtland. To keep harmony in the slave community, Randall secured permission from the owner, William Wirt, to effect the purchase.[18] When the Wirtland nurse, Betsy, asked to marry Noah, a slave living on a nearby plantation, that request was also honored.[19]

Not all planters were so lenient about spouses or visitors from other plantations. Douglas Dorsey's master was uncompromising concerning slave visitations. A slave who was caught off plantation, Dorsey remembered, would be tied to a whipping post and "lashed on the bare back."[20] Although planters such as Zephaniah Kingsley, John and Robert Gamble, William Wirt, George Noble Jones, and others tried to discourage their slaves from visiting or marrying slaves from other plantations, they were forced to compromise as the population of male slaves on some of their properties began to out-number females. Still, they used the possibility of marriage as a re-ward. Slaves were permitted to marry off the plantation in exchange for loyalty and efficient work.[21]

Absentee planters like George N. Jones often permitted overseers to make decisions concerning slave marriages. After facing disci-plinary problems, John Evans, the overseer of the Chemonie plan-tation in Jefferson County, refused to allow any slave to marry off the plantation. Later, Evans compromised by allowing Chemonie's workers to marry slaves from Jones's other plantation, El Destino. In 1851 Evans informed Jones that he had given Peggy permission to marry Ansler at El Destino provided that he took her to El Des-tino with him to marry. The next year, the overseer permitted two couples, James and Martha and Lafayette and Lear, to marry. Even-tually so many slaves married that Jones directed Evans to send him a list of "all the names of the Negroes on Chemonie in Famleys."[22]

Even among planters who objected to visitations and marriage off the plantation, some seemed willing to allow their slaves to marry bondsmen from plantations owned by the planters' family members. John and Robert Gamble gave several slaves from their Waukee-nah and Welaunee plantations permission to marry on the Wirtland plantation of their brother-in-law William Wirt. Wirt reciprocated.

Former slaves from northeast Florida, ca. 1875. This family of six included both parents, three small children, and a nursing child. Courtesy of the St. Augustine Historical Society.

Although a black minister usually performed the marriage ceremony, Wirt's son Henry performed several himself. Slave weddings allowed planters to demonstrate their paternalism. George N. Jones had a cabin built for Chesley and his wife, and the Gamble brothers purchased articles for housekeeping, as well as new dresses, trousers, and shirts for their newly-married slave couples.[23]

On occasion gifts were given for less honorable reasons. An uproar ensued at El Destino, for example, when slaves learned that Jonathan Roberson, the sawmill overseer, was courting favors from one of the slave women. The woman admitted that Roberson had given her "gifts of whiskey on several occasions in exchange of certain favors." Since slave men of marrying age outnumbered such women at El Destino and Chemonie, male bondsmen saw Roberson as an unfair competitor and an intruder in the plantation courtship rituals. Roberson's authority was compromised after this incident. Slaves working at the mill became overtly resistant and so unproductive that the owner considered dismissing Roberson as his agent, an action urged by overseers on both plantations.[24]

Just as slaveholders tried to control the religious behavior and interpersonal relations of the slaves, they also sought to regulate their work patterns. Even though it gave planters absolute power, the legal system could not ensure effective control of the quality or quantity of work performed. Alteration of entrenched patterns and customary levels of production often proved difficult because slaves resisted. When El Destino's overseer, Moxley, flogged many slaves for "coming up short" on their cotton picking, four slaves fled from the plantation.[25] Planter Jones asked Evans, the overseer at Chemonie, to investigate. Not surprisingly, Evans supported his colleague although he admitted to Jones that the whippings had been rather severe. Evans could hardly judge Moxley's actions objectively since he was having his own slave problems and also had resorted to frequent floggings. As Evans wrote in frustration to Jones, "I am doeing all I knoe [to make the slaves work]."[26]

Poor supervision exacerbated problems. Both Evans and Moxley blamed their difficulties in punishing slaves on Jonathan Roberson, the sawmill overseer, who seemed incapable of supervising or masking his dependence upon the fifteen or more slaves under his control. This group took every opportunity to challenge his power. In an effort at compromise, Roberson allowed the slaves to report to work after sunrise and to work under less immediate supervision than was permitted other bondsmen on the two plantations.[27] Since the slaves had permission to visit either plantation and to party together on occasion, they likely discussed their newly won autonomy with the other slaves. The outcome was predictable. "If they see negroes around them Ideling," Evans reported, "why they want to doe so two [sic]."[28]

Evans and Moxley followed the path trod by many other overseers and were unyielding in pushing slaves to work more efficiently. In time, Chemonie and El Destino slaves tried to undermine their overseers' authority by communicating directly with their owner during his intermittent visits. This practice so frustrated Evans that he wrote to his employer in 1856, "Your negroes behave badly behind my back and then run to you and you appear to beleave what they say." After serving Jones for over a decade, Evans tendered his letter of resignation that year.[29]

The methods used to make slaves work productively and efficiently varied from place to place. In the eastern and southern areas of Florida, where sugar, cotton, and tobacco were grown, planters employed the task system; in Middle Florida, where most of the larger plantations were located, they used the gang system. Of the two systems, slaves seemed to prefer the former. Zephaniah Kingsley wrote that his slaves were pleased with the task system, worked more efficiently, and were less rebellious when allowed to complete the assigned tasks by two or three o'clock each day. No records suggest disciplinary problems among Kingsley's workers.[30] Achille Murat also employed the task system. He claimed that his workers were usually finished with their work around three or four o'clock and were then allowed to attend to their private concerns.[31]

In Middle Florida some plantations, such as Wirtland, were sizable enough to employ both systems, but this duality led to power struggles over the work regime and the type of activity that slaves found appropriate.[32] A new Wirtland slave, Henry Minor, was accustomed to a degree of independence since he had previously been hired out. When Minor was instructed to plant trees, he complained about outdoor work and finally asked to be sold. Mrs. Wirt was compelled to remind her agent that she had absolute power over Henry's life and that "he is not his own master, to come and go as he pleases, to the arrogance [sic] of his owner."[33]

Despite such assertions, owners sometimes acknowledged slaves' attempts to define the terms of their labor. In 1843 Ellen Wirt discussed Lucy's proposed assignment in the field and noted that she was "unfit for the field, yet, she makes no objection to cooking." When Ellen attempted to sell Charles, who had worked at the sawmill as a field hand, Charles "took it upon himself to tell [the prospective buyer] that he had never been in the field and done any hard work." Ellen noted, "Of course, Mr. Crong decline[d] closing the bargain."[34] Another of Wirt's slaves, Eliza, believed that her task was to cook, "and [she had] the notion that nothing else [is] to be expected of her."

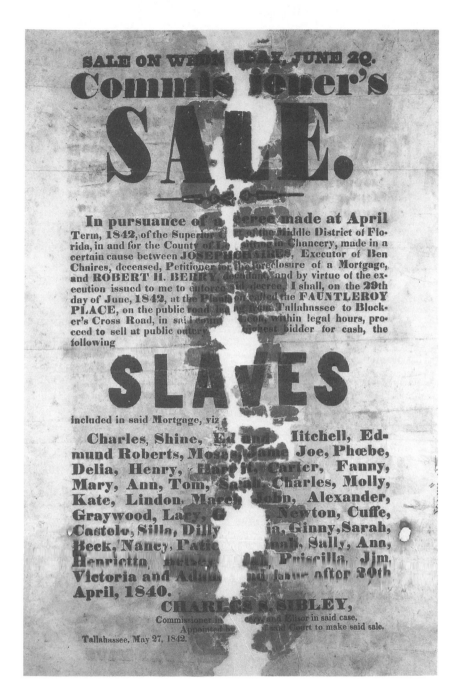

Advertisement for the sale of slaves belonging to the estate of planter Ben Chaires, Leon County, Florida, 1842. African and Spanish names appear in the list of slaves to be sold.

The slave never completely fulfilled her owners' expectations even after repeated corporal punishment.[35] The Wirts finally threatened to sell Eliza to "Cherokee Planters without one feeling of regret."

When planters failed to allow a degree of autonomy, slaves resisted with patterns of poor performance. Not only did they challenge the gang system repeatedly, but they even challenged less demanding assignments. One owner complained that a house servant worked to her own "liking" and that another, Emaline, "has turned out so badly that she has been ejected from the kitchen. She was not only impudent to Rosetta [the white worker] and unmanageable . . . [but] dishonest." John, who took care of the carriage and horses, was "lazy and inefficient," the same frustrated owner accused.[36]

In the face of such challenges, some owners and overseers used force to enhance their authority. Louis Goldsborough whipped a disgruntled slave who packed cotton poorly. "The packer has been punished severely, and too in as formal and inspiring a manner as I thought the occasion deserved," Goldsborough recorded. "The punishment I inflicted in the presence of all the colored people on the plantation . . . and by telling them of the offense committed, and giving them to understand what each and all might expect for such a similar conduct." [37]

But even fear of severe punishments did not coerce all bondsmen. Former slave Margrett Nickerson remembered that her sister Holly, who worked on William Carr's plantation, refused to be driven at any pace other than the one she had established for herself. "Holly didn' stand back on non' uv em," Nickerson recalled, "when dey'd git behin' her, she'd git behin' dem; she wuz dat stubbo'n and when dey would beat her she wouldn' holler and jes take it and go on." [38]

When corporal punishment failed, as it often did, slavemasters were left with few options except threatening to sell rebellious blacks. Former slave Acie Thomas of Jefferson County recalled that it did not take "tearing the hid[e] off" a slave to get him or her to behave; instead, the suggestion that the master would "sell him to some po' white trash . . . allus brougt good results." [39]

Over time many slaveholders learned that neither severe punishment nor threat of sale would modify behavior or work patterns of some bondsmen. They learned that their laborers, at least occasionally, required positive inducements. Rewards for good work or good behavior might include extra days off during the holidays, additional food allotments, additional free time, or money. According to Douglas Parish, his master "fed his slaves well, [and] gave them comfortable quarters in which to live . . . and if the slaves failed to do their work, they were reported to him and not to the overseer for punishment." Acie Thomas recalled, "Slaves were often given time off for frolics, dances, and quilting-weddings." She also claimed that some Jefferson County slaveholders prided themselves on giving their slaves "the finest parties."[40]

Rewards and inducements varied widely and often were tailored to address personal needs and special circumstances. Wally, one of the Wirtland overseers, gave money to an old slave named Quak as a reward for work well done. In 1850, he presented Jud Poll with $2 to purchase an outfit for his wife-to-be. A year later, he purchased cooking utensils for certain slaves for good conduct. Laura Randall gave two of her father's slaves dresses for them to wear when they married men on her uncle John Gamble's plantation in Jefferson County.[41] As a cooperative gesture, J. K. Gibbs, Kingsley's nephew and overseer at Fort George, gave bondsmen time off to plant and harvest their crops, noting that it "is a rule which we have, to give all the Negroes one day in the Spring to plant and one in the fall to reap." Gibbs also gave the slaves extra rations and four days off during the Christmas holidays. "[I] got the Beef for the people on yesterday," he recorded on December 25, 1841, "and gave out double allowances of corn and salt also, so that the Negroes could feed their holliday visitors—of course, no work for anybody."[42]

While slaves no doubt welcomed such gifts, they also worked hard to lessen their dependence on their masters. When assigned tasks were completed, slaves on the Kingsley plantation, for example, tended their gardens and fished as a way of feeding themselves and their families. According to Murat, blacks on his plantation raised poultry and pigs for themselves, grew their own vegetables, and could sell them at market.[43]

Other slaves stole food and other items. One overseer claimed that a slave named Mugin was up to his "old trade of stealing chickens [at night]."[44] A slave named Dick was noted for stealing watermelons and stopped his thefts only after a dog seized him by the "seat of his pants."[45] Two "trusted" slaves of the Eppes family, Molly and

Randall Junior, conspired to steal bacon from the smokehouse to exchange for whiskey when Randall journeyed to Tallahassee with a delivery of cotton. The theft was discovered and although the slaves' punishments are not known, Eppes noted that "this may not have been Randall's first offense, but it was certainly his last."[46] Planters regularly punished thefts by slaves but failed to prevent further losses or the repeated challenges to their authority.

Realizing that overt opposition to a master's control would lead to punishment, slaves developed alternative, less easily countered forms of resistance. They learned early that feigning illness was one simple, yet difficult-to-disprove evasion. According to the overseer of the El Destino mill, four or five of the slaves under his control normally were "sick." During one four-month period about one-third of the workforce was confined to the quarters because of illness. The Wirt plantations were likewise afflicted. Chemonie's overseer, A. R. McCall, reported that Ellen was not sick but trying to "deceive" him.[47] Alexander Randall reflected McCall's sentiments when he said that Nelly "is not much sick . . . and supposes herself privileged [by not having to work]."[48] The number of slaves who became ill rose during the planting and harvesting seasons. In September 1839 Ellen Wirt Voss complained that "almost every man, woman, and child with two exceptions have been sick."[49] Louis Wirt recorded that his mother's bondsmen were constantly sick during the warm season. Henry Wirt summed up the illness on the Wirtland plantation in 1843 by stating, "I think Charlotte [a slave] told me there was more sickness during the months of May, June, and July among the negroes that she had ever known."[50]

In addition to feigning illness, slaves found other means of manipulating their masters. When Squire Jackson's master came upon him reading, the bondsman quickly turned the paper upside down and began to shout, "The Confederates don won the War." The master laughed at what he heard and walked away without disciplining the slave.[51] A quiet-acting slave at Chemonie was so overjoyed by the news of her freedom that she dropped her crutches and began to walk. The former master was quite disgusted with this revelation since he had excused her from doing any "real work" for seven years.[52] Some apparently compliant bondsmen showed different sides of their personalities when there was little chance of being punished. According to the daughter of a Middle Florida planter, the cook and faithful servant, Emeline, changed overnight after learning of her freedom. When asked to cook for her former master, Emeline replied, "Take dem keys back ter yer mother an' tell her [I] don't never 'spects ter cook no more, not while I lives—tell her I's free, bless de Lord!" Despite repeated requests, Emeline refused to change her mind.[53]

Not all resistance was covert, however. Some slaves openly defied the power and authority of their masters, sometimes by attempts to physically harm owners and overseers. Laura Randall claimed in 1832 that three of her slaves had conspired to poison their overseer. One of the accused, Sally, was "banished" from the house and two other slaves were sold. After witnessing the brutal treatment of his mother, another slave, Douglas Dorsey, plotted to serve his master strychnine with his coffee. Fortunately for both, as Dorsey remembered, "Freedom had saved him of this act which would have resulted in his death." [54] When four women from the El Destino plantation who had run away to escape flogging were captured and returned, the overseer started to whip one of the runaways. Her brother, Aberdeen, then attacked the overseer with an axe. Aberdeen afterwards was given a "genteel flogging" in front of the entire slave community.[55] When Chemonie's overseer attempted to whip Winter, the slave confronted him, saying that he "would not take it," and ran off to the neighboring plantation of El Destino, where he stayed for at least four days before returning.[56]

Every member of the planter class knew that running away was the disgruntled slave's immediate and most effective way of resisting his master's control. Donorena Harris noted in her study of Florida runaways between 1821 and 1860 that only a small percentage of slaveowners regularly advertised their runaways because those who frequently absconded were usually caught within a few days.[57] Of 742 identified slaves who fled Florida farms and plantations, 148, or 20 percent, were repeaters, and a few were habitual offenders. Those slaves who had been on a plantation for only a brief period were most prone to escape. Of the 742 runaways, 77 percent were males, averaging twenty-nine years of age. Some left when new masters or overseers took control of the enterprise; others fled out of anger or frustration. Still others ran away because of the separation of a family member, and some absconded out of a simple desire to be free.[58]

"Mauma Mollie," ca. 1850s. Mauma Mollie was brought from Africa to South Carolina on a slave ship and became nursemaid for the children of John and Eliza Partridge of Jefferson, Florida, in the 1830s. Henry Edward Partridge wrote in his diary in 1873 that "We buried either in 57 or 58 our faithful old 'Mauma' Mollie—her who had nursed nearly all of the children of the family; been a friend as well as a faithful servant to my Mother; in whose cabin we had often eaten the homely meal of fried bacon & ash cake and where we always had welcome and sympathy and whom we loved as a second mother. Black of skin but pure of heart, she doubtless stands among the faithful on the right of the King." Courtesy of the Florida State Archives.

TEN DOLLARS REWARD.

RAN AWAY from the sub-
scriber, a *Negro man* named *Charles*, and a *Negro woman* named *Dorcas*. The man
is about forty years old, and
the woman thirty-eight. The
man is very black—about five
feet nine inches in height,—
with the African marks on his face of his native country. The woman is about five feet
nine inches, and rather thick set. Any person returning them shall receive the above
reward.   **HENRY W. MAXEY.**
Cedar Point, March 4.   1w10

Runaway slave advertisement from the *Jacksonville Courier*, April 16, 1835, in which planter Henry Maxey described the facial scarification of his African-born slave Charles, who escaped with a female companion, Dorcas. Courtesy of the Florida Historical Society.

Slaves ran away throughout the year, and although Harris concluded that more left the plantation in February, April, May, and June than at any other time, other contemporary sources indicate that most escapees fled during June, July, August, and September.[59]

Interestingly, many planters revealed a gross misperception of their chattel's personality in describing their runaways. Susan Bradford Eppes expressed great surprise when a trusted and reliable plowhand, Laurence, left the Bradford plantation. She remembered that he was not provoked in any way but had just "disappeared" one day.[60] Another slave master insisted that Tom was "usually very polite and pausible when spoken to" but displayed more insight when he added that Tom was an "artful scamp, if he thought it to his advantage might deny he belonged or knew me or even change his name."[61]

Edward Houston admitted that his runaway was "forward in speaking and not timid," as well as being well-dressed when he escaped.[62] Although only a tiny portion of Florida's slave population resorted to illegal flight in any given year, the problem nonetheless plagued slaveholders throughout the period.[63]

Once a slave had fled his master's control, his or her destination varied according to several factors. Young, married slaves were more likely to remain within Florida. Ties of family and affection rated high as a cause of slave flight, as bondsmen and -women often left in search of family members or loved ones. One runaway, Hannah, was "believed to be headed for Tallahassee where her mother lives." Other slaves like George and John were thought to be "lurking at Black Creek where they have Wives." One owner offered a handsome $200 reward for the return of two children who had run away to seek their "freed mother." Abram, a Leon County slave, was at large looking "for his wife." Levenia left Tallahassee for Quincy where "she has a husband." In some cases entire families vanished, as did Nelson, his wife Jinny, and their son and daughter.[64]

Those runaways with fewer familial ties to bind them did not linger in Middle Florida, but moved on to central or southern Florida or to the Bahamas. Aware of traditional alliances forged between slaves, free blacks, and Seminole Indians during the late-eighteenth and early-nineteenth centuries under both Spanish and British rule, slaves from the plantations throughout Florida logically made their way to black and Indian settlements scattered throughout the peninsula. Slave hunters such as John Winslett pursued runaways living among the peninsular maroons at the risk of their lives.[65]

Some runaways looked beyond the peninsula for a haven in the Bahamas. In 1842, several slaves escaped from St. Augustine on boats belonging to the local pilots of the harbor. They headed to the Bahamas, robbing and murdering a Key Biscayne man en route to their destination. After arrival in the islands, the runaways remained safe under British jurisdiction despite pleas from planters for their return to Florida.[66]

Inevitably, some planters came to believe that their runaways were being assisted by abolitionists in Florida, although these reformers were never a threat to the institution of slavery in the territory or state. White assistance to slave flight often was an individual act, not a well-planned conspiracy to aid in the escape of "large" numbers of slaves. In many such cases no records exist on the sentence of the guilty party, although many offenders were not punished to the highest extent of the law. According to former slave Shack Thomas, some alleged abolitionists were simply run out of town.[67] One celebrated 1844 case involved Jonathan Walker, a Boston abolitionist, who abetted the escape of seven Pensacola slaves. All of the culprits were apprehended and returned. The slaves went back to their respective masters, while Walker stood trial and was found guilty of "aiding and abetting" runaways. The court ordered that he be placed in the pillory, branded on the hand with the letters *SS*, imprisoned for fifteen days, and fined $150.[68]

Not all master-slave relationships were characterized by conflict—at least according to the WPA accounts of elderly Florida freedmen. Some bondsmen seemed to identify with the master as a father figure, while others may have remained loyal in hopes of manumission. Bolden Hall recalled that his master had been "very good to his slaves . . . and provided them with plenty of food and clothing, and always saw to it that their cabins were liveable."[69] Louis Napoleon stated that "his master and mistress were very kind to the slaves and would never whip them"; if a black was whipped, the slave had only to report the incident to the "master and the 'driver' was dismissed."[70] Willis Williams reminisced that his master was kind, and that he had no "unpleasant experiences as related by some other ex-slaves." He was never flogged, and he was pleased to sit in the balcony at the same church attended by his owner.[71] The promise of eventual freedom kept Cato loyal to his master, Jesse Potts, until his death. Other Middle Florida planters also freed loyal slaves in their wills, provided they "left" the country upon their owner's death.[72]

Slaves in Middle Florida were, indeed, a "troublesome property," and the master-slave relationship was continually contested. The master, who was supported by law, social institutions, and established regional values, demanded obedience. Although slaves had no legal redress and few social supports, they nevertheless realized that the master's reliance upon slave labor was an effective source of power for them. Despite their "social death," Florida slaves creatively and persistently used this knowledge to modify the conditions of their enslavement.

Notes

1. See, for example, Eugene D. Genovese, *Roll, Jordan, Roll: The World the Slaves Made* (New York: Random House, 1974); John W. Blassingame, *The Slave Community: Plantation Life in the Antebellum South* (New York: Oxford University Press, 1972); Robert W. Fogel and Stanley L. Engerman, *Time on the Cross*, 2 vols. (Boston: Little, Brown, 1974); George P. Rawick, *From Sundown to Sunup: The Making of the Black Community*, 19 vols. (1941; reprint, Westport, Conn.: Greenwood, 1972); and Herbert Aptheker, *American Negro Slave Revolts* (New York: Columbia University Press, 1938).

2. Julia Smith, *Slavery and Plantation Growth in Antebellum Florida: 1821–1860* (Gainesville: University of Florida Press, 1972), 17–20, 101–20; Jane Landers, "Gracia Real de Santa Teresa de Mose: A Free Black Town in Spanish Colonial Florida," *American Historical Review* 95 (February 1990): 9–30; Canter Brown, Jr., "The Sarrazota, or Runaway Negro Plantations: Tampa Bay's First Black Community, 1812–1821," *Tampa Bay History* 12 (Fall/Winter 1990): 5–19; James W. Covington, "The Negro Fort," *Gulf Coast Historical Review* 5 (Spring 1990): 80; Larry E. Rivers, "Slavery in Microcosm: Leon County, Florida, 1824–1860," *Journal of Negro History* 46 (Fall 1981): 244–45; Larry E. Rivers, "Dignity and Importance: Slavery in Jefferson County, Florida—1827 to 1860," *Florida Historical Quarterly* 61 (April 1983): 425–27; Larry E. Rivers, "Slavery and the Political Economy of Gadsden County, Florida: 1823–1861," *Florida Historical Quarterly* 70 (July 1991): 18.

3. Pensacola's population in 1860 was 2,876. Key West residents numbered 2,832, and Jacksonville's total came to 2,118. Roland Harper, "Antebellum Census Enumerations in Florida," *Florida Historical Quarterly* 6 (July 1927): 51; Canter Brown, Jr., *Florida's Peace River Frontier* (Gainesville: University Presses of Florida, 1991), 8.

4. Kenneth W. Stampp, *The Peculiar Institution* (New York: Random House, 1956), 86–140; Genovese, *Roll, Jordan, Roll*, 361–64. Several Florida slaveholders considered their slaves to be a troublesome property. See Hardy B. Groomes to Henry Gaskin, June 20, 1837, Hardy B. Groomes Papers, Florida Collection, State Library of Florida, Tallahassee (hereafter, Florida Collection); A. R. McCall to George Noble Jones, May 16, 1856, in *Florida Plantation Records from the Papers of George Noble Jones*, ed. Ulrich B. Phillips and James David Glunt (St. Louis: Missouri Historical Society, 1927), 68, 154 (hereafter, *Florida Plantation Records*).

5. Zephaniah Kingsley, *A Treatise on the Patriarchal or Cooperative System of Society as it exists in some Governments, and Colonies in America, and in*

the United States Under the name of Slavery with its Necessity and Advantages (Freeport, 1829), 14–15.

6. *The American Slave: A Composite Autobiography,* vol. 17, *Florida Narratives,* ed. George P. Rawick (Westport, Conn.: Greenwood, 1972–79), 166 (hereafter, *Florida Slave Narratives*). See also Gary R. Mormino, "Florida Slave Narratives," *Florida Historical Quarterly* 66 (April 1988): 411–12.

7. D. N. Moxley to George N. Jones, October 8, 1854, *Florida Plantation Records,* 106–7.

8. Jonathan Roberson, the overseer of the mill at El Destino, had given slaves permission to be baptized by James Page two years prior to Moxley's arrival in 1854. Jonathan Roberson to G. Jones, May 21, 1852, and D. N. Moxley to Jones, October 8, November 21, 1854, *Florida Plantation Records,* 31, 108, 118–19.

9. Thomas Randall to William Wirt, April 13, 1828, and Wirt to Laura and Thomas Randall, ca. 1828, William Wirt Papers, microfilm copy at Maryland Historical Society, Baltimore (hereafter, Wirt Papers).

10. Susan B. Eppes, "Recollection of Slavery on the Pine Hill Plantation," mss. in Pine Hill Plantation Papers, Florida Collection. See also N. W. Eppes, *The Negro of the Old South: A Bit of Period History* (Chicago, 1925), 3–4.

11. *Florida Slave Narratives,* 355–56.

12. Ibid., 165.

13. Ibid., 252–53, 352–53; Laura Randall to Elizabeth Wirt, December 17, 1829, Wirt Papers.

14. *Florida Plantation Records,* 97–98.

15. Ibid., 244–45.

16. Will of Emmula Bellamy, April 12, 1851, 34–36, and Will of William Bailey, Jr., July 16, 1862, 160, in Jefferson County Wills, Letters, and Testamentary Book B, Florida State Archives, Tallahassee; Rivers, "Slavery in Leon County," 244; Rivers, "Slavery in Jefferson County," 415.

17. Kingsley, *Treatise,* 8–9. For more on slave and free black families, see James Roark and Michael Johnson, "Strategies of Survival: Free Negro Families and the Problem of Slavery," and Brenda Stevenson, "Distress and Discord in Virginia Slave Families, 1830–1860," in *In Joy and In Sorrow: Women, Family, and Marriage in the Victorian South, 1830–1900,* ed. Carol Bleser (New York: Oxford University Press, 1991), 103–24.

18. Thomas Randall to William Wirt, December 20, 1828, November 20, 1829, Wirt Papers; Blassingame, *Slave Community,* 173.

19. H. Louise Anderson to Catherine Wirt Randall, December 1, 1842, Ellen McCormick to Elizabeth Wirt, October 12, 1842, Wirt Papers.

20. *Florida Slave Narratives,* 97.

21. John Gamble Diary, January 26, 1847, Jefferson County Historical

Society, Monticello (hereafter, Gamble Diary); Thomas Randall to William Wirt, April 13, 1828, Wirt Papers; John Evans to George N. Jones, July 16, 1851, *Florida Slave Narratives*, 137–41; Kingsley, *Treatise*, 14–15.

22. John Evans to George Jones, May 3, 1851, April 2, 1852, *Florida Plantation Records*, 63, 74.

23. Gamble Diary, passim; Louisa Anderson to Catharine W. Randall, December 1842, Ellen McCormick to Elizabeth Wirt, October 12, 1854, *Florida Plantation Records*, 19; "Diary of David L. White, July 1835–June 1842," typescript, Work Projects Administration, Jacksonville, 1939; *Florida Slave Narratives*, 327–31.

24. Robert White to George Jones, September 10, 1850, *Florida Plantation Records*, 60; Kathryn T. Abbey, "Documents Relating to El Destino and Chemonie Plantations, Middle Florida, 1828–1868, Part 3," *Florida Historical Quarterly* 8 (July 1929): 3–46; *Florida Slave Narratives*, 166–67.

25. D. N. Moxley to George Jones, September 8, 1854, John Evans to Jones, October 18, 1854, Jones to Moxley, April 20, 1856, April 20, 1857, *Florida Plantation Records*, 97, 110, 152–53; Ellen McCormick to Catharine Randall, October 20, 1854, Wirt Papers.

26. John Evans to George Jones, September 2, 1852; October 18, 1854; January 10, 1856, *Florida Plantation Records*, 78, 80, 111–12.

27. Ibid., October 8, 1854, June 15, 1855, 107, 130–31.

28. Despite these charges, Roberson enjoyed a fifteen-year tenure at the saw mill at El Destino, and no available information suggests that he physically abused any of his hands. John Evans to George Jones, June 30, 1852, June 15, 1855; D. N. Moxley to Jones, October 18, 21, November 8, 1854, *Florida Plantation Records*, 71, 74, 111–13, 115–16. See also Louis Goldsborough to Elizabeth Goldsborough, January 24, 1834, in Louis Goldsborough Papers, Library of Congress, Washington, D.C. (hereafter, Goldsborough Papers).

29. John Evans to George Jones, January 10, 1856, *Florida Plantation Records*, 150.

30. Kingsley B. Gibbs Journal, 1840–1843, 22–23, Florida Collection.

31. Achille Murat, *The United States of North America* (London, 1833), 98.

32. Catharine Wirt to Louis Goldsborough, January 3, June 8, 1839, Wirt Papers.

33. Ibid., Ellen McCormick to Family, March 18, September 8, 1842.

34. Ibid., Ellen McCormick to Catharine Wirt, June 14, September 10, 1843.

35. Ibid., Ellen McCormick to Catharine Wirt, October 1, 1843.

36. Ibid., Laura Randall to Elizabeth Wirt, February 9, July 11, 1828, Ellen McCormick to Laura Randall, October 12, 1842.

37. Louis Goldsborough to Elizabeth Wirt, June 28, 1834; Goldsborough to Gracie, Prime and Company, June 24, 1834, Goldsborough Papers.

38. *Florida Slave Narratives*, 253.

39. Murat, *United States*, 96; *Florida Slave Narratives*, 328.

40. *Florida Slave Narratives*, 330; Thomas Randall to William Wirt, February 10, 1828, Wirt Papers.

41. Jerrell H. Shofner, *History of Jefferson County* (Tallahassee, 1976), 130; Gamble Diary, passim; Thomas Randall to William Wirt, March 20, April 7, 1833; Elizabeth Wirt to Laura Randall, November 13, 1827, Wirt Papers.

42. Kingsley B. Gibbs Journal, 1840–1843, especially December 25, 1841, 24.

43. Ibid.; Murat, *United States*, 98.

44. John Evans to George Jones, September 17, 1852, *Florida Plantation Records*, 80.

45. Joshua Hoyst Frier, "Journal of Reminiscences of the War Between the States, 1859–1865," 35–36, MSS collection, Florida State Archives.

46. Eppes, *Negro in the Old South*, 89–90.

47. A. R. McCall to George Jones, May 31, 1856, John Evans to Jones, June 15, 1852, July 31, August 6, 1854, September 14, October 2, 1855, *Florida Plantation Records*, 71–72, 88–91, 154–55.

48. Alexander Randall to Elizabeth Wirt, September 11, 1841, Wirt Papers; John Evans to George Jones, June 1, 1852, September 14, 1855, *Florida Plantation Records*, 70–77, 145.

49. Ellen Voss to Catharine Wirt, September 4, 1839, Wirt Papers.

50. Thomas Randall to William Wirt, April 13, October 14, 1828, Elizabeth Wirt to Laura Randall, October 12, 1837, Louis Goldsborough to William Wirt, February 1, 1834, Ellen McCormick to Elizabeth Wirt, April 15, 1842, Louisa A. Wirt to Elizabeth Wirt, July 14, 1844, Wirt Papers. For numerous entries describing the health and welfare of bondsmen and -women, see also Charles W. Bannerman Diary, 1837–1868, MSS collection, Florida State Archives.

51. *Florida Slave Narratives*, 178; Thomas Randall to William Wirt, April 13, 1828, Ellen McCormick to Catharine W. Randall, March 16, 1849, Louisa A. Wirt to Elizabeth Wirt, November 26, 1845, Wirt Papers.

52. Kathryn T. Abbey, "Documents Relating to El Destino and Chemonie Plantations, Middle Florida, 1828–1868, Part 4," *Florida Historical Quarterly* 8 (October 1929): 80.

53. Eppes, *Negro in the South*, 116–17; Ellen McCormick to Elizabeth Wirt, September 8, 1842, Wirt Papers.

54. Laura Randall to William Wirt, June 30, 1832, Wirt Papers; *Florida Slave Narratives*, 94–95.

55. John Evans to George Jones, October 8, 1854, *Florida Slave Narratives*, 110.

56. Ibid., February 9, 1848, 57.

57. Donorena Harris, "Abolitionist Sentiment in Florida 1821–1860" (M.A. thesis, Florida State University, 1989), 99.

58. To identify slave runaways, the author consulted the principal diaries, journals, letter collections, memoirs, and state and local histories covering the period 1821–60, as well as the principal extant newspapers published within Florida during the period. Particularly helpful were *Florida Plantation Records*; "Diary of David L. White"; "Diary of William D. Moseley"; Eppes, *Negro in the Old South*; Shofner, *History of Jefferson County*; Jerrell H. Shofner, *Jackson County, Florida: A History* (Marianna, Fla.: Jackson County Heritage Association, 1985); William Wirt Papers; Louis Goldsborough Papers. Notes as to specific references are in collection of the author, Florida A&M University, Tallahassee.

59. Harris, "Abolitionist Sentiment," 102.

60. Eppes, *Negro in the Old South*, 99–100.

61. *Jacksonville Florida News*, March 12, 1853. See also *Pensacola Gazette*, October 14, 1828.

62. *Tallahassee Florida Watchman*, April 28, 1838.

63. An exception to the small percentage of slaves fleeing occurred in the period 1835–36, when the Second Seminole War began. Joshua R. Giddings, Kenneth W. Porter, and Canter Brown, Jr., have stressed that hundreds, if not 1,000 or more, slaves deserted to the hostiles during the period. Joshua R. Giddings, *The Exiles of Florida: or, The Crimes Committed by Our Government Against the Maroons, Who Fled from South Carolina and Other Slave States, Seeking Protection Under Spanish Laws* (Columbus, Ohio, 1858; reprint ed., Gainesville, 1964), 97–134; Porter, "Negro Abraham," 17–18; Brown, "Race Relations."

64. *Tallahassee Floridian and Journal*, April 12, June 12, 1851, July 31, 1852; *Jacksonville Courier*, August 9, 1835, January 4, 1851.

65. Clarence E. Carter, ed., *Territorial Papers of the United States*, vols. 22–26, *Florida Territory* (Washington, D.C., 1956–1962), 22:763; *American State Papers: Military Affairs*, 7 vols. (Washington, D.C., 1832–60), 6:453; Louis Goldsborough to William Wirt, February 1834, Thomas Randall to Wirt, October 13, 1827, Randall to Mrs. Wirt, December 29, 1827, Wirt Papers; Louis Goldsborough to Catharine Goldsborough, November 2, 1827, Goldsborough Papers.

66. *St. Augustine News*, April 13, 1839, September 17, 1842, March 18, June 3, October 23, 1843, January 20, 1844; *St. Augustine Florida Herald and Southern Democrat*, July 11, 1843; *Tallahassee Floridian*, November 1, 1845; *Tallahassee Floridian and Advocate*, July 12, 1834.

67. In 1844 James Kelly was found guilty in a Leon County court of aiding a runaway. Charles S. Powell was accused of assisting a "slave with an escape," but found not guilty of the charge in Jackson County. Jefferson County's Irwin Ganger aided in the unsuccessful escape of a slave belonging to Nicholas Branch. Leon County Circuit Court Minute Book 4, 247, Leon County Courthouse, Tallahassee; Jackson County Circuit Court Order Book A, November 1844, Jefferson County Courthouse.

68. Jonathan Walker, *Trial and Imprisonment of Jonathan Walker at Pensacola, Florida, for Aiding Slaves to Escape From Bondage* (Boston, 1845; facsimile ed., Gainesville, 1974), 32–73; *Tallahassee Floridian and Journal*, February 20, 1858; *Tallahassee Floridian*, January 6, 1836, September 2, 1848.

69. Blassingame, *Slave Community*, 304; *Florida Slave Narratives*, 165.

70. *Florida Slave Narratives*, 243, 257–59.

71. Ibid., 348. For other bondsmen and -women who felt an attachment to the master and his family, see Laura Wirt to Elizabeth Wirt, July 14, 1844, Catharine W. Randall to Ellen McCormick, September 11, 1844, Wirt Papers; John Evans to George Jones, June 15, 1855, *Florida Plantation Records*, 128–29.

72. Will of Jesse Potts, August 4, 1829, and will of Robert S. Edmund, August 3, 1850, Gadsden County Will Book A, Gadsden County Courthouse, Quincy. See also wills of slaveholders in Madison, Leon, Jackson, and Jefferson counties concerning manumission of slaves upon the master's death (all on microfilm at Florida State Archives)

6

Blacks and the Seminole
Removal Debate, 1821–1835

George Klos

HE RISE OF Jacksonian democracy in the United States during the 1820s and 1830s led to a national program of Indian displacement for the benefit of white settlers and land speculators. Disputes between whites and Native Americans over the possession of black slaves was a very prominent feature of Indian removal from Florida. Unlike Indian removal in other parts of the United States, land was not the main issue; thousands of acres of public land could be had in Florida without dispossessing the Seminoles. Mediation of white-Seminole disputes over slaves failed, in part, because the federal Indian agents often owned and speculated in slaves themselves and thus were compromised by personal interests. Also, many blacks worked for the Seminoles as influential interpreters and advisers.

Even before the acquisition of Florida by the United States in 1821, blacks were involved in white-native conflicts. The combination of blacks and Seminoles was important in the international affairs of the region from the 1810–14 plot to take East Florida from the Spanish by force to the 1816 Negro Fort incident on the Apalachicola River and Andrew Jackson's Florida campaign of 1818.[1] After 1821, the problems between whites, Seminoles, and black allies of the Seminoles changed from an international issue to an internal one; the Florida Indians could now be dealt with unilaterally by the United States.

Settlers coming into Florida found, according to a correspondent in *Niles Weekly Register*, "the finest agricultural district within the limits of the United States." He described the area between the Suwanee and St. Johns rivers as "combining the advantages of a mild and healthy climate, a rich soil, and convenient navigation."[2] William P. DuVal, Jackson's successor as territorial governor of Florida, warned Secretary of War John C. Calhoun that "it will be a serious misfortune to this Territory if the Indians are permitted to occupy this tract of country." DuVal recommended moving the Indians of Florida to the domain of the Creeks, "to whom they properly belong," or to land west of the Mississippi River.[3] Writing to Florida Indian agent John R. Bell, Calhoun noted, "The government expects that the Slaves who have run away or been plundered from our Citizens or from Indian tribes within our limits will be given up peaceably by the Seminole Indians when demanded." Calhoun instructed Bell to convince the Seminoles either to join the Creeks or "to concentrate . . . in one place and become peaceable and industrious farmers."[4]

Governor DuVal, along with Florida planters James Gadsden and Bernard Segui, met with Indian representatives in September 1823 at Moultrie Creek south of St. Augustine. The Seminoles agreed to cede their land in north Florida to the United States and to receive a large tract with recognized boundaries farther south. Part of the negotiations required the listing of Indian towns and a census of their inhabitants. Neamathla, the leader of the Seminole delegation, listed thirty-seven towns with 4,883 natives. He objected, however, according to Gadsden, to specifying "the number of negroes in the nation."[5]

The Moultrie Creek agreement reserved for the Seminoles the area from the Big Swamp along the Withlacoochee River south to the "main branch of the Charlotte [Peace] river," some fifteen to twenty miles inland from the coasts. The Indians were to receive $5,000 per year for twenty years. Article 7 bound the Indians to be "active and vigilant in preventing the retreating to, or passing through, of the district assigned them, of any absconding slaves, or fugitives from justice" and to deliver all such people to the agent, when they would be compensated for their expenses.[6]

The U.S. government representatives, in their report accompanying the treaty, recommended that military posts be established around the contours of Indian country "to embody such a population within prescribed limits, and to conquer their erratic habits . . . [and to] further induce an early settlement of the country now open to the enterprise of emigrants."[7]

In giving up their North Florida land, the Indians were relinquishing an area of fertile soil, good rainfall, and temperate climate. Many of the early settlers migrated from elsewhere in the South and, with slaves that they brought with them, established cotton, sugar, and tobacco plantations and farms. Many Piedmont and Tidewater elites moved to Florida and created a new hierarchy in the territory.[8] Between 1825 and 1832, 433,751 acres of public land were sold in Florida; some 5 million acres were still available in 1833. The territorial Legislative Council, in an 1828 resolution to Congress, requested that the price per acre for public land be reduced so as to attract more settlers. The legislators argued it was a national security move to increase population.[9]

The 1830 census listed 34,730 Floridians, of whom 15,501 were slaves and 844 "free colored."[10] The Comte de Castelneau, a French visitor to Florida in the 1830s, observed the local planter as being "accustomed to exercise absolute power over his slaves[;] he cannot endure any opposition to his wishes." Whites of modest means, he said, were "brought up from childhood with the idea that the Indians are the usurpers of the land that belongs to them, and even in times of peace they are always ready to go hunting savages rather than deer hunting. . . . These men know no other power than physical force, and no other pleasure than carrying out their brutal passions."[11]

Blacks living with the Seminoles became a point of contention for whites because the Seminole system of slavery was not as harsh or rigid as the Anglo-American system; a comparatively lenient system in such close proximity might offer slaves of whites an alternative that their owners could not tolerate. A Seminole was more of a patron than a master; the Seminole slave system was akin to tenant farming. Blacks lived in their own villages near Indian villages and paid a harvest tribute, a percentage of the yield from their fields, to the chief. Blacks, an Indian agent reported, had "horses, cows, and hogs, with which the Indian owner never presumed to meddle."[12]

In the 1820s, when there were approximately four hundred blacks living with the Seminoles, only some eighty could be identified as fugitive slaves. Jacob Rhett Motte, an army surgeon stationed in

Florida in the 1830s, noted, "They had none of the servility of our northern blacks, but were constantly offerring their dirty paws with as much hauteur and nonchalance as if they were conferring a vast deal of honor." [13] They could "speak English as well as Indian," the trader Horatio Dexter reported, "and feel satisfied with their situation. They have the easy unconstrained manner of the Indian but more vivacity, and from their understanding of both languages possess considerable influence with their masters." [14] Only a few black Seminoles were bilingual, and those who were became influential in Indian councils. Although much has been made of the "equality" of the black Seminoles, it would be more accurate to say that some blacks were more equal than others. Seminole society had blacks of every status—born free, or the descendants of fugitives, or perhaps fugitives themselves. Some were interpreters and advisers of importance, others were warriors and hunters or field hands. Intermarriage with Indians further complicated black status. But even a black of low status among the Seminoles felt it was an improvement over Anglo-American chattel slavery.

People living near the Seminoles usually became acquainted with the Indians and their black interpreters through trade. Seminoles visited stores and plantations despite the legal prohibition on leaving the reservation. Blacks often crossed the prescribed boundaries, and some white-owned slaves had spouses and other relatives living in Indian country. John Philip, a middle-aged "chief negro" to King Philip, leader of an Indian band, had a wife living on a St. Johns River plantation. Luis Fatio, owned by Francis Philip Fatio, one of the most prominent planters in East Florida, made his first contact with the Seminoles on the plantation. His older brother ran away to Indian country, and Luis learned one of the Indian languages during his brother's periodic visits to the slave quarters. One day Luis went on a visit to Seminole country and never returned. [15]

There were others like Luis. Alachua County slaveowners estimated one hundred runaways among the Seminoles, complaining that the black Seminoles (the planters apparently saw a difference between them and runaways) "aided such slaves to select new and more secure places of refuge." [16] Owen Marsh, who visited several "Negro Villages" looking for runaways, noted that the number of runaway slaves among the Seminoles could not be determined "from the Cir-

Gopher John, Seminole Interpreter. Reprinted from Joshua R. Giddings, *The Exiles of Florida* (Columbus, Ohio, 1858). Africans living among the Seminoles in Florida adopted Seminole dress and ways of life.

cumstances of their being protected by the Indian Negroes. . . . These Indian Negroes are so artfull that it is impossible to gain any Information relating to such property from them." [17]

Governor DuVal admonished the Seminoles in January 1826 for not returning runaway slaves.

> You are not to mind what the negroes say; they will lie, and lead you astray, in the hope to escape from their white owners, and that you will give them refuge and hide them. Do your duty and give them up. They care nothing for you, further than to make use of you, to keep out of the hands of their masters. Thus far the negroes have made you their tools, and gained protection, contrary to both justice and the treaty, and at the same time, laugh at you for being deceived by them. Your conduct in this matter is cause of loud, constant, and just complaint on the part of the white people. . . . Deliver them up, rid your nation of a serious pest, and do what, as honest men, you should not hesitate to do; then your white brothers will say you have done them justice, like honest, good men.

Should the Seminoles refuse, DuVal warned, the army will take the blacks by force, "and in the confusion, many of you may lose your own slaves." [18]

Tuckose Emathla (John Hicks), a principal spokesman for the Indians, replied, "We do not like the story that our people hide the runaway negroes from their masters. It is not a true talk. . . . We have never prevented the whites from coming into our country and taking their slaves whenever they could find them and we will not hereafter oppose their doing so." At another meeting that year, Tuckose Emathla voiced the main Indian complaint regarding slaves: "The white people have got some of our negroes, which we expect they will be made to give up." [19]

Besides the black communities on Seminole land, other groups of blacks and Indians lived outside the treaty boundaries, and still others left Florida altogether. Owen Marsh, in his investigation of Seminole country, reported that many runaway slaves had departed for the Bahamas and Cuba, and a Darien, Georgia, slaveowner complained to the secretary of war that his escaped slaves left Florida via "West India wreckers" working the Atlantic coast.[20] Two other settlements in southwest Florida were described by John Winslett, who was tracking three slaves of a Georgia planter. He was told at Tampa Bay that "it would not be safe to pursue them much farther without force; that a band of desperadoes, runaways, murderers, and thieves (negroes and Indians, a majority runaway slaves)" lived on an island south of Charlotte Harbor. Blacks and Indians who had been there told Winslett of "another settlement of lawless persons (Indians and absconded slaves) on a creek between Manatia [Manatee] River and Charlotte's Harbor, some miles west of the latter." [21] The island community was a haven for some survivors of the Negro Fort on the Apalachicola River, and existed until the war for Seminole removal.[22] The residents cut timber and fished, shipping their goods to Havana, where they were traded for rum and firearms. The Seminoles also traded with Cuban fishermen, and Indian agent Gad Humphreys reported that runaway slaves were shuttled to Havana this way, sometimes bound for freedom and sometimes for sale.[23]

The legal mechanisms for settling slave disputes between whites and Indians failed. DuVal proposed that the government buy Seminole slaves, as individual whites were prohibited from slave trading with Indians, but he was told by the superintendent of Indian Affairs that agents should not involve themselves in slave trade with their charges. When whites took slaves from Indians, Florida agents were instructed to use due process to get the slaves back. When Indians held slaves claimed by whites, the burden of proof was on the whites. In accordance with the Moultrie Creek treaty, the Seminoles did return some runaway slaves, and in other cases, Humphreys explained to the representative of a Georgia slaveowner, they welcomed investigation "by a competent tribunal." [24] For the most part, however, the Seminoles refused to surrender the slaves in question before the trial. "Their own negroes that have been taken from them are held by white people who refuse to dilliver them up," DuVal told the superintendent of Indian Affairs. "I have felt asshamed while urgeing the Indians to surrender the property they hold, that I had not power to obtain for them their own rights and property held by our citizens. . . . To tell one of these people that he must go to law for his property in our courts with a white man is only adding insult to injury." [25]

Indians resisted surrendering slaves to public (white) custody as a precondition for resolving disputes because they knew they had no rights in court. "The Indian, conscious of his rights, and knowing that he paid the money, though incapable of showing the papers executed under forms of law, as he had received none, and relying upon the honesty of the white man, protested most earnestly against these demands, and resolutely expressed a determination to resist all attempts thus to wrest from him his rightfully acquired property," explained John T. Sprague in his history of the Second Seminole War. "Deprived as they were of a voice in the halls of justice, the surrender of the negro at once dispossessed them, without the least prospect of ever getting him returned." The commander of the army post at Tampa Bay, Colonel George M. Brooke, observed in 1828 that "so many claims are now made on them, that they begin to believe that it is the determination of the United States to take them all. This idea is strengthened by the conversations of many of the whites, and which they have heard." [26]

Whites, however, saw it differently. Samuel Cook, Abraham Bellamy, and other planters complained that "whilst the Law furnishes to the Indians ample means of redress for the aggressions of Whitemen, we are Constrained to look with patience, whilst they possess and enjoy the property most justly and rightfully Ours." They also objected to being prevented from taking from Indian country "even those negroes that are unclaimed and unpossessed by the Indians." [27] Cook also voiced another frontier slaveowner's complaint, that slaves purchased from the Seminoles often slipped back to Indian country. DuVal reported to McKenney that "the persons who have been most clamorous about their claims on the Indians and their property are those who have cheated them, under false reports, of their slaves, who have since gone back to the Indians." [28] Alfred Beckley, an army lieutenant stationed in Florida in 1825, noted that planters sought any opportunity to use force against the Seminoles "so that the whites might possess themselves of many valuable negroes." [29]

DuVal favored withholding treaty annuities until the Indians returned runaway slaves, and the Indian Office did so in 1828 but later reversed the policy and forbade it in the future. Since some white claims were indisputable, DuVal said, the slave in question ought to be given by the Indians to the agent, or the owner "ought to receive

Billy Bowlegs and Chiefs of the Seminole Indians: Billy Bowlegs, Chocote Tustenuggee, Abram [sic], John Jumper, Fasatchee Emanthla, Sarparkee Yohola, on a state visit to Washington, D.C., in 1826. Abraham, fourth from the left, escaped from slavery and became an adviser to Chief Micanopy. He helped negotiate the treaties of Paynes Landing and Fort Gibson and urged the Seminoles to resist deportation to the Indian Territory. He was eventually exiled with them in 1839. Courtesy of the Florida State Archives.

the full value of him from the nation." [30] Local slaveowners, however, advocated "adequate military force" to "recover pilfered property" from the Seminoles.[31]

If, in the critical role of the agents as mediators between Indians and frontier whites, "the success of the work depended upon the character of the man," then the agents assigned to the Seminoles exacerbated rather than allayed conflict.[32] Ample evidence shows that, contrary to orders, Gad Humphreys engaged in slave trade with his charges, and planters accused him of dragging his feet on their complaints about runaways. In one case, a woman in St. Marys, Georgia, claimed that a slave and the slave's children were living with the Seminoles. A man dispatched to retrieve them found it "next to an impossibility" to get them back due to the Seminoles' "natural reluctance to give it up and the wish of their agent to speculate." [33]

"The negroes this man is after are ours, and the white people *know* it is so," said the subchief Jumper to Humphreys.[34] When Humphreys reported the Seminoles' determination not to allow the contested slaves out of their possession, interested parties petitioned Washington for an investigation, charging Humphreys with colluding with a local planter to prevent transfer of the slaves, in the expectation that the claim would be abandoned with the passage of time, as expenses mounted.[35]

McKenney also received accusations that Humphreys had worked fugitive slaves on his own land for several months before returning them to their owners. Secretary of War Peter B. Porter informed President John Quincy Adams of allegations that Humphreys had "connived with the Indians in the concealment of runaway slaves, and in that way affected purchases of them himself, at reduced prices."[36]

Humphreys explained to Alex Adair, the investigator of the allegations, that he bought slaves from Indians so that claimants could prove ownership in court, an impossibility as long as the slaves were in Indian possession.[37] Adair concluded that while Humphreys in fact probably had billed the government for sugar kettles installed on his land, the other charges were difficult to prove since "those who had been most clamorous appeared most disposed to evade the inquiry." Humphreys apparently had made reasonable settlements with his accusers when he learned that he was to be investigated. Zephaniah Kingsley, who claimed that Humphreys had held one of his slaves for over a year, "stated he had settled his business with the Agent in his own way. . . . His property had been surrendered to him some months back and he cared no more about it."[38]

An Alachua County resident reported to Governor DuVal that Humphreys possessed blacks belonging to Indians, and that he bought Indian cattle with IOUs he later refused to honor. Humphreys was a liability, McKenney noted, because those opposing him in Florida "make his services in that quarter of but little, if any, use to the Government, whilst his dealing in slaves is in direct violation of an express order forbidding it." Both Governor DuVal and the territory's Congressional Delegate Joseph White wanted Humphreys replaced, and he was dismissed in March 1830.[39]

Humphreys's slave problems, however, continued, as DuVal had received complaints from Indians that Humphreys held their slaves. Humphreys's replacement, John Phagan, attempted to return the slaves, but Humphreys refused to release them unless Phagan was willing to purchase them.[40] In another case, stemming from his role as Indian agent, Humphreys sought government assistance in recovering two black men claimed by an Indian woman named Culekeechowa. She had inherited from her mother a slave named Caty, who later bore four children. Horatio Dexter, a trader, persuaded Culekeechowa's brother and Caty's husband, to sell Caty and her two daughters and two sons in exchange for whiskey. Humphreys, as agent, who had agreed to help the Indian woman, went to St. Augustine, where Dexter was offering the slaves for sale. Humphreys maintained that he had to buy them to prevent their sale to a Charleston buyer. But then, instead of returning them to Culekeechowa, he kept the slaves for himself. When the boys grew older and became aware of what had happened, they left for Seminole country in 1835.[41]

Slave disputes between Seminoles and whites frequently went unresolved because the interpreters in these negotiations were sometimes former slaves themselves. DuVal observed that the blacks were "much more hostile to the white people than their masters," and were "constantly counteracting" advice to the Indians. In several instances, he said, chiefs had agreed to a white demand in council but later were talked out of compliance by their black advisers.[42] The problem, as Humphreys saw it in 1827, was that "the negroes of the Seminole Indians are wholly independent, or at least regardless of the authority of their masters; and are Slaves but in name." Indians considered blacks "rather as fellow Sufferers and companions in misery than as inferiors," Humphreys wrote, and the "great influence the Slaves possess over their masters" enabled them to "artfully represent" whites as hostile to people of color.[43] The first step in moving the Seminoles out of Florida, DuVal told the commissioner of Indian Affairs in 1834, "must be *the breaking up of the runaway slaves and outlaw Indians.*"[44]

When Andrew Jackson was elected president, public opinion in the South was demanding stricter control over Indians. Whites wanted land, of course, but they also saw Indians as possible allies of foreign powers (as in the War of 1812), and the presence of fugitive slaves among them was viewed as a threat to internal security. Jackson

Ben Bruno, *Harper's Weekly*, June 12, 1858. Like Abraham, Bruno served as interpreter and adviser to the Seminoles. He was a confidant of Chief Billy Bowlegs. Courtesy of the Florida State Archives.

urged Indian removal legislation in his December 1829 annual message to Congress, and he tried to sooth opposition by assuring that removal would be voluntary and peaceful. In May 1830, Congress appropriated $500,000 for the negotiation of removal treaties. The territory north of Texas and west of Arkansas that was designated for resettlement was considered at the time the only available location where the Indians would not be in the way of white expansion.[45]

Floridians had been voicing removal sentiment since early in the territorial period.[46] As indicated in a message to Congress, the main reason for ousting the Seminoles from Florida was unchanged through the years: "A most weighty objection" to the presence of Indians in the territory was "that absconding slaves find ready security among the Indians and such aid is amply sufficient to enable them successfully to elude the best efforts by their masters to recover them."[47]

Territorial government wholeheartedly supported the white slave interests. The Legislative Council requested removal in July 1827, and Acting Governor James Westcott asked the council to strengthen the militia because "we have amongst us two classes who may possibly at some future period, be incited to hostility, and . . . it behooves us always to be prepared." He believed the only humane solution was to move the Indians away from whites, without moving their slaves.[48]

An 1826 Florida law to regulate Indian trade in general imposed the death penalty on anyone who "shall inveigle, steal, or carry away" any slave or "hire, aid, or counsel" anyone to do so. That this section—which does not mention Indians—appears in a bill relating to Indian trade shows slaveowners' concern over the black-Indian connection. In 1832, the territory prohibited "Indian negroes, bond or free," from traveling outside the Indian boundaries. Also, in light of the Gad Humphreys episodes, the council set limits to the amount of the reward Indian agents could collect for capturing runaway slaves, established accounting requirements in slave cases, and required agents to advertise fugitive slaves in their custody.[49]

In January 1832 Secretary of War Lewis Cass instructed James Gadsden, Florida planter and Jackson supporter, to arrange a treaty with the Seminoles providing for their removal west to the new Creek country, with all annuities in the West to be paid through the Creeks.[50] Gadsden met with the Seminole leaders at Paynes Landing on the Ocklawaha River. Among the first orders of business was selection of interpreters satisfactory to the Seminoles. Gadsden brought along Stephen Richards for that purpose, while the Seminoles chose Abraham, "a faithful domestic of Micanope, the Head Chief. In addition the interpreter of the agent, Cudjo, was present."[51] As advisers and interpreters in Indian-white negotiations, these two men were perhaps the most influential blacks in Florida at the time.

Abraham was regarded as more than an interpreter; he was frequently called a "chief Negro" in official dispatches, and army surgeon Jacob Rhett Motte described him as "a perfect Tallyrand of the savage court."[52] How he arrived among the Seminoles is speculative, but judging by his manners and knowledge of English, he may have been an Englishman's house servant prior to the U.S. acquisition of Florida. His wife was Bowleg's half-black widow, by whom he fathered three or four children.[53] Abraham's influence is usually described in comparison to that of his "master" or patron, Micanopy, "a large, fat man, rather obtuse in intellect, but kind to his people and his slaves."[54] Micanopy was described by McCall as "rather too indolent to rule harshly"; he tended to leave official business to what he called his "sense-bearers," one of whom was Abraham.[55] Despite the prevailing opinion of Micanopy, no one underestimated Abraham. John Lee Williams, one of the first Florida historians and a figure in territorial politics, said Abraham had "as much influence in the nation as any other man. With an appearance of great modesty, he is ambitious, avaricious, and withal very intelligent."[56] Thin and over six feet tall with a broad, square face and a thin moustache, Abraham was "plausible, pliant, and deceitful," according to Mayer Cohen, who also noted, "and, under an exterior of profound meekness, [he] cloaks deep, dark, and bloody purposes. He has at once the crouch and the spring of the panther."[57] Captain John C. Casey, who spent much time with Abraham during the war and knew him better than most whites, described him as having "a slight inclination forward like a Frenchman of the old school. His countenance is one of great cunning and penetration. He always smiles, and his words flow like oil. His conversation is soft and low, but very distinct, with a most genteel emphasis."[58]

Cudjo was described as a "regular interpreter at the Seminole agency," although it is not known when his relationship with the government began. As late as 1822 he was "one of the principal characters" of a black Seminole town in the Big Swamp area, according to William Simmons, who spent a night in his house.[59] One Indian agent complained of his "very imperfect knowledge of the English language," yet John Bemrose, a soldier in Florida in the 1830s, described his speech as "the common negro jargon of the plantation." [60] Bemrose mentioned that partial paralysis afflicted Cudjo, while another contemporary caustically remarked on the "little, limping figure of *Cudjoe* . . . with his cunning, squinting eyes; and his hands folded across his lap, in seemingly meek attention to the scene around him." Of all the blacks to figure prominently in Seminole removal and the ensuing war, Cudjo was the first to side with the government. Porter attributes this to "his physical deficiency of partial paralysis [that] predisposed him toward association with those who could give him the medical attention and comforts which his condition called for and which would have been inaccessible among the hostile Indians and Negroes." [61] By the time of the meeting at Paynes Landing, Cudjo was drawing a salary and rations from the Indian agency at Fort King and probably living there as well.

Gadsden's main obstacles to a successful conclusion of the treaty negotiations were slave claims and the idea that the Seminoles should combine with the Creeks. He told the assemblage that as bad as emigration sounded to them, their situation would only be worse under local jurisdiction, which would be their fate if they refused to sell their land. He offered to include in the treaty an article earmarking $7,000, over and above the main payment for relinquishing their land, for the government to settle property claims against them. The sum "will probably cover all demands which can be satisfactorily proved," Gadsden said. "Many claims are for negroes. . . . The Indians allege that the depredations were mutual, that they suffered in the same degree, and that most of the property claimed was taken as reprisal for property of equal value lost by them." [62] Finally, Gadsden conferred privately with Abraham and Cudjo and added $400 to the Seminole payment specifically for the two black men. It was "intended to be a bribe," recalled one disgusted army captain; Gadsden "could not have got the treaty through if he had not bribed the negro interpreter." [63]

The Seminoles believed they had forestalled giving up their land.

All they had agreed to, they thought, was to send a delegation to the Indian territory to examine the proposed new land. The group would report back to the larger body of Seminoles, and then the final decision would be made. This interpretation was also held at the highest levels of the federal government. The secretary of war, in his annual report to the president, said the treaty was "not obligatory on [the Indians'] part" until a group examined the land "and until the tribe, upon their report, shall have signified their desire" to move. "When they return, the determination of the tribe will be made known to the government." [64]

Seven Seminoles, Abraham, and agent John Phagan went to the proposed new Seminole land during the winter of 1832–33. At Fort Gibson on the Arkansas River, Phagan and three other federal agents prepared a document for the group's signatures. It stated that the group was satisfied with the country to be assigned to the Seminoles, that they would live within the Creek nation but have a separate designated area, and that they would become "a constituent part of the Creek nation." [65] The Seminoles balked. They had no authority to sign anything, and it is reasonable to assume that Oklahoma in the winter was not very appealing to natives of Florida. According to one version, Phagan threatened to refuse to guide them home until they signed. Jumper, Holata Emathla, and Coi Hadjo later claimed never to have signed, but they probably said that to protect themselves from Seminoles violently opposed to removal. Abraham's part at Fort Gibson went unrecorded and is unclear, but obviously a combination of trickery and duress was employed to hasten emigration. Hitchcock, who later had to fight in the resulting war, called the Seminole treaty process "a fraud upon the Indians." [66]

When the group returned and reported to the Seminole council what they had seen, Micanopy informed agent Wiley Thompson that the Seminoles had decided to decline the offer. Thompson told him that the delegation had signed away Florida and to prepare his people for emigration. Abraham brought the chief's answer the next day. "The old man says today the same he said yesterday, 'the nation decided in council to decline the offer.'" Captain McCall, with several years service in Florida, knew the interpreter to be "crafty and artful in the extreme" and thus did not doubt that he had "as usual, much to do in keeping the chief, who was of a vacillating character, steady in his purpose." [67] Abraham, however, was not the only influence on Micanopy; "not an Indian would have consented to the relinquishment of their country" had the Paynes Landing agreement worked the way they thought it would, according to Sprague. The Seminoles who had signed at Fort Gibson were, in fact, "ridiculed and upbraided by all classes, male and female, for being circumvented by the whites." Resistance sentiment was so strong that the Fort Gibson signatories feared for their lives.[68]

Aside from the overt fraudulence of the recent treaties, the two major obstacles to Seminole removal remained their opposition to living with the Creeks and their rejection of the designs of others on their slaves. The first problem was destined to continue as a part of the removal treaties; the second was supposedly settled by the stipulation that the United States settle property claims against the Seminoles. Nevertheless, plans were still afoot to keep the Seminoles' blacks in Florida as the Indians were moved out.

The Seminoles gradually separated themselves from the Creek Confederacy, a process virtually complete by the Red Stick War, but the Creeks often included the Seminoles in their treaties even though no Seminoles were signatories.[69] The Seminoles, in fact, adamantly denied the Creeks' right to do so. These treaties usually had articles indemnifying American citizens for slaves taken by Indians as part of the Creek annuity; thus the Creeks claimed black Seminoles as their own, and their demands for the "return" of slaves further complicated Indian removal. Though the Seminoles recognized a political separation between themselves and the Creeks, clan ties bridged the two groups.[70]

Even Seminoles who favored emigration objected to uniting with the Creeks. The Creeks wanted, according to Lieutenant Woodbourne Potter, to bring the Seminoles into their nation "evidently with a view to dispossess the Seminoles, in the easiest manner, of their large negro property, to which the former had unsuccessfully urged a claim." [71] Colonel Duncan Clinch, leader of the U.S. forces in the 1816 Negro Fort battle and by the 1830s owner of 3,000 acres in Alachua County, explained that the Seminoles feared for their property because the Creeks greatly outnumbered them. They also believed they would have no justice in the West if there were no separate agent to attend to Seminole interests. However, the authorities in Washington, ignoring the advice of those at the scene, continued to plan for combining the Creeks and Seminoles on the same land, under one agency.[72] The Seminoles argued that the slave claims made by the Creeks were covered by the sixth article of the Paynes Landing treaty, in which the United States agreed to pay for such claims. "As it would be difficult, not to say impossible, to prove that the negroes claimed by the Creeks, now in the possession of the Seminole Indians, are the identical negroes, or their descendants. . . . I cannot conceive that the Creeks can be supposed to have a fair claim to them," said agent Thompson.[73]

The Creeks were but one group asserting the right to enslave black Seminoles. After President Jackson agreed with his Florida supporters that it might be a good idea for the government to permit the selling of the black Seminoles to whites, Thompson expressed his fear to the acting secretary of war that such a policy would "bring into the nation a crowd of 'speculators,' some of whom might resort to the use of improper means to effect their object, and thereby greatly embarrass our operations."[74]

Governor Richard Keith Call, who had served under Jackson in the Florida campaign of 1818, initiated the plan to sell the blacks. "The negroes have a great influence over the Indians; they are better agriculturalists and inferior huntsmen to the Indians, and are violently opposed to leaving the country," he explained to Jackson. "If the Indians are permitted to convert them into specie, one great obstacle in the way of removal may be overcome." Carey A. Harris, head of the Office of Indian Affairs, explained to Thompson that such a move would rid the Seminoles of one certain point of conflict in the West "which . . . would excite the cupidity of the Creeks." Harris believed, furthermore, that it would not be an inhumane act as "it is not to be presumed the condition of these slaves would be worse than that of others in the same section of the country."[75] To Thompson, a policy of allowing Seminole slave sales was yet one more problem blocking peaceful removal. He had to counteract rumors spread by "malcontent Indians" that he had his own designs on the blacks, "and the moment I am called upon to meet this new difficulty, a party of whites arrives at the agency with what they consider a permission from the War Department to purchase slaves from the Indians." Should this continue, he warned, "it is reasonable to suppose that the negroes would en masse unite with the malcontent Indians." Instead, he proposed that the government persuade the blacks "to exert their known influence" on behalf of removal by assuring the security of their existing relations with the Indians and not "classing them with skins and furs." In the end, Thompson was permitted to deny any trader entry to Seminole country by refusing him a license, and Thompson could issue licenses at his own discretion.[76]

Army officers in Florida agreed with Thompson that black opposition to being sold to whites would bring energy to the Seminole resistance, as blacks did not see themselves benefiting under white control. The commander of U.S. troops in Florida, Lieutenant Colonel A. C. W. Fanning, worried that "the cupidity of our own citizens" might ruin removal plans because the blacks, "who are bold, active, and armed will sacrifice some of them to their rage."[77] When Thompson asked chiefs friendly to removal to conduct a preremoval census of their people, including slaves, blacks became alarmed that the compilation of their names and numbers was the first step in the effort to put them under white control. At the same time, Thompson said, whites came to the agency with the War Department's affirmative response to Call's inquiry about Seminole slaves.[78]

The majority of Indians opposed emigration, regardless of the agreement made by a handful of chiefs. As General Thomas S. Jesup explained in the midst of the war, "Even when a large portion of the heads of families should assent to a measure, those who dissented did not consider themselves bound to submit to or adopt it." Some headmen, including Jumper, Coi Hadjo, Charley Emathla, and Holata Emathla, knew that U.S. power made resistance futile and thus privately favored emigration, but their people so opposed it that they threatened the lives of any Indians who complied with the removal plan. Osceola emerged as a leader of the militant resistance and, though not a hereditary Seminole leader, he collected followers who agreed with what he said. His ascent to leadership also owed as much to action as talk; Thompson jailed Osceola briefly for threatening him with a knife, and in 1835, a month before the onset of the Second Seminole War, Osceola killed Charley Emathla for preparing for removal regardless of the sentiment of the people.[79]

Thompson tried to explain to the Seminoles how much worse their condition would be if they remained in Florida without federal protection. He also offered assurances that the government would protect their property from the Creeks. Micanopy held firm on the twenty-year term of the Moultrie Creek treaty, which would not expire for nine more years. Other Indian speakers complained that the Paynes Landing Treaty had not been explained to them correctly, that they had meant only to evaluate the western land, which had turned out to be no good. Nothing was resolved at this October 1834 meeting, and Thompson noticed that the Indians, "after they had received their annuity, purchased an unusually large quantity of powder and lead." [80]

Duncan Clinch, who met with the Seminoles in April 1835, got no further than had Thompson. Jumper proceeded to make a lively two-hour speech, and Bemrose recorded "Cudjo's short and abrupt elucidation of doubtless a noble harangue. . . . 'When he look upon the White man's warriors, he sorry to injure them, but he cannot fear them, he had fought them before, he will do so again, if his people say fight.' . . . When asked to elucidate more fully the speaker's meaning, it tended only to his imperfect grunt of 'he say he no go, dat all he say.'" Clinch, exasperated, finally told the council if they did not emigrate voluntarily, they would be removed by force. A number of chiefs agreed, but not Micanopy or Jumper.[81]

Abraham, who had interpreted the removal treaties, was now counseling resistance, and Thompson believed the cause lay in the actions of Thompson's predecessor at the Seminole agency, John Phagan.[82] Abraham fumed that he had never been paid, as Thompson explained: "He has (in my possession) Major Phagan's certificate that he is entitled for his service to $280 for which Major Phagan, on the presentation of Abraham's receipt at the Department received credit. Abraham says he never gave a receipt; that he has been imposed upon, and he is consequently more indifferent upon the subject of emigration than I think he would otherwise have been. I have little doubt that a few hundred dollars would make him zealous and active." The money, Thompson said, should be given only "on the production of the effect desired." [83]

Secretary of War Cass declined this opportunity to influence a useful ally. "Major Phagan having filed here the proper receipt for Abraham for his pay as interpreter, and received credit for the amount, it would be unsafe and inconsistent with the rules of the De-

"Aunt Jane" and her charge, Sarah Walker Palmer, ca. 1850s. Jane, nurse-maid for the children of Dr. J.D. Palmer of Fernandina, was a survivor of the Seminole attack on Indian Key during the Second Seminole War. Courtesy of the Florida State Archives.

partment to set aside the receipt, and pay the claim now presented," he told Thompson.[84]

While the blacks, especially the influential ones, sided with the resistance, the murder of Charley Emathla by Osceola frightened those Indians inclined to cooperate with removal, and there was sudden abandonment of the Seminole communities. Clinch and Thompson perceived that trouble was imminent. The Florida frontier might

Abraham, adviser to Chief Micanopy, ca. 1830s. From Joshua R. Giddings, *The Exiles of Florida* (Columbus, Ohio, 1858)

be destroyed, Clinch told the adjutant general of the army, "by a combination of the Indians, Indian Negroes and the Negroes on the plantations." Reinforcements arrived in December, and a plan was made to move by force on the Seminole country after New Year's Day to round up the Indians for emigration.[85]

The eruption of hostilities in the last week of 1835 owed much to the alliance of blacks with the Seminoles. Luis Pacheco, the former slave of the Fatio family who had subsequently lived in Indian country, was the guide for Major Francis L. Dade's fateful encounter with the Seminole warriors who were determined to resist removal. Whether or not he colluded with the attackers, as he denied to his death, other blacks assisted the warriors who ambushed Dade's troops. Major F. S. Belton published in the *Niles Register* his account of the battle, in which he stated that "a negro . . . named Harry, controls the Pea Creek band of about a hundred warriors, forty miles southeast of [Fort Brooke] . . . who keep this post constantly observed, and communicate with the Mickasukians at Wythlacoochee." [86]

At the same time that Dade's force was wiped out, blacks and Indians assaulted plantations near St. Augustine, and approximately three hundred slaves joined them. One leader of the raids, John Caesar, was a black Seminole with family connections on one plantation. Another was John Philip, who lived with King Philip and had a wife on Benjamin Heriot's sugar plantation.[87]

Thus began the longest and most expensive Indian war the U.S. government was to wage. Ultimately the war for removal could not be resolved without a guarantee by Major General Thomas Jesup that blacks would be permitted to go to the West with the Seminoles rather than being sold into slavery. Obviously, the events leading up to the war were distinctly influenced by blacks sympathetic to Seminole resistance.

Notes

1. Kenneth W. Porter wrote extensively on blacks and Seminoles. His *Negro on the American Frontier* (New York: Arno Press, 1971) is a compilation of articles first published in *Florida Historical Quarterly* and *Journal of Negro History*, among others. Rembert W. Patrick, *Florida Fiasco* (Athens: University of Georgia Press, 1954), covers the East Florida campaign of 1811–1813, and includes a chapter on the blacks living with the Seminoles of Alachua. Mark F. Boyd, "Events at Prospect Bluff on the Apalachicola River, 1808–1818," *Florida Historical Quarterly* 16 (October 1937): 55–96, and John D. Milligan, "Slave Rebelliousness and the Florida Maroon," *Prologue* 6 (Spring 1974): 4–18, descriptively cover the Negro Fort incident.

2. *Niles Weekly Register* 21 (September 29, 1821): 69.

3. William DuVal to John C. Calhoun, September 22, 1822, in *Territorial Papers of the United States*, ed. Clarence E. Carter, 27 vols. (Washington, D.C.: Government Printing Office, 1934–69), 22:533–34 (hereafter cited as *Territorial Papers*).

4. Calhoun to John R. Bell, September 28, 1821, *Territorial Papers* 22:219–21.

5. *American State Papers–Indian Affairs*, 2 vols. (Washington, D.C.: Gales and Seaton, 1832–61), 2:439.

6. The treaty is printed in full in *Indian Affairs: Laws and Treaties*, ed. Charles J. Kappler (Washington, D.C.: Government Printing Office, 1904), 2:203–6.

7. Indian Commissioners to Calhoun, September 26, 1823, *Territorial Papers* 22:750.

8. Julia F. Smith, *Slavery and Plantation Growth in Antebellum Florida, 1821–1860* (Gainesville: University of Florida Press, 1973), 18; Michael G. Schene, *Hopes, Dreams, and Promises: A History of Volusia County, Florida* (Daytona Beach: News-Journal Corp., 1976), 30–39, details the sugar enterprises set up in a county near the Seminole boundary.

9. *American State Papers–Public Land*, 8 vols., 6:630, 663; 5:375.

10. *Abstract of Returns, 5th Census* (Washington, D.C.: Duff and Green, 1832), 44. Indians, and the blacks living among them, were not counted.

11. "Essay on Middle Florida, 1837–38," trans. Arthur R. Seymour, *Florida Historical Quarterly* 26 (January 1948): 236, 239.

12. Wiley Thompson to Secretary of War, April 27, 1835, *American State Papers–Military Affairs*, 7 vols., 6:534 (hereafter cited as *American State Papers–MA*).

13. Jacob Rhett Motte, *Journey Into Wilderness*, ed. James F. Sunderman (Gainesville: University of Florida Press, 1953), 210.

14. Mark F. Boyd, "Horatio Dexter and Events Leading to the Treaty of Moultrie Creek with the Seminole Indians," *Florida Anthropologist* 6 (September 1958): 81–92.

15. Kenneth W. Porter, *Negro on the American Frontier*, 240–41; Kenneth W. Porter, "The Early Life of Luis Pacheco Née Fatio," *Negro History Bulletin* 7 (December 1943): 52.

16. House Misc. Document 271, 24th Cong., 1st Sess., 31.

17. Owen Marsh to Thomas L. McKenney, May 17, 1826, Office of Indian Affairs–Letters Received, National Archives microcopy 234, roll 800 (hereafter cited as OIA–LR).

18. House Misc. Doc. 17, 19th Cong., 2nd Sess., 18.

19. Ibid., 20; Tuckose Emathla to James Barbour (transcribed by Gad Humphreys), May 17, 1826, OIA–LR roll 800.

20. Marsh to McKenney, May 17, 1826, and John N. McIntosh to Calhoun, January 16, 1825, OIA–LR roll 800. See also John M. Goggin, "The Seminole Negroes of Andros Island, Bahamas," *Florida Historical Quarterly* 24 (January 1946): 201–6; Kenneth W. Porter, "Notes on the Seminole Negroes in the Bahamas," *Florida Historical Quarterly* 24 (July 1945): 56–

60; and Harry A. Kersey, Jr., "The Seminole Negroes of Andros Island Revisited: Some New Pieces to an Old Puzzle," *Florida Anthropologist* 34 (December 1981): 169–76.

21. Statement of John Winslett, sworn to by Augustus Steele, Jr., December 21, 1833, OIA–LR roll 290.

22. James Forbes and James Innerarity, searching for slaves known to have been at Negro Fort, got as far as Tampa Bay, where they were informed that the runaways were in the Charlotte Harbor area. William Coker and Thomas Watson, *Indian Traders of the Southeastern Spanish Borderlands* (Pensacola: University of West Florida Press, 1986), 309.

23. DuVal to Calhoun, September 23, 1823, *Territorial Papers* 22, 744; Gad Humphreys to Calhoun, January 31, 1826, *Territorial Papers* 23, 203; James W. Covington, "Life at Fort Brooke, 1824–1836," *Florida Historical Quarterly* 36 (April 1958): 325–26.

24. Humphreys to Horatio Lowe, September 17, 1828, OIA–LR roll 800.

25. DuVal to McKenney, March 20, 1826, *Territorial Papers* 23, 483; McKenney to DuVal, May 8, 1826, *American State Papers–Indian Affairs* 2:698; Mark F. Boyd, *Florida Aflame* (Tallahassee: Florida Board of Parks and Historic Memorials, 1951), 36.

26. John T. Sprague, *Origin, Progress, and Conclusion of the Florida War* (New York: Appleton, 1848), 34, 43, 52–53.

27. *Territorial Papers* 22:763.

28. *Territorial Papers* 23:473, 483.

29. "Memoir of a West Pointer in Florida," ed. Cecil D. Eby, Jr., *Florida Historical Quarterly* 41 (October 1962): 163.

30. *Territorial Papers* 24:452; Boyd, *Florida Aflame*, 42; DuVal to Lewis Cass, May 26, 1832, OIA–LR roll 288.

31. Memorial to the President by Inhabitants of St. Johns County, March 6, 1826, *Territorial Papers* 23:462–63. Three members of the Fatio family signed the memorial.

32. Francis Paul Prucha, *American Indian Policy in the Formative Years* (Cambridge: Harvard University Press, 1962), 56.

33. James Dean to Archibald Clark, September 20, 1828, OIA–LR roll 800.

34. Sprague, *Origin, Progress, and Conclusion*, 51. The Indians maintained, and white witnesses later confirmed, that the slave woman in question had been sold to an Indian by the claimant's father twenty years earlier.

35. Archibald Clark to McKenney, October 20, 1828, OIA–LR roll 800.

36. McKenney to Peter Porter, November 1, 1828, *Territorial Papers* 24:95–97; Porter to John Quincy Adams, December 6, 1828, OIA–LR roll 800.

37. Humphreys to Alex Adair, April 27, 1829, OIA–LR roll 800.

38. Adair to John Eaton, April 24, 1829, OIA–LR roll 800.

39. Marsh to DuVal, May 29, 1829, *Territorial Papers* 24:234; McKenney to Porter, November 1, 1828, *Territorial Papers* 24:95–97.

40. DuVal to Phagan, October 9, 1830; Phagan to Lewis Cass, February 6, 1832, OIA–LR roll 800. The blacks in this case were claimed by an Indian woman, Nelly Factor, and by two whites named Floyd and Garey. DuVal told Phagan to seize the slaves and deliver them to Floyd and Garey. DuVal to Phagan, February 7, 1832, ibid.

41. Wiley Thompson to Cass, July 19, 1835, *American State Papers–Military Affairs* 6:460; a copy of the bill of sale is in the Florida Negro Collection of the Florida Historical Society Archives, University of South Florida Library, Tampa. Later, Caty and one of her daughters also ran away, as Humphreys listed them (and the sons) as slaves "taken" by the Indians in the war. Caty, one son, and one daughter are listed in 1838 muster rolls of captured blacks en route to Indian Territory.

42. If the Seminoles were to be taken out of Florida and sent west, DuVal recommended, "The Government ought not to admit negros to go with them. . . . I am convinced the sooner they dispose of them the better." DuVal to McKenney, January 12, 1826, *Territorial Papers* 23:414; DuVal to McKenney, March 2, 1826, ibid., 454.

43. Humphreys to Acting Governor William McCarty, September 6, 1827, ibid., 911.

44. DuVal to Elbert Herring, January 26, 1834, House Misc. Doc. 271, 24th Cong., 1st Sess., 18. Emphasis in original.

45. Ronald N. Satz, *American Indian Policy in the Jacksonian Era* (Lincoln: University of Nebraska Press, 1975), 3–11; Prucha, *Formative Years*, 225–38.

46. Joseph Hernández to Thomas Metcalfe (Chairman, House Committee on Indian Affairs), February 19, 1823, *American State Papers–Indian Affairs* 2:410. Hernández, like many slaveowning petitioners to the government from Florida, was a naturalized U.S. citizen who had been living in Florida since the Spanish period.

47. Memorial to Congress by Inhabitants of the Territory, March 26, 1832, *Territorial Papers* 24.679.

48. *Territorial Papers* 23.897; *St. Augustine Florida Herald* January 26, 1832.

49. *Acts of the Legislative Council*, 5th Sess. (1827), 79–81; *Acts*, 6th Sess. (1828), 104–107; *Florida Herald*, July 1, 1830, February 2, 1832.

50. *American State Papers–Military Affairs* 6:472.

51. James Gadsden to Cass, November 1, 1834, OIA–LR roll 806.

52. Woodbourne Potter, *The War in Florida* (Baltimore: Lewis and Coleman, 1836; facsimile ed., Ann Arbor: University Microfilms, 1966), 9; Motte, *Journey*, 210.

53. Porter, *Negro on the Frontier*, 296–305.

54. John Lee Williams, *Territory of Florida* (New York: A. T. Goodrich, 1837; facsimile ed., Gainesville: University of Florida Press, 1962), 214.

55. George A. McCall, *Letters from the Frontiers* (Philadelphia: Lippincott, 1868), 146.

56. Williams, *Territory of Florida*, 214.

57. Mayer M. Cohen, *Notices of Florida and the Campaigns* (Charleston, 1836; facsimile ed., Gainesville: University of Florida Press, 1964), 239.

58. Casey quoted in Charles H. Coe, *Red Patriots* (Cincinnati, 1898), 46.

59. William Simmons, *Notices of East Florida* (Charleston: A. E. Miller, 1822; facsimile ed., Gainesville: University of Florida Press, 1973), 41.

60. Thompson to Elbert Herring, October 28, 1834, House Misc. Doc. 271, 24th Cong., 1st Sess., 154; Lt. Joseph W. Harris to Cass, October 12, 1835, ibid., 217; John Bemrose, *Reminiscences of the Second Seminole War*, ed. John K. Mahon (Gainesville: University of Florida Press, 1966), 17.

61. Kenneth W. Porter, "Negro Guides and Interpreters in the Early Stages of the Seminole War," *Journal of Negro History* 35 (April 1950): 175, 177.

62. Potter, *War in Florida*, 31–32.

63. Ethan Allen Hitchcock, *Fifty Years in Camp and Field* (New York and London: G. P. Putnam's, 1909), 79; John K. Mahon, "Two Seminole Treaties: Paynes Landing, 1832, and Fort Gibson, 1833," *Florida Historical Quarterly* 41 (July 1962): 1–11; Paynes Landing Treaty printed in full in *Indian Affairs* 2:344–45.

64. *Niles Weekly Register* 43 (January 26, 1833): 367.

65. Fort Gibson treaty printed in *Indian Affairs* 2:394–95.

66. Mahon, "Two Treaties," 11–21; Hitchcock, *Fifty Years*, 80, 122; Grant Foreman, *Indian Removal* (Norman: University of Oklahoma Press, 1932), 322.

67. McCall, *Letters*, 301–302.

68. Sprague, *Origin, Progress, and Conclusion*, 79.

69. The treaty the Creeks made in New York in 1790 and the Indian Springs Treaty of 1821 are two examples.

70. Gadsden warned Gad Humphreys that "disaffected" Creeks were prone to move to the Seminoles "whenever their irregularities earned them to chastizement." Gadsden to Humphreys, November 11, 1827, OIA–LR roll 806. Creeks unwilling to move West, he said, will seek refuge in Florida, and the letters of the Office of Indian Affairs during the war and the diary of Major General Thomas Jesup (in the State Archives of Florida) show that many did indeed seek their escape in Florida. Cases also exist of Florida Indians—such as the chief Neamathla—moving to Creek country in Alabama to forestall removal.

71. Potter, *War in Florida*, 43.

72. Boyd, *Florida Aflame*, 52; Duncan Clinch to Cass, August 24, 1835, House Misc. Doc. 271, 24th Cong., 1st Sess., 104; Acting Secretary of War C. A. Harris to Thompson, May 20, 1835, OIA–LR roll 806; Rembert W. Patrick, *Aristocrat in Uniform: General Duncan L. Clinch* (Gainesville: University of Florida Press, 1963), 61.

73. Potter, *War in Florida*, 41; Thompson to DuVal, January 1, 1834, *American State Papers—Military Affairs* 6:454.

74. Thompson to Harris, June 17, 1835, *American State Papers–Military Affairs* 6:471.

75. Potter, *War in Florida*, 46–49; Harris to Thompson, May 22, 1835, OIA–LR roll 806.

76. Thompson to Cass, April 27, 1835, House Misc. Doc. 271, 24th Cong., 1st Sess., 183–84; Harris to Thompson, July 11, 1835, OIA–LR roll 806.

77. Alexander C. W. Fanning to Adjutant General, April 29, 1835, *Territorial Papers* 25:133.

78. Potter, *War in Florida*, 45–46; Thompson to Harris, June 17, 1835, OIA–LR roll 800.

79. Boyd, *Florida Aflame*, 47–56; Williams, *Territory of Florida*, 216; Thomas S. Jesup to Secretary of War Joel Poinsett, October 17, 1837, *American State Papers–Military Affairs* 7:886.

80. Thompson to Herring, October 28, 1834, House Misc. Doc. 271, 24th Cong., 1st Sess., 54–65.

81. Bemrose, *Reminiscences*, 17–24; *American State Papers–Military Affairs* 6:75.

82. Phagan had been fired in 1833 when a Treasury Department comptroller found in Phagan's accounts twelve invoices that had been altered by $397.50 over the true amount, with Phagan paying the contractor the true amount and then pocketing the remainder. J. B. Thornton to Cass, August 29, 1833, OIA–LR roll 800. A year previously, Phagan had found himself in trouble for openly campaigning against Joseph White in the delegate election, conducting card games in the office, and hiring his own slave at the agency smithy at government expense. Phagan to Cass, February 6, 1832, OIA–LR roll 800.

83. Thompson to George Gibson (Commissary General of Subsistence), September 21, 1835, House Misc. Doc. 271, 24th Cong., 1st Sess., 214.

84. Cass to Thompson, October 28, 1835, ibid., 227. The Paynes Landing treaty specifically stated that Abraham and Cudjo were "to be paid on their arrival in the country they consent to remove to"; thus Phagan had no business invoicing the government for Abraham's payment while the Seminoles were still in Florida. Cudjo also had been victimized when Phagan sent to Washington a bill for $480 (although Cudjo was due only $180), then paid the interpreter nothing. Cudjo complained that in three years with Phagan

he had received only $175. Thompson to Herring, March 3, 1835, OIA–LR roll 800.

85. *American State Papers–Military Affairs* 6:61; Patrick, *Aristocrat*, 71.

86. *Niles Weekly Register* 49 (January 30, 1836): 367.

87. Motte, *Journey*, 118.

7

Freedom Was as Close as the River
African Americans and the Civil War
in Northeast Florida

Daniel L. Schafer

FOLLOWING THE Federal occupation of northeast
Florida in March and April of 1862, slaveowners in the region began complaining of slave runaways. Although Union forces
stayed only briefly in Jacksonville during this first of four occupations, navy gunboats remained on station at the mouth of the St.
Johns River and regularly patrolled upriver as far as Lake George.
African Americans in the region immediately identified the gunboats
as a path to freedom. Waving white flags from shore, paddling canoes
and poling rafts out into the currents, slaves and free blacks alike
hailed the vessels and embarked on journeys to liberty. For black
Floridians, freedom became as close as the St. Johns River.[1]

This chapter examines slaves who escaped from bondage in northeast Florida during the Civil War, particularly those who enlisted in
Federal regiments and returned to Florida to fight for Union. Also
discussed is the influence of slave runaways on Confederate and
Union activities in the region. Evidence is drawn from contemporary
newspapers, personal correspondence and diaries, census data and
plantation records, and from the records of the 1st, 2d, and 3d South
Carolina Volunteers, later mustered into regular service as the 33d,
34th, and 21st regiments of the U.S. Colored Infantry (USCI). More
than a thousand slaves and free blacks from northeast Florida joined
these regiments during the war. The records of their military careers
and of their subsequent efforts to obtain pensions provide valuable

insights into the lives of black soldiers and the world of slavery in northeast Florida at the time of its demise.

Beyond the occasional standard newspaper advertisements for runaways, there is little evidence that slaves were absconding in sufficient numbers to prompt unusual anxiety among their owners during the early months of the war. In May 1861 sawmill owner Samuel Fairbanks criticized Confederate training officers for concentrating on marching drills rather than high-visibility picket duty intended to intimidate slaves contemplating escape.[2] The Federal seizure of Port Royal in November and the ensuing activity of the Union naval blockading squadron off the Florida coast prompted some planters to send their chattels away from the coastal zone for security.[3] When rumors of slave insurrection plots spread throughout the region in December, owners accelerated security measures, but the surviving evidence indicates that northeast Florida slaveowners were not unduly alarmed that their chattels might escape—at least not in 1861.[4]

The editor of Jacksonville's *Southern Confederacy*, for example, had appeared unconcerned on February 1, 1861, when he commented on free blacks who volunteered to help build Fort Steele at the mouth of the St. Johns River: "We understand that their patriotic example will be followed by all the other free colored men in this place. What will Messrs. Seward, Greeley, and Co. say to this? Gentlemen, are we not reposing on a mine?" With only thirty-one males between the ages of fourteen and ninety, Jacksonville's free blacks made at best a minimal contribution to the work, as Captain Holmes Steele recognized in May when he solicited "the contribution of slave laborers, for a week or 10 days, for most important work on the fort at the mouth of the river."[5] According to soldier Willie Bryant there was still plenty of "dirty smutty work going on" at Fort Steele on October 1, when an officer left for Jacksonville with a conscription list for slave laborers.[6]

The alarm bells sounded for northeast Florida's slaveowners in March 1862 when Yankee troops captured Fernandina, St. Augustine, and Jacksonville. For weeks preceding departure of the thirty-three-vessel flotilla under command of Flag Officer Samuel Du Pont, escaped slaves and white Union supporters had been arriving at Port Royal carrying valuable information about northeast Florida's coastal defenses. Isaac Tatnall, a former slave pilot of the steamer *St. Marys*, proved to be the most effective informant. As the Confederate defenders had recently been ordered to the west by General Robert E. Lee to stop Union penetration in Kentucky and Tennessee, U.S. forces captured the northeast Florida ports while facing only scattered and disorganized resistance.[7]

As soon as Brigadier General Horatio G. Wright and the Third Brigade, U.S. Expeditionary Force, reached Fernandina, runaway slaves began crossing their picket lines. Wright observed on March 10: "Some of these people are left behind, and others are presenting themselves daily, coming in from different directions."[8] From St. Augustine, Lieutenant J. W. A. Nicholson sent a similar report on March 21: "Several contrabands have delivered themselves to, or been arrested by, the guard at the entrance to the city. They have fled their masters who are in rebellion."[9]

Lieutenant Thomas Holdup Stevens was sent to Jacksonville with orders to "examine the condition of things" but not to "occupy any point on the St. Johns River." But once in the town, Stevens became so impressed by the numbers and sincerity of the remaining Unionists that he decided to take possession of the town. General Wright also concluded it would be wise to hold the town, as did the senior commander, General Thomas W. Sherman, who saw in Jacksonville the germ of a regeneration policy that might bring Florida back into the Union. Flag Officer Du Pont was willing to use naval force to protect the Jacksonville Unionists even if the infantry companies were withdrawn. This strong Union presence, coupled with the wide-ranging patrols of the gunboats, galvanized the black slaves of the region into action.[10]

Samuel Fairbanks hurriedly took his Negroes upriver when he learned of the Union incursion, and left them at what he thought to be a secure location in Clay County. After Fairbanks departed, however, his slaves John and Frank, a sawmill engineer and a laborer, stole a boat and paddled back to Jacksonville. Fairbanks tracked them down, but they refused to return to Clay County. Jacksonville's still-functioning civil authorities, many of them slaveowners, jailed the slaves for their "saucy behavior." Within days, John and Frank escaped from the jail and found refuge with naval vessels at Mayport, managing somehow to bring along John's wife, Charlotte.[11]

Frank continued on to Fernandina, but Fairbanks located John and Charlotte before they left Mayport and persuaded a Union officer to return them to his custody. While Fairbanks looked for a boat to carry the couple back to Clay County, however, the Federals evacuated Jacksonville and carried Unionists and runaway slaves along with them. When the navy transports departed the St. Johns River on April 8, they carried away nine of Fairbanks's slaves. John and Frank later joined the Union army and died while serving their country.[12]

Friends of Fairbanks suffered even heavier losses, prompting planters to resort to harsh measures. In one escape, twenty-three men and women from three neighboring plantations fled together, pursued by an armed vigilante posse. One escapee was shot in the head and killed during the chase, prompting Confederate cavalry officer Winston Stephens to inform his slaves of the draconian measures being used to discourage runaway attempts. He also warned his wife to watch for three fugitives thought to be lurking near Welaka searching for the wife of one of the men. Stephens wanted them shot if recapture efforts failed.[13]

Union military records provide the names of some of the escapees. Joseph Cryer and his son Andrew escaped to Union lines from the Palm Valley plantation of Jacob Mickler, while James and Henry Adams fled Francis Richard's plantation on the St. Johns River. Andrew Murray, a native of St. Augustine, belonged to Joseph Finegan when he fled to Fernandina after hearing rumors of Federal forces there. Thomas Long and Charles McQueen made their way to Jacksonville and were aboard the Union transports when the city was evacuated on April 9, 1862. Each of these men later volunteered for service in the Union army.[14]

The free African American population of northeast Florida also sought protection behind Union lines. Benjamin Williams was living in Jacksonville in 1860, listed in the census as a native of Maine. Alonzo H. Phillips, born in Jacksonville, became a commissary sergeant in Company A, 3d South Carolina. Henry Hanahan, born free in 1833 at Pablo Beach, became a sergeant-major in the same company. Lewis Forester, born a slave but freed as a boy when purchased by his father, escaped to Fernandina in 1862. He volunteered for service in Company A, 1st South Carolina, on June 3, 1863. His brother, George Forester, joined the U.S. navy in 1862, as did Henry Johnson and James P. Lang. Other Duval County free Negroes who joined Union regiments were Albert Sammis, George

Floyd, Frank and Alexander Hagen, John Lacurgas, Charles Lang, Levi and William H. McQueen, Samuel Petty, John B. Richard, Walter Taylor, James Simmons, and Henry and James Williams.[15]

Union volunteers from St. Augustine in Company D, 1st South Carolina, included Samuel Osborn and his son Samuel, Jr., free black residents since at least 1850. In an unusual occurrence, another Osborn son, Emmanuel, volunteered for the St. Johns Grays, a Confederate militia company formed in St. Augustine. It appears that free black families, like white families, could be divided by Civil War loyalties.[16]

Abraham Lancaster enlisted in Company F, 1st South Carolina, in 1863. Other free blacks from St. Augustine who joined Union regiments were Pablo Rogers, James Lang, James Hills, James Ash, George Garvin, William Morris, Alexander Clark, and the Pappy brothers, Antony, Frank, and William.[17]

By the time the Jacksonville evacuation fleet reached Fernandina in April 1862, the exodus of black laborers had reached alarming proportions. But local slaveowners still thought they could regain control of their chattels. Fairbanks and Stephen Bryan, a wealthy Clay County planter, sailed to Fernandina on April 21 to test Union policy on this issue. They carried a letter from Lieutenant Stevens that described them as "gentlemen of character and influence" and urged Union officers to "give them whatever facilities your official position may afford toward securing the object of their mission."[18] Disdaining the letter, an "abolitionist Lt. Colonel" refused to grant an interview. The slaveowners remonstrated that General Wright had "afforded every facility for masters to claim and take away their negroes" in Jacksonville, even towing boats up the river with them." And in fact, two of Fairbanks's slaves had been aboard a Union vessel that returned from Fernandina to Jacksonville after the evacuation, under orders from General Wright to return fifty-two slaves to their owners.[19]

Before July 1862 Union policy on slave refugees had often been confusing and inconsistent, depending on whether the officer in charge opposed or favored slavery. Logs of the St. Johns River gunboats document that black refugees picked up during patrols were routinely considered property of Confederates and were not returned to their owners. On April 1 and 2, 1862, for example, the *Seneca* picked up eleven "contrabands" and carried them to freedom at Hilton Head.

Yet Lieutenant Stevens, naval commander on the St. Johns, tended to be extremely cooperative with Unionist slaveowners.[20]

General Wright also cooperated with Unionist slaveowners who remained behind Federal lines. Rebels were not accorded these privileges, with the exception of Wright's action in returning fifty-two slaves to Confederate command at Jacksonville. Before the transports left Jacksonville on April 10, 1862, Wright had ordered every runaway removed and left at the town wharf. But his own men smuggled the escapees back aboard the ships and hid them during the journey to Fernandina.[21] When Wright discovered the stowaways, he ordered they be returned to Jacksonville and left at the wharf to await their owners.

At this late point in the war, such variations in policy should not have existed. The original congressional confiscation act of August 6, 1861, had authorized commanders to refuse requests for the return of slaves, but only if they had been utilized by Confederate forces. Abolitionist officers interpreted this act with wide latitude, while their conservative colleagues sometimes excluded all black refugees from Union lines. By March 13, 1862, the growing power of radicals in Congress brought a tougher policy, which barred return of slaves to any claimant, even to Union loyalists. If guidelines were subject to individual interpretation before March 13, they were as clear as the possibility of court martial after that date. If the orders had not traveled as far as Jacksonville by April 10, they had certainly reached Admiral Du Pont by July, and henceforth no runaway slaves would be returned in northeast Florida.[22]

Until that time, Jacksonville slaveowners attempted to exploit the individual interpretations of Union policy. In late April, they sent Judge Burritt to Hilton Head to confer with General Hunter, hoping to obtain the return of slave runaways. Hunter, an avowed abolitionist, was not encouraging. The audacious Burritt continued on to Washington, where he arranged to meet with President Lincoln. According to Fairbanks, Burritt found the president still a reluctant emancipator who would "not commit himself. But Burritt says that he thinks Lincoln is not an abolitionist and that the negroes will be returned at the end of the war." [23]

Burritt must have been surprised to discover later that year that he had misjudged the president. At the time of their interview, Lincoln was still worried about losing the border states. In August 1861 he had rescinded John C. Fremont's declaration of martial law in Missouri, which freed the slaves of Confederates in that state, while commenting on the importance of holding on to Kentucky. In October 1861 he forced Secretary of War Simon Cameron to retract a statement advocating the freeing of rebel-owned slaves and arming them to fight for the Union. As late as May 1862 Lincoln rebuked General Hunter and revoked his order abolishing slavery in Florida, South Carolina, and Georgia. Lincoln was playing a cautious hand so as not to alienate slaveowners in the border states.

But the president was also being pressured by radicals in Congress to free the slaves as a military necessity. For months Lincoln privately contemplated an emancipation proclamation, but in public he attempted to persuade the border states to accept gradual and compensated emancipation. When that policy was emphatically rejected by congressmen from the border states on March 13, 1862, Lincoln embraced the more radical position, still privately, and began working on a preliminary emancipation statement. He finally issued it in September, following the Northern victory at Antietam In his address, Lincoln declared that all slaves in regions still in rebellion on January 1, 1863, would be forever free. On New Year's Day he made it official and announced that the United States would begin enlisting blacks in its armed forces. Samuel Burritt need not ponder again the vagaries of Union contraband policy; in the future Federal armies would free his slaves. If Burritt had misread the president, so had many Northern abolitionists.

In the meantime, slaves in northeast Florida continued to run away from their owners, even after Jacksonville was evacuated on April 10, 1862. Late in May, a gunboat anchored off Stephen Bryan's plantation on Doctor's Lake, galvanizing "twenty-four of his negroes to escape and take refuge." The next day Bryan drove the remainder of his chattels, along with sixty-two from neighboring estates, to unoccupied land in the interior. Although Winston Stephens was able to capture two runaways from Ocala who were trying to get to the gunboats near Jacksonville, he estimated that 1,500 black refugees had gathered in Fernandina by July 1862.[24]

Fairbanks predicted that 15,000 to 20,000 bushels of corn in the coastal area would go unharvested for lack of laborers. Winston

Stephens agreed, saying planters would "not be able to save their crops." Late in August, Fairbanks was still complaining that "Negroes are gradually getting away—singley and by two's and three's—the coast is pretty near drained." Union military records attest to Fairbanks's accuracy. One of the singles escaping in July was David Flemming, who made it safely to Mayport, where he found freedom in a gunboat.[25]

In Tallahassee, Ellen Call Long received a letter from a friend in Jacksonville, saying her father had decided it was "impossible to keep negroes on the river now." After he "discovered our servants about to bid farewell to the place [the] next morning he packed them all off to the interior. Can you imagine how we get along without a single servant? . . . Father determined it was better to have a home without servants than servants without a home. So we stay here living on cornbread and hope, our only consolation that we are no worse off than our neighbors."[26]

All the Jacksonville area slaveowners could share the anguish of a former St. Augustine merchant who lost fifteen slaves to the Union. Christian Boye wrote to his son:

> Those slaves of mine were worth to me a year ago, seventeen thousand dollars and there was some 10 young ones among them who increased in value every day. My yearly income from them was not less than $2000.00 to $2500.00. I could afford to send you and your sister to expensive schools. . . . This income is stopped, and God knows when it will begin again. I am obliged to use strictest economy, turn a penny a dozen times before I spend it. The loss of our slaves forces me to take Mary from school . . . as I cannot make enough to pay her school bills.[27]

Confederate General Joseph Finegan was one who sympathized. A long-time slaveowner in northeast Florida who had lost bondsmen to Union gunboats, Finegan understood the importance of slavery to Florida's economy and was willing to tailor Confederate strategy to protect that vital connection. In May 1862 Finegan began moving men and artillery to the lower St. Johns in an effort to stop the Union gunboat incursions. If he was successful future escapees, forced inland, would encounter military security and vigilantee patrols.

Finegan had never accepted the truce delivered at the town wharf to Lieutenant Colonel John Maxwell of the 3d Florida as Union forces left Jacksonville on April 10. The terms presented by gunboat commander William Budd called for the U.S. navy to move its gunboats to the mouth of the St. Johns River to avoid further confrontation, but the Union intended to retain control of the major waterway in northeast Florida. Two or more gunboats would be based at Mayport to guard against blockade runners and to patrol upriver as far as Palatka. Residents were free to move in and out of Jacksonville providing that Confederate forces did not fortify the town nor harm Union loyalists who remained.[28]

Following the evacuation, three Confederate infantry companies moved into Jacksonville. Among the ranks of Company C of the 4th Florida was Washington Ives, an eighteen-year-old from Lake City. Until May 27, Ives's duty was on the waterfront, where he counted five gunboats pass the town with guns at the ready. In his diary, Ives recorded an uneasy truce, with armed pickets patrolling the town and cavalry and infantry companies drilling in camps to the west, while along the waterfront armed adversaries watched each other suspiciously across the water. But there was no fighting and people began returning to the town.[29]

Union officers tolerated these Confederate activities in Jacksonville but were alarmed when bands of regulators began organizing throughout the countryside and harassing Unionists. There were newspaper reports of "bands of guerrillas" conducting a "reign of terror" in the area, "murdering and destroying property."[30] Lieutenant Daniel Ammen's investigation in late April confirmed that Unionists were in peril; he said of the refugees at Mayport: "They are wholly destitute, and I am obliged to feed them or see them starve."[31]

Late in June, Union Lieutenant J. W. A. Nicholson met in Jacksonville with Colonel John C. Hately of the 5th Florida Infantry to discuss violations of the truce. He warned that the navy would retaliate if the town was fortified or if the gunboats were fired upon. General Finegan later repudiated the agreement with a rebuke of Federal terms: "The threat of shelling our undefended town, containing only women and children, is not consistent with the usages of war between civilized nations."[32]

These events had a marked effect on the future conduct of the war along the St. Johns. Until then, the Federals had tended to respect private property, including slaves, except when the owners were suspected of maltreating Unionists or engaging in guerrilla activities. But the increased guerrilla activity placed this Federal policy in a questionable light. On June 17 Lieutenant Nicholson reported to his superiors that "the whole of the banks of the river as far as one can see is planted with corn. They say corn enough is in Florida for all of the Southern rebel States. If we carry their darkies off they can not gather it." [33]

Admiral Du Pont was in agreement. After considering the matter for several weeks, he made his decision on July 3.

> In reference to the contraband question, my instructions are to surrender none, no matter whether the parties asking for them profess to be loyal or not. There has been so much abuse of this privilege that it can no longer be granted. A glaring instance of it occurred in the case of the regulator Huston, whose slaves were returned to him on the false pretense of a neighbor that they belonged to a Union man. Even supposing the claimant may be loyal, yet if he takes his slaves among the rebels . . . [they are] liable to be seized at any moment and put to work erecting fortifications against our forces.[34]

By the time Du Pont came to this conclusion, the Confederate plan to close the St. Johns River to Union gunboats was already underway. Aware that he could succeed only if he was able to "evade the vigilance of the enemy," and convinced that Union sympathizers were the main source of enemy intelligence, General Finegan ordered all small boats belonging to Unionists confiscated or destroyed and decreed that anyone suspected of harboring a Union loyalist was to be moved inland at least ten miles.[35]

With great ingenuity Finegan pulled together a rag-tail military force from around the state and during the first week of September installed it at St. Johns Bluff to "relieve the valley of the St. Johns from the marauding incursions of the enemy and . . . to establish a base for operations against St. Augustine." It was a promising beginning, but Finegan was plagued by a shortage of men and arms, and despite repeated requests he was not to receive reinforcements.

When the Union gunboats next came up the river, they were stopped by Finegan's batteries on St. Johns Bluff. Samuel Fairbanks was ecstatic. Had this action been taken sooner, Jacksonville would not have fallen to the Yankees in March and the slaves would never have escaped, Fairbanks proclaimed. He did, however, "hope that the negroes will go along without too much trouble." [36]

Finegan's measures proved only a temporary respite. On October 1, 1862, as gunboats bombarded the Confederate gun installations, Yankee troops landed along the Pablo River and marched toward St. Johns Bluff from the land side, led by "Israel, our faithful Negro guide who ran away from Jacksonville a few weeks since and is thoroughly acquainted with all the country." [37] The bluff was hastily abandoned while rebel troops retreated towards the interior. Union forces continued upriver to occupy Jacksonville again on October 5.

During the second occupation of Jacksonville, the navy scoured the St. Johns for small boats and rafts, destroying several hundred in order to prevent their use by Finegan's troops. During these operations the gunboats roamed at will along the St. Johns, shelling the potentially dangerous structures along the river banks. Rebel-owned property was destroyed and confiscated, and endangered Union supporters were evacuated. At Palatka, Commander Maxwell Woodhull of the *Cimarron* was concerned for the safety of several black refugees who volunteered as river pilots and guides. Threats had been issued that they would be hanged and their families abused if the gunboats abandoned them. Woodhull thus evacuated several families of "about thirty persons." [38]

While Finegan worked feverishly to regroup his demoralized troops and establish lines west of the town, slaves in the region realized that the chaotic conditions again favored escapes to freedom. Recognizing this, Samuel Fairbanks announced: "They shall probably steal what few negroes there are left and destroy at will." [39] Fairbanks was furious to learn that the Federals had destroyed a thousand boats along the St. Johns, but after reconsideration he welcomed the act, saying that it might keep blacks from rowing to the gunboats.

One group of enterprising contrabands found it possible to gain freedom without small boats. Lieutenant S. S. Snell and a small naval force worked in the Palatka area for two days to raise two barges sunk by the rebels. As soon as the barges were floating, forty-nine runaway slaves appeared on the shore, boarded the barges and were towed to Mayport. [40]

Most escaped alone or with their families. Men like James Bagley, James Bagley, Jr., Henry Harrison, Jackson Long, Lewis McQueen, and Benjamin Turner made their escapes to Jacksonville. Thomas Holzendorf escaped with his family to Fernandina. All of these men would later join Union regiments.[41]

At A. M. Reed's Mulberry Grove plantation south of Jacksonville, a mass runaway attempt was thwarted when the conspirators were discovered by a white neighbor. A family friend said of the event:

All of Mr. Reeds negroes had packed up to go off at night and they were seen by [Peyre] Pearson and he ordered one of the men to stop and he then got Mr. Reed up and he went in the kitchen and there everything was ready and Perry attempted to run off and he was shot in the legs and I think they are sent off to be sold. Long legged Jake got to the Gunboat and the Yankees went back with him after his family but they had moved out in the country and Jake made a terrible fuss.[42]

A. M. Reed recorded the same event in his diary: "About 12 p.m. found my negroes preparing to leave. In the melee, Jake and Dave escaped carrying off my boat, the Laura Shaw." [43] Reed acted swiftly to save his remaining slaves. His diary entry for October 6 states: "Started all the negroes . . . for the interior."

Reed must have been astonished on October 7 when the "U. S. Gunboat, Patroon, stopped at my wharf. Sent up Lieutenant Potts of the flagship, [and] Captain Steadman, with a file of men bringing the runaway, Jake, to get his family and things." Learning that his wife, Etta, had been sent into the interior, Jake could only remonstrate and return with the gunboat. But A. M. Reed had not seen the last of Jake.

Union troops stayed in Jacksonville less than a week during the second occupation, leaving on October 11, 1862. As the transports steamed downriver, they carried what one naval officer judged to be "the most tangible result" of the entire expedition: the 276 "contrabands" who had reached Union lines. Looking back from one of the decks was the man A. M. Reed knew as "long-legged Jake." He would return the following summer wearing the uniform of the U.S. army.[44]

After the second occupation terminated, Finegan lamented: "The Yankees have taken all the negroes, free and slave, they could find in the place."[45] He ordered cavalrymen under Captain J. J. Dickison to round up all blacks—free or slave—and to remove them "from the St. Johns River into the interior at a safe distance from the enemy." Winston Stephens complained that the Yankees stole and vandalized, acting "more like black hearted scamps in Jacksonville than they ever have on the river."[46] He also reported in mid-October that several blacks had been shot in Jacksonville, and that others were being harassed by Confederate cavalry. Samuel Fairbanks finally gave up in despair; concluding that slave property was no longer safe on the St. Johns, he took his two remaining slaves to be sold in Georgia. Other planters followed his example.[47]

Fairbanks, Finegan, Stephens, and the coastal African American slave population had all learned that freedom was no longer an impossible dream. It was as close as the St. Johns River and as sure as the power of the Federal gunboats that stood ready to receive and protect escapees. General Finegan would work diligently to keep runaways from reaching the gunboats, but his range of options had narrowed substantially. After the attempt to bar the gunboats from the St. Johns River had failed at the bluffs south of Jacksonville, Finegan knew that Uncle Sam was on the river to stay.

While Finegan and his Confederate command struggled to reassert control, contrabands flocked into Union-occupied Fernandina, St. Augustine, and Key West. Many found their way to Beaufort, South Carolina, where Union officers had been attempting since May 1862 to organize an experimental phalanx of black soldiers from the swelling ranks of refugees. On August 25, 1862, Secretary of War Edwin M. Stanton, prompted by a shortage of men for operations in the South, issued orders to General Rufus Saxton to arm and equip up to five thousand "volunteers of African descent."[48]

By November 3, 1862, Saxton was ready to test the men of the 1st South Carolina Volunteers, sending Company A to raid the Florida and Georgia coasts. Saxton called the expedition a "perfect success. . . . The negroes fought with a coolness and bravery that would have done credit to veteran soldiers. . . . They seemed like men who were fighting to vindicate their manhood and they did it well."[49] The commander of the raid, Lieutenant Colonel Oliver Beard, said: "I started from Saint Simon's with 62 colored fighting men and returned to Beaufort with 156 fighting men (all colored). As soon as we took a slave from his claimant we placed a musket in his hand and he began to fight for the freedom of others." [50]

General Saxton saw in the expedition the germ of a larger war policy, one that could cripple plantation production and force the Confederate command to divert manpower from northern battle-fields. Calling the raid "one of the important events of the war, one that will carry terror to the hearts of the rebels," Saxton proposed to arm and barricade a number of light draft vessels, each manned by one hundred black soldiers, to run up the coastal rivers and capture plantations. Expecting hundreds of slaves to flock to the gunboat whistles, Saxton could "see no limit to which our successes might not be pushed[,] up to the entire occupation of States." [51]

Lieutenant Colonel Beard led his black troops on another Georgia coastal raid on November 13, but further application of Saxton's plan was delayed by the arrival of a new regimental commander. The man chosen to lead what would become the first black regiment officially mustered into the Union army was Thomas Wentworth Higginson, famed abolitionist, novelist, Unitarian preacher, and a captain in the Fifty-first Massachusetts Regiment. Sensing that a dramatic chapter in the history of the nation was about to be written, Higginson said: "I had been an abolitionist too long, and had known and loved John Brown too well, not to feel a thrill of joy at last on finding myself in the position where he only wished to be." [52]

A stickler for drill and discipline, Higginson put his troops through a rigorous training schedule that stressed order and military disci-pline. But he was also able to implement some of his abolitionist ideals through daily talks to the troops on the meaning of freedom. They often followed the theme of his November 25 speech: "You are fighting for your own liberty and the liberty of your children. Nobody can make you free unless you have the courage to fight for your own freedom. And if you resolve to be free nobody can make you slaves." [53]

In his diary on December 2, 1862, Higginson wrote: "Today General Saxton has returned from Fernandina with seventy-six recruits, and the eagerness of the captains to secure them was a sight to see." The following day he commented on a special company of "all Florida Men" who appeared to be "the finest looking company I ever saw, white or black; they range admirably in size, have remarkable erectness and ease of carriage, and really march splendidly. Not a visitor but notices them; yet they have been under drill only a fortnight." [54]

Higginson probably referred to Company G, which included fifty-seven Florida-born men among the first 106 enrollees. Samples from the regimental muster rolls indicate that the three loyal South Carolina regiments enlisted more than a thousand men who had lived in northeast Florida before the war. Considering that the 1860 Census listed 11,756 slaves, of both sexes and all ages, for Clay, Duval, Nassau, and St. Johns counties, and that many owners either sold their chattels or moved them to more secure locations in the interior of the state prior to the arrival of Union troops, the 1,000 volunteers represent a significant percentage of the adult male slaves living in the region in 1862. [55]

The volunteers came from surprisingly diverse circumstances. Based on a sample of 364 recruits from the region, the median age was twenty-four, yet forty-two gave their ages at the time of muster as forty through sixty years. The majority of the recruits, 65 percent, were engaged in some form of agricultural enterprise. Ten percent were employed in skilled crafts: twelve were carpenters, two were machinists, two were tailors, one was a shoemaker, and one was a bricklayer. Two who had been free before the war were engineers. Fourteen men gave teamster, drayman, wagoneer, hosteler, or coachman as their occupations, while nine said they had been lumbermen or sawyers, and twelve said they were boatmen or sailors. Fifty-seven said they had been cooks, waiters, or servants in towns that drew business travelers and tourists. From St. Augustine alone came twenty-five waiters and three cooks.

The loyal South Carolina regiments were often on duty in northeast Florida. Higginson's first expedition into Florida came in January 1863 in the form of a raid up the St. Marys River on a mission to carry the Emancipation Proclamation into the interior, to plunder lumber mills, ransack the countryside, and gain needed supplies. It was a highly successful mission called by a Confederate in the Second Florida Cavalry a "general thieving expedition." Following a skirmish in which the Confederates were forced to withdraw, the soldier wrote: "What makes it more maddening is they are all nigger soldiers, officered by white men." [56]

The St. Marys River raid convinced General Saxton to send Higginson and his black troops up the St. Johns River. Saxton wrote: "I have reliable information that there are large numbers of able-bodied negroes in that vicinity who are watching for an opportunity to join us. The negroes from Florida are far more intelligent than any I have yet seen. . . . They will fight with as much desperation as any people in the world."[57]

The Second South Carolina would be formed primarily from soldiers recruited during this Florida campaign. Colonel James Montgomery recruited his first two companies at Key West, where numerous northeast Florida refugees had congregated. In March 1863 Montgomery took his "raw recruits" north for military training "at the mouth of the St. Johns River where they were allowed to fire a few shots to get used to their guns."[58]

On March 9, 1863, Higginson's expedition arrived off the mouth of the St. Johns, waiting until 2 A.M. on March 10 before starting up-river for Jacksonville under a bright moon. As they approached the city the Florida men became, in Higginson's words: "wild with delight" and called out: " 'too much good.' "[59]

To the surprise of everyone, Jacksonville was occupied without a shot in opposition. There were about five hundred civilians in the town at the time, mostly whites who regarded the occupation by their former slaves as the "crowning humiliation" in their wartime experiences. The black soldiers were insulted and sworn at, particularly by the women of the town. After claiming to be in "perpetual fear," several hundred people were permitted to leave the town in one forty-eight-hour period.[60]

Some residents had good reason to be fearful. Hattie Reed was frightened by a soldier who had only recently been the property of her father. She wrote to a family friend that Jake had returned a "bold soldier boy" after escaping to a Union gunboat in October 1862. Jake was looking for Hattie's father, threatening to take vengeance for the sale of his wife to buyers in Georgia. Hattie said that Jake wanted "to meet Pa face to face to teach him what it is to part man and wife." Reed was so frightened that he would not stay at his town residence. "We are moving away as many things as possible," Hattie said. Jake also put a gun to the head of a man who had helped deter the October runaway attempt by the Reed slaves. Later, when Jake was overheard threatening to burn the Reeds' home, he was arrested and confined for the duration of the Union occupation.[61]

Another slaveowner savored the misfortunes of his former chattels who returned, writing: "Our negro Ted was among the troops at Jacksonville, also Mrs. Duval's boy Henry. Henry was mortally wounded in one of their skirmishes and has since died. So out of five who left our plantation last year only two are well and strong. . . . Does this not seem a just retribution?"[62]

Higginson realized that many of his men "had private wrongs to avenge," but he kept a tight discipline, noting that they rarely talked of revenge. He later wrote: "I shall never forget the self-control with which one of our best sergeants pointed out to me, at Jacksonville, the very place where one of his brothers had been hanged by the whites for leading a party of fugitive slaves. He spoke of it as a historic matter, without any bearing on the present issue."[63]

While the 33d USCI held Jacksonville against Confederate forays during the third occupation, Colonel Montgomery's incomplete 34th regiment took part in numerous skirmishes and battles, all the while recruiting heavily in the field to fill their ranks. Higginson vividly described these forays:

> In Colonel Montgomery's hands these upriver raids reached the dignity of a fine art. His conceptions of foraging were rather more Western and liberal than mine, and on these excursions he fully indemnified himself for any undue abstinence demanded of him when in camp. I remember being on the wharf, with some naval officers, when he came down from his first trip. The steamer seemed an animated hencoop. Live poultry hung from the foremast shrouds, dead ones from the mainmast, geese hissed from the binnacle, a pig paced the quarter deck, and a duck's wings were seen fluttering from a line which was wont to sustain duck trousers.[64]

On March 27 Montgomery and 120 black troops started on an expedition upriver toward Palatka, raiding plantations along the way. Planter Thomas T. Russell reported that six landings were made while the black troops carried off slaves, horses, carts, poultry, hogs, cotton, salt, and "everything else they could lay their hands upon."[65]

The raids were anything but amusing to the Confederates. "They are robbing and plundering everything on the east bank," Finegan wrote, "[and plan] to occupy Jacksonville with white troops and send the negroes . . . to Palatka and then attempt to move amongst the plantations." [66]

But Abraham Lincoln was delighted. On learning of the northeast Florida troops' activities, Lincoln wrote to General Hunter: "I am glad to see the accounts of your colored force at Jacksonville. . . . I see the enemy are driving at them fiercely, as is to be expected. It is important to the enemy that such a force shall not take shape and grow and thrive in the South, and in precisely the same proportion it is important to us that it shall." [67]

Shaken by the "celerity and secrecy" by which Lincoln's "abolition troops" seized Jacksonville, Finegan ordered troops from around Florida to concentrate to the west of the town to check Federal progress into the interior. "To do this," he wrote, "I am compelled to leave with entirely inadequate protection many important points on the coast where negroes may escape in large numbers to the enemy and where they have easy access to the interior." [68] Recognizing that once again freedom was as close as the St. Johns River, Finegan warned the Confederate command that if a means to hold the river were not found, the entire slave population would be lost. He wired Richmond:

> The entire negro population of East Florida will be lost and the country ruined . . . unless the means of holding the St. Johns River are immediately supplied. . . . To appreciate the danger of the permanent establishment of these posts of negro troops on the St. Johns River I respectfully submit to the commanding general that a consideration of the topography of the country will exhibit the fact that the entire planting interest of East Florida lies within easy communication of the river; that intercourse will immediately commence between negroes on the plantations and those in the enemy's service, that this intercourse will suffice to corrupt the entire slave population of East Florida.[69]

Well aware of Confederate reactions to the black troops, General Saxton informed Secretary of War Stanton: "The Negroes are collecting in Jacksonville from all quarters." [70] Saxton was convinced that "scarcely an incident in this war has caused a greater panic throughout the whole Southern coast than this raid of the colored troops in Florida." In tallying the successes of the mission, Saxton noted that two regiments had been augmented in numbers, that the occupation had received extensive coverage in the Northern press, and that white and black troops had served together for the first time during the war.

Despite these successes the Union command decided to terminate the third occupation of Jacksonville. The troop transports steamed back to Beaufort carrying battle-tested veterans alongside raw recruits. Fernandina's burgeoning black population swelled beyond 15,000, prompting Colonel Milton S. Littlefield to recruit the first 101 volunteers for the 3d South Carolina (21st USCI) from the refugee camps.[71]

The USCI regiments continued fighting for freedom in South Carolina until the war ended. The 34th regiment returned to Jacksonville in February 1864 and took part in the tragic battle of Olustee, suffering heavy casualties alongside black and white regiments from the North. Following Olustee the regiment stayed in Jacksonville, continuing to raid plantations for supplies and recruits.[72]

On September 4, 1864, for example, Colonel William R. Noble led men from the 34th, the 35th, and the 102d USCI and white troops of the Ohio Mounted Infantry, along with the 3d Rhode Island Artillery on a four-day raid from Black Creek to the north of Lake George. The previous day, Dr. Esther Hill Hawks witnessed the concluding scenes of a mass runaway: thirty black refugees were seen south of Magnolia on the banks of the St. Johns River. They waved a flag until one of the gunboats picked them up and carried them to freedom in Jacksonville.[73]

The military record of the African Americans from northeast Florida is impressive. By escaping they had passed a test of courage; for the lure of freedom some would-be escapees paid with their lives at the hands of Confederate troops and vigilantes. Not content to have broken their personal chains of slavery, many who escaped joined the U.S. army and fought for the freedom of others, even knowing that the Union government paid them substantially less each month than it paid the white soldiers.

The black troops also knew that they and their white officers were subject to execution by Confederate authorities if captured and detained as prisoners of war, and to reenslavement if the Union cause

Black soldiers in the Union Army. This illustration from *Frank Leslie's Illustrated Newspaper*, January 16, 1864, shows the variety of wartime functions performed by African Americans serving in the Union Army. Hundreds of Florida slaves escaped from plantations along the St. Johns River to join the Union forces.

failed. "They had more to fight for than the whites," Colonel Higginson felt. "Besides the flag and the Union, they had home and wife and child. They fought with ropes round their necks."[74]

Private Thomas Long of northeast Florida, serving in the 33d USCI, captured in a brief speech the spirit of the black refugees that joined Union forces. Speaking to his regiment as lay chaplain for the day, Long said that becoming soldiers had had helped prepare them for American citizenship.

> If we hadn't become sojers, all might have gone back as it was before; our freedom might have slipped through two houses of Congress and President Linkum's four years might have passed by and notin' been done for us. But now tings can neber go back, because we have showed our energy and our courage and our naturally manhood.
>
> Anoder ting is, suppose you had kep your freedom witout enlisting in dis army; your children might of growed up free and been well cultivated . . . but it would have been always flung in dere faces, 'Your fader never fought for he own freedom' — and what could day answer? Neber can suy dat to dis African Race no more.[75]

Private Long settled in Jacksonville after being discharged from the army, became a preacher, and served three terms in the Florida Senate.

Many other veterans of the loyal South Carolina regiments came back to northeast Florida after the war, settling in the towns and farms of the region. These veterans entered civilian life with a rudimentary education provided by their abolitionist officers to prepare them for a life of responsible citizenship. Throughout the fourth occupation of Jacksonville, which began February 7, 1864, hundreds of black soldiers attended the flourishing "free school" run by Dr. Esther Hawks and the American Missionary Society. Dr. Hawks began teaching the men of the 33d in Beaufort on January 15, 1863. She founded another free school for children, which was racially integrated until the white women of the town withdrew their children.[76]

Some of the black veterans joined in a communal farming venture on the northern outskirts of Jacksonville founded by a surgeon with the 34th USCI, Dr. Daniel Dustin Hanson. Leasing or selling plots to soldiers and other black families, Hanson also helped the freedmen market their crops and pool their earnings for further land purchases. Today, this section of Jacksonville is still known as Hansontown.[77]

Hanson later joined with Colonel William W. Marple and Lieutenant Colonel William L. Apthorp, both of the 34th USCI, in the purchase of several thousand acres of land for the establishment of a larger communal settlement for freedmen in what became known as Arlington. Little is known about the fate of the colony.[78]

Evidence in the military pension records indicates that most black veterans from the region made diverse individual adjustments to postwar life. South Carolina–born Henry Allen mustered out of the 34th USCI and settled in Jacksonville and later in Pablo Beach, working variously as a laborer, oysterman, fisherman, raftsman, and porter in a store. Silas Forman made his living snaring rattlesnakes and milking their venom for home remedies. David Hall became a drayman, William Johnson became a farmer at Chaseville, and Henry Adams returned to Jacksonville to resume his work in area sawmills. William Josey, a carpenter before the war, became a mechanic after, while James Lang settled in Fernandina as a grocer, oysterman, and carpenter. William Pappy returned to St. Augustine to work as a barber. Charles Wilson cut timber across northeast Florida, Simon Primus returned to the Mandarin area as an agricultural laborer, and James Lain worked as a blacksmith. Charles Knabb returned to Nassau County and became a successful cotton farmer and agent for a wealthy landowner. Thomas Holzendorf gave up shoemaking and farming at Kings Ferry to become a preacher. Harry and Smart Tillman invested in Union surgeon John Milton Hawks's Florida Land and Lumber Company at Port Orange in Volusia County.[79]

Veterans who had been free men before 1861 also returned to northeast Florida, many to jobs not unlike those they had worked at before the war. Henry Hanahan of Pablo Beach resumed his life on the area waterways, working as a steward on the steamer *Dictator*. Alonzo H. Phillips returned to Jacksonville to work again as a merchant. Lewis McQueen found employment as a mason. Lewis Forester and his wife, Affa, went back to Magnolia to the farm they had worked before the Yankee gunboats came upriver in 1862. Nearby, George Floyd farmed along the St. Johns opposite Black Creek. Samuel Osborn II, a waiter in St. Augustine before the war, afterward became a waiter at the Pulaski House in Savannah, then returned to St. Augustine in 1884.

By fall 1865, black veterans in Jacksonville had organized a series of public meetings to discuss the needs of the poor in the community. They also purchased a farm outside the town to use as a home for the aged and infirm. Other issues discussed were rights and duties of black citizens and their educational needs. On September 22, 1865, the *Jacksonville Herald* reported that black soldiers were planning to circulate petitions to help them gain the right of suffrage. During Reconstruction many of the veterans participated actively in the affairs of the Republican party, some filling appointive and elective offices.

These trained soldiers, veterans of bloody battles throughout the Southeast, equipped with rudimentary educations and an expectation that they were to become equal citizens of the nation soon after the guns stopped firing, would not acquiesce easily to the white supremacist politics that came to Jacksonville after 1865. The extent to which their lives reflected a spirit of "hope and encouragement" is worthy of a separate study, one that could benefit from perusal of the military pension records kept in the National Archives. The roles played played by the black veterans in the dramatic events of the immediate postwar years would be an interesting sequel for researchers concerned with the few successes and many failures of Reconstruction.

Notes

1. An earlier version of this chapter appeared in *El Escribano: The Journal of the St. Augustine Historical Society* (1986). The title comes from a line by Richard A. Martin in Martin and Daniel L. Schafer, *Jacksonville's Ordeal by Fire: A Civil War History* (Jacksonville: Florida Publishing Company, 1984).

2. A. Fairbanks to G. Fairbanks, May 24, 1861, Strozier Library, Special Collections, Florida State University.

3. A. Fairbanks to G. Fairbanks, November 21, 1861.

4. Winston Stephens to Octavia Stephens, December 12, 1861, Bryant-Stephens Collection, P. K. Yonge Library, University of Florida, discusses rumors of a plot by slaves of former Governor Moseley to free themselves if President Lincoln failed to do so by the end of January 1862.

5. *St. Johns Mirror*, May 7, 1861.

6. Willie Bryant to Davis Bryant, October 30, 1861, Bryant-Stephens Collection. For the local economy and idle bondsmen, see Andrew Fairbanks to

George Fairbanks, August 30, 1860, and Martin and Schafer, *Jacksonville's Ordeal*, chap. 2.

7. Brig. Gen. J. H. Trapier to Maj. T. A. Washington, March 28, 1862; Lee to Trapier, Feb. 24, 1862, *The War of the Rebellion: A Compilation of the Official Records of the Union and Confederate Armies* (Washington, D.C.: GPO, 1880–1901), series I, 6:93–94, 398–99 (hereafter ORA). See also "Report of S. F. Du Pont," March 4, 1862, *Official Records of the Union and Confederate Navies in the War of Rebellion* (Washington, D.C.: GPO, 1894–1927), series I, 12:573 (hereafter ORN); *New York Times* Jan. 14, March 15, 1862. Also, Du Pont to Capt. J. L. Lardner, March 1, 1862; Du Pont to Comdr. P. Drayton, March 2, 1862; Du Pont to Sec. of Navy Gideon Welles, March 1, 1862; Lt. T. H. Stevens to Du Pont, March 7, 1862, ORN 1:12, 581–85.

8. Brig. Gen. H. G. Wright to Capt. Louis H. Pelouze, March 10, 1862, ORA 1:6, 143–44.

9. Report of Lt. J. W. A. Nicholson, March 21, 1862, ORN 1:12, 643.

10. Du Pont to Stevens, March 7, 1862, ORN 1:12, 586–87; Sherman to Adj. Gen. L. Thomas, March 16, 1862, ORA 1:6, 248–50; *New York Times*, March 20, 24, 26, 31, April 2, 1862; Calvin Robinson, "An Account of Some of My Experiences," undated typescript, p. 29, Jacksonville Historical Society Library, Jacksonville University; John Daniel Hayes, ed., *Samuel Francis Du Pont, A Selection From His Civil War Letters* (Ithaca, N.Y.: Cornell University Press, 1969), 1:373; and Martin and Schafer, *Jacksonville's Ordeal*, chap. 3.

11. S. Fairbanks to G. Fairbanks, April 21, 29, 1862.

12. When Fairbanks heard in July 1863 that John, "our engineer," had been shot, he wished the same fate for Frank. S. Fairbanks to G. Fairbanks, April 21, 29, May 4, 1862; July 4, 1863. Muster and Descriptive Books, Co. G, USCT, Record Group 94, National Archives, Washington, D.C. Both men served in Co. A, 33d Regiment.

13. Winston to Octavia Stephens, October 23, 1862. "Old Banjo" was the slave shot in the head; his son was Burrell, Stephens's plantation manager during the war. Banjo belonged to James W. Bryant, Stephens's father-in-law.

14. Regimental Muster and Descriptive Books for the 33d, 34th, and 21st regiments, U.S. Colored Infantry, are in the National Archives, Record Group 94. Pension Records are RG 15, Records of Veterans Administration. Pension records used here are Cryer: 452,263; J. Adams: 254,507; H. Adams: 874,759; Murray: 689,587; Long: 125,870; McQueen: 343,261

15. Many identified here as free before 1861 were in one or more of the censuses from 1830 to 1860; others have been traced tentatively through relatives of corresponding ages in a census. Regimental Muster and Descriptive Books sometimes identify volunteers as free blacks, as do Union pension

files. Pension records are important sources of pre-1861 information, since investigations were rigorous for black applicants, prompting fifteen to twenty veterans to testify for their wartime comrades with data concerning occupations, families, etc. See pension records for Phillips: 839,924; Hannahan: 721,857; Forrester: 808,976 and 288,415.

16. See Pension Records 998,333; 778,686; 998,312. See also the 1850 and 1860 censuses of St. Johns County.

17. Pension Records, Pappy: 363,496; Thomas Long: 1,125,870; J. Lang: 1,166,518.

18. S. Fairbanks to G. Fairbanks, April 21, 1862.

19. Stevens to Drayton, April 3, 1862, ORN 1:12, 705.

20. Logbook of the *Seneca*, Daniel Ammen, Lieutenant Commanding. Select List of U.S. Navy Logbooks, Record Group 24, National Archives. See also Logbooks for the *Ottawa* and *Water Witch*.

21. Wright, report of April 13, 1862, ORA 1:6, 124–25, and Dilworth to Washington, ORA 1:6, 131.

22. McPherson, in *Battle Cry of Freedom*, pp. 352–58, and chap. 16, discusses changing Union policies and Lincoln's path to the Emancipation Proclamation.

23. S. Fairbanks to G. Fairbanks, July 10, 1862.

24. Winston to Octavia Stephens, July 24, 1862.

25. Ibid., and Fairbanks to Fairbanks, August 27, 1862; Flemming pension file, 273.637.

26. Ellen Call Long, *Florida Breezes* (Gainesville: University of Florida Press, 1962), 331.

27. Christian Boye to son, September 23, 1862, typescript, Biographical File, St. Augustine Historical Society.

28. Stevens to Du Pont, Stevens to Budd, April 10, 1862, ORN 1:12, 728–729; Budd to Stevens, April 12, 1862, ORN 1:12, 738–39.

29. Washington Ives, Journal, April 17–May 27, 1862, Dorothy Dodd Room, Florida State Archives.

30. *New York Times*, April 2, 1862; *New York Tribune*, March 24, 1862; *New York Herald*, September 12, 1862. See also Lt. Daniel Ammen to Du Pont, May 3, 1862, ORN 1:12, 749–50.

31. Ammen to Du Pont, May 3, 1862. There is evidence of guerrilla activity in Sproston to Ammen, April 28, 1862, ORN 1:12, 749–51; Davis Bryant to Willie Bryant, July 27, 1862; Winston Stephens to Octavia Stephens, July 17, 1862; Stephens Collection.

32. Nicholson to Du Pont, June 27, 1862, ORN 1:13, 147–48; and Hately to Nicholson, and Nicholson to Hately, ibid.

33. Nicholson to Du Pont, June 17, 1862, ORN 1:13, 110.

34. Du Pont to Nicholson, July 3, 1862, ORN 1:13, 167.

35. *Florida A Hundred Years Ago*, ed. Samuel Proctor, April 29, 1862; Nicholson to Du Pont, July 14, 1862, ORN 1:13, 163.

36. The story of St. Johns Bluff is told in part in Martin and Schafer, *Jacksonville's Ordeal*, 100–117. The key accounts are Brannan to Mitchel, October 4, 1862, and Hopkins to Finegan, October 8, 1862, ORA 1:14, 127–32, 138–41.

37. Valentine Chamberlain to (unidentified), October 10, 1862, MS Box 7, P. K. Yonge Library.

38. Woodhull to Steedman, October 7, 11, 1862, ORN 1:13, 361, 367; Steedman to Du Pont, October 14, 1862, ORN 1:13, 362–64; Williams to Steedman, October 19, 1862, ORN 1:13, 366–67. Brannan had intended to destroy the rich crops of corn growing along the St. Johns River but evacuated before doing so. Woodhull also noted the corn crops and the abundance of cattle in the region. See Brannan to Prentice, October 13, 1862, ORA 1:14, 130, and Woodhull to Steedman, October 7, 1862, ORN 1:13, 367–70.

39. Samuel Fairbanks to George Fairbanks, October 6, 1862.

40. Snell to Steedman, October 14, 1862, Steedman Collection, P. K. Yonge Library. That not all Union officers reacted favorably to blacks in the Union army can be seen by Steedman's March 20, 1863, letter to his wife, concerning his duty in Jacksonville: "The duty has been by no means to my taste as the army force was composed entirely of niggers."

41. Muster and Descriptive Books, 33d and 34th Regiments, USCI, RG 94; and pension record 752.605, Thomas Holzendorf.

42. Winston to Octavia Stephens, November 4, 1862. See also S. Fairbanks to G. Fairbanks, October 7, 1862.

43. "The Diary of A. M. Reed, 1848–99" (copy prepared by the Historic Records Survey, Works Progress Administration), William R. Perkins Library, Duke University.

44. When Lieutenant S. W. Preston summarized the importance of the campaign, he reported "that upward of 2,000 negroes from the territory adjacent to the river have sought the protection of our arms." See his report to Du Pont, Oct. 11, 1862, ORN 1:13, 379.

45. Finegan to Cooper, Oct. 9, 1862, ORA 1:14, 633 and 661.

46. Winston to Octavia Stephens, November 4, 1862. See also October 15, 23, 1862; Davis Bryant to Willie Bryant, December 21, 1862.

47. Brannan to Prentice, October 13, 1862, ORA 1:14, 131; Boatner, *Civil War Dictionary*, 81; Captain Wilkerson Call, Special Orders No. 1342, October 30, 1862, ORA 1:14, 661.

48. This story is best told in Thomas Wentworth Higginson, *Army Life in a Black Regiment* (Boston: Fields, Osgood, 1870; reprint, Boston: Beacon Press, 1962); Dudley Taylor Cornish, *The Sable Arm: Negro Troops in the*

Union Army, *1861–1865* (New York: Longmans, Green, 1956); George W. Williams, *A History of Negro Troops in the War of the Rebellion, 1861–1865* (New York: Harper and Bros., 1888); Joseph T. Wilson, *The Black Phalanx: A History of the Negro Soldiers of the United States in the Wars of 1775–1812, 1861–'65* (Hartford, Conn.: American Publishing Co., 1980); Susie King Taylor, *Reminiscences of My Life in Camp* (Boston: privately printed, 1901); Rupert S. Holland, *Letters and Diary of Laura M. Town; Written from the Sea Islands of South Carolina, 1862–1884* (Cambridge: Riverside Press, 1912).

49. Saxton to Stanton, November 12, 1862, ORA 1:14, 189–92.

50. Ibid., Beard to Saxton, November 10, 1862.

51. Ibid., Saxton to Stanton, November 12, 1862.

52. Howard N. Meyer, "Introduction," in T. W. Higginson, *Army Life in a Black Regiment* (New York: Collier Books, 1962), 7–23, 29.

53. Higginson to Co. G, November 25, 1862, General Order No. 1, Order Books, 33d Regiment, USCI, RG 94. Such addresses were routine.

54. Higginson, *Army Life*, 42.

55. Muster and Descriptive Books, 33d, 34th, and 21st regiments, USCI, RG 94. The estimates come from Muster and Descriptive Books and from the pension records cited later in the chapter. See also the *Eighth Census of the United States, 1860*, Florida, Slave Schedules.

56. W. Stephens to O. Stephens, February 8, 1863, and D. Bryant to W. Bryant, February 14, 1863. Higginson's account is in *Army Life*, 84–90.

57. Saxton to Stanton, March 6, 1863, ORA 1:14, 423.

58. Montgomery to Mrs. George Stearns, April 25, 1863, Papers of George Luther Stearns and Mary Elizabeth Stearns, MSS 171, Kansas State Historical Society, Topeka.

59. Higginson, *Army Life*, 97.

60. Ibid., 115–16. See also W. Stephens to O. Stephens, March 16, 1863.

61. Hattie Reed to D. Bryant, March 22, 1863, and O. Stephens to D. Bryant, April 2, 1863.

62. Anonymous to Loulie Tydings, April 4, 1863, Bryant-Stephens Collection.

63. Higginson, *Army Life*, 236.

64. Ibid., 120.

65. Russell to Finegan, April 2, 1863, in Higginson, *Army Life*, 860 61.

66. Finegan to Brig. Gen. Thomas Jordan, March 14, 1863, ORA 1:14, 226–29.

67. Lincoln to Hunter, April 1, 1863, in John G. Nicolay and John Hay, *Abraham Lincoln; Complete Works* (New York: Century Co., 1902), 2:321.

68. Finegan to Jordan, March 14, 1863, ORA 1:14, 227–28.

69. Ibid., 229.

70. Saxton to Stanton, March 14, 1863, ORA 1:14, 227. See also Martin

and Schafer, *Jacksonville's Ordeal*, chap. 5, and Richard A. Martin, "The *New York Times* Views Civil War Jacksonville," *Florida Historical Quarterly* 53 (April 1975): 409–27.

71. Calvin Robinson, "Ms of Robinson concerning his residence in Jacksonville during the Civil War," MS Box 51, P. K. Yonge.

72. See Cornish, *Sable Arm*, and Higginson, *Army Life*, and the letters from Colonel Montgomery to his wife, especially August 25, 29, 30, 31, 1863, James Montgomery Collection, Kansas State Historical Society. Also helpful is Frederick H. Dyer, *A Compendium of the War of the Rebellion* (Des Moines, Iowa: Dyer Publishing Co., 1908), vol. 3.

73. Col. William R. Noble to J. P. Hatch, Sept. 4, 1864, MS Box 4, P. K. Yonge Library. Gerald Schwartz, ed., *A Woman Doctor's Civil War: Esther Hill Hawks' Diary* (Columbia: University of South Carolina Press, 1984), 77. See also Gerald Schwartz, "An Integrated Free School in Civil War Florida," *Florida Historical Quarterly* 61 (October 1982), and the Esther and John Milton Hawks Papers, Library of Congress.

74. Higginson, *Army Life*, 237.

75. Ibid., 19–20. For Long's postwar life see "The Black Facts Handbook," ed. Theresa Dive, University of North Florida History Committee (1985), 14–15, and Jerrell H. Shofner, *Nor Is It Over Yet: Florida in the Era of Reconstruction, 1865–1887* (Gainesville: University Presses of Florida, 1974), 143.

76. Schwartz, *A Woman Doctor's* and "Integrated Free School."

77. Daniel D. Hanson, pension record 362,152, RG 94.

78. Ibid. The land in today's Arlington section was purchased from John S. Sammis. Following the death of Hanson in 1870 and the failure of the other buyers to satisfy the mortgage, the land reverted to Sammis.

79. John Milton Hawks, "Prospectus of the Florida Land and Lumber Company," MS Box 3, no. 2, P. K. Yonge Library.

8

LaVilla, Florida, 1866–1887
Reconstruction Dreams and the Formation of a Black Community

Patricia L. Kenney

EMPTY LOTS, boarded-up and condemned buildings, sagging houses, litter and debris scattered along the streets, locks and iron bars protecting the businesses of those who have chosen to stay: This is the LaVilla of today, a mile-square, blighted area adjacent to downtown Jacksonville, Florida. It has been in decline for a long time, the origins of its slow death deep in the history of this predominantly black neighborhood. Indeed, the roots of decline are tangled in the decade of the 1880s, when LaVilla, along with the town of Fairfield and eight unincorporated suburbs, was annexed to Jacksonville during a political expansion linked to a need to fund the growing demands for public works improvements in that burgeoning city. The physical deterioration of LaVilla today, however, belies a period of vitality and growth in the two decades following the Civil War—a time when the need for economic redevelopment intersected with the emancipation of black slaves.[1]

Prior to the Civil War LaVilla was sparsely settled and its few black inhabitants were slaves. But the war dramatically altered the social composition of the area. Freedmen, seeking shelter and work, took advantage of the inexpensive housing and proximity to employment offered by nearby Jacksonville and, by 1870, became the majority population. In 1869 LaVilla incorporated, an act that provided a political dimension to the freedmen's future. When LaVilla lost its political autonomy in 1887, it lost as well a symbiotic relationship that had developed between the freedmen and whites, primarily

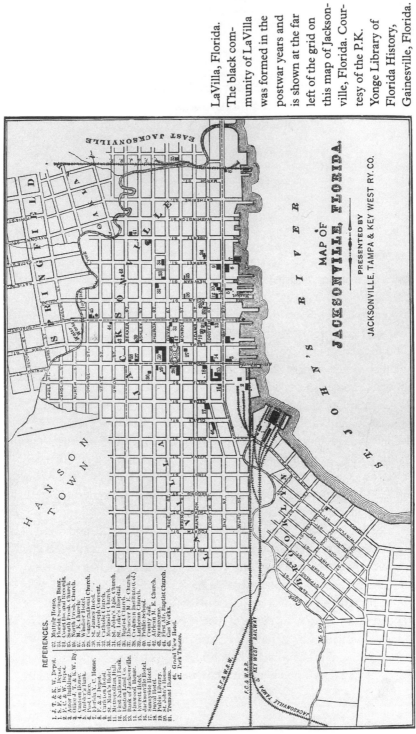

LaVilla, Florida. The black community of LaVilla was formed in the postwar years and is shown at the far left of the grid on this map of Jacksonville, Florida. Courtesy of the P.K. Yonge Library of Florida History, Gainesville, Florida.

MAP OF JACKSONVILLE, FLORIDA.

PRESENTED BY

JACKSONVILLE, TAMPA & KEY WEST RY. CO.

REFERENCES.

1. J. T. & K. W. Depot.
2. S. F. & W. Depot.
3. F. C. & W. Depot.
4. Astor Building.
5. Office J. T. & K. W. Ry.
6. Custom House.
7. Ambler's Bank.
8. Post Office.
9. F. & J. Depot.
10. Florida Y. C. House.
11. Carleton Hotel.
12. St. Mark's Hotel.
13. Metropolitan Hall.
14. First National Bank.
15. Bisalon Land Co.
16. Bank of Jacksonville.
17. Hanwood House.
18. Everett Hotel.
19. Jacksonville Hotel.
20. Sunnyside Hotel.
21. Duval Hotel.
22. Public Library.
23. St. John's House.
24. Tremont House.

22. Mataie House.
23. Florida Savings Bank.
24. Court Ho. and Records.
25. South Presb. Church.
26. M. E. Church.
27. North Presb. Church.
28. Windsor Hotel.
29. Congregational Church.
30. St. James Hotel.
31. St. Joseph Convent.
32. Catholic Church.
33. McClenn's Church.
34. St. John's Epis. Church.
35. St. Luke's Hospital.
36. Baptist Church.
37. Ebenezer M. E. Church.
38. Cookman Institute (col.)
39. Lutheran Church.
40. Public School.
41. Grace Hall.
42. A. M. E. Church.
43. Synagogue.
44. First Afr. Baptist Church.
45. Gas Works.
46. Grand View Hotel.
47. Park Theatre.

focused on interaction in local government. Together, black freedmen and whites had enacted laws, set and collected taxes, controlled crime, voted public improvements, and formed a community.

In LaVilla, as in other southern communities, prewar patterns of paternalism meshed with but oftentimes were challenged by the newly acquired independence of black urban dwellers—an independence reinforced by a tightly knit web of black relationships.[2] The social dimension of freedmen's and -women's lives was articulated through segregated social networks of family, kin, and friends. These social networks were anchored in and strengthened by the black church, school, and voluntary associations. Although blacks in the main worked for white employers, the workforce was frequently integrated. But, unlike most white workers, blacks found themselves restricted to the lower level of urban occupations—a condition that severely inhibited their ability to advance in the urban economy. Participation in local affairs, however, brought blacks and whites together and afforded black males power and influence in the civic decisions of their community.

Most studies of the black experience in the urban South have concentrated on social, economic, and political trends. This study of LaVilla, from its inception in 1866 through its demise as an independent entity in 1887, examines the details of that experience: from choosing a place to settle, finding work, securing shelter, and creating political organizations.[3]

The Civil War was a wellspring of change in Jacksonville, and the change subsequently affected LaVilla. At war's end the city teemed with newly freed slaves, former Confederates, and northern entrepreneurs. Like other southern cities, Jacksonville attracted freedmen because the Federal forces headquartered there offered safety, the Freedmen's Bureau offered education and welfare services, and a postwar commercial boom offered employment. Jacksonville, on the St. Johns River, was ideally located for a quick economic recovery through port development to supplement existing rail and steamship connections to major cities.[4] While the city had suffered extensive damage during the war years, its need to rebuild stimulated the construction and timber industries.[5] Jacksonville was also acquiring a reputation as a health and vacation resort. The opening on January 1, 1869, of the plush St. James Hotel signaled a new era of prosperity for entrepreneurs. Thus, this bustling city in northeast Florida assured a variety of job opportunities for hundreds of hopeful freedmen.

The earliest recorded black residents of LaVilla were forty-one freedmen who received ninety-nine-year leases in 1866 from Francis F. L'Engle, a prominent lawyer who had purchased a portion of the area in 1856. The quarter-acre lots were located in the southeast quadrant, immediately south of Spring and Mansion streets, where L'Engle and other white families lived. L'Engle played an important role in the development of black LaVilla: Not only did he provide the initial opportunity for the freedmen to secure housing, but as the first mayor of LaVilla, he was instrumental in creating political ties between blacks and whites. It is not clear why L'Engle, a former slaveowner (perhaps of some of the lessees), opted to encourage black settlement in LaVilla. An ardent Confederate, L'Engle was prepared to emigrate to Brazil in 1865 rather than remain in Florida under "enemy" Republican rule. An opportunity to cut crossties for the Pensacola and Georgia Railroad altered his plans, and possibly L'Engle hoped to employ the freedmen in his new business venture.[6]

Inexpensive housing and LaVilla's close proximity to employment favored rapid development; by 1870 the community numbered nearly eleven hundred, of whom 77 percent were black. Over the next ten years, LaVilla's black population nearly doubled.

The rapid rise in the number of African Americans resulted from immigration.[7] Arriving blacks were largely Florida-born. For example, Samuel Spearing, a former slave owned by Elisha Green of neighboring Baker County, brought his wife Percilla, six children, and one grandchild to LaVilla in 1866, purchased a lot, and settled on Bay Street.[8] Frank Andrews moved to LaVilla with his wife and five children and leased two lots from L'Engle. Other newcomers, like James Johnson, came from distant places. Johnson, a free black born in Virginia, had moved to Nassau at the onset of the Civil War and had become headwaiter at the Royal Victorian Hotel. Informed by American guests of the economic opportunities to be found in the winter resort of Jacksonville, Johnson moved his wife, infant daughter, in-laws, and the family nurse and cook to the "small, insignificant, and, for the most part, crude and primitive" town of LaVilla, because he was aware that northern people and capital were interested in Jacksonville.[9] For $300, Johnson purchased a corner lot

This unidentified African American family of six was photographed outside their log cabin in St. Augustine in 1893. Archaeologists have theorized that chimneys were deliberately constructed to lean away from wooden cabins so that in the event of fire they could be easily pushed away. Courtesy of the St. Augustine Historical Society.

with a "four- or five-room dwelling, old, rough, and unpainted" on Lee Street.[10]

An additional source of immigration was the Union army. As Daniel Schafer's essay in chapter 7, "Freedom Was as Close as the River" points out, many male slaves from northeast Florida had joined the three black regiments originating in Beaufort, South Carolina, in 1862.[11] Black soldiers from the 33d and 34th Regiments had occupied Jacksonville for a brief time in March 1863, and at war's end the 34th Regiment was headquartered there until September 1865.[12] Conceivably, the black soldiers' military experience affected their decision to settle in the Jacksonville area.[13] Thirty-five LaVilla residents have been identified as former soldiers.[14] An examination of pension records of the black soldiers indicates the existence of friendship among those who had lived as slaves on the same or nearby plantations. In addition, the records document friendships that con-

Table 1. Social Network of Fred Hamilton, LaVilla

Source of Network Link	Fred Hamilton's Connections†												
	1	2	3	4	5	6	7	8	9	10	11	12	13
Prewar	★	★	★										★
Military	★	★	★	★		★	★	★	★	★	★	★	★
Neighbor	★		★										
Friend	★	★		★	★			★	★	★	★	★	★
Church		★											
Work											★		

Source: PR 575.251, Pension Records, Veterans Administration, National Archives, Washington, D.C.

Note: †Numbers listed in table correspond to individual connections listed below.

1 William Benjamin	6 John Ryals	11 Isaac Middleton
2 Augustus Dorsey	7 Benjamin Turner	12 Scipeo Middleton
3 Abram Grant	8 Joseph Holder	13 Florida Singleton
4 David Hall	9 Chancey Jones	
5 William Baker	10 Richard Masters	

tinued as male slaves joined the Union army in groups or that were created out of common military experience. Thomas Holzendorf, Company D, 34th Regiment, is a representative case. Born a slave in Fernandina, Florida, Holzendorf had several owners before Samuel Sweringen purchased him and brought him to Kings Ferry. At age twenty he married Harriet, a slave from a neighboring plantation, and they had two children before the war. Harriet subsequently testified that "my said husband and I ran away from our masters and went to the white federal soldiers who had come into the King's Ferry neighborhood [and they] took us to Fernandina where my husband enlisted right away." Discharged from service in Jacksonville, Holzendorf leased a lot from L'Engle, began preaching, and remained in LaVilla with his family until 1872.[15]

Other freedmen arrived in LaVilla in kin groups. Brothers and their respective families frequently settled near one another. Stacio and Stephen Benjamin leased a single lot from L'Engle. Scipeo and Lymus Middleton, brothers who served together in the army, moved from Fernandina and leased adjacent lots. Benjamin, another

Middleton brother, moved in with Lymus's young family. William McRae leased a lot three streets south of his brother Absolom.

Friendship networks also brought settlers to LaVilla.[16] Fred K. Hamilton's network exemplifies the paths of such connections among residents of LaVilla (table 1). Hamilton, a mulatto, was born in Nassau County, Florida, in 1830 and mustered into Company G, 33d Regiment, in 1862. Discharged from the service, Hamilton moved his family to LaVilla. Hamilton's friendships were an important part of his life in LaVilla. Four of Hamilton's connections—to William Benjamin, Augustus Dorsey, David Hall, and Florida Singleton— had been established during slavery and continued in military service. William Benjamin, who had known Hamilton for more than thirty years, "lived near him in this country about six years and saw him nearly every day during that time." Florida Singleton had known Hamilton's wife, Fanny, for fifty years and "knew them both before they were married." Augustus Dorsey "knew Fred Hamilton in 1862 before he enlisted . . . [and] was with him all during the war . . . [and in LaVilla] lived about three blocks or so apart." Frederick Hamilton met Isaac Middleton "soon after my enlistment" and "kept up my acquaintance with [him] at the brickmason trade and we met each other most every Sunday at Church."[17]

Each of the former soldiers leased lots from L'Engle in LaVilla and maintained contact with one another through friendship, work, church, and leisure activities. The social networks of other soldiers revealed similar links. Networks based on kinship, friendship, and comradeship not only influenced the process of settlement, but structured the social web of relationships that defined LaVilla's black community as well. During times of need family, friends, and neighbors came to the aid of one another with food, shelter, and occasionally money.

The social web, moreover, was shaped by demographic factors. In 1870 the average age of all residents in LaVilla was twenty-one. This youthful population was nearly evenly distributed by sex, with black women slightly outnumbering black males. The age structure of blacks in 1870 indicates a large number of children from birth to fourteen years, suggesting that young families resided in LaVilla, and the nuclear family was the predominant household unit in LaVilla from 1870 to 1885 (table 2).

Table 2. Black Household Composition, LaVilla

Household Composition	1870		1885	
Nuclear	97	(57.7)	93	(47.9)
Extended	26	(15.5)	34	(17.5)
Augmented	33	(19.6)	45	(23.2)
Irregular	12	(7.1)	22	(11.3)
Total	168	(100.0)	194	(100.0)

Source: LaVilla Database.
Note: Nuclear: one or both parents and children; extended: nuclear family with kin; augmented: nuclear with nonkin members; irregular: single or nonkin. Percentages in parentheses.

Uneducated and largely unskilled, LaVilla's newcomers were dependent upon a white social structure that controlled access to jobs and home ownership. While a small number of black entrepreneurs became financially secure and bought homes, the majority of LaVilla's black residents relied on low-paying jobs and rented their homes. Tax records for Duval County, Florida, from 1866 to 1877 indicate that blacks paid taxes on property in LaVilla, but such payments do not necessarily imply ownership of property.[18] Moreover, the property of the majority of black taxpayers was valued below $500, whereas the majority of white taxpayers had property valued above $600.

During LaVilla's incorporated period, job opportunities steadily improved. Entry into the expanded economy, however, did not necessarily translate into improved social conditions: Low wages, unemployment, and poor housing plagued the lives of most former slaves.[19] Both the type of work open to them and the quality of housing available not only affected the workers' livelihood, but defined the character of the urban black community. Freedmen generally found employment as day laborers, earning between $1.50 and $2.00 per day when work was available.[20] Throughout the period, the majority of black workers were relegated to unskilled or personal and domestic service (table 3), but by the 1880s options for work had improved greatly. More blacks were successful in securing skilled and semiskilled jobs and the number of black professionals and businessmen

Table 3. Occupational Status of Black Workers, LaVilla

Occupational Status	1870		1880		1887	
Professional	3	(1.0)	8	(1.5)	19	(2.3)
Proprietor, manager, official	1	(0.3)	20	(3.8)	30	(3.6)
Clerical	5	(1.7)	4	(0.8)	1	(0.1)
Skilled	24	(8.2)	60	(11.5)	158	(18.9)
Semiskilled	34	(11.6)	127	(24.3)	126	(15.1)
Unskilled	153	(52.4)	191	(36.5)	313	(37.5)
Domestic service	72	(24.7)	113	(21.6)	188	(22.5)
Total	292	(100.0)	523	(100.0)	835	(100.0)

Sources: U.S. Census Bureau, *Ninth Census, 1870*, and *Tenth Census, 1880*; *Richards' Jacksonville Duplex City Directory* (Jacksonville, Florida: John R. Richards Co., 1887). Occupational status from Kenneth L. Kusmer, *A Ghetto Takes Shape: Black Cleveland, 1870–1930* (Urbana: University of Illinois Press, 1976), 275–80.
Note: Percentage figures given in parentheses.

increased. This socioeconomic change occurred as black workers from LaVilla found employment in the hotel, timber, port, construction, and railroad industries (table 4). For example, only one black male was employed by the railroad in 1870; seventeen years later, 114 (14 percent) of LaVilla's black males worked for railway concerns such as the Florida Railway and Navigation Company, Jacksonville Tampa and Key West Railway, or Savannah Florida and Western Railroad, Wharves, and Warehouse.

Between 1870 and 1887 the spatial landscape of LaVilla changed dramatically. Extant maps and city directories show the addition of family dwellings, boardinghouses, tenements, churches, schools, small manufactories, and neighborhood businesses. A commercial district had developed along Bay Street, in part as an extension of Jacksonville's business district. The shift toward commerce and manufacturing in the southeast quadrant of the town enhanced LaVilla's place in the larger urban economy and provided additional employment for the town's residents, but at the same time reduced the availability of housing.

Table 4. Black Workers Employed in Local Industry, LaVilla

Industry	1870		1880		1887	
Civic/						
professional	4	(1.3)	18	(3.4)	27	(3.2)
Business/						
artisan	6	(2.0)	52	(10.0)	122	(14.6)
Railroad	1	(0.3)	36	(6.9)	114	(13.7)
Port	3	(1.0)	23	(4.4)	11	(1.3)
Construction	16	(5.4)	39	(7.5)	104	(12.5)
Service	102	(35.0)	127	(24.3)	231	(27.7)
Timber	7	(2.3)	44	(8.4)	2	(0.2)
Brick mfg.	8	(2.7)	12	(2.3)	13	(1.6)
Hotel	2	(0.7)	10	(1.9)	12	(1.4)
Misc.	1	(0.3)	53*	(10.0)	15†	(1.8)
Unknown‡	142	(49.0)	109	(20.8)	184	(22.0)
Total	292	(100.0)	523	(100.0)	835	(100.0)

Source: U.S. Census Bureau, *Ninth Census, 1870* and *Tenth Census, 1880*; *Richards' Duplex Jacksonville Directory*, 1887.
Note: Percentage figures given in parentheses.
*Includes twenty-nine farmers and farmhands.   †Includes three farmers.
‡Day laborers.

LaVilla's businesses and manufactories were owned principally by whites, but by 1886 a small number of black businessmen had emerged: Wyatt J. Geter and his brothers, Jacob and Madison, owned a blacksmith and wheelwright shop on Forsyth Street; Robert F. Comfort owned the New Palace Shaving Saloon and Bathrooms on Bridge Street, which was "opened to the public, both white and colored"; Thomas Claiborne owned a saloon and a furniture store; other blacks operated grocery stores and restaurants.[21] The addition of black-owned businesses represented an important alternative in work relations, as black workers could now work for black employers.

While male workers were able to expand into various industries in the urban economy, black females who lived in LaVilla, with few exceptions, remained in domestic service. But between 1870 and 1885 the composition of the labor force in LaVilla changed. In 1870 no female over the age of twenty-five worked outside her home; by

Middle-class African American family in Gainesville, circa 1900s. Like LaVilla, Gaines-ville's black community flourished following the Civil War. The relative prosperity of this unidentified black family is evident by the dress of the mother and children and the toys arrayed for the photograph. Courtesy of the Florida State Archives.

1885, however, 73 percent of all black working women were twenty-five years of age or older (table 5). And while 80 percent of all black female workers were single in 1870, ten years later married women dominated the workforce. Moreover, by 1885 a significant number of widows were employed (table 6). A survey of black working females in 1885 reveals that 46 percent headed households without husbands, while the remainder either lived with their husbands and family or boarded. Male absence in the black household has been attributed to death, desertion, or out-of-town employment.[22]

Job security was tenuous for many urban black workers, and un-employment was a common reality in the financial burdens on the household. Urban black males compensated for the precarious nature of employment by working out of town or changing occupations. In

Table 5. Employment of Black Females, by Age Groups, LaVilla

Age (years)	1870		1880		1885	
13–20	32	(59.3)	45	(52.9)	13	(12.0)
21–24	22	(40.7)	15	(17.6)	16	(14.8)
24–34	0		11	(12.9)	37	(34.2)
35–44	0		5	(5.9)	18	(16.7)
45 & older	0		9	(10.6)	24	(22.2)
Total	54	(100.0)	85	(100.0)	108	(100.0)

Sources: U.S. Census Bureau, *Ninth Census, 1870,* and *Tenth Census, 1880;* Florida Census, 1885 (incomplete).
Note: Percentage figures given in parentheses.

1887 Isaac Middleton, a brickmason, traveled to Key West because "work had got dull here and he could get work there and better wages." Middleton's wife, Diana, and his two children from a previous marriage remained in LaVilla.[23] James Johnson adjusted his employment according to the tourist season. During the winter months he worked as headwaiter for the St. James Hotel, but during the summer months he often worked in northern hotels.[24] Unemployment was especially harsh when more than one worker in a family went without work. In 1885 Jack Butler, a sixty-one-year-old carpenter, was unemployed for three months. Living in his household were his wife, Maria, and their three sons, Jonathan (24), William (20), and Samuel (15). Jonathan, a laborer, was unemployed for half the year, and William, a fireman, for two months.

During its eighteen years of incorporation, LaVilla experienced many of the problems found in other urban areas during the late nineteenth century. Jacksonville's rapid growth and economic development benefited LaVilla, but it also contributed to poverty, unemployment, health hazards, municipal corruption, and crime. By 1885 a significant number of black males between the ages of twenty and twenty-four were living in LaVilla. Most of them were single, a change that modified the otherwise family-oriented community. In addition to the economic and demographic changes, an increase in the number of saloons, gambling houses, and houses of prostitution strained the community infrastructure and its ability to cope.

Table 6. Marital Status of Black Female Workers, LaVilla

Marital Status	1870		1880		1885	
Single	43	(79.6)	8	(9.4)	29	(26.8)
Married	5	(9.3)	57	(67.1)	35	(32.4)
Widowed	6	(11.1)	12	(14.1)	37	(34.2)
Divorced	0		0		1	(0.9)
Unknown	0		8	(9.4)	6	(5.5)
Total	54	(100.0)	85	(100.0)	108	(100.0)

Sources: 1870 Federal Census; 1885 Florida State Census; *Jacksonville City Directory,* 1871 and 1876–77; *Webb's Jacksonville Directory,* 1880; *Richards' Jacksonville City Directory,* 1887.
Note: Data were accumulated for seven elections. Percentage figures given in parentheses.

The black response to such urban problems can be viewed on two levels: social and political. On the social level, blacks functioned independently from the whites. Blacks looked to family, kin, friends, and neighbors in time of personal need, and they had established an institutional framework of churches, schools, and voluntary associations to undergird their collective needs. On the political level, blacks allied with whites and shared in decision-making with respect to the civic needs of the community. Thus, in the first twenty years of freedom, blacks had organized a duality in their associational life. When annexation to Jacksonville in 1887 shut them out of political power in their community, they came to rely even more heavily on the existing social institutions.

Black institutions cushioned the harshness of urban life by providing a means for religious expression, education, aid, and social interaction. After emancipation, blacks throughout the South established their own churches, and LaVilla followed this pattern. After the family, the church became "the central and unifying institution in the postwar black community," serving not only religious needs, but political and educational needs as well.[25]

The freedmen also built schools to educate their children. In 1868 leading blacks from Jacksonville and its suburbs organized as the Trustees of the Florida Institute, with the intent of establishing a school in LaVilla. With financial assistance from the Freedmen's Bureau, the Trustees purchased land, and within a year Stanton Normal School was dedicated. Throughout the year recitals, plays, and lectures held at the school brought black members of the community together.

In addition, black benevolent associations, many of which met in Jacksonville, responded to the social and welfare needs of the black community of LaVilla. Among them were the Daughters of Israel, who assisted in the burial of the poor; the Benevolent Association of Colored Folks, who cared for the aged; the Colored Law and Order League, which encouraged "orderly conduct"; and the Colored Medical Protective Health Association.[26] Blacks also associated less formally through festivals, picnics, excursions, dances, and parades.

Black voluntary associations served one set of social needs for LaVilla's blacks. Their participation in local government served another. Throughout LaVilla's incorporated period, blacks held political office, fulfilling an aspiration born in freedom.[27] In 1867 Samuel Spearing, member of the Union Republican Club, publicly addressed "the colored citizens of Jacksonville" and urged the crowd to "be united in support of the Republican party." In addition, he eloquently enumerated the political goals of the freedmen: "We have not the right to sit in the jury box. On every jury there should be six white and six colored men. . . . We have a right to appointments on the police, for we have lives and property as well as white men, and an equal right to protect them. We also have a right to hold a few offices. . . . we have a right to colored Justices of the Peace."[28] In LaVilla, black males served not only as marshal and policemen but at all levels of public office.

When LaVilla incorporated in 1869, it severed itself from Jacksonville politically. Thereafter, annual elections filled the offices of mayor, marshal, tax collector, tax assessor, clerk, treasurer, and alderman. In six of the seven elections for which results are known, the office of mayor was held by a white resident who figured prominently in LaVilla's social and economic hierarchy (table 7).[29] But on at least one occasion a black was elected mayor: Alfred Grant, an Alabama native, who held the mayor's office in 1876.

Aldermen on LaVilla's city council were frequently black, and, like their white counterparts, represented a cross section of occupa-

Table 7. Elected Officials, by Race, LaVilla, 1870–1871, 1876, and 1884–1887

Office	Black	White	Unknown
Mayor	1	6	0
Marshal	6	0	0
Tax collector	6	0	0
Tax assessor	1	3	2
Treasurer	4	1	0
Alderman	37	14	5
Clerk	5	0	1

Sources: 1870 Federal Census; 1885 Florida State Census; *Jacksonville City Directory,* 1871 and 1876–77; *Webb's Jacksonville Directory,* 1880; *Richards' Jacksonville City Directory,* 1887.
Note: Data were accumulated for seven elections.

tions (table 8). The office of alderman conferred status and power on those elected. Described as the "voice" of the neighborhoods, aldermen served neighborhood needs and became "the means by which residents obtained services, improvements, permits, exemptions, and sometimes jobs."[30] In LaVilla, for example, Alderman Jones requested permission for Squire English and Thomas Clairborne to grade the streets in their neighborhood; Dinah Tucker brought a complaint, through the president of the council, "that the prisoners were suffering considerable in the LaVilla jail for the want of blankets"; and Captain J. W. Fitzgerald asked permission, through Alderman Jones, "to lay water pipes on Adams Street to Bridge Street from the City of Jacksonville."[31]

Aldermen were especially powerful in recommending and approving various municipal jobs for local constituents. They controlled the hiring of policemen who, in 1886, were paid between $30 and $40 dollars per month. Other city jobs included sanitary inspector, street lamp lighter, scavenger, and jail guard. For a few of the aldermen, power resulted from longevity in office; for others power was temporary. Fifty-nine males held positions on seven LaVilla city councils examined. The majority (61 percent) served only one term, 25 percent two terms, 10 percent three terms, and 3 percent at least five terms. But the offices of marshal and treasurer were held by indi-

Table 8. Occupations of Elected Officials, by Race, LaVilla, 1870, 1871, 1876, 1884–1887

Office	Occupation	
	Black	White
Mayor	Dray proprietor	Lawyer
		Brick manufacturer
		Merchant
Tax collector	Blacksmith	Merchant
	Furniture dealer	
Tax assessor	Carpenter	Merchant
		Clerk
Treasurer	Clerk	Real estate agent
Alderman	Laborer	Laborer
	Carpenter	Carpenter-builder
	Stevedore	Contractor
	Clerk	Clerk
	Retail grocer	Retail grocer
	Brakeman	Brakeman
	Butcher	Painter
	Bricklayer	
	Railroad worker	
	Drayman	

Sources: LaVilla Database; city directories.
Note: Occupations are a select representation of officeholders.

vidual blacks for an extended period, and their length of service generated considerable influence within the community.

The town council saw to LaVilla's day-to-day needs. Street lamps were installed, water and sewer pipes laid, sidewalks constructed, trash and dead animals removed from the streets, and police protection ensured. On certain occasions, the LaVilla Council undertook philanthropic efforts. For example, in 1886 donations and a letter of condolence were sent to the earthquake victims of Charleston, South Carolina. Despite such activities, LaVilla seemed beset with problems, from governmental corruption to malfeasance to annexation attempts.

Jonathan C. Gibbs. Gibbs was born free in Philadelphia and after the Civil War opened a school to teach the newly freed slaves. He moved to Florida in 1867 and was appointed secretary of state during the Radical Reconstruction. Courtesy of the Florida State Archives.

Annexation was a constant threat to LaVilla's political autonomy. As early as 1873, movements were afoot to enlarge Jacksonville's tax base. The editor of the *Weekly Florida Union* complained that "the city needs ten times the capital and energy it now possesses and all public spirited citizens should endeavor to promote this step." To this end, he recommended that "the city should now take steps for extending its limits." [32] Ten years later, to finance public health improvements, the Jacksonville Board of Sanitary Trustees recommended the "annexation of the suburbs in order to broaden the city's tax base to pay for ongoing municipal services." [33]

During Jacksonville's 1887 municipal elections, annexation was promoted by the Citizens' Ticket, a coalition of reform Democrats, Republicans, and the Knights of Labor, who advocated municipal reform. This time support from LaVilla's prominent property owners, who saw the move as "an absolute necessity for the protection of their property, etc.," guaranteed the success of annexation.[34] By the 1880s, LaVilla was notorious as an unsavory place to live and had become the locus for gambling, drunkenness, prostitution, and frequent fighting. By 1885 Florida's Democrats had gained sufficient power to abolish the 1868 Constitution and write a new state constitution that allowed annexation by means of a simple majority in the state legislature. Jacksonville's Board of Trade, eager to boost economic growth and development as well as broaden the tax base, submitted a bill to the state legislature that would allow for a new city charter and concomitantly abolish the charters of both LaVilla and Fairfield. By aligning with Jacksonville's reform movement for annexation, law and order, a full-time mayor, conservative fiscal policies, and a paid fire department, many of LaVilla's residents hoped to rid the town of its problems.[35]

Annexation in 1887 dealt a severe blow to the African American residents of LaVilla. Participation in the political sphere was dramatically reduced, to a single representative on the Jacksonville City Council who would have to compete with other wards for services. This fact, in conjunction with newly passed Jim Crow legislation, restricted the leadership roles available for blacks.

The freedmen who arrived in Jacksonville following the Civil War had hopes and dreams for their future: job and home security, education for their children, and social and political equality. In LaVilla, as elsewhere, they struggled to act upon their aspirations. They entered "freedom" unskilled, uneducated, and poor. But their social networks became rooted in the grid of the urban landscape and matured into relationships that would mitigate the harsh realities that fractured their dreams. In the city, the freedmen structured their lives around family, kin, friends, neighbors, and wartime comrades, while the political organization of LaVilla served as the locus of joint efforts by both white and black residents. The gains made during the first two decades of freedom were small, however, and blacks found their lives still controlled by white society.

Black participation in government was essential to the freedmen's dream and to the success of Reconstruction in the South. Twenty years in LaVilla had fulfilled this dream, but when removed from the political arena, the blacks of LaVilla were disjoined from the civic decision-making process. Although supported by strong social institutions and networks of family, friends, and neighbors, blacks lost the ability to control both their own fate and the ultimate fate of LaVilla when they lost direct political participation in community affairs .

Notes

I would like to thank Dr. Darrett B. Rutman and Anita H. Rutman for their encouragement and criticism in the writing of this essay, which summarizes the findings of a master's thesis and is the basis for a dissertation-in-progress.

1. Originally part of a land grant to John Jones by the Spanish government in 1801, LaVilla underwent a succession of owners until the early 1850s, when it was subdivided and portions were sold to several whites. The area received its name in 1851 from J. McRobert Baker, who called his plantation house LaVilla. For a description of ownership, see T. Frederick Davis, *History of Jacksonville, Florida and Vicinity, 1513 to 1924* (Jacksonville: Florida Historical Society, 1925), 42–44; and Archibald Abstracts, Duval County Courthouse, Jacksonville, Florida.

2. Race relations in northeast Florida were influenced by the multicultural nature of its past. On race relations during the second Spanish period, which acknowledged both slave and free black rights and afforded legal protection, see Jane Landers, "Black Society in Spanish St. Augustine, 1784–1821," (Ph.D. diss., University of Florida, 1988). On the replacement of the relaxed racial policies under the Spanish Crown with a more rigid and strictly regulated policy under the United States, see Daniel L. Schafer, " 'A Class of People Neither Freeman Nor Slaves': From Spanish to American Race Relations in Florida, 1821–1861," *Journal of Social History* 26 (Spring 1993): 587–609.

3. On studies of the urban black experience in the South, see John W. Blassingame, "Before the Ghetto: The Making of the Black Community in Savannah, Georgia, 1865–1880," *Journal of Social History* 4(Summer 1973): 463–88; Blassingame, *Black New Orleans, 1860–1890* (Chicago: University of

Chicago Press, 1973); Zane L. Miller, "Urban Blacks in the South, 1865–1920: An Analysis of Some Quantitative Data on Richmond, Savannah, New Orleans, Louisville, and Birmingham," in *The New Urban History*, ed. Leo F. Schnore (Princeton: Princeton University Press, 1975); Robert Francis Engs, *Freedom's First Generation: Black Hampton, Virginia, 1861–1890* (Philadelphia: University of Pennsylvania Press, 1979); and Howard N. Rabinowitz, *Race Relations in the Urban South, 1865–1890* (Urbana: University of Illinois Press, 1980).

4. Richard Martin, *Consolidation: Jacksonville/Duval County* (Jacksonville, Florida: Crawford Publishing, 1968), 45; Jerrell H. Shofner, *Nor Is It Over Yet: Florida in the Era of Reconstruction, 1863–1877* (Gainesville: University Presses of Florida, 1974), 20.

5. James R. Ward, *Old Hickory's Town* (Jacksonville: Florida Publishing Co., 1982), 90–91; Richard A. Martin and Daniel L. Schafer, *Jacksonville's Ordeal by Fire: A Civil War History* (Jacksonville: Florida Publishing Co., 1984), 260.

6. Shofner, *Nor Is It Over Yet*, 21–22.

7. The federal census of 1860 counted only 908 slaves and 87 free blacks living in Jacksonville. See Barbara Ann Richardson, "A History of Blacks in Jacksonville, Florida, 1860–1895: A Socio-Economic and Political Study" (Ph.D. diss., Carnegie-Mellon University, 1975), 10.

8. Unless stated otherwise, all information regarding the residents of LaVilla comes from LaVilla Database. This database is comprised of information gathered from the 1870 and 1880 Federal Manuscript Census, Duval County, Florida; 1885 State Census; city directories; county court records; and the state and county tax rolls, Duval County, 1866–77. In addition, information was found in an obituary written by Spearing of his former owner, reprinted in *Columbus Drew: Something of His Life and Ancestry and Some of His Literary Work* (Jacksonville, Florida: The Drew Press, 1910), 17–18; Archibald Abstracts, Book A, 139.

9. James Weldon Johnson, *Along This Way* (New York: Viking Press, 1933), 6.

10. Johnson, *Along This Way*, 6–7.

11. Daniel L. Schafer, "Freedom Was as Close as the River: The Blacks of Northeast Florida and the Civil War," *El Escribano* 23(1986): 91.

12. *Jacksonville Herald*, August 31, 1865, and September 22, 1865.

13. Howard N. Rabinowitz has found a similar pattern of black soldiers residing in Nashville, Tennessee, where the 12th and 15th U.S. Colored Infantry was mustered out and many of the soldiers remained. See *Race Relations in the Urban South*, 23.

14. Identification of black soldiers was possible by compiling an index of all black males who resided in LaVilla from 1870 to 1885 and who were of age

to serve in the military. This index was cross-referenced with the *Register of Deceased Veterans of Florida*, no. 16, Duval County (prepared by the Veterans' Graves Registration Project, WPA, 1940–41); *Compiled Service Records of Volunteer Soldiers Who Served with United States Colored Troops*, Muster Rolls and Regimental Descriptive Books for the South Carolina Regiments; and the Pension Records, Records of Veterans Administration, National Archives, Washington, D.C.

15. Descriptive Roll, Company D, 34th Regiment, U.S. Colored Infantry; Pension Record (hereafter PR) 752.605.

16. Evidence detailing these networks can be obtained from the pension records of black soldiers. An examination of these records indicates the existence of friendship among slaves living on the same or nearby plantations. In addition, the pension records document friendships that continued when male slaves joined the Union army in groups, or those created among soldiers out of their common military experience.

17. PR 575.251.

18. Identification of black property owners who lived in LaVilla was difficult because many blacks who entered into lease agreements were required to pay state and county taxes. Thus, blacks listed on the tax rolls were not necessarily homeowners. The Archibald Abstracts suggest that at least twenty-five blacks owned property in LaVilla between 1866 and 1881.

19. Barbara Richardson, "A History of Blacks in Jacksonville," 68–90; Joe M. Richardson, *The Negro in the Reconstruction of Florida*, 70; Rabinowitz, *Race Relations in the Urban South*, 61–62; and John W. Blassingame, "Before the Ghetto," 465–70.

20. Barbara Richardson, "A History of Jacksonville," 102.

21. *Richards' Jacksonville Duplex City Directory*, 1887.

22. On the phenomenon of the rise of black-female-headed households, see Herbert G. Gutman, *The Black Family in Slavery & Freedom, 1750–1925* (New York: Pantheon Books, 1976), 444–45; Orville Vernon Burton, *In My Father's House Are Many Mansions: Family and Community in Edgefield, South Carolina* (Chapel Hill: University of North Carolina Press, 1985), 284–87; and Frank F. Furstenberg, Jr., Theodore Hershberg, and John Modell, "The Origins of the Female-Headed Black Family: The Impact of the Urban Experience," in *Philadelphia: Work, Space, Family, and Group Experience in the 19th Century*, ed. Theodore Hershberg (Oxford: Oxford University Press, 1981).

23. PR 550.921.

24. James Weldon Johnson, *Along This Way*, 15.

25. Leon F. Litwack, *Been in The Storm So Long: The Aftermath of Slavery* (New York: Vintage Books, 1979), 471.

26. Barbara Richardson, "A History of Blacks in Jacksonville," 110–18.

27. During the years of incorporation, several of LaVilla's African American residents were politically active at the local, county, and state level. Although beyond the scope of this essay, the construction and nature of political networks (among blacks and between blacks and whites) and their function in the formation of an urban community will be addressed in my forthcoming dissertation. On the success of blacks in local government during Reconstruction, see Eric Foner, *Reconstruction: America's Unfinished Revolution, 1863-1877* (New York: Harper & Row, 1988).

28. *Florida Union*, June 1, 1867.

29. Data were gathered from select years: 1870, 1871, 1876, and 1884-1887.

30. Jon C. Teaford, *The Unheralded Triumph: City Government in America, 1870-1900* (Baltimore: Johns Hopkins University Press, 1984), 25 and 36.

31. Town Council Minutes, May 19, 1884; December 6, 1884; and January 21, 1885.

32. *Weekly Florida Union*, January 23, 1873.

33. Richard Martin, *City Makers*, 129.

34. *Times Union*, February 24, 1887.

35. In his study of post-Reconstruction politics, Edward N. Akin argues that although 1876 represented a shift to Redeemer rule, Jacksonville's urban character and its black majority population fostered the continuation, albeit limited, of a biracial polity. For a detailed examination of the political climate in Jacksonville and its ramifications for blacks, see Akin's "When a Minority Becomes the Majority: Blacks in Jacksonville Politics, 1887-1907," *Florida Historical Quarterly* 53 (October 1974): 123-45.

9

Black Violence in the New South
Patterns of Conflict in
Late-Nineteenth-Century Tampa

Jeffrey S. Adler

IOLENCE PERMEATED urban life in the New South. Like other late-nineteenth-century Southerners, white Floridians believed that blacks were prone to sudden, unprovoked bursts of violence and that such behavior posed a growing threat to social order —particularly to the safety of white women. Conservative southerners justified segregation, at least in part, as a response to their concern that blacks might at any moment become savage and vicious. Moreover, many whites argued that lynching, which became increasingly common at the end of the century, was a reaction to mounting black violence. Although influential newspaper editors and public officials often denounced vigilantism and affirmed their belief in the rule of law, they were also quick to defend lynching as a necessary evil—as long as black violence persisted.[1] In short, the perception that blacks were unusually violent sparked aggressive white efforts at racial control, thus reordering race relations in Florida.

Urbanization, according to many whites, exacerbated the problem. As Florida cities grew at the end of the century and blacks migrated to the state's urban centers, black violence, according to whites, became more common. Many prominent observers suggested that blacks were somehow better suited to rural life; the thrall and confusion of city life, white commentators argued, overwhelmed members of a group long accustomed to the slower and more regulated rhythms of the country.[2] Others proclaimed that the social and racial controls that had maintained "harmony" and inculcated "civilized ways" in the region for over a century collapsed—or at least became more relaxed—when blacks migrated to urban centers.[3] Freed from the constraints that had operated under the slave system and emboldened by the inflammatory efforts of northern radicals, blacks, according to this line of reasoning, "degenerated" during the late nineteenth century, becoming more aggressive and more violent.[4]

Historians have devoted relatively little attention to black violence in the South during the late nineteenth and early twentieth centuries.[5] Much of the best research on southern violence has focused on the Old South.[6] Historians and criminologists of the New South, by contrast, have more often studied white responses to changes in race relations, producing important studies of lynching, whitecapping, and the Ku Klux Klan.[7] Although white fears of black violence triggered lynchings and related campaigns of repression, southern historians have seldom analyzed the nature or the level of black violence.[8]

The most sophisticated studies of the history of black violence have focused on northern cities. The leading authority on the subject, Roger Lane, examined Philadelphia prior to the "Great Migration" of southern blacks to the North. Lane concluded that the social and economic conditions of northern urban life bred black violence. City life, he argued, transformed the behavior of newcomers.[9] The regimen of the factory and the school as well as the active hand of the State (through the police and the courts) encouraged immigrants and other migrants to become more orderly and less violent.[10] For Philadelphia's black residents, however, the process worked differently. Excluded from industrial work, mired in poverty, and confronted with rising levels of racism, the city's blacks became accustomed to "self-help" solutions and reliant on violent methods of dispute resolution. During the late nineteenth century, the black homicide rate was five times that of white Philadelphians, and as the exclusion and isolation of black residents increased, the gap widened. By the middle of the twentieth century, according to Lane, the black homicide rate had risen to fourteen times the white rate.[11] Other scholars, particularly criminologists and sociologists, have also noted the unusually high homicide rate among blacks and have often formulated theories that complement Lane's analysis.[12]

The most powerful analyses of the history of black violence rely on a conceptual model rooted in the dynamics of northern industrial society. Basic questions about black violence in the South remain largely unanswered. For example, were southern blacks unusually violent by the standards of the era and the region? Or were high levels of violence a response to northern conditions? How did urbanization in the New South affect violent behavior? Finally, and perhaps most important, the paucity of research on the history of black violence has prevented historians from understanding the ways in which white perceptions may have influenced black violence.[13] An exploration of black violence in the late nineteenth century promises to shed light on southern race relations. Such an analysis might suggest the ways in which the social and institutional changes of the New South, particularly the rise of Jim Crow, affected twentieth-century patterns of black violence.

Late-nineteenth-century Tampa is a good setting in which to explore these issues. Like other New South cities, Tampa experienced explosive growth during the closing decades of the nineteenth century.[14] Between 1880 and 1900 it grew from a small town with just over seven hundred residents to a bustling city of nearly 16,000. The black population surged as well, increasing by 168 percent during the final decade of the century. In 1900 black residents comprised almost 28 percent of the city's population.[15] Race relations in the city were badly strained; lynchings and other forms of brutality punctuated Tampa's growth, as they did that of other cities in the region.[16] Tampa also became an ethnically diverse city during this period, with sizable numbers of Italian, Spanish, and Cuban newcomers, and it grew to be an industrial center, with flourishing cigar factories.[17]

Relatively few sources provide detailed information on violent behavior.[18] Coroner's records contain data on homicides, though murder was—and is—an unusual and relatively infrequent outcome of violent behavior.[19] For this reason, analyses of low-level violence are particularly useful.[20] Police reports provide information on arrests for low-level violence, but, typically, police blotters merely list names and offenses. Similarly, court records often identify only the name of the defendant and the verdict; missing is any discussion of the context in which the violence occurred. Jurisdictional boundaries also make court records a difficult source. In cities such as Tampa, cases involving violence were divided among municipal, county, and federal courts, depending on the discretion of law enforcers and the nature of the offense. Seldom are the records for all of the courts either available or similar in form.

Newspapers are the best single source for studies of nineteenth-century violence.[21] Accounts of fights and assaults in newspapers, such as the *Tampa Morning Tribune*, included not only the names of the participants but also the race and often the ethnicity, as well as the location of the altercation and the circumstances that sparked the battle.[22] Furthermore, newspapers, particularly in their daily coverage of municipal courts, reported on violent behavior that did not result in criminal charges.[23] Thus, newspapers contain more information on violent episodes than any other source. To be sure, late-nineteenth-century white newspaper editors and reporters seldom presented neutral or unbiased accounts of violence, particularly when blacks were involved. With rare exceptions, reports of black violence during this period were written by white journalists, and racist assumptions informed their accounts. The biases of editors and reporters, however, provide important clues about white perceptions of race relations and about the operation of the criminal justice system. Moreover, although police-beat reporters offered distorted explanations for black violence, these journalists provided relatively reliable data on the number of arrests, the nature of charges, and the names and backgrounds of those involved. When homicide rates computed from newspaper accounts are compared with those calculated from other sources, such as the reports of medical examiners, the figures are quite close.[24] The foundation of this study, therefore, is an analysis of every incident involving black violence that was reported in the *Tampa Morning Tribune* between 1895 and 1897.[25]

At a time when violent behavior was becoming increasingly rare in other parts of the country, informal and aggressive methods of dispute resolution flourished in the South. Both contemporary observers and modern analysts have noted the enduring connection between the South and violence. According to an 1880 study, "the number of homicides in the Southern States is proportionately greater than in any country on earth the population of which is rated as civilized."[26] The homicide rate—perhaps the most objective measure of violence—in the South was between five and fifteen times greater than that of other parts of the United States during the late nineteenth and early twentieth centuries.[27] Florida was remarkably violent. Data for 1870 indicate that homicides in the state were "over one hundred and fifty times more frequent [per hundred thousand residents] than in New Hampshire and Vermont."[28]

Southern cities experienced particularly high rates of violent crime. When homicide rates in northern cities varied from two per hundred thousand to twelve per hundred thousand residents and averaged approximately five per hundred thousand, the rates for southern cities often exceeded thirty and averaged approximately fifteen per hundred thousand residents.[29] One study, based on data for the first decade of the twentieth century, revealed that the average homicide rates for southern cities were more than three times those for northeastern cities.[30]

But violence committed by southern blacks, particularly black city dwellers, far exceeded the norms for the region.[31] In 1897 Cesare Lombroso, the leading authority on "scientific criminology," argued that the "colored race furnishes to the statistics of this crime [homicide] proportionately more than five times as many cases as whites."[32] The gap proved to be greater, however, in southern cities. Studies of homicide in southern urban centers during the early twentieth century revealed that the rates for black city dwellers were often six or seven times greater than for white urbanites. In Atlanta during the early 1920s, the homicide rate per hundred thousand black residents exceeded 107, while the rate for white residents was 9.[33] Tampa conformed to these patterns. The homicide rate for blacks in Hillsborough County during the mid-1890s was 112; according to local law enforcers, blacks killed 41 people in the county between 1895 and 1897.[34] Although historians have not constructed standardized measures for other forms of violence, less serious violence was also widespread among black Tampans.

Residents of the city, both white and black, commented on the high level of conflict.[35] Many white observers insisted that black Tampans were impulsive and hostile to whites. Thus, the editor of the *Tampa Morning Tribune* suggested in 1893, "It requires only the slightest provocation to kindle that fire into a burning flame which results in riot and bloodshed [by black residents]."[36] Again and again, the newspaper urged blacks to stop "jerking out a pistol, or using a knife for the most trivial causes." [37] Black Tampans occasionally offered a similar explanation. During his trial for assault with intent to murder, Robert Miller, for example, argued that the "goosie," a kind of reflex, caused him to draw his pistol and fire at a friend who had "playfully struck him in the back." Black residents, Miller explained and a court reporter summarized, "are so constituted that if suddenly startled by a touch . . . the goosie will strike the nearest one in front of, or near him, involuntarily." The jury accepted Miller's analysis but nonetheless found him guilty of assault with intent to murder.[38]

More frightening to whites than Miller's assault on his friend were incidents in which black Tampans seemed to have attacked whites.[39] "Out of pure wickedness," according to a local writer, John Towles shoved a white passerby off a sidewalk and struck, then choked him.[40] Such reports sparked outrage and hysteria in the city. Black residents of Tampa, white journalists argued, seemed to be vicious and prone to unprovoked attacks on whites.

Black rapists generated particular concern. According to many white southerners, rape was the "most atrocious of all crimes." [41] Leading ministers, politicians, and newspaper editors insisted that an "epidemic" of black rape had hit the region during the 1890s.[42] As a result of the end of slavery and the machinations of northern interlopers, they argued, the savage passions of blacks had been unleashed. Rape became the "New Negro Crime" and the "Black Shadow in the South." Atticus Haygood reported in *Forum*, for example, that over "three hundred white women had been raped by negroes" during one three-month period in the South in 1893.[43]

This epidemic appeared to strike Tampa with enormous force. The *Tampa Morning Tribune* reported a dozen rapes or attempted rapes by blacks in the city between 1895 and 1897, and five of the victims were white. The newspaper also devoted considerable coverage to rapes and attempted rapes elsewhere in the South, adding to the local hysteria. No other crime sparked such an emotional response. "What has gotten in some negro men in this country," the *Tribune*'s editor beseeched, "that a decent white woman cannot go by herself, or be out walking or riding, that some brutish, lustful black demon does not suddenly arise like a moving apparition from hell, burning with carnal passion." [44] "No Home is safe from invasion," the newspaper warned in 1896, "if these things are allowed to go unrevenged."[45] Respectable residents, according to local editors, must be "ready with the rope."[46] George Hendry, in a letter to the *Tribune*, asserted that critics of lynching should persuade "negroes to stop murdering and raping our wives, daughters and sisters, and then we will stop lynching them and not till then."[47]

The hysteria, however, made the fear of the black rapist self-perpetuating. Law enforcers treated nearly every episode of violence involving a black man and a white woman as an attempted rape. Tampa policemen, judges, and jurors assumed that the goal or purpose of every such encounter was an "unmentionable offense." But seldom did the sexual assault in fact take place, and it is unlikely that many of the episodes were, in fact, attempted rapes.

Despite the widely celebrated strength and power of the "black beasts," the "fragile and delicate" white women of Tampa almost always repelled the savage attack. A "negro brute" named Virgil Jones, the *Tribune* reported in 1897, forced his way into a Mr. Whitehead's home. When the "black fiend" determined that Mrs. Whitehead was alone, he attempted to "accomplish his diabolical purpose." After throwing Mrs. Whitehead to the floor, however, he heard a noise and fled. Jones then forced his way into the home of a Mrs. LaRosa, who resisted the attack. Once again, Jones fled.[48] In other incidents, Mrs. Candido Alvarez successfully resisted an attempted rape, as did Mrs. Timberlake, and Mrs. Knowles.[49] By contrast, when black men attempted to rape black women, their attempts more often succeeded, according to newspaper reporters.[50] Law enforcers generally ignored these distinctions and treated all black men who assaulted white women as rapists.

The "evidence" against those charged with attempting to ravage white women was almost always the same. A black man, according to police-beat reporters, had grabbed or choked a white woman. Often he was alleged to have pushed her to the ground.[51] It is unlikely that journalists simply omitted graphic descriptions of the crime, as editors were skilled at describing the details of a rape while protecting the sensibilities of their readers.[52] One account of an intraracial rape, for example, noted that the victim's "thigh was broken and badly mangled, her eyes were protruding, and there was every evidence of a fearful outrage having been committed."[53] When a black

The Tampa Police Department in 1899. The all-white municipal police force worked to establish order and preserve white supremacy in the face of rapid demographic and economic change in Tampa. Courtesy of the Tampa–Hillsborough County Public Library.

man was charged with raping a white woman, however, the *Tribune* usually indicated that the attacker fled immediately after choking his white victim. Rarely did such incidents involve sexual assaults. In one case, the *Tribune* acknowledged "a conflict of opinion as to the purpose of the negro. Some believe that the motive was robbery, as Mr. Pipkin [the victim's father] had been robbed of some money a few days before." [54] White perceptions of black character, therefore, often transformed attempted robberies and assaults—as well as violations of racial conventions—into attempted rapes, thereby providing apparent confirmation of the epidemic and fueling the hysteria. The locations of the alleged sexual assaults intensified white fears as well. Attempted rapes most often occurred at the homes of white women. "Respectable" men believed that their homes and neighborhoods were being invaded. [55]

Sensational murders, which commanded enormous attention from local newspapers, reinforced white perceptions of the vicious black man. According to the editors of the *Tribune* and other observers, irrational young blacks, most of whom were newcomers to Tampa, committed the majority of the homicides in the city and comprised "about 90 percent of the criminals that crowd our courts."[56] Because these migrants tended to be highly impulsive and extremely violent, the editors proclaimed, no one was safe.[57]

Although the black homicide rate in the city was extraordinarily high, white Tampans misunderstood the nature of black violence in important ways. Murder rarely crossed racial lines in Tampa. In only one homicide of every six in which a black resident was charged was the victim white.[58] Nor did lesser forms of black violence frequently involve whites. Even though residents reported black-on-white violence more consistently than black-on-black violence, only 24 percent of the black violence recounted in the *Tribune* had a white victim. Between 1895 and 1897 the newspaper reported thirty-three incidents in which blacks assaulted whites in the city; whites attacked other whites far more frequently than blacks attacked whites.

The particular details of newspaper accounts of interracial violence, however, shaped white reactions. The circumstances of black-on-white conflict reflected the strained nature of race relations in Tampa during the age of Jim Crow. While most fights in Tampa —and elsewhere—occurred between friends or relatives, black-on-white violence had a formal, stilted character, revealing the new and growing separation of the races. Black-on-white violence, which was committed by men in more than 97 percent of cases, most often occurred between strangers or acquaintances, individuals who had little or no personal relationship with one another.

More than 13 percent of black-on-white violence occurred in the workplace, when black men fought with their coworkers, employers, or former employers. John McDuffee, for example, slashed his former boss, Walter Spitler, during a dispute over wages.[59] Similarly, "a negro named Stanley" crushed the skull of his supervisor at the docks with a cant hook, and Richard Webb, a black porter, ended an argument with the yard master by means of a "shooting bee."[60]

Black men, according to police-beat reporters, also engaged in occasional rows with strangers. In fact, black men who fought with white men were seven times more likely to be involved in an altercation with a stranger than were black men who fought with other black men.[61] Attacks against strangers occasionally occurred during

Workers at Tampa cigar factory, ca. 1900. As they had in Cuba, black and white cigarmakers in Tampa worked side by side in the cigar industry, which dominated the city's economy and was the largest single employer of black Tampans. Courtesy of the University of South Florida, Special Collections.

robberies. On July 24, 1895, for example, "a big burly negro" robbed and shot an Italian grocer.[62] Robberies, however, accounted for only 3 percent of the black violence reported in the *Tampa Morning Tribune*.[63] Similarly, battles over control of the streets and sidewalks sparked skirmishes between strangers. White shopkeepers or policemen sometimes became involved in affrays with black men after attempting to displace pedestrians or vagrants from street corners or alleys.[64] The night watchman José Martinez, for example, attempted to arrest Elijah Ferguson, "a colored rascal," for "sitting on a box inside an enclosure." Ferguson resisted the watchman's efforts and struck Martinez with "a huge club." [65] Although such violence was hardly random, the participants were often strangers or, at best, acquaintances.

Because black Tampans neither lived near white residents nor spent private or leisure time in multiracial settings, contact between black and white residents of the city was confined to streets, alleys, markets, or other public places. Nearly 60 percent of black-on-white violence occurred on the street or in the workplace—compared with only 29 percent of black-on-black fights. Moreover, black-on-white conflict was concentrated in the central business district and other congested areas.

The physical setting in which interracial violence erupted distorted white images of black crime in two important ways. First, black-on-white violence was a public spectacle, unlike the overwhelming majority of intraracial violence, which occurred in more private settings.[66] Although intraracial violence most often took place late at night, interracial violence usually occurred during the morning or early evening. In fact, over one-third of all black-on-white violence took place during the early evening, when the streets of the city were crowded—compared with 14 percent of black-on-black violence. White Tampans, therefore, often witnessed black violence, reinforcing and exaggerating perceptions of black aggressiveness. A crowd of "reputable" whites, for example, saw "a big burly negro" shoot Hosa Galinda on July 31, 1895.[67] Second, black-on-white violence involved more bystanders or nonparticipants than other forms of violence. Stray shots occasionally struck or grazed passersby, adding to the belief that no white Tampan was safe from the random aggression of the city's black residents.

Equally significant, black men disproportionately relied on weapons, particularly firearms, when they fought with white men. In late-nineteenth-century Tampa, the closer the relationship between offender and victim, the lower the level of firepower. Lovers, for example, most often used only their fists, and men engaged in barroom brawls with friends usually relied on fists or knives and rarely used lethal force. Casual acquaintances or strangers, however, were much more likely to use guns. The growing estrangement between the races in Tampa ensured that guns would become the weapons of choice in interracial battles, and black Tampans were nearly twice as likely to use firearms in fights with whites as in battles with other blacks.[68] Similarly, the more public the setting, the greater the inclination to use deadly force.[69] Fights between relatives usually occurred in the presence of other family members, some of whom were likely to intercede before the conflict escalated. Rows in saloons most often took place when friends were in close proximity. The presence of allies may have emboldened the participants in barroom brawls, but it also increased the chances that partisans—or anxious saloon

Tampa Urban League. Blacks in Tampa organized the Harlem Branch of the Urban League, which met in the Tampa Public Library. Courtesy of the Tampa–Hillsborough County Public Library.

keepers—would stop the battle before the level of carnage became too great. When black Tampans fought white Tampans in the streets, however, there were few friends or relatives to intercede.

The lack of alternatives seen by blacks contributed to the use of guns. Black Tampans recognized that the legal system, both criminal and civil mechanisms, offered scant protection.[70] They knew that criminal courts sided with white residents as a matter of course.[71] Thus, once a fight with a white man had begun, a black man in Tampa was in many ways doomed. If he relied on formal institutions to mediate the dispute, he placed his fate in the hands of a legal system rife with overt discrimination, and he might face a prison sentence or even hanging. Aggressive self-help seemed to be a more viable option. Guns, even if they were used only to intimidate, represented the great equalizer for members of a group denied access to formal means of redress.[72] Racial discrimination, therefore, promoted self-help solutions and the use of lethal force.

These conditions also discouraged black men from engaging in spontaneous battles with white men. Contrary to white impressions that black Tampans were volatile and impulsive, black men, according to court testimony, often planned their encounters with white enemies and borrowed guns for the occasions.[73] The resulting battles with whites tended to be rehearsed and purposeful. On April 20, 1897, for example, the *Tampa Morning Tribune* reported that "a Cuban negro who goes by the name of Juan Arango has held a grudge against a Spaniard for some time, and finding him out yesterday opened fire on him."[74]

Ironically, the forces that encouraged black Tampans to rely on firearms limited the lethality of interracial fights. Considerable physical distances usually separated the participants. Angry black residents shot their weapons across streets and down alleyways. As a result, they fired much more often than they struck their enemies. Arango's "hot lead," for example, "went wide of the mark and no damage was done more than to create a great sensation."[75] Sam Gordon "pumped five shots" at a policeman in 1895. None of the bullets hit its mark, though the skirmish "made things rather lively," the *Tribune* reported.[76] Thus, while black men used guns more frequently when they fought with whites, they inflicted greater harm—drew more blood and committed a greater proportion of homicides—when they fought with one another, using fists, knives, or clubs at close proximity. Fifty-five percent of black-on-white violence resulted in injuries, compared with 60 percent of black-on-black violence; similarly, the ratio of homicides to total violent encounters was slightly greater for black-on-black fights.[77] Nonetheless, the use of firearms in interracial violence "create[d] a great sensation" and contributed to the idea that black men were impulsive and violent.

If black-on-white violence was relatively uncommon and was likely to occur in downtown settings, involve firearms, entail planning, include strangers, and alarm white Tampans, black-on-black violence was, in every way, the opposite. The overwhelming majority of fights involving local blacks grew out of ordinary social relations; where social activities were most vigorous, violence flared most often.[78] Black Tampans usually fought in the "Scrub" (the largest black neighborhood in the city). Moreover, violence occurred in settings in which black residents spent the majority of their time, particularly in the home and in the saloon. Fights usually erupted between relatives or friends, and the combatants relied on their fists more than any other weapons.

Black men committed nearly three-fourths of the violent acts, and in more than 71 percent of such episodes they fought with other men. Conflict between black men most often occurred during leisure hours. More than one-third of the fights took place between 8:00 P.M. and midnight, and more than 42 percent of such violence occurred in the streets—usually within the Scrub and close to "blind tigers" (saloons). Not surprisingly, men tended to fight on Saturday evenings, a traditional leisure time.[79] They were nearly as aggressive, however, on Tuesdays.

The typical fight between black men, according to police-beat reporters, involved friends and occurred near a barroom. One Tampan, for example, received a cut during a "friendly scuffle" outside Salter's saloon.[80] Similarly, Jim Norman and William Williams traded punches in front of Balbentin's saloon.[81] White observers, insensitive to the complexities of black society, seldom fully understood the causes of such affrays, though many rows, the *Tribune* concluded, grew out of disagreements over money or out of drinking quarrels. Arthur Sapp fought with Edward Williams during a game of pool at the "colored bar in Mugge's saloon." Sapp quickly terminated the fight by cracking his "twenty ounce cue" over Williams's head, hitting him with such force that bystanders "thought the latter's skull was fractured."[82]

Such extreme violence was not unusual. In fact, the level of injury was surprisingly high when men fought other men.[83] Although brawls between men resulted in no injuries in 40 percent of episodes, the combatants drew significant amounts of blood in 31 percent of the fights. In part, the severity of the violence reflected the choice of weapons and the physical proximity of the participants. When black men fought other black men, they sometimes used knives or other sharp objects. For example, on April 14, 1897, Charley Osteen and Camico Bigtree had a dispute over money at the "colored department of the Turf Exchange Saloon." Bigtree chased Osteen through the "white department" of the tavern, caught him, and "drove a big knife in the muscle of the left arm making a hole large enough to run three fingers into." [84] H. H. Jackson relied on a glass bottle when he slashed William Bell just outside the same saloon.[85]

Black violence often crossed gender lines. In more than 20 percent of the black violence reported in the *Tribune* during the mid-1890s, a man attacked a woman. Such fights almost always occurred between loved ones; men assaulted either their wives or their lovers. "A negro by the name of Hutchinson," for example, "beat up his wife unmercifully" after she had "found him in company with another woman." [86] Similarly, Charles Kelly assaulted "an unfortunate creature" who "had the misfortune to be connected with him in some way." [87]

Spouse abuse in late-nineteenth-century Tampa among black residents occurred in the home, during the early evening, and disproportionately on Thursdays. Husbands and wives (or lovers) spent the early evening hours together at home. During the morning and afternoon men, and many women, were at work, and black Tampans seemed to spend late evening hours engaged in public, leisure activities. The concentration of domestic violence on Thursdays, however, is less easily explained. More than 32 percent of assaults on women occurred on Thursdays. This pattern probably reflected the particular ways in which economic pressures affected family life.[88]

Although men rarely killed their wives or lovers, they often inflicted very serious wounds on the women. Over half of the assaults produced significant bloodshed. In part, this reflected the very personal nature of spouse abuse. Unlike other kinds of violence that occurred in the home, wife beating often took place beyond the gaze of bystanders who could intercede. Alternatively, reporting biases were enormous; only very severe beatings came to the attention of outsiders such as the police or newspaper reporters. In fact, many cases of spouse abuse resulted in criminal proceedings only because they sparked other fights. Neighbors who tried to stop the assaults sometimes became embroiled in the quarrels. Despite reporting biases, however, it is clear that domestic violence was both common and brutal.[89]

Black women also contributed significantly to the high level of violence in Tampa. Although they committed only 5 percent of the homicides in the city during the mid-1890s, women were responsible for 27 percent of the city's black violence. Just as discord between black men reflected the rhythms of daily life, black women engaged in aggressive conduct in the settings where they spent the largest amounts of time and with the companions with whom they spent the majority of the day.

The aggressiveness of black women shocked white Tampans. Again and again, the *Tribune* commented on the willingness of these residents to fight. Reporters frequently described black women as "colored viragos" or "regular viragos."[90] To be sure, white commentators tended to view all aspects of black society with disdain. By comparison with women in other areas of the nation during the late nineteenth century, however, the black women of Tampa disproportionately resorted to violence.[91]

Nor did they refrain from attacking men. Nearly one-fifth of the violence committed by black women was directed against black men —such violence rarely crossed racial lines. Some women committed violent acts while defending themselves, doing so in remarkably aggressive ways. Laura Moore, for example, grew wary of the behavior of her abusive husband. One morning, as J. P. Moore lay asleep on a lounge, she resolved "to do something to make him treat her better." Thus, she shot at her sleeping husband and "chased him out of the house" with another volley of shots. Moore explained to a local judge that she "only intended to frighten" her spouse.[92] Sarah Dickerson demonstrated still greater tenacity. Dickerson quarreled with "a colored man named Bob Fisher." The woman, however, abruptly suspended the altercation, explaining to Fisher that "if he would wait until she could go home and change her dress, she would fight him." To Fisher's astonishment, Dickerson returned some time later, wearing a different dress and brandishing a razor, with which she slashed Fisher's face and arm.[93]

More often, however, black women fought with one another. More than 77 percent of women's violence remained within gender lines, and such conflict occurred in ways that reflected social relations. Most of the fights between women took place in or around the home.[94] Black women also battled only with people they knew. As a result, fights were common; bystanders were usually present to separate the combatants; and the level of hostility was relatively low. Over half of the fights between black women that were recounted in the *Tribune* resulted in no injuries, and only 7 percent ended in homicides—compared with 17 percent of the fights between black men and 11 percent of the fights between black men and white men.

These clashes, police-beat writers concluded, were often spontaneous, forcing women to use whatever weapons were readily available. Thus, they relied on their fists in half of the cases. Razors were present in every household, and more than one-fourth of the violence committed by women involved the use of a razor.[95] Similarly, two-thirds of the conflicts in which razors were used involved women. Newspaper editors often began accounts of such episodes with the headline "The Razor Again."[96] Other household items, such as hot spoons and pans, were also frequently employed.[97] Women, however, seldom used guns, which were reserved for the most serious and festering encounters.

Black women fought over romantic entanglements, the behavior of children, and the full range of other issues that arose between people living in close proximity. The high population density of the Scrub gave black women support networks, but it also increased the chances of friction between the residents, and many fights grew out of disputes between neighbors. Alice Gregory and Lettie Birts and their families shared a house and a close friendship. When Birts told Gregory's husband that his wife had purchased whiskey in Ybor City, the women quarreled. Gregory reached for a "sad iron" and struck her neighbor on the forehead.[98] Other disputes concerned sexual relationships. Amy Foster slashed Lizzie Gibbs with a razor because the latter had been "galavanting" with Sam Brown.[99] Because many black women worked in the home (often taking in washing), work-related disputes tended to erupt in that setting.[100]

But black women also spent more time away from their homes than their white counterparts. As a consequence, the violence committed by black women occurred in a wide variety of settings. Occasionally romantic disagreements erupted in the streets. Ida Bird, for example, confronted Josephine Jackson on the corner of a busy street one evening. While they argued about the affections of Charles Thorton, Bird stabbed Jackson in the shoulder. When Victoria Bastian "attempted to interfere," Bird sent the dagger into Bastian's left breast.[101] Moreover, black women often frequented saloons and became involved in barroom brawls, usually with other women. Fifteen percent of women's violence took place in taverns. Mamie Carter and

Minnie Eubanks, for example, fought at Mugge's saloon, a frequent site of brawls between men.[102] As with men, the barroom brawls involving women tended to occur late at night and on Saturdays. But unlike the violence committed by black men and the violence that crossed racial lines, fights between black women occurred throughout the day and throughout the week.

The range of settings and contexts of women's violence no doubt reflected the expanded role that women played in black social life.[103] More often than their white counterparts, black women worked and spent leisure time outside the home. Thus, they committed violent acts in a wide range of settings and engaged in aggressive behavior more often than white women, most of whom led more proscribed lives. Relatively greater autonomy in combination with high levels of poverty and a lack of access to the legal system produced high rates of violence for black women. Although black women's violence differed from that of black men, the gap between the two was much smaller than that between white men and white women.

In short, black residents of Tampa were extremely violent, though the levels of violence occurred in inverse proportion to white perceptions. White Tampans most feared interracial conflict, which was rare. They cared little about black-on-black conflict, which was common. Measured against northern city dwellers, black Tampans committed violent acts at a considerably higher rate. Black Tampans were also more violent than black Philadelphians or New Yorkers. Furthermore, blacks in the Florida city were unusually violent by the standards of the South. Black Atlantans, black Memphians, black Tampans, and the black residents of other New South cities, however, engaged in violent encounters at roughly comparable rates. Thus, high levels of black violence preceded the Great Migration. Far from being exclusively a reaction to conditions in the northern ghetto, high rates of black violence were a part of urban life in the New South.

White perceptions of black social life in Tampa—and probably throughout the region—influenced black violence in two far-reaching ways. First, fears of the "black brute" ensured that whites would overreact to interracial conflict. White officials treated black assaults against white women as attempted rapes in nearly all cases. Such a reaction simultaneously inflated rape statistics and lent apparent credence to white fears, thereby reinforcing the hysteria that spawned the reaction. Similarly, fights between blacks and whites were typically transformed into black assaults. Policemen and prosecutors, already frightened by the specter of black-on-white violence, tended to hold black men responsible for interracial fights and to charge black men who fought white men with "assault," a criminal offense. When whites fought other whites, law enforcers more often charged the combatants with "fighting" or disorderly conduct, both of which were violations of local ordinances. This tendency exaggerated perceptions of interracial violence, provided apparent evidence that white fears were well founded, contributed to the wave of lynchings that exploded during the 1890s, and generated support for efforts to segregate black Floridians.

Second, the criminal justice system distorted black social life. Policemen, judges, and prosecutors in late-nineteenth-century cities influenced social relations. Police efforts, for example, often discouraged certain kinds of conduct. To reduce public drunkenness, law enforcers in northern cities often arrested rowdy young men; to discourage casual prostitution, the police arrested streetwalkers, thereby privileging brothels and full-time, professional prostitutes. Moreover, the criminal justice system, by providing formal, bureaucratic mechanisms for defusing conflict, transformed the nature of dispute resolution. Civil and criminal courts, according to a host of recent studies, supplemented and gradually supplanted traditional, informal means of redress, particularly violence. Immigrants quickly learned that the courts and the political system, often through the intervention of the ward boss, offered an alternative to older methods of problem solving.[104] For black Tampans, however, legal institutions provided no such alternatives.

Rather, the peculiar logic of the criminal justice system in late-nineteenth-century Tampa encouraged aggressive forms of dispute resolution among the city's black population. The courts, for example, offered scant protection for black residents. When blacks fought with whites, the verdict in court proceedings was seldom in doubt. Nor was this fact unknown to black Tampans. From the gallows, for example, the convicted murderer Harry Singleton, who had killed a white resident while attempting to stop a man from beating a young woman, indicted the criminal justice system. "I am guilty," Singleton charged. "But you are not hanging me because I was convicted by the court. You are hanging me because I am a negro and killed a white man." [105] Johnny Johnson echoed Singleton's complaint. Pronounced guilty of raping a white woman and sentenced to hang, Johnson commented that "if God was black and came before this jury you would find him guilty." [106] By contrast, white Tampans often received "generous" treatment from local law enforcers. When Tom Kersey, a white resident, shot a young black man in the face during a scuffle, killing him instantly, the jury of inquest ruled the death a "suicide." [107] "Whenever a Negro feels himself grievously wronged by a white man and at the same time believes that an appeal to law will be worse than useless," a leading writer on southern violence concluded in 1934, "the setting is prepared for an interracial homicide." [108] Thus, it was hardly surprising that black Tampans sometimes relied on firearms when they fought with white residents. Instead of looking to the legal system, a black man, according to another early-twentieth-century observer, recognized that he "must shift for himself." [109]

At the same time, white law enforcers in late-nineteenth-century Tampa routinely ignored or minimized black-on-black violence.[110] The police were often content to stop fights—without arresting the combatants. Furthermore, the courts imposed scant sanctions on black residents who assaulted "members of their own race." For example, when Sophia Banks bit "a piece out of the physiognomy of one Sarah Simpson," a neighbor, a local judge dismissed the charge.[111] Similarly, John and Dan Patterson beat John Henderson with the butt of a gun; a municipal judge fined Dan Patterson $5. Alice Gregory, the woman who struck her neighbor with an iron, inflicting a gash on her former friend's head "a couple of inches long clear to the bone," was fined $12.85.[112] Blacks who assaulted other blacks usually faced a fine of $5, and blacks who killed other blacks were often acquitted.[113] The effect of such practices was to condone black-on-black violence.[114] In the eyes of the law enforcers, black violence in general posed a threat to society only when the victim was white.[115] Far from discouraging informal, aggressive mechanisms of dispute resolution, the legal system reinforced self-help methods among black Tampans.

Urbanization also affected black Tampans in unusual ways. Studies of migration indicate that as rural dwellers moved to cities during the late nineteenth century, the potential for violent behavior increased.[116] Newcomers often arrived in the city accustomed to resolving disputes without the assistance of legal institutions. Moreover, the urban setting weakened many of the social patterns that limited violence in the country. If villagers were quick to come to blows, they were in familiar settings where relatives and neighbors could prevent an assault from becoming a homicide. Rural migrants, who brought an aggressive style into the city, found themselves without the social networks that reduced the severity of fights. The urban setting, thus, created the potential for conflict by placing violent newcomers in unfamiliar situations, isolated from the social context that limited violence. For most groups of newcomers, violent behavior increased immediately after their arrival in the city but fell sharply thereafter. The police, employers, property owners, and the courts discouraged aggressive, violent conduct; urban life gradually reduced violence.[117]

For southern blacks, however, only half of this process occurred.[118] Like other Tampans, black residents, most of whom hailed from rural settings, found themselves in unfamiliar circumstances, which increased the likelihood for discord. But unlike other residents, black Tampans encountered a criminal justice system that failed to discourage the most common forms of violent conduct. Put differently, as a result of racial discrimination, formal constraints against violence were barely applied. Legal, bureaucratic mechanisms, therefore, failed to supplant informal, self-help mechanisms. Not only did the potential for conflict increase, but the constraints on violent conduct decreased. Black Tampans migrated from a rural setting with high levels of violence to an urban setting with even higher levels of violence.[119] For blacks, perhaps unlike any other group of urban newcomers, city life exaggerated self-help remedies.

Sociologists, criminologists, and other social scientists have struggled to explain the high levels of black violence in modern America. Although scholars have not reached a consensus, the most influential model proposes that in some cultural settings aggressive behavior and violent means of dispute resolution are accepted and even expected.[120] In such a "subculture of violence," minor disagreements can spark explosions of rage and aggression. Critics of this theory note that the model devotes scant attention to structural or historical forces; the theory fails to account for the origin or source of the subculture.[121] Perhaps the quick resort to intraracial violence described by late-nineteenth-century white Tampans represented the early stages in the development of a social and cultural milieu that encouraged aggression and self-help. As the police and the courts overreacted to some kinds of black violence and ignored other kinds of black conflict, aggression may have become an increasingly viable source of protection and form of dispute resolution. The world of the New South city, with its growing black population, its surging levels of racism and racial oppression, and its emerging arsenal of institutional mechanisms to enforce Jim Crow, may have produced a tradition of aggressive self-help among black residents and thus forged the roots of modern black violence.

To be sure, these interpretations are suggestive more than definitive. A larger sample would provide a clearer sense of the "sanctioning threshold" — the point at which formal constraints were imposed. Moreover, black violence should be analyzed within the context of black culture. In order to assess the relationship between aggressive behavior and black social life, research on violence needs to be wedded to work on black social networks, institutions, and family life. How, for example, did black religious and political leaders respond to aggressive methods of dispute resolution? And how did class and gender relations affect the character of conflict? Finally, other studies of black violence must be undertaken. Until scholars extend their frames of analysis beyond homicide (to examine behavior rather than the outcome of behavior) and until historians examine a broad range of cities and towns, it will remain difficult to interpret the significance of high levels of black violence in Tampa — or in Philadelphia. But despite the tentative nature of these conclusions, the larger pattern seems clear: Jim Crow and Judge Lynch promoted black violence in late-nineteenth-century Tampa.

Notes

1. For example, see *Tampa Morning Tribune*, April 11, 1893; January 29, 1895; February 23, 1895; September 2, 1896; September 3, 1896; July 30, 1897; Frederick L. Hoffman, *Race Traits and Tendencies of the American Negro* (London: Macmillan, 1896), 230–31; Atticus G. Haygood, "The Black Shadow in the South," *Forum* 16 (October 1893): 168; James E. Cutler, *Lynch-Law*

(New York: Longmans, Green 1905). Also see Joel Williamson, *A Rage for Order* (New York: Oxford University Press, 1986), 70–151; Herbert Shapiro, *White Violence and Black Resistance* (Amherst: University of Massachusetts Press, 1988), 30–63.

2. *Tampa Morning Tribune*, September 20, 1895; July 23, 1895.

3. Ibid., August 10, 1893.

4. Ibid., August 10, 1893, December 29, 1893, April 4, 1895, and September 20, 1895; Haygood, "The Black Shadow in the South," 173–74; Alfred Holt Stone, *Studies in the American Race Problem* (New York: Doubleday, Page, 1908), 93; Walter F. Willcox, "Negro Criminality," in Stone, *Studies in the American Race Problem*, 474. Also see Williamson, *A Rage for Order*, 83–89.

5. For a notable exception, see Edward L. Ayers, *Vengeance & Justice* (New York: Oxford University Press, 1984). Also see Howard N. Rabinowitz, *Race Relations in the Urban South, 1865–1890* (New York: Oxford University Press, 1978); Raymond D. Gastil, "Homicide and a Regional Culture of Violence," *American Sociological Review* 36 (June 1971): 412–27; Sheldon Hackney, "Southern Violence," *American Historical Review* 74 (February 1969): 906–25; Richard Maxwell Brown, *Strain of Violence* (New York: Oxford University Press, 1975), 185–235.

6. For example, see Dickson D. Bruce, Jr., *Violence and Culture in the Antebellum South* (Austin: University of Texas Press, 1979); Bertram Wyatt-Brown, *Southern Honor* (New York: Oxford University Press, 1982); Victoria E. Bynum, *Unruly Women* (Chapel Hill: University of North Carolina Press, 1992); Michael Stephen Hindus, *Prison and Plantation* (Chapel Hill: University of North Carolina Press, 1980).

7. For a few examples of this rich literature, see Williamson, *A Rage for Order*; Shapiro, *White Violence and Black Response*; Stewart E. Tolnay and E. M. Beck, "Racial Violence and Black Migration in the American South, 1910–1930," *American Sociological Review* 57 (February 1992): 103–16; James L. Massey, "The Ideology of Lynch Law," paper presented at the annual meeting of the American Society of Criminology, Baltimore, November 8, 1990.

8. A number of late-nineteenth- and early-twentieth-century scholars, however, examined this issue. See John Dollard, *Caste and Class in a Southern Town* (New York: Doubleday, Anchor, 1937); H. C. Brearley, "The Pattern of Violence," in *Culture in the South*, ed. W. T. Couch (Chapel Hill: University of North Carolina Press, 1934), 691; Frederick L. Hoffman, *The Homicide Problem* (Newark: Prudential Press, 1925); Horace V. Redfield, *Homicide, North and South* (Philadelphia: Lippincott, 1880).

9. Roger Lane, "Urban Homicide in the Nineteenth Century: Some Lessons for the Twentieth," in *History and Crime*, ed. James A. Inciardi and

Charles E. Faupel (Beverly Hills: Sage, 1980), 91–109; id., "On the Social Meaning of Homicide Trends in America," in *Violence in America*, ed. Ted Robert Gurr (Newbury Park: Sage, 1989), 1: 55–79; id., *Violent Death in the City* (Cambridge, Mass.: Harvard University Press, 1979); id., *Roots of Violence in Black Philadelphia, 1860–1900* (Cambridge, Mass.: Harvard University Press, 1986).

10. See Lane, *Roots of Violence in Black Philadelphia*, 5, 12–16. Also see Eric H. Monkkonen, "A Disorderly People? Urban Order in the Nineteenth and Twentieth Centuries," *Journal of American History* 68 (December 1981): 539–59; Howard Zehr, *Crime and the Development of Modern Society* (London: Rowman and Littlefield, 1976); Eric A. Johnson, "Cities Don't Cause Crime," *Social Science History* 16 (Spring 1992): 129–76; Louise I. Shelley, *Crime and Modernization* (Carbondale: University of Southern Illinois Press, 1981), 26–34.

11. Lane, *Violent Death in the City*, 113, and *Roots of Violence in Black Philadelphia*, 134, 163–64. In his study of homicide in Philadelphia between 1948 and 1952, Marvin E. Wolfgang found that the black homicide rate was fourteen times the white rate. See *Patterns in Criminal Homicide* (New York: Wiley, 1958), 33. O'Carroll and Mercy, analyzing data for the late 1970s and early 1980s, found that black Americans were six times more likely to die from homicide than white Americans. See Patrick A. O'Carroll and James A. Mercy, "Patterns and Recent Trends in Black Homicide," in *Violence: Patterns, Causes, and Public Policy*, ed. Neil Alan Weiner, Margaret A. Zahn, and Rita J. Sagi (San Diego: Harcourt, Brace, Jovanovich, 1990), 56.

12. See Eric H. Monkkonen, "Diverging Homicide Rates: England and the United States, 1850–1875," in *Violence in America*, 91–94; James Q. Wilson and Richard J. Herrnstein, *Crime and Human Nature* (New York: Simon and Schuster, 1985), 459–86; William Julius Wilson, *The Truly Disadvantaged* (Chicago: University of Chicago Press, 1987), 21–26; Marvin E. Wolfgang and Franco Ferracuti, *The Subculture of Violence* (London: Tavistock, 1967); Lynn A. Curtis, *Violence, Race, and Culture* (Lexington, Mass.: D. C. Heath, 1975); O'Carroll and Mercy, "Patterns and Recent Trends in Black Homicide," 55–59.

13. Lane's work, of course, is the principal exception to this pattern.

14. For an overview of Tampa's growth, see Gary R. Mormino and Anthony P. Pizzo, *Tampa: The Treasure City* (Tulsa: Continental Heritage, 1983).

15. The black population of the county increased by 189 percent during the 1890s. See *Twelfth Census of the United States: Population* (Washington, D.C., 1901), 1:532.

16. U.S. Bureau of the Census, *Negro Population, 1790–1915* (Washington, D.C., 1918); Jerrell H. Shofner, "Custom, Law, and History: The Enduring

Influence of Florida's Black Code," *Florida Historical Quarterly* 55 (January 1977): 277–98; Jesse Jefferson Jackson, "The Negro and the Law in Florida, 1821–1921" (master's thesis, Florida State University, 1960), 82–107; Robert P. Ingalls, "Lynching and Establishment Violence in Tampa, 1858–1935," *Journal of Southern History* 53 (November 1987): 613–44.

17. See Gary R. Mormino and George E. Pozzetta, *The Immigrant World of Ybor City* (Urbana: University of Illinois Press, 1987); Robert P. Ingalls, *Urban Vigilantes in the New South* (Knoxville: University of Tennessee Press, 1988).

18. For a general discussion of this issue, see Ted Robert Gurr, "Historical Trends in Violent Crime," in *Violence in America*, 21–54.

19. Lane, in *Violent Death in the City*, made excellent use of coroner's records.

20. For extremely perceptive analyses of working-class violence in nineteenth-century New York City, see Pamela Haag, "The 'Ill-Use of a Wife': Patterns of Working-Class Violence in Domestic and Public New York City, 1860–1880," *Journal of Social History* 25 (Spring 1992): 447–77; Elliot J. Gorn, "Good-Bye Boys, I Die a True American," *Journal of American History* 74 (September 1987): 388–410.

21. For a thoughtful discussion of this issue, see Monkkonen, "Diverging Homicide Rates," 81–83, 96–98. A number of rich sources of information on white violence provide little information on black violence. For example, pardon files and death warrants contain much material on the nature of conflict. But most cases involving black violence, at least in Tampa, did not move through different levels of the criminal justice system. Rather, lower court judges, often relying on summary proceedings, decided such cases, and these rulings were seldom appealed. Coverage of crime, particularly black violence, in the *Tampa Morning Tribune* was somewhat uneven. Although the newspaper usually devoted some attention each day to local crime, major news stories occasionally displaced crime coverage. The most extreme example occurred in 1898, when the Spanish-American War so dominated the news that reports of the war completely displaced crime stories.

22. The newspaper devoted relatively greater attention to serious crime, particularly to interracial violence. Minor crime was underreported and is, therefore, underrepresented in my sample. But interracial violence also exerted the greatest influence on race relations in the city. Biases in reporting were both a cause and an effect of white perceptions.

23. The newspaper reported many cases of wife beating, few of which resulted in court proceedings. This reporting indicates that the newspaper did indeed cover a broad range of violent incidents.

24. Relying on reports in the *Tampa Morning Tribune*, I calculated a

black homicide rate of 112 per hundred thousand for Tampa. Researchers using medical examiner's reports and similar data have reported that black homicide rates for southern cities during the early twentieth century were clustered between 80 and 120. Brearley's study, which relied on government vital statistics for the early 1920s, reported black homicide rates for Birmingham of 104; Little Rock, 118; Tampa, 102; Jacksonville, 89; Atlanta, 107; New Orleans, 75; Jackson, 113. See H. C. Brearley, *Homicide in the United States* (Chapel Hill: University of North Carolina Press, 1932), 217–19. Other comparative data support the patterns determined through an analysis of the violence reported in the *Tribune*. Also see Arthur F. Raper, *The Tragedy of Lynching* (1933; reprint ed., New York: New American Library, 1969), 33; Haag, "The 'Ill-Use of a Wife,'" 450; Hoffman, *The Homicide Problem*, 14.

25. I recorded material on every violent episode for which the newspaper provided a description. Robberies in which there was no personal violence were not included in the database, nor were cases of property destruction, disorderly conduct, drunkenness, cruelty to animals, or other criminal acts that did not involve personal violence. In all, I compiled detailed information on 140 cases. The data were then analyzed to determine frequency distributions and correlations between variables (cross-tabulations). The rates of violence are consistent with those found in other studies, indicating that the database is large enough to yield reliable statistics. Biases in reporting would tend to result in the underreporting of black-on-black violence, since such conflict generated less concern among white Tampans. The *Tribune*, however, devoted considerable attention to such violence. Without question, the newspaper did not report every violent episode, but its coverage of black violence provides a revealing sample of patterns of conflict. Black newspapers for Tampa during this era have not survived, and black national newspapers did not cover Tampa news in sufficient detail to be useful for the quantitative analysis.

26. Redfield, *Homicide, North and South*, 10.

27. Ibid., 10–20; Brearley, *Homicide in the United States*, 19–20; Austin L. Porterfield, "Indices of Suicide and Homicide By States and Cities," *American Sociological Review* 14 (August 1949): 481–90. For late twentieth-century homicide figures, see Dane Archer and Rosemary Gartner, *Violence and Crime in Cross-National Perspective* (New Haven: Yale University Press, 1984). Also see Patricia L. McCall, Kenneth C. Land, and Lawrence E. Cohen, "Violent Criminal Behavior: Is There a General and Continuing Influence of the South?" *Social Science Research* 21 (September 1992): 286–310.

28. Redfield, *Homicide, North and South*, 174. It should be noted, however, that New Hampshire and Vermont had extremely low homicide rates. Thus, Redfield compared an unusually violent state in an especially violent region with two unusually nonviolent states in a notably nonviolent region. Half

a century later the homicide rate in Florida was more than thirty-one times greater than that in either of the two New England states. See Brearley, *Homicide in the United States,* 70.

29. See Hoffman, *The Homicide Problem,* 14, 75; Raper, *The Tragedy of Lynching,* 33; Brearley, "The Pattern of Violence," 691.

30. Hoffman, *The Homicide Problem,* 14. Although a number of scholars have computed homicide rates for southern cities, few historians or other social scientists have attempted to analyze violence in late-nineteenth-century southern cities.

31. See Brearley, "The Pattern of Violence," 691.

32. Cesare Lombroso, "Why Homicide Has Increased in the United States," *North American Review* 165 (December 1897): 647.

33. Brearley, *Homicide in the United States,* 217, and "The Pattern of Violence," 691; Raper, *The Tragedy of Lynching,* 33. For a superb study of homicide in the modern city, see Henry P. Lundsgaarde, *Murder in Space City* (New York: Oxford University Press, 1977).

34. I used county rather than city figures in order to arrive at a more cautious estimate. The newspaper did not restrict its coverage to city events, and it was often impossible to determine whether a homicide had occurred within the corporate boundaries of Tampa. Thus, county population figures provided a safer base for the computation of rates. But even these figures are estimates because I did not have population data for the 1895–97 period. Analyzing data for the entire period reduced the likelihood of any serious distortion. For early-twentieth-century figures, see Brearley, *Homicide in the United States,* 217. According to Brearley's data, the black homicide rate in Tampa during the early twentieth century was more than five times the white homicide rate.

35. *Tampa Morning Tribune,* January 16, 1896.

36. Ibid., December 29, 1893.

37. Ibid., June 28, 1896. Also see Brearley, "The Pattern of Violence," 690, and *Homicide in the United States,* 112; Lane, *Roots of Violence in Black Philadelphia,* 149. Authorities on modern violence have noted that "most homicides are impulsive." See Reynolds Farley, "Homicide Trends in the United States," in *Homicide Among Black Americans,* ed. Darnell F. Hawkins (Lanham, Md.: University Press of America, 1986), 20.

38. *Tampa Morning Tribune,* May 7, 1896. For similar discussions, see ibid., August 24, 1895; Brearley, "The Pattern of Violence," 690; Ayers, *Vengeance & Justice,* 233.

39. The *Tribune* routinely identified the race of those involved in fights. Occasionally the newspaper also noted the ethnicity of the combatants. Thus, for editors and police-beat reporters, race comprised the principal division in Tampa society; white Tampa appeared rather monolithic when

racial tensions surfaced. Social life—as well as the morphology of conflict—was undoubtedly more complex. Black violence probably assumed a unique character when "Latins" were involved, for example. Put differently, Latins interacted with black Tampans in different ways than did blacks or other whites. The sources, however, do not permit a full analysis of this dimension of urban violence. Similarly, an examination of the age structure—and sex ratios—of the city's population might provide clues about the nature of conflict. Furthermore, reporting biases make it very difficult to determine who initiated a violent encounter. For interracial violence, this bias in the sources is particularly pronounced. Many black Tampans were no doubt defending themselves when they fought with white residents. The accounts in the *Tribune* do not permit historians to determine who sparked the fight, even though these news stories do identify episodes of interracial conflict.

40. *Tampa Morning Tribune*, February 17, 1895.

41. Hoffman, *Race Traits and Tendencies of the American Negro*, 220.

42. Haygood, "The Black Shadow in the South"; Hoffman, *Race Traits and Tendencies of the American Negro*, 227; Williamson, *A Rage For Order*, 83–89.

43. Haygood, "The Black Shadow in the South," 169.

44. *Tampa Morning Tribune*, August 10, 1893.

45. Ibid., September 2, 1896.

46. Ibid., July 2, 1897.

47. Ibid., August 30, 1895.

48. Ibid., December 25, 1897.

49. Ibid., July 28, 1897; June 6, 1895; July 2, 1897.

50. Ibid., September 4, 1897; June 8, 1897.

51. For example, see ibid., July 3, 1897; July 28, 1897; June 7, 1895; July 31, 1897.

52. Perhaps the editors hoped that such descriptions would avoid embarrassing or sullying the reputations of rape victims. Thus, attempts to protect the sensibilities of readers may have distorted the reports. Editors, however, had other methods of protecting both readers and crime victims and of drawing the distinction between rapes and attempted rapes. Reports of rapes, for example, often indicated that the victim had been rendered unconscious, leaving unstated the events that subsequently transpired.

53. *Tampa Morning Tribune*, July 27, 1893. Both the victim and the rapist in this incident were black, according to the newspaper.

54. Ibid., June 6, 1895.

55. For this fear, see ibid., September 2, 1896.

56. Ibid., June 14, 1896; April 4, 1895.

57. For example, see ibid., June 28, 1896.

58. Scholars analyzing modern data have found a similar pattern. The overwhelming majority of homicides are intraracial. See John A. Humphrey and Stuart Palmer, "Race, Sex, and Criminal Homicide Offender-Victim Relationships," in *Homicide Among Black Americans*, 57; William Wilbanks, "Criminal Homicide Offenders in the U.S.," in *Homicide Among Black Americans*, 48.

59. *Tampa Morning Tribune*, June 13, 1895. Again, it is impossible to determine precisely why the fight occurred or who initiated it. It is clear, however, that a violent struggle occurred between McDuffee and Spitler.

60. Ibid., March 12, 1896; June 22, 1893.

61. Research on modern homicide has revealed a similar pattern. See Humphrey and Palmer, "Race, Sex, and Criminal Homicide Offender-Victim Relationships," 63.

62. *Tampa Morning Tribune*, July 25, 1895; also see June 17, 1896.

63. Lane found a similar pattern. See *Roots of Violence in Black Philadelphia*, 103.

64. For example, see *Tampa Morning Tribune*, April 16, 1897.

65. Ibid., March 27, 1895.

66. Less than 17 percent of black-on-white violence occurred in a domestic setting, compared with 47 percent of black-on-black violence.

67. *Tampa Morning Tribune*, August 1, 1895.

68. For a similar analysis, see Steven F. Messner and Reid M. Golden, "Racial Inequality and Racially Disaggregated Homicide Rates," *Criminology* 30 (August 1992): 439.

69. According to Wolfgang, the street was "the most dangerous single place." See *Patterns in Criminal Homicide*, 322.

70. For analyses of race and the municipal police in the New South, see Howard N. Rabinowitz, "The Conflict Between Blacks and the Police in the Urban South, 1865–1900," *Historian* 39 (November 1976): 62–76; George C. Wright, "The Billy Club and the Ballot," *Southern Studies* 13 (Spring 1984): 20–41.

71. For a similar analysis, see Dollard, *Caste and Class in a Southern Town*, 279.

72. See Lane, *Roots of Violence in Black Philadelphia*, 136.

73. For example, see *Tampa Morning Tribune*, April 11, 1895.

74. Ibid., April 20, 1897.

75. Ibid.

76. Ibid., November 5, 1895.

77. Sociologists and criminologists studying modern America have also noted that "injuries were sustained more often by victims who knew their assailants." See Neil Alan Weiner and Marvin E. Wolfgang, "The Extent and

Character of Violent Crime in America, 1969 to 1982," in *American Violence and Public Policy*, ed. Lynn A. Curtis (New Haven: Yale University Press, 1985), 31.

78. For a more theoretical perspective on this pattern, see William J. Goode, *Explorations in Social Theory* (New York: Oxford University Press, 1973), 148–49.

79. In her study of white working-class men, Haag found a similar pattern. See "The 'Ill-Use of a Wife,' " 450, 455.

80. *Tampa Morning Tribune*, October 10, 1895.

81. Ibid., June 23, 1896; also see December 4, 1895.

82. Ibid., August 17, 1897.

83. As is always the case, the police and the courts were more likely to become involved when fights resulted in bloodshed or serious injury. For a similar analysis, see Wolfgang, *Patterns in Criminal Homicide*, 323.

84. *Tampa Morning Tribune*, April 15, 1897. This news story suggested that the conflict reflected a division within the black community—between West Indians and native Tampans. Also see ibid., June 6, 1896, which noted that a fight was rooted in political fissures within the black community. Such hints about the internal world of black Tampa, however, were rare.

85. Ibid., August 16, 1896.

86. Ibid., November 23, 1894.

87. Ibid., August 21, 1895.

88. The concentration of domestic violence on Thursdays might have been related to the rhythms of *bolita*, the popular game of chance. There is some evidence that winning numbers were drawn on Thursday evenings, and black women, the *Tribune* frequently observed, often quarreled with their husbands over money used for gambling. According to the newspaper, black "washerwomen" protested when their husbands attempted to sell their soaps for money to play bolita. See Mormino and Pizzo, *Tampa*, 176. Alternatively, the pattern of Thursday violence may have been related to the work schedules of black women, particularly domestic servants. Haag, in her study of New York City, also found that domestic violence surged on Thursdays, and she suggests that the pressures of the end of the pay week may have triggered it, though she does not provide information about pay cycles. See Haag, "The 'Ill-Use of a Wife,' " 450. Tampa's leading employer, the cigar industry, usually paid its workers on Saturday. Thursday night, therefore, was probably not the end of the pay week in Tampa. For other studies of domestic violence, see Linda Gordon, *Heroes of Their Own Lives* (New York: Penguin, 1988); Ellen Ross, " 'Fierce Questions and Taunts': Married Life in Working-Class London, 1870–1914," *Feminist Studies* 8 (Fall 1982): 575–602; Nancy Tomes, "A 'Torrent of Abuse': Crimes of Violence

between Working-Class Men and Women in London 1840–1875," *Journal of Social History* 11 (Spring 1978): 328–45.

89. Virtually every study of homicide has concluded that the rate for black Americans has been considerably greater than that for white Americans. A comparison of my data on violence in Tampa with Haag's data on violence in New York City suggests that the gap between the races was enormous with regard to women's violence but relatively modest with regard to spouse abuse. For Tampa, the ratio of man-on-man violence to man-on-woman violence was 100:41. For New York City, it was 100:30. See Haag, "The 'Ill-Use of a Wife,' " 450. Although the *Tampa Morning Tribune* contained much information about wife beating, the newspaper seldom reported — or even mentioned — child abuse, suggesting that such violence was considered a more private matter.

90. *Tampa Morning Tribune*, October 9, 1897, and June 16, 1896. Also see ibid., February 21, 1895, and August 4, 1895.

91. For other studies that have noted the relatively high level of violence committed by black women, see Wolfgang, *Patterns in Criminal Homicide*, 33; Dollard, *Caste and Class in a Southern Town*, 269, 271; O'Carroll and Mercy, "Patterns and Recent Trends in Black Homicide," 56. Robert A. Taylor found that black women in late-nineteenth-century Jacksonville were often arrested. See "Crime and Race Relations in Jacksonville, 1884–1892," *Southern Studies*, new ser., 2 (Spring 1991): 20. For white women during this period, see Lawrence M. Friedman and Robert V. Percival, *The Roots of Justice* (Chapel Hill: University of North Carolina Press, 1981), 107–8. Friedman and Percival found that white women were rarely arrested in Alameda County. Haag found a similar pattern of infrequent arrests in New York City. See "The 'Ill-Use of a Wife,' " 450. In Tampa, the ratio of man-on-man violence to woman-on-woman violence was 100:43 among blacks. Haag's research on New York City revealed a ratio of 100:8.

92. *Tampa Morning Tribune*, March 26, 1898.

93. Ibid., April 28, 1895.

94. Scholars examining violence in modern America have found that the overwhelming majority of homicides by women are committed in the home. See Jeffrey H. Goldstein, *Aggression and Crimes of Violence* (New York: Oxford University Press, 1986), 77.

95. Also see Dollard, *Caste and Class in a Southern Town*, 271.

96. *Tampa Morning Tribune*, May 29, 1895.

97. For example, see ibid., November 16, 1894.

98. Ibid., August 18, 1896.

99. Ibid., October 26, 1894.

100. Ibid., January 6, 1895; July 29, 1896.

101. Ibid., March 8, 1898.

102. Ibid., April 27, 1895.

103. See Lane, *Violent Death in the City*, 109; Jacqueline Jones, *Labor of Love, Labor of Sorrow* (New York, 1985), 104.

104. See Allen Steinberg, *The Transformation of Criminal Justice* (Chapel Hill: University of North Carolina Press, 1989); Robert A. Silverman, *Law and Urban Growth* (Princeton: Princeton University Press, 1981).

105. *Tampa Morning Tribune*, January 8, 1898.

106. Ibid., July 31, 1897; August 13, 1897.

107. Ibid., February 13, 1897.

108. Brearley, "The Pattern of Violence," 690.

109. Dollard, *Caste and Class in a Southern Town*, 279. Also see Raper, *The Tragedy of Lynching*, 34–35.

110. For more broadly cast discussions of this phenomenon, see *Negro Population, 1790–1915*, 438; Brearley, "The Pattern of Violence," 690. Experts on the modern criminal justice system have noted a similar pattern. See Darnell F. Hawkins, "Black and White Homicide Differentials," in *Homicide Among Black Americans*, 119–20.

111. *Tampa Morning Tribune*, September 22, 1897; also see ibid., July 24, 1896.

112. Ibid., August 18, 1896.

113. See ibid., August 28, 1896; May 10, 1896; April 23, 1895; May 8, 1895.

114. According to Dollard, "this differential application of the law amounts to a condoning of Negro violence." See *Caste and Class in a Southern Town*, 280.

115. For a related analysis, see Henry P. Lundsgaarde, "Public Policy and the Differential Punishment of Homicide," in *Homicide Among Black Americans*, 205.

116. See, for example, Lane, *Violent Death in the City*; Zehr, *Crime and the Development of Modern Society*.

117. For a discussion of this process, see David J. Bodenhamer, "Law and Disorder on the Early Frontier: Marion County, Indiana, 1823–1850," *Western Historical Quarterly* 10 (July 1979): 323–36.

118. See Lane, *Roots of Violence in Black Philadelphia*; Olivier Zunz, *The Changing Face of Inequality* (Chicago: University of Chicago Press, 1982), 373–98.

119. For figures on urban versus rural homicide rates, see Brearley, *Homicide in the United States*, 99.

120. Wolfgang and Ferracuti, *The Subculture of Violence*; Hawkins, "Black and White Homicide Differentials," 126. According to the subculture hypothesis, violence is not random. Instead, it is regulated by culturally defined rules and traditions that tolerate and encourage the use of violence in cer-

tain situations (such as the defense of "honor"). Although conflict may unfold according to "cultural guidelines," to those outside the subculture or unaware of its rules, such violence appears irrational and random.

121. Hawkins, "Black and White Homicide Differentials," 111–13. Other critics of the subculture hypothesis have emphasized the difficulty of identifying the nature and the boundaries of the subcultural group. See Lundsgaarde, *Murder in Space City*, 17; Howard S. Erlanger, "The Empirical Status of the Subculture of Violence Thesis," *Social Problems* 22 (December 1974): 280–92.

10

No Longer Denied
Black Women in Florida, 1920–1950

Maxine D. Jones

*Whether it be my religion, my aesthetic taste,
my economic opportunity, my educational
desire, whatever the craving is, I find a
limitation because I suffer the greatest known
handicap, a Negro — a Negro woman.*
Mary McLeod Bethune

ALTHOUGH PROGRESS has been made in recounting the history of blacks in Florida, the role of black women has long been neglected and remains, for the most part, unwritten. While the careers of Zora Neale Hurston and Mary McLeod Bethune are now well known, the achievements of thousands of other teachers, nurses, social workers, business owners, and activists are hidden from view. Yet they too have played a major role in the African American community and in the history and development of the Sunshine State. They not only constituted a large segment of the labor force, but they also facilitated the agricultural and industrial development of Florida. All these women shared in the social, political, and economic life of the state, and it is their lives and contributions from 1920 to 1950 that are recounted in this chapter.

In the 1920's Florida's population rapidly expanded and in the process the state became a major tourist center. Northerners traveled south to get away from harsh winters, but many also migrated to Florida for reasons other than climate, and by 1930 the state's population was rapidly approaching 1.5 million. Florida's African American population also expanded in this period. The 329,487 African

Americans living in Florida in 1920 represented 34 percent of the population. Natural increase was responsible for only part of the growth, however, as large numbers of blacks migrated to Florida from Georgia, Alabama, and South Carolina in search of job opportunities and a better life.[1]

For African Americans, life had not changed much in the past half-century. They had discovered that surviving in freedom was almost as difficult as surviving slavery. They were reminded almost daily of their place in society, and the violence against the entire black communities of Ocoee in 1920 and Rosewood in 1923 remained permanently etched in their minds. Lynching and violence against African Americans remained a constant threat in the segregated communities of Florida. Often forced out of jobs that traditionally had been

Table 1. Florida Population, 1900–1950[2]

Year	Total	White	Black
1900	528,542	297,333	230,730
1910	752,619	443,634	308,669
1920	968,470	638,153	329,487
1925	1,263,549	854,585	401,733
1930	1,468,211	1,035,205	431,828
1935	1,606,842	1,139,063	463,205
1940	1,897,414	1,381,986	514,198
1945	2,250,061	1,695,301	554,760
1950	2,771,305	2,166,051	603,101

Table 2. Black Male and Female Population of Florida, 1900–1950[3]

Year	Male	Female	Total
1900	120,199	110,531	230,730
1910	161,362	147,307	308,669
1920	167,156	162,331	329,487
1930	215,148	216,680	431,828
1940	252,799	261,399	514,198
1950	293,137	309,964	603,101

Zora Neale Hurston. Hurston was born in the all-black town of Eatonville, Florida. She studied anthropology and used her training in writing about African American life in Florida. She won literary acclaim during the famous Harlem Renaissance, but died in poverty. Courtesy of the Carl Van Vechten Papers, Beinecke Rare Book Room, Yale University.

theirs, African Americans found it difficult to get ahead economically. In urban areas especially, black men had a hard time finding steady work. They faced discrimination and resentment from white competitors.[4] Black women, however, remained a major part of the unskilled and semiskilled workforce in the South, including Florida. For example, the number of nonwhite women at least fourteen years old in Florida's labor force in 1940 was 48.6 percent. This was higher than both the South's (37.1 percent) and the country's (37.3 percent) averages. Only New York (49.5 percent) had a higher percentage than Florida.[5]

African American women performed essentially the same labor they always had. Racism and discrimination limited employment opportunities outside of agricultural, domestic, and personal service, thus continuing the longstanding pattern of relegating black women to the "more menial, the lower paid, the heavier and more hazardous jobs."[6] Black women undertook "a man's share in the field, and a woman's part at home," working alongside their husbands as farmers and sharecroppers or as domestics, cooks, and personal servants for whites. After an exhausting day, whether working in the field or in someone else's house, they returned to do the washing, sewing, cooking, cleaning, and nurturing in their own homes.[7]

Although Florida's urban population outnumbered rural residents by 1930, it was not until 1940 that more black Floridians lived in urban rather than rural areas.[8] Following the national trend, Florida's black farm operators decreased in number between 1920 and 1950, but large numbers of black women continued to work on Florida's farms.[9]

Approximately one-fourth of all black farm laborers worked on truck farms, which provided seasonal employment for thousands of

Table 3. Negro Urban and Rural Population, 1920–1950[10]

	Urban	Rural Nonfarm	Rural Farm
1920	120,596	121,289	87,602
1930	210,292	146,067	75,469
1940	287,047	147,998	79,153
1950	395,703	151,257	56,141

black women in South and Central Florida. They harvested tomatoes, cucumbers, celery, beans, peppers, melons, cantaloupes, strawberries, corn, potatoes, and peanuts. During the 1930s and 1940s, blacks in the Boca Raton area were employed on the Butts, Raulerson's, Strickland and Chesebro farms. Generally paid by the hamper when picking beans, workers could make between $10 and $15 dollars a day. One woman earned a reputation for picking fifty bushels of beans a day. Another woman reported making as much as $60 a week by bunching greens and celery on a muck farm.[11] Since workers were often paid by the amount of vegetables they picked, some women earned as much as men.

Compensation varied from farm to farm. Martin Richardson of the Florida Writers Project reported that the strawberry farms in Hillsborough County paid above average wages, while those in Polk County paid at the subsistence level. Young girls and women in Plant City earned between $7 and $9 a week in 1939. Richardson found both the lowest and highest wages in St. Lucie County. Blacks in the Miami area, however, refused to pick tomatoes for $2.50–3.00 a day in 1934, and owners were forced to transport workers from Georgia. Wages were so poor in St. Johns County that blacks declined to work for one potato farmer. They could earn more for less work if they took relief jobs.[12]

Working conditions on truck farms varied significantly. Some truck farms, such as the Butts farm in Boca Raton, provided living quarters for their workers. Approximately three hundred African American workers and their families lived on the Butts farm, which was reputedly the third largest employer in the area. One tenant recalled that "living on Butts Farm there was no light bill, no rent, no nothing. You would just be ready to go to the bean field in the morning."[13] Most farms, however, were like those in St. Lucie County, where several hundred black men, women, and children worked long hours under appalling conditions. One farm laborer declined to work there not only because of the "sunup to sundown" working hours but also, as he said, " 'them people on that farm work so hard they look like African wildmen.' " It was rumored that those unable to do the work were beaten.[14]

Although the number of black female workers declined significantly after 1910, more than 12,000 black females at least ten years old were listed as agricultural workers in 1930. Of this number 1,247 were owners and tenants, and more than 11,000 were farm laborers.[15] In 1950 17,605 nonwhite[16] women, or 15.9 percent, toiled in some capacity at farm work in Florida. This was considerably higher than the national average of all females at least fourteen years old who either owned or worked on farms. In 1950 2.7 percent of the country's females were owners or tenants and 6.3 percent were farm managers.[17]

Often gender played no role in the type of work done by farm laborers. "During potato season in Hastings or Bunnell one sees nearly as many women as men handling the heavy potato hoes," an observer noted in 1937. One Marion County woman farmed thirty acres and looked forward to getting her crops in.[18] As farmers, sharecroppers, and tenants, black women worked their own land or alongside their husbands trying to eke out a living. Growing cotton, tobacco, peanuts, and potatoes and raising livestock often proved unprofitable for many farmers and they generally lived from hand to mouth. Rarely paid in cash, their compensation was in livestock feed, fertilizer, seed, and other supplies, including cornmeal, salt pork, and molasses.[19]

Bessie and George Derrick were tenant farmers in Plant City, where they cultivated three acres rented from E. J. Marshall, overseer for the Swift Company, for $45 a year. The parents of four children, the Derricks struggled to make a decent living. They grew strawberries, cucumbers, beans, sugar cane, okra, tomatoes, and other vegetables. In a good year they cleared $100 after paying for their land, fertilizer, and seedlings. "The best I can do is keep some food on the table. If we have a good season we live nicely, if not we fare pretty hard. If I didn't raise some vegetables on this place I couldn't make a go of it," George Derrick claimed. In spite of their difficulties, Bessie Derrick loved farming and professed that there was not a lazy bone in her body. "After all you get out of work what you put into it."[20]

Ed and Ida Gray made enough to support themselves on their Beasville, Florida, farm. With the help of two of their daughters, nineteen-year-old Bessie and twenty-eight-year-old Rosa Lee, they grew strawberries and beans as their major cash crops. They raised hogs and chickens and grew Irish and sweet potatoes, corn, peppers, cucumbers, okra, and tomatoes to supplement their table fare, as well as peanuts to fatten their hogs. Another daughter, Fennie, liked farm work and cultivated three acres with her husband about a mile from her parents. They grew strawberries and other vegetables to sell. "Farming is nice when you have every thing to farm with," Ed Gray declared, but concluded that "a poor colored man sees a hard time on the farm." [21]

Not all farmers lived at the subsistence level. Luck and hard work produced a good crop and a profit for some. Mr. and Mrs. Haynes Brooks of Alachua County, who owned and operated a small poultry farm, in 1939 made $741 from selling eggs and poultry.[22] Dairy farmer George Philpot of Hamilton County cleared $1,346.00 in 1939 and $1,963.91 in 1941.[23] Octavia Hodges owned a hog farm in Marion County in the 1930s and grew peanuts to feed them. She got fifty tons of peanuts to the acre and could have made a sizable profit if she had sold them, but she boasted that if the price of pork remained stable she could double her profit by using the peanuts to fatten her hogs.[24]

African American Farm and Home Demonstration agents played a critical role in efforts to improve the lives of black farmers and their families. Home Demonstration agents such as Mary Todd McKenzie, Floy Britt, Idella R. Kelley, Diana Bouie, Ethel Powell, and Alice Poole spent many hours aiding rural black women. They gave lessons in nutrition, needlework, cooking, preserving and canning foods, health and sanitary measures, home improvement, and dressmaking. In addition, women were instructed and encouraged to raise poultry, while their husbands were advised on planting crops and other farm matters. These agents were instrumental in raising the standard of living for many farmers and other rural blacks.[25]

Although agriculture provided employment for thousands of African American women in Florida and across the South as a whole, the national trend was that more and more women, both black and white, were leaving the fields to work as domestics. In 1940 17.7 percent of the nation's females at least fourteen years old worked as domestics and 11.3 percent as service workers. Florida's figures were higher than both national and regional averages. Almost 30 percent of Florida's females in that age bracket found employment as domestics, and 13.5 percent labored as service workers in 1940.[26] Between 1920 and 1950 the majority of black women in Florida worked as domestics or personal servants. Florida employment statistics for 1930 show that, out of a total of 77,040 gainfully employed black females, 52,387 worked as servants.[27] In 1950, 97,994 black women at least fourteen years old were employed in Florida, 42,913 of whom were private household workers and 16,646 service workers. Service workers included waitresses, practical nurses, midwives, cooks, janitors, charwomen, hotel housekeepers, and attendants in hospitals and other institutions.[28]

Service work was an occupational category dominated by black women. For example in the Tampa–St. Petersburg metropolitan area in 1940, 6,915 (out of 9,363) nonwhite but only 3,050 (out of 21,711) white women fourteen and older worked in personal services.[29] In 1950 more than half (5,260) of the 10,278 employed black females fourteen and older were private household workers. Only 850 (out of 36,543) white women were thus employed.[30] The same held true in other areas. In Jacksonville in 1940, 9,375 (out of 13,557) nonwhite women worked in personal service, as compared with 1,847 (out of 14,729) white women. In 1950, 6,175 (out of 13,305) black women worked as domestics but only 399 (out of 25,226) white females. This trend was also evident in the Miami and Orlando metropolitan areas.[31]

The average salary for domestics and personal servants varied from city to city. In Tampa during the 1920s, the average weekly salary for domestic servants was $8.50, but maids at the local tourist hotels generally made more. The Tampa Floridan Hotel employed fifteen chamber maids in 1927 at $10 a week. However, black women employed as maids in dormitories at the University of Florida in Gainesville in 1932 earned $5 a week.[32] As late as 1940, domestics and maids in Tallahassee received only $4 to $6 a week. Cooks and maids in Jacksonville earned between $15 and $22 a week in 1946.[33] Sometimes employers supplemented these low salaries with bus fare, old clothes, furniture, and meals.[34]

Relationships between black women and their white employers probably did not differ much from the master-slave relationship of the antebellum South. A study conducted in 1927 found that many employers expressed a "genuine interest" in their employees, but many of the relationships were paternalistic, with blacks going to their white employers for financial and other help during emergencies.[35] This sometimes continued long after the employer-employee relationship had ended. Mandy MaQuay remained in close contact with her former employer, Mrs. L. A. Fraleigh of Madison County, long after she retired. Even though teased by some in the black community for doing so, Mrs. MaQuay frequently visited the Fraleighs and referred to them as her "white folks." When MaQuay died, Mrs. Fraleigh attended her funeral and identified herself as MaQuay's "faithful friend and employer." [36]

Most private household workers did not live in the homes of their employers. Of the 6,972 private household workers in the Miami area in 1950, only 529 lived in. The same was true in Orlando, where only 31 of 2,198 lived.[37] Mrs. Rosa Lee Henry lived on the premises of four Tallahassee families. She recalls living on Mitchell Street with Irene Wells, her three children, and her father during the 1940s. While Mrs. Wells worked at a local department store, Mrs. Henry took care of her children and their invalid grandfather, besides cleaning, cooking, and doing laundry. She received $6 a week plus meals and accommodations and was generally given Sundays off to attend church.[38] The majority of black women, no doubt, preferred living in their own communities among family and friends, with time away from their white employers. Often, however, salaries were so low that some could not afford to live off premises.[39]

The hours of work varied for domestics and personal servants. Those who lived in were basically on call twenty-four hours a day. Some employers even placed buzzers or bells in their servants' quarters so that they could easily summon them when needed. In Tampa during the 1920s, the average workday was eleven and a half hours for a cook, ten hours for a nurse, and eight hours for maids. Some domestics received two afternoons off during the week. Those in Jacksonville had Sunday and either Thursday or Saturday afternoons off.[40]

Domestic work was often seasonal and irregular. Many found steady employment with whites who came South for the winter but still had to find other means of support for the remainder of the year. Women who picked vegetables on truck farms during the winter months worked as domestics during the summer, when farm work was slow. Some women performed what was referred to as "days work," working for several white women on different days of the week.[41]

In addition to domestic positions, black women filled other unskilled positions in the area of personal service. They even assumed several posts that had been traditionally held by black men. During World War I, when black men entered the military, and during the 1930s, when many migrated North, women replaced them as chauffeurs, laundry workers, and, in Miami and Tampa, as elevator operators.[42]

Although black women labored as charwomen, cleaning office buildings at night, as well as kitchen workers, cooks, and maids in many of Florida's year-round establishments, most women employed in the seasonal businesses, according to a study in 1928–29, were northern and white. Employers believed that northern whites preferred having other whites wait upon them. In seasonal establishments only 17.9 percent of the women workers were black, while 82.1 percent were white. Conversely, black women represented 56 percent and white women 44 percent of those who worked in year-round businesses.[43] The median weekly wages for black women, $8.80, were higher than the $7.05 for whites employed in Florida's hotels and restaurants, for several reasons, including compensation for the likelihood that white women would receive tips, lodging, and meals in addition to wages.[44]

While African Americans had difficulty locating work in seasonal industries, some found steady employment in Florida industries. Although the phosphate industry was a male-dominated field, a few African American women worked in a phosphate rock mill near Dunnellon in 1936–37. For ten hours a day these women sat over a chute picking foreign substances out of a passing stream of rocks. Even though they did not complain about the difficulty of the job, their foreman considered the work too "gruelling" for women and threatened to quit if the women stayed on. The women averaged between $4 and $7 a week, while men earned between $8 and $10.[45] Women typically lived with their husbands in company towns operated by phosphate companies, such as the American Agricultural Chemical Company in Polk County, and eventually began doing manual labor. Since they could be hired at lower wages, they began gradually to replace men especially in the processing of phosphate.[46]

According to Martin Richardson, the citrus industry was the "mainstay of Negro employment," with "whole communities of Negroes liv[ing] on citrus work for a few months, each year, then

African American women working on the Johnson-Wolfe Tobacco Company farm, four miles north of Tallahassee, ca. 1910. Field labor was still a way of life for many African Americans in Florida well into the twentieth century. Courtesy of the Florida State Archives.

'Relief' until citrus season returns."[47] However, state figures reveal that most workers in Florida's citrus industry were white. The 1935 state census shows that, of the 11,260 persons employed in the citrus industry, 8,176 were white men, 1,301 black men, 1,548 white women, and only 44 black women.[48]

Women did not pick fruit, as the work was considered too strenuous. They were more likely to be packers, graders, and canners.[49] However, even these positions were dominated by white women. Blacks generally were not hired even for menial tasks in the packinghouses and canning plants.[50] A few black women were observed working as graders and a few as separators or peelers in canning plants. Although rarely hired as "cold peelers," several black women found employment as "hot peelers," in a process that steamed the fruit before the peel was removed.[51] Wages varied across the citrus belt, but they were as characteristically low as the hours were long.[52]

The tobacco industry in Florida employed the greatest number of African American women. In North and West Florida women labored on tobacco plantations, growing and harvesting shade and bright tobacco. Born in 1929, Lucille Love of Quincy went to work on a tobacco plantation when she was only thirteen. For 15 cents a day she pulled weeds and worked as a "toter," carrying tobacco leaves to a wagon stationed at the end of a row for transport to the barn.[53] In 1944, when she was fifteen, she earned 75 cents a day wrapping and pushing down tobacco loops, a task she described as particularly strenuous:

> Yeah, pushing them [loops of string] down from around the stalk so that the tobacco could grow up and you could wrap that string around that tobacco so it wouldn't fall down as it growed up. You know the wind blow against it and would blow it down. But you see, if you had it wrapped when the wind and rain would fall that string what we had wrapped around it would help support it and Lord Have Mercy in looping tobacco those that wrapped and pushed down that loop went behind the person that was wrapping. Now that's up and down, up and down looping all day handing the person what's on a bench above you looping that stalk with that string bring it up to the fellow up there he tie it and you go back down the loop, that's all day.[54]

Lucille Love received her social security card at age sixteen and joined some seventy-five other women in making cigars and cigarillos at the Florida Cigar Company in Quincy. This was considered a good job, at top pay. A relative taught her how to roll cigarillos:

> My aunt taught me because I never would have learned if I had went there not knowing. But my aunt, Leola Watson, taught me how to make those cigarillos. You know she would slip and bring them home and she would teach me how to roll them. She would slip and bring home the wraps and the paste and the blade. We had to have a blade to cut that wrapper with and she would slip and bring home because she would say that way I . . . wont have to go to the farm if you learn how to make, to roll those cigarillos

Women tobacco workers, Havana, Florida, 1956. Gussie Richardson is shown packing tobacco and Annie Lee Jones is "lugging," or carrying tobacco leaves. Courtesy of the Florida State Archives.

and that's what she did she would bring it home in her hand bag and would teach me all afternoon how to do it. . . . If I had to wait for an instructor I never would have learn how to do it.

When the Florida Cigar Company closed, she returned to work on tobacco farms until the early 1950s.[55]

According to the 1930 census, fewer than seven hundred black women worked in the state's cigar and tobacco factories. Cigar manufacturing was largely concentrated in Tampa, Jacksonville, and Quincy. In one Jacksonville establishment, African American women performed more than 75 percent of the tasks. Cubans, both black and white, dominated the industry in Tampa, where women accounted for 43 percent of the employees in 1930 and 55 percent in 1939; the numbers of blacks are not known. The majority of the women labored as cigar makers or strippers. In 1927 most blacks in Tampa's cigar industry worked in the factories that produced the "cheap and medium" price products.[56]

A study of women in Florida's industries conducted by the Women's Bureau during 1928–29 identified 155 (8.2 percent) black and 2,680 (45 percent) white women employed in the cigar industry. More than a third of the black women were under twenty years of age. Black women generally worked as strippers and worked longer hours and earned less than their white counterparts. The median weekly earnings were $16.65 for white women but only $7.10 for blacks.[57]

Although African American women constituted a majority of those employed in the laundry business, they also worked longer hours for less pay than their white counterparts. In 1928 75.3 percent of African Americans and 61.1 percent of white women worked at least ten hours a day. Median weekly earnings were $7.85 for black women and $12.30 for white.[58] Statistics from the 1950 census showed 2,992 white and 5,511 black women working in laundries and dry cleaners statewide.[59] More black women than white labored as pressers and hand ironers, while white women were employed as flatwork ironers, shakers, feeders, folders, and markers and sorters.[60]

Not all African American women were sentenced to a lifetime of menial tasks. The teaching profession called many women of color. There were 539 black teachers in 1930 and 3,796 in 1950. Many also served as principals and administrators in segregated schools. There

Warnell Lumber and Veneer Company No. 17 Laundry, ca. 1890s. This unidentified woman was employed as a laundress for the company in the 1890s. Here she beats the clothes while keeping an eye on her young daughter. Courtesy of the Florida State Archives.

were at least eight female principals in Miami in 1942 and some five in Pensacola in 1950.[61] Since state funds for education were not distributed equally, African American teachers had to work with inadequate facilities and insufficient supplies. Black women received less pay, not only because of their color but also because of their gender. In 1930, the average monthly salary for white males was $169.20, for black males $84.20, white females $115.80, and black females $61.60. In spite of salary increments in following years, the gap remained and discrimination continued. The average annual salary for whites in 1939—40 was $1,145 but for blacks $583. Salaries during the 1949—50 school year averaged $3,030 for white teachers and $2,616 for African Americans.[62]

Various organizations and individuals condemned the low wages that black teachers received. A study of blacks in Tampa commissioned by the Tampa Welfare League, the Urban League, and the Tampa Young Men's Christian Association in 1927 denounced the unfairness:

The negro teacher must keep neat, clean, and wear good clothes. The teacher's position demands that he conform to certain standards in society, and this he cannot do with such meager income. Furthermore, the times demand that teachers attend summer school and improve themselves. This they can hardly do, in view of the fact that it takes all they earn teaching, and more besides, to meet the ordinary requirements of life. The salaries should be large enough to induce the best minds to qualify for a teacher's position, and to make it possible for teachers to devote themselves wholly to their work and not have to worry about 'wherewithal shall they be clothed.'[63]

D. E. Williams, the superintendent of Negro Schools in Florida, considered the salaries of black teachers "appallingly low." Acknowledging that salaries in general were poor, Williams pointed out that it was easier for white teachers to supplement their income than it was for blacks. Many jobs were not open to blacks because of their color, and competition was so keen, Williams claimed, that it was impossible for black teachers to work on a part-time basis. In addition, many of the state's black teachers had to attend school during the summer.[64]

African American educators in Escambia, Brevard, Duval, Hillsborough, and Palm Beach counties filed salary equity suits during the 1940s. Two women were among them. In 1941 sixty-nine-year-old Mary Blocker of Jacksonville became the third African American and the first woman to file a lawsuit against Duval County for discrimination in teacher salaries. Even though she was forced to retire, the court ruled in her favor the following June. In appreciation of her tenacity, the Duval County Teachers' Association, composed of African American teachers, voted to continue Blocker's salary. They did so for more than twenty years. Similarly, Hilda Turney Turner sued the Hillsborough County School Board in November 1942, but the court ruled against her.[65]

Beyond teaching, black women found remarkably few opportunities in the professional fields. Their lack of success was due in part to traditional views about the role of women in such fields and in part to discrimination against blacks who sought advanced degrees and training in such fields. Nevertheless, as early as 1908 Dr. Effie Carrie Mitchell Hampton became the first black female physician to practice in Florida. Born in Fernandina in 1886, Mitchell grew up in Ocala and attended Howard Academy and the Orange Park School

This unidentified woman was the oldest member of the adult education classes at Washington School in Pensacola, 1935. African Americans of all ages recognized the value of education. Courtesy of the Florida State Archives.

for girls at Orange Park. She entered Meharry Medical School in 1904 and received her medical degree in 1908, then set up practice in Ocala. She reputedly practiced only until her marriage in 1915 to a dentist, L. R. Hampton, but in 1916 she served as secretary for the Florida Medical, Dental and Pharmaceutical Association.[66] Census records show that there were only 257 African American women medical doctors in the United States in 1950, of whom 103 practiced in the South. There were no female physicians in the state in 1930, but four in 1950. Two of the four practiced in Miami.[67]

Black women were also represented in small numbers in other medicine-related fields, including pharmacy, dentistry, and nursing. In 1942 Dr. Henrietta Jones worked as a pharmacist in what was billed as "the largest drug store owned by a Negro in Florida," the Economy Drug Store in Miami. Mabel Ervin Latson was a dental hygienist in Jacksonville in 1942, and more than twenty-two black women practiced as medical and dental technicians in the state in 1950.[68] By 1930 273 trained or professional black nurses worked in Florida, including Clara Draughan Frye, the Sunshine State's most famous African American nurse. The daughter of a southern black man and a white woman from England, Frye was born in New York in 1872. When she was ten, her family moved to Montgomery, Alabama. She studied nursing in Chicago for two years and practiced her profession for sixteen years in Montgomery. In 1908 she moved to Tampa, where she earned a reputation as the city's "best fever nurse."[69]

Frye opened Tampa's first hospital for blacks in 1908 in a rented building on Lamar Avenue. Aided by both blacks and whites, she was able to expand the facility and to purchase the property. Both black and white patients were admitted and treated by both black and white doctors. In 1930–31, the City of Tampa took over the hospital and changed the name to Municipal Hospital for Negroes. Frye died penniless in 1937, but a new medical facility for blacks was built in 1938 and dedicated as the Clara Frye Municipal Negro Hospital in honor of her remarkable service.[70]

By 1950 423 African American professional nurses practiced in Florida, out of 12,550 nationwide. Most were employed in the larger metropolitan areas, where job opportunities were greatest and where they were less likely to encounter racial discrimination. Ninety-six worked in Jacksonville, 95 in Miami, 57 in Tampa–St. Petersburg, and 18 in Orlando. African American nurses worked in many of the black hospitals across the state, including Brewster Hospital in Jacksonville, the Clara Frye Tampa Municipal Negro Hospital, Mercy Hospital in St. Petersburg, and the Pine Ridge Hospital in West Palm Beach.[71] They also found employment in private establishments, as well as county health departments.[72] Unfortunately, trained black and white nurses did not receive the same pay. In 1953 the annual salary for a white general-duty hospital nurse in Tampa ranged from $2,401 to $2,518 but was only $1,984 for black nurses. Several nurses of color in the Tampa Bay area protested the lower salaries, and in 1953 a suit was filed in their behalf against the City of Tampa.[73]

Most African American women working in medical care were practical nurses and midwives. According to the 1950 census, more than 450 worked in these two fields.[74] The "Granny" midwife, however, had to struggle against racism and the increasing professionalization of medical practice. A study of midwives in Tampa in 1927 concluded, "The average Negro Midwife is illiterate, and coupled with this illiteracy, is obscessed [sic] with ideals and methods regarding the practice of midwifery that too often prove detrimental to mother and child."[75] Many in the health profession agreed. A statewide effort was made to regulate and ultimately to eliminate the practice of midwifery.[76] Florida's black midwives came under scrutiny and were required to take courses and attend midwives institutes such as those held at Florida Agricultural and Mechanical College in Tallahassee from 1933 to 1946.[77]

After a 1931 law required that midwives be licensed, more than seven hundred black midwives registered with the state. According to Debra Susie, who has studied midwifery in Florida, "It was never the state's objective to enhance the midwife profession. Midwives would be tolerated where the poor needed medical care." This increased control meant that the number of black women practicing midwifery steadily decreased. For the most part, midwives were allowed to practice where they would not compete with physicians and medical establishments.[78]

Highly respected in the black community, midwives provided a service that many poor rural blacks and whites could not do without. In many areas of Florida there were no medical facilities for blacks and, in any case, a midwife's services were certainly cheaper than

Professional midwives attending a seminar at Edward Waters College in Jacksonville, ca. 1940s. African American midwives were respected members of their communities. Courtesy of the Florida State Archives.

a physician-attended birth. Hillsborough County midwives charged $25 for their services as compared with the $35 fee for a doctor in 1927. As late as 1952, midwives delivered more than one-fourth of all black infants not born in a hospital in Hillsborough County.[79]

Black women also toppled barriers and created their own opportunities in fields unrelated to health care. Arnolta Johnson of Jacksonville worked as a reporter and served as her city's representative for the Associated Negro Press. She also anonymously reported news of the Jacksonville black community for the *Pittsburgh Courier*. Margaret Simms, also of Jacksonville, was editor of the "colored page" of the *Jacksonville Journal* in 1939.[80]

Despite the enormous disadvantages they faced, a few black women also entered the art world. Augusta Savage was Florida's best-known artist, but others, including Savanna Roy of Pensacola, attempted to make a living from their work. Roy had received training at Florida Agricultural and Mechanical College, and during the 1930s her paintings included still scenes done in oils and watercolors that were both "striking in their blending and subject material." [81]

Although segregation was an enormous obstacle to black opportunity, it also ensured black business owners a clientele. Thriving black business districts developed in Miami, Jacksonville, Tampa, and other Florida cities, and some African American women operated successful enterprises. Several, including Pauline Pratt and Mrs. R. H. Walker of Jacksonville, Mrs. Preston Pughsley of Tampa, and Mrs. M. L. Rogers of Bradenton, were owners and managers of funeral homes.[82] Among the female business owners in Jacksonville in 1942 were Anna Reed, who owned and operated a tailor's shop; Mabel L. McClendon, owner and manager of Broad Street Cleaners; florist Alex Skinner; and Mrs. Alice Kirkpatrick, who operated the forty-eight room Richmond Hotel.[83] Tampa black business-women operated dry cleaners, florist shops, beauty parlors, and rooming houses in 1950. Photographer Amelia J. Hicks owned the Harlem Studio in West Palm Beach during the 1940s, and Mrs. M. D. Potter, along with her husband, owned and edited the *Tampa Bulletin*.[84]

In spite of the success experienced by some black women, the majority remained mired in poverty, even while they worked long hours. Black women were often forced to search for ways to supplement their low salaries. Many took in laundry and worked at more than one job away from home. They lamented that their sons and daughters had to quit school to work as domestics, servants, and unskilled laborers to supplement the family income.[85]

Tallahassee teachers, disturbed by the widespread poverty in the black community and the increase in marriage among the city's youth in 1945, charged that "the wages earned by mothers and fathers are often too low to provide all of the home comforts and other things needed by large families." As a result "many girls drop out of school before completing the 9th grade. They take jobs in order to increase the family earnings." The teachers concluded that adult responsibilities at such an early age led to a "mature social life and eventually [too-early] marriage." [86]

Poor people were often ingenious in finding ways to make ends meet. To raise additional money, black women and their families

African American women working at the Jacksonville Negro Mattress Factory, 1935. Courtesy of the Florida State Archives.

gathered and cured Spanish moss, which was used to stuff mattresses. During the Depression years, Moss sold for between 2 and 4 cents a pound, and some families received as much as $70 at a time.[87] Miami women supplemented their incomes by making baskets, brushes, jams, and jellies and selling them to tourists and white residents of the area. Others fished in Florida's bountiful lakes and along the coastline, not only to provide food for their own table but also to sell. Those who lived near the coast hunted turtles for food and gathered their eggs, which were considered a delicacy and brought a good price.[88]

Black heads of households struggled to improve their circumstances and to provide a decent life for their families, but often they could afford little more than food on the table and a roof over their heads. They had little money for medical care and other necessities. Unsatisfactory working conditions and subsistence wages contributed to the poor health of African Americans. E. H. DeBose, a black dentist in Gainesville, contended that the low wages and long hours were responsible for the undernourishment and general unhealthiness apparent among blacks in that city.[89] Similarly, physician C. Frederick Duncan singled out three factors largely responsible for the poor health of African Americans in Jacksonville—politics, economic conditions, and ignorance:

> The latter may well be classified as the central point from which the other two radiate. State vital statistics harp upon the proneness to disease and numerical surplus of Negro mortality in comparison to that of whites. Yet the state politics through individuals who are armed with state authority mercilessly and consistently relegate the Negro into a situation of impotence in denying him the practical means of protection by disfranchising him. The municipality steals from him his right to go to the polls to vote, thus denying him a voice in the formation of laws which concern him. Therefore we have the segregated Negro districts and Negro ghettos, the former characterized by poorly laid out, unpaved, sandrutted, and non-lighted streets; inadequate and poor sanitary conditions; lack of properly arranged playgrounds and swimming pools; lanes that are physical and moral hazards. Moreover, almost all the Gehennas [places of misery] are in the Negro sections of the community. With such state and municipal settings, is it to be wondered at that Negroes are more exposed to contagious and infectious diseases than are the non-Negro groups?[90]

Ignorance, hazardous working conditions, and the long hours that women were compelled to work—all contributed to a large number of stillbirths. Black women accounted for 96 of the 204 stillbirths in Tampa in 1926. Of the 1,753 stillbirths in the state in 1930, 1,006 were among black women; in 1931, the figure for blacks was 833 of 1,523.[91] Maternal and infant deaths were twice as high among African Americans as among whites in Jacksonville in 1943, and Jacksonville statistics mirrored those of the state. In 1947 more nonwhite females died of diseases of pregnancy, childbirth, and the puerperium than did whites.[92]

African Americans never placidly accepted poverty, substandard living conditions, and resulting poor health. Women such as Eartha

White of Jacksonville, Viola T. Hill of Orlando, Alice Mickens of West Palm Beach, and Tampan Blanche Armwood Beatty made valiant efforts to improve the quality of life among their sisters. As president of the Florida Baptist Convention, Viola Hill labored for the "uplift and advancement" of her people. She organized girls and women according to age and marital status into clubs, including the Matron's Circle, Young Women's Auxiliary, and the Young Women's Business and Professional Association. She stressed leadership training, raised scholarship money, and led a movement to provide more recreational opportunities for African American youth. In 1941 she was appointed supervisor of the National Youth Administration project among blacks in Orlando.[93]

Blanche Armwood Beatty devoted herself to making life better for downtrodden blacks in Tampa and Hillsborough County. For eight years she served as supervisor of Negro schools and brought about major changes in black education. She secured new facilities, increased the length of the school year, organized parent-teacher associations in the black community, and established a vocational school for blacks. Beatty was also largely responsible for the opening of the first secondary school for blacks in Tampa. In 1931 she relinquished her position as supervisor of Negro schools to work with the city's unemployed black women.[94] In doing so she organized successful schools of household arts and played a pivotal role in the organization of the Tampa Gas School, which helped black women make the transition from wood to gas stoves. Beatty also established a branch of the American Red Cross in the black community and set up a family welfare program with a trained social worker. She secured a cemetery for World War I veterans and organized the Helping Hand Day Nursery and Kindergarten for working mothers. The Blanche Armwood Comprehensive High School opened in 1984 and was dedicated in February 1985.[95]

Eartha White's work in Jacksonville to ameliorate conditions in the black community is well documented. Referred to as the "Jane Addams" of her race and as the "Angel of Ashly Street," White was an indefatigable social worker. In 1922 she established the Clara White Mission, where thousands of needy blacks found clothing, food, and shelter. White also operated an orphanage, a rest home for the elderly and the tubercular, and a day nursery. She earned the admiration of whites as well as blacks and played a role in maintaining peaceful race relations in the city.[96]

While some black women worked within the system to improve the quality of life for their race, others challenged segregation. Blanche S. Brookins of Orlando sued the Atlantic Coast Line Railroad and the Pullman Company in 1926 after she was arrested and jailed in Palatka for refusing to ride in the car for blacks. Brookins, on a return trip from New York to Orlando, encountered no trouble until the train left Jacksonville. When she refused to ride in the "colored" car, the conductor wired officials in Palatka, where she was arrested, tried, found guilty and fined $500 and court costs.[97] Aided by the National Association for the Advancement of Colored People (NAACP) through a defense team led by Arthur Garfield Hayes, who argued that passengers in interstate commerce were not subject to segregation laws in southern states without equal accommodations, Brookins won her case and was awarded $2,750.[98] Berta Mae Watkins won a similar petition in 1946 against the city of Jacksonville, when she was removed from a train and arrested for not moving to the "colored" section.[99]

Although Virgil Hawkins is generally recognized as the first to challenge the Jim Crow system in higher education when he applied and was denied admission to the University of Florida's law school in 1949, he was only one of several African Americans who sought entrance into the state university's professional schools that year. Rose Boyd sought admission to the University of Florida's pharmacy school in April 1949. Denied entrance on the basis of her skin color, she appealed to the Florida Supreme Court. In *State ex rel. Boyd v. Board of Control et al.*, the court offered Boyd the option in August 1950 of attending pharmacy school in another state or of enrolling in the recently established school of pharmacy at Florida Agricultural and Mechanical College for Negroes.[100]

Not only did African American women in Florida use the legal system to fight their own personal battles against discrimination, but they were also active in organizations that attempted to bring an end to racism and color discrimination. Black women in Florida were extensively involved in the state chapter of the NAACP as members, recruiters, and officers. Mary McLeod Bethune, for example, served as vice president of the NAACP in 1940. Bethune, Eartha White, and Blanche Armwood Beatty also worked for organizations such as the National Association of Colored Women (NACW) whose purpose was to combat racial discrimination. From 1924 to 1928 Bethune served as president of that organization.[101]

Bethune, Beatty, and White vigorously fought racism and discrimination and campaigned for equal opportunity in Florida and throughout the nation. In many of Bethune's talks, the *New York Times* reported, she "went straight to the heart of the race problem, pleaded for social justice, pointed out injustices being practiced upon her race, and did it with such sincerity and zeal that her remarks were followed by applause, instead of the derogatory comment that often follows when a Negro speaks with such candor." [102] In a speech entitled "The High Cost of Keeping the Negro Inferior," Bethune stressed how much it cost Florida in dollars and cents to keep the Negro in his place. No doubt Bethune's steadfastness and refusal to submit to the segregated South played a part in her being named the recipient of the prestigious Spingarn Award in 1935.[103]

Considered aggressive and a rebel by some, Blanche Armwood Beatty fought for political, economic, social, and educational equality for blacks in Florida. A charter member and the first secretary of Tampa's National Urban League, Beatty was forthright and quite outspoken on many issues. "She did not ask favors— she demanded rights—the same rights for all American citizens." [104] She joined Eartha White, the Florida director of the Anti-lynching Crusaders Committee in 1922, and Mary McLeod Bethune in denouncing lynching.[105] She engaged in a debate on the editorial page of the Tampa *Morning Tribune* with a white reader who opposed the Dyer Anti-Lynching bill because he believed it would protect the " 'bad nigger' " rapists who were "usually of 'high color' and 'high eddication.' " [106] Beatty responded:

> The premium that white men put on their womanhood is worthy of the commendation of any people. Making criminals of hundreds of fathers of the future womanhood of their race who participated in mob murders is rather inconsistent, however. Please let us say further, Mr. Editor, that we do not know any case where educated Negroes have been lynched save in race riots like the ones in Arkansas and Oklahoma, where the blood-

thirsty mob found pleasure in destroying the lives and property of the best Negro citizens as a means of humiliating the entire race. Nor do we understand what is meant by the Negro of 'high color.' Surely, the writer does not refer to mulattoes whose color proves the disregard our Southern white men have had for racial purity and the value of virtuous womanhood even among the Negroes, their humble loyal friends. . . . Yours of peace and civic righteousness.[107]

White, Beatty, and Bethune were also active in politics. Eartha White served as a precinct worker for the Republican party in Jacksonville, headed the Negro Republican Women Voters in 1920, and was state chairperson of the National League of Republican Colored Women in 1928. At one point, White was the only female member of the Duval County Republican Executive Committee.[108] The national Republican party took advantage of Blanche Beatty's speaking ability and influence among blacks. She spoke on behalf of several Republican candidates around the country and in 1924 gave a speech on a Pittsburgh radio station entitled "The National Republican Convention from the American Negro's Viewpoint." She strongly endorsed the Republican platform against lynching and mob violence.[109]

Beatty, Bethune, and White all supported the right of women to vote and encouraged African American women to do so. When women of color were compelled to stand in long lines in the hot sun to register to vote in 1920, Eartha White kept their spirits high by serving them cold lemonade. Her efforts helped ensure that black female registrants outnumbered white women in four Jacksonville wards.[110] In a sense all three women were patronage politicians, dependent upon those in office for support for their programs. Unlike Bethune and White, however, Beatty did not readily accept the policies of whichever party was in power. She remained a staunch Republican throughout her career.[111]

Because of their gender, the three African American women accomplished more than any black male could during their day. They were perceived as less of a threat than black men by the power structure, were allowed to say things that might have gotten a black man lynched or run out of town, and were occasionally praised by whites as outstanding citizens and peacemakers in race relations. Black men who won such praise from whites were generally more accommodating and less vocal in denouncing racism. The men who challenged the injustices and racism faced by blacks and who encouraged other blacks to do the same often lost their jobs or were even beaten or killed, like NAACP president Harry T. Moore.[112]

Bethune, Beatty, White, and hundreds of other strong and independent-minded women helped ameliorate the plight of African Americans in Florida and gave voice to their concerns. Although they were not able to relieve the oppression of segregation and the poverty faced by most black families, they refused to yield to racism. Augusta Savage, Effie Carrie Mitchell Hampton, and others turned deaf ears to those who told them they were powerless because they were black. The contributions of these and countless other, less noted women helped maintain the black family and set in motion after World War II efforts to dismantle segregation.

Although the vast majority of African American women remained mired in poverty and oppressed by segregation, they refused to accept white society's view of them and their people. These women kept alive the hopes and aspirations of black Americans for racial change, accelerated the dialogue within the black community for racial advancement, and, by their labor, maintained some stability in the black family and the black community. Where the future would take them, their families, and members of their race was not clear in 1950, but these women were determined to persevere.

Notes

The author wishes to acknowledge a Black Faculty Support Grant and a Foundation Grant from the Florida State University.

1. *Government and Politics In Florida*, ed. Robert J. Huckshorn (Gainesville: University of Florida Press, 1991), 30–46; U.S. Bureau of the Census, *Negro Population in the United States, 1920–32* (Washington, D.C.: U.S. Government Printing Office, 1935), 15, 46.

2. Compiled from U.S. Bureau of the Census, *Negro Population, 1790–1915*, (Washington, D.C.: U.S. Government Printing Office, 1918); U.S. Bureau of the Census, *Negro Population, 1920–32*; Florida State Department of Agriculture, *The Sixth Census of the State of Florida, 1935* (Winter Park: Orange Press, 1936); Florida State Department of Agriculture, *The Seventh Census of the State of Florida, 1945* (Tallahassee, 1946); U.S. Bureau of the

Census, *Sixteenth Census of the United States, 1940*, vol. 2, *Characteristics of the Population*, part 2, "Reports by States Florida-Iowa" (Washington, D.C.: U.S. Government Printing Office, 1943); U.S. Bureau of the Census, *A Report of the Seventeenth Decennial Census of the United States. Census of Population: 1950*, vol. 2, *Characteristics of the Population*, part 10, "Florida." (Washington, D.C.: U.S. Government Printing Office, 1952).

3. Compiled from U.S. Bureau of the Census, *Negro Population, 1790–1915*; U.S. Bureau of the Census, *Negro Population, 1920–1932*; U.S. Bureau of the Census, *Sixteenth Census, 1940*, vol. 2, part 2; U.S. Bureau of the Census, *Seventeenth Decennial Census, 1950*, vol. 2, part 10, "Florida."

4. Jacqueline Jones, *Labor of Love, Labor of Sorrow: Black Women, Work, and the Family from Slavery to the Present* (New York: Basic Books, 1985), 75.

5. U.S. Bureau of the Census, *Sixteenth Census, 1940*, vol. 2, part 1, "U.S. States Summary," 93.

6. Monroe N. Work, *Negro Year Book: An Annual Encyclopedia of the Negro, 1937–39* (Tuskegee: Negro Year Book Publishing Co., 1937), 63–64.

7. Jones, *Labor of Love*, 85.

8. "Rural nonfarm population" included those who lived outside urban areas but not on farms. U.S. Bureau of the Census, *Statistical Abstract of the United States: 1950* (Washington, D.C.: U.S. Government Printing Office, 1950), 49.

9. U.S. Bureau of the Census, *Negroe Population, 1920–32*, 596, 583; Barbara R. Cotton, *Lamplighters: Black Farm and Home Demonstration Agents in Florida, 1915–65* (Tallahassee: U.S. Department of Agriculture in cooperation with Florida Agricultural and Mechanical University, 1982), 38, 101.

10. Compiled from U.S. Bureau of the Census, *Negro Population, 1920–32*; *Sixteenth Census, 1940*, vol. 2, part 2; *Seventeenth Decennial Census, 1950*, vol. 2, part 10, "Florida."

11. Arthur S. Evans, Jr., and David Lee, *Pearl City, Florida: A Black Community Remembers* (Boca Raton: Florida Atlantic University Press, 1990), 12, 13–14, 20, 21; Martin Richardson, "What the Florida Negro Does," typescript, 1937, Florida Writers Project, P.K. Yonge Library of Florida History, University of Florida, 4, 19; Daisy Jerry, *My Life Story—A Sharecropper's Daughter* (Rochester, N.Y.: Eastern Printing and Publishing Company, 1984), 14.

12. Richardson, "What the Florida Negro Does," 20; Paul Diggs, "Plant City Biographies," typescript, 1939, Florida Writers Project, P.K. Yonge Library of Florida History, University of Florida, 11; St. Augustine *Record*, March 21, 1934, 4; March 22, 1934, 2.

13. Evans and Lee, *Pearl City*, 128, 14–16.

14. Richardson, "What the Florida Negro Does," 20.

15. More than 8,000 of these farm laborers received a salary. U.S. Bureau

of the Census, *Negro Population, 1920–32*, 304, and *Negro Population, 1790–1915*, 521.

16. "Nonwhite" may include Japanese, Chinese, and Indian.

17. Only slightly more than seven hundred were either owners or managers of farms. U.S. Bureau of the Census, *Seventeenth Decennial Census, 1950*, vol. 2, part I, "U.S. Summary," 261.

18. Richardson, "What the Florida Negro Does," 38–39.

19. Ibid., 15.

20. Diggs, "Plant City Biographies," 1–2, 5–6.

21. Ibid., 1–4, 6–7, 9.

22. *Report of General Activities for 1939* (Silver Anniversary Report), Florida Agricultural Extension Service, 89.

23. Ibid.; *Report of General Activities for 1941*, Florida Agricultural Extension Service, 60.

24. Fifty tons to the acre seems unusually high. Richardson, "What the Florida Negro Does," 17–18.

25. *Report of General Activities for 1940*, Florida Agricultural Extension Service, 82; Cotton, *Lamplighters*, 5, 16; *Report of General Activities for 1934*, Cooperative Extension Work in Agriculture and Home Economics, 95.

26. U.S. Bureau of the Census, *Sixteenth Census, 1940*, vol. 2, part 1, "U.S. States Summary," 98.

27. U.S. Bureau of the Census, *A Social-Economic Grouping of the Gainful Workers of the United States, 1930* (Washington, D.C.: U.S. Government Printing Office, 1938), 60–61.

28. U.S. Bureau of the Census, *Seventeenth Decennial Census, 1950*, vol. 2, part 10, "Florida," 237.

29. Personal services included domestic work, hotels and lodging places, laundering, cleaning and dyeing services, and miscellaneous personal services; U.S. Bureau of the Census, *Sixteenth Census, 1940*, vol. 2, part 2, 178–179.

30. U.S. Bureau of the Census, *Seventeenth Decennial Census, 1950*, vol. 2, part 10, "Florida," 243.

31. U.S. Bureau of the Census, *Sixteenth Census, 1940*, vol. 2, part 2, 164–65; *Seventeenth Decennial Census, 1950*, vol. 2, part 10, "Florida," 240.

32. "A Study of Negro Life in Tampa," made at the request of the Tampa Welfare League, the Tampa Urban League, and the Tampa Young Men's Christian Association, March 8–April 13, 1927 (typescript, University of South Florida Library, n.p.); Edward Loring Miller, "Negro Life in Gainesville: A Sociological Study" (M.A. thesis, University of Florida, 1938), 41.

33. Two months after the birth of her son in 1939, white Tallahasseean Hermine Pegram Love was forced to return to work. She hired a black woman for $4 a week to look after her house and child. Two more were hired

in subsequent years, including Estelle Hudnell at $6 a week. Interview with Hermine Pegram Love, September 28, 1992, Tallahassee, Florida; *Jacksonville Looks at Its Negro Community* (Jacksonville: Council of Social Agencies, 1946), 63.

34. Interview with Hermine Pegram Love; "A Study of Negro Life in Tampa," pages not numbered; Jones, *Labor of Love*, 6.

35. "A Study of Negro Life in Tampa," pages not numbered.

36. Madison County Historical Society Annual, 1941; mimeograph, 15–16. Mrs. Rosa Lee Henry, now almost eighty-nine years old, still receives telephone calls and visits from the men and women she helped raise when she worked as a domestic in Tallahassee. Interview with Mrs. Rosa Lee Henry, September 28, 1992, Tallahassee, Florida.

37. U.S. Bureau of the Census, *Seventeenth Decennial Census, 1950*, vol. 2, part 10, "Florida," 240, 243.

38. Interview with Mrs. Rosa Lee Henry, September 28, 1992, Tallahassee, Florida; Jones, *Labor of Love*, 6.

39. "A Study of Negro Life in Tampa," pages not numbered.

40. Ibid.; *Jacksonville Looks at Its Negro Community*, 63.

41. Evans and Lee, *Pearl City*, 14, 30–31.

42. Richardson, "What the Florida Negro Does," 38, 39; U.S. Department of Labor (USDL), Women's Bureau, *Women in Florida Industries* (Washington, D.C.: U.S. Government Printing Office, 1930), 61. The weekly median salary for black women working as hotel elevator operators in 1928–29 was $9.75.

43. USDL, Women's Bureau, *Women in Florida Industries*, 55.

44. Ibid., 61.

45. Richardson, "What the Florida Negro Does," 33–34.

46. Paul Diggs, "A Negro Community—Pierce, Florida," typescript, 1938, Florida Writers Project, Florida Historical Collection, University of South Florida, 1–4; Florida Works Progress Administration, *Florida: A Guide to the Southernmost State* (New York: Oxford University Press, 1939), 94.

47. Richardson, "What the Florida Negro Does," 9.

48. Allison Clay Kistler, "The History and Status of Labor in the Citrus Industry of Florida" (M.A. thesis, University of Florida, 1939), 198, 201.

49. Ibid., 102, 153.

50. Women could be hired at lower wages than men. Kistler, "Labor in the Citrus Industry of Florida," 161, 173.

51. Richardson, "What the Florida Negro Does," 10, 12.

52. White women sectioners and peelers averaged $2.50 a day during the 1930s. It is likely that black women received the equal pay or less than their white counterparts. Kistler, "Labor in the Citrus Industry of Florida," 222–23; Richardson, "What the Florida Negro Does," 10.

53. Interview with Mrs. Lucille Love, September 20, 1992, Quincy, Florida; Ennis Lee Chestang, "The Shade-Grown Cigar Wrapper District of Gadsden County, Florida," Ph.D. diss., Indiana University, 1965, 66.

54. Interview with Mrs. Lucille Love, September 20, 1992, Quincy, Florida.

55. Interview with Mrs. Lucille Love, September 20, 1992, Quincy, Florida.

56. U.S. Bureau of the Census, *Negroe Population, 1920–1932*, 304; Richardson, "What the Florida Negro Does," 38; Archer Campbell, *The Cigar Industry of Tampa*, Bureau of Economic and Business Research, University of Florida, September 1939, 165, 141; "A Study of Negro Life in Tampa," pages not numbered; "Negro Population for Tampa Local Guide," typescript, March 1938, Records of the Works Progress Administration in Tampa, 1938–43, Florida Historical Collection, University of South Florida.

57. *Women in Florida Industries*, 4– 5, 10, 22.

58. Ibid., 25, 34, 50.

59. Ethel L. Best and Ethel Erickson, *A Survey of Laundries and Their Workers in 23 Cities* (Washington, D.C.: U.S. Government Printing Office, 1930), 8; U.S. Bureau of the Census, *Seventeenth Decennial Census, 1950*, vol. 2, part 10, "Florida," 237.

60. USDL, Women's Bureau, *Eleventh Annual Report, 1929* (Washington, D.C.: U.S. Government Printing Office, 1929), 11.

61. U.S. Bureau of the Census, *Negro Population, 1920–1932*, 304, and *Seventeenth Decennial Census, 1950*, vol. 2, part 10, "Florida," 237; *Crisis* 49 (March 1942): 92; Charlene Hunter, "A History of Pensacola's Black Community" (student paper, Fish University, n.d., pages not numbered).

62. Anna May Cleek, "The Development of Negro Education as an Integral Part of Public Education in the State of Florida" (M.A. thesis, University of Cincinnati, 1933), 93; *Biennial Report*, Superintendent of Public Instruction, State of Florida, July 1, 1950–June 30, 1952, 262.

63. "A Study of Negro Life In Tampa," pages not numbered.

64. D. E. Williams, A. R. Ward, and Hal G. Lewis, "A Study of Economic Status of Negro Teachers," Bulletin no. 10, Bureau of Educational Research, University of Florida, Gainesville, June 1939, 1–2.

65. Barbara H. Walch, "Sallye B. Mathis and Mary L. Singleton: Black Pioneers on the Jacksonville, Florida, City Council" (M.A. thesis, University of Florida, 1988), 75–76; J. Irving Scott, *The Education of Black People in Florida* (Philadelphia: Dorrance & Company, 1974), 72, 74, 77–78; *Crisis* 50 (May 1943): 151; Gilbert L. Porter and Leedell W. Neyland, *History of the Florida State Teachers Association* (Washington, D.C.: National Education Association of the United States, 1977), 69.

66. J. M. Johnson, "Negro History, Ocala," typescript, 1936, Florida

Writers Project, P. K. Yonge Library of Florida History, University of Florida, 4– 5; *Crisis* 12 (May 1916): 12.

67. U.S. Bureau of the Census, *Seventeenth Decennial Census, 1950*, vol. 2, part 1, "U.S. Summary," 278, 402. U.S. Bureau of the Census, *Negro Population, 1920–1932*, 304; U.S. Bureau of the Census, *Seventeenth Decennial Census, 1950*, vol. 2, part 10, "Florida," 237, 240.

68. *Crisis* 49 (March 1942): 85, (January 1942): 33; U.S. Bureau of the Census, *Seventeenth Decennial Census, 1950*, vol. 2, part 10, "Florida," 237.

69. "A Study of Negro Life In Tampa," pages not numbered; Lottie Montgomery Clark, "Negro Women Leaders of Florida," M.A. thesis, Florida State University, 1942, 86–87.

70. Tampa Mayor R. E. L. Clancey described Frye as one of Tampa's outstanding citizens. In 1991 a nine-floor patient care wing was renamed the Clara Frye Pavilion at Tampa General Hospital. Tampa *Tribune*, February 24, 1991, and April 5, 1959.

71. U.S. Bureau of the Census, *Negro Population, 1920–1932*, 293, and *Seventeenth Decennial Census, 1950*, vol. 2, part 10, "Florida," 237, 240, 243; *The Negro Handbook, 1946–47*, ed. Florence Murray (New York: Current Books, Inc., 1947), 79–80, 86; U.S. Bureau of the Census, *Seventeenth Decennial Census, 1950*, vol. 2, part 1, "U.S. Summary," 278.

72. Estelle Bonner worked for the St. Johns County Welfare Federation in 1931. In January 1931 alone she made 244 visits in the black community. In addition, Bonner conducted six home hygiene classes and made ten trips into rural areas of the county. St. Augustine *Record*, February 11, 1931.

73. Warren M. Banner, "Cultural and Economic Survey, Tampa, Florida," typescript, Advisory Committee, Tampa Urban League, 1953, 18, 41.

74. Miller, "Negro Life in Gainesville," 29; Banner, "Cultural and Economic Survey, Tampa," 43; U.S. Bureau of the Census, *Seventeenth Decennial Census, 1950*, vol. 2, part 10, Florida, 237.

75. "A Study of Negro Life in Tampa," pages not numbered.

76. Debra Anne Susie, *In the Way of Our Grandmothers: A Cultural View of Twentieth-Century Midwifery in Florida* (Athens: University of Georgia Press, 1988), 33, 38–39, 41, 49; "A Study of Negro Life in Tampa," pages not numbered; Banner, "Cultural and Economic Survey, Tampa," 36.

77. Susie, *In the Way of Our Grandmothers*, 42–43.

78. Ibid., 47.

79. Banner, "Cultural and Economic Survey, Tampa," 36; Evans and Lee, *Pearl City*, 60; *Contributions of Black Women to America*, ed. Marianna W. Davis (Columbia, S.C.: Kenday Press, 1982), 2:360. African American midwives included Mary Jenkins of Pearl City, who delivered more than a hundred black and white babies, and Marie Francis Jones, who claimed to

have delivered more than 40,000 babies during her thirty-two-year career.

80. *Crisis* 49 (January 1942): 18; Walch, "Sallye B. Mathis and Mary L. Singleton," 52; *Crisis* 46 (December 1939): 381.

81. Martin Richardson, "Pensacola Art," typescript, n.d., Florida Writers Project, P. K. Yonge Library of Florida History, University of Florida, 6.

82. Program of the Twelfth Annual Session of the Florida Negro Embalmers and Funeral Directors Association, May 5–7, 1936, Tampa, Florida; *Crisis* 49 (January 1942): 27.

83. *Crisis* 49 (January 1942): 18, 13, 11.

84. Banner, "Cultural and Economic Survey, Tampa," 147; *Crisis* 49 (April 1942): 122; Clark, "Negro Women Leaders of Florida," 94.

85. "A Study of Negro Life In Tampa," pages not numbered.

86. *The Evolution of Susan Prim: A Story Developed by the Lincoln High and Elementary School Faculties in Cooperation with the Staff of the Secondary School Study of the Association of Colleges and Secondary Schools for Negroes* (Tallahassee: Lincoln High School, 1945), 39.

87. Richardson, "What the Florida Negro Does," 43; *Report of General Activities for 1942*, Florida Agricultural Extension Service, 59; Works Progress Administration, *Florida: A Guide to the Southernmost State*, 417.

88. Martin Richardson, "Unusual Negro Occupations," typescript, 1937, Florida Writers Project, Florida Historical Collection, University of South Florida, 8–9; Richardson, "What the Florida Negro Does," 41–42.

89. Miller, "Negro Life In Gainesville," 160.

90. *Crisis* 49 (January 1942): 29, 32.

91. U.S. Bureau of the Census, *Negro Population, 1920–32*, 376.

92. *Jacksonville Looks at Its Negro Community*, 2, 3; National Office of Vital Statistics, *Vital Statistics of the United States, 1947*, part 2 (Washington, D.C.: U.S. Government Printing Office, 1949), 457.

93. Clark, "Negro Women Leaders of Florida," 83–86.

94. Ibid., 66; *Tampa Tribune*, February 26, 1983.

95. Clark, "Negro Women Leaders of Florida," 66–67; *Tampa Tribune*, July 20, 1983; *Florida Sentinel Bulletin*, February 5, 1983, Blanche Armwood Comprehensive High School Dedication Program, February 10, 1985, Blanche Armwood Papers, University of South Florida.

96. Wilson Rice, "Negro Churches," typescript, 1936, Florida Writers Project, Florida Historical Collection, University of South Florida, 14; Paul Diggs, "Little Angel of Ashly Street—Miss Eartha M. M. White," typescript, 1938, Florida Writers Project, Florida Historical Collection, University of South Florida; *Crisis* 49 (September 1942): 289, (January 1942): 19.

97. *Crisis* 33 (February 1927): 194.

98. *Crisis* 36 (January 1929): 14.

99. Walch, "Sallye B. Mathis and Mary L. Singleton," 54.

100. Florida Supreme Court, *Southern Reporter*, 2d series 47 (St. Paul: West Publishing Co., 1951), 619–20.

101. Walch, "Sallye B. Mathis and Mary L. Singleton," 42, 44, 46; *Crisis* 46 (July 1939): 216, 47 (February 1940): 53.

102. *New York Times*, February 18, 1931, in Mary McLeod Bethune Papers, Amistad Research Center, Tulane University, New Orleans.

103. Ibid.; paper written by Mary McLeod Bethune, n.d., Mary McLeod Bethune Papers. When whites attended programs at Bethune-Cookman College in Daytona Beach, they found no special seats reserved for their use and sat among blacks in the audience. *Philadelphia Tribune*, June 6, 1935, in Mary McLeod Bethune Papers.

104. Clark, "Negro Women Leaders of Florida," 63, 67, 70–71.

105. Beatty helped to organize the Anti-Lynching Crusaders in 1922. *Tampa Tribune*, February 26, 1983; Walch, "Sallye B. Mathis and Mary L. Singleton," 52. See "Interracial Cooperation In Florida" in Mary McLeod Bethune Papers.

106. *Crisis* 25 (February 1923): 183.

107. *Ibid.*

108. Walch, "Sallye B. Mathis and Mary L. Singleton," 47–48.

109. Clark, "Negro Women Leaders of Florida," 70; *Tampa Tribune*, February 26, 1983.

110. Walch, "Sallye B. Mathis and Mary L. Singleton," 46–47; *Crisis* 21 (January 1921): 109.

111. Walch, "Sallye B. Mathis and Mary L. Singleton," 48; *Tampa Tribune*, February 26, 1983.

112. For more details about the murder of Harry T. Moore, see Caroline Emmons Poore, "Striking the First Blow: Harry T. Moore and the Fight for Black Equality in Florida" (M.A. thesis, Florida State University, 1992). Moore and his wife were silenced on Christmas Day, 1951, when a bomb, set by white racists, exploded under the bedroom of his home in Mims, Florida.

◇ 11

Under a Double Burden
Florida's Black Feeble-Minded, 1920–1957

Steven Noll

THE DECEMBER 19, 1921, edition of the *Gainesville Sun* proudly reported in a full-page article that the newly opened Florida Farm Colony for Epileptic and Feeble-Minded would make a "quaint and beautiful picture." The institution opened as an all-white facility but administrators planned a "negro department . . . [which] will be located on the same tract of land about one mile from the white group." [1] In spite of this implied promise of erecting facilities for African American individuals on the grounds of Florida Farm Colony, the state of Florida took little notice of its black feeble-minded population. Fourteen years after the *Sun* article, Dr. J. H. Colson, the superintendent of the Florida Farm Colony, answered an application regarding admission for a black patient this way: "I regret to advise that we have no provisions for the care of colored patients at the Colony." [2] Indeed, throughout the first half of the twentieth century, African American feeble-minded residents of Florida suffered under the double burden of a debilitating mental condition and life within a system of enforced racial segregation.

From 1921 to 1957, Florida Farm Colony for Epileptic and Feeble-Minded operated as the state's only public institution for the care and training of persons labeled feeble-minded, mentally defective, or mentally deficient. [3] For all but the last four of those years, the facility served only white patients. In 1953, black patients were finally admitted to the Farm Colony, but only in segregated facilities located at the back of the institution's grounds. Four years later, the state reached a turning point in its institutionalized treatment of mentally handicapped individuals. In 1958 state officials renamed the colony "Sunland Training Center," and more important, the legislature authorized the establishment of a second public institution in Fort Myers. With that development, Florida Farm Colony was no longer the centerpiece of the state's mental retardation policy.

Florida's lack of concern about its black feeble-minded population reflected region-wide attitudes about the efficacy of providing facilities for their care and training. In the fifteen-year period from 1910 to 1925, nine southern states, including Florida, opened new institutions to house mentally handicapped individuals, and another state, Kentucky, enlarged and revamped drastically its existing structure. Only two of these facilities, the Kentucky Feeble-Minded Institute in Frankfort and the Louisiana State Training School in Alexandria, housed feeble-minded residents of both races, albeit in segregated quarters (see table 1). In 1939 Virginia became the only southern state to operate a separate institution "for the purpose of caring for and training mentally defective Negroes" when it opened the Petersburg State Colony.[4] The remaining seven states, again including Florida, either housed African American feeble-minded individuals in institutions designed for the care of the black insane or made no provisions at all for their care and training. That exclusionary policy finally ended by the early 1950s, when all these states finally admitted black patients into their institutions, albeit in limited numbers and in segregated facilities.

The treatment of black patients in institutions for the feeble-minded such as Florida Farm Colony generally followed the patterns of facilities throughout the South that were designed for the insane and mentally ill. Virginia's Eastern State Hospital, founded in 1773 as the first public mental hospital in what would become the United States, admitted its first free black patient only a year after its opening. In 1846, the Virginia legislature voted to allow slaves admission to Eastern State in apparently nonsegregated quarters. This episode in racial liberalism was short-lived, however. By 1869 blacks were excluded from the institution and shipped to the new Central State Hospital in Petersburg, which housed only African American patients.[5] The segregation of black mental patients reflected the hardening of racial attitudes in the postbellum South in the face

Table 1. Institutions in the South for the Feeble-Minded

State	Institution	First White Patients	First Black Patients
Alabama	Partlow State School for Mental Defectives, Tuscaloosa	1919	1947
Florida	Florida Farm Colony for Epileptic and Feeble-Minded, Gainesville	1921	1953
Georgia	Georgia Training School for Mental Defectives, Gracewood	1921	1951
Kentucky	State Institution for the Feeble-Minded, Frankfort	1860	1887
Louisiana	State Colony and Training School, Alexandria	1922	1922
Mississippi	Ellisville State School, Ellisville	1923	1951
North Carolina	Caswell Training School, Kinston	1914	1948
South Carolina	State Training School, Clinton	1920	1950
Tennessee	State Home & Training School for Feeble-Minded Persons, Donelson	1923	1953
Virginia	Lynchburg State Colony, Colony	1914[1]	1961
	Petersburg State Colony, Petersburg	1961	1939[2]

[1] Colony opened in 1908 as an institution for epileptic persons. Feeble-minded individuals were admitted in 1914.
[2] Petersburg was the South's only separate institution for black patients.

of emancipation. No southern institution allowed integrated wards, and black patients remained isolated in separate wings and facilities. In Florida, the sprawling mental hospital in Chattahoochee, founded in 1867, relegated blacks to wards at the rear of the institution. By the 1920s, institutional segregation led Virginia, North Carolina, and South Carolina to open separate institutions for black mental patients. In a period when southern states provided a level of mental health care deemed "medieval" by a prominent southern psychiatrist, blacks received the lowest percentage of funding.[6]

Southern treatment of feeble-minded individuals mirrored white attitudes toward blacks in the early years of the twentieth century. Historian George Fredrickson's observation concerning upper-class whites and their relationship to black southerners could easily have been applied to the organizers and advocates of southern institutions for the feeble-minded. "This conservative ethos," Fredrickson argued, "promoted Christian charity, noblesse oblige, and a quasiparental form of guardianship over people who were thought of as inherently child-like."[7] Of course, this benevolent paternalism had another, darker side. Whites also viewed blacks as atavistic brutes, controlled by emotions and driven to sexual excess.

The two sides of this paternalist equation were also applied to feeble-minded individuals. In 1912 Dr. Ira Hardy, the first superintendent of North Carolina's Caswell Training School for the Feeble-Minded, addressed the Southern Medical Association in Jacksonville, Florida. He exorted Floridians to follow North Carolina's example and establish an institution for the feeble-minded as protection for society. "Take wise and prompt measures to prevent as well as mitigate," he warned, "the great evils which already accrue or may accrue from the feeble-mindedness in your midst, so as to prevent its expression in pauperism, harlotry, and crime."[8]

Florida legislators followed Hardy's admonitions and passed a bill in April 1919 establishing the Florida Farm Colony for Epileptic and Feeble-Minded, to be located on the outskirts of Gainesville. The institution admitted its first patients, all of whom were white, in November 1921.[9] While institutions such as the Farm Colony often served as agencies of social control, superintendents saw another function. Institutions offered the opportunity, according to Farm Colony superintendent Dr. J. H. Hodges in a 1922 speech, "to take these feeble-minded children while they are still young and trainable and guard their habits . . . , and if possible, teach them to do something useful."[10]

As the southern color line solidified in the first two decades of the twentieth century, the state officials responsible for the establishment of Florida Farm Colony ignored the needs and concerns of black residents. In a state where spending for general social services was inconsequential and where race consistently influenced state spending policies, funding for the problems created by black feeble-minded individuals simply was not made available. Feeble-minded black persons involved in antisocial or criminal behavior were often adjudicated through the criminal justice system and not considered for placement in Florida Farm Colony. Others, usually those causing no community problems, were provided for through African American charities and churches, were placed in the segregated back wards of the state insane asylum at Chattahoochee, or were simply cared for—or not cared for—at home by parents or other family members.

Public apathy and legislative penury toward the feeble-minded generally, and toward feeble-minded blacks specifically, frustrated the institutional leaders and social workers concerned about protection for and from these persons. Inability to define policy goals clearly, as well as the fetters of a strictly segregated society, characterized Florida's public policy for the African American feeble-minded during the first sixty years of the twentieth century.[11]

By the second decade of the twentieth century, southern states, following their northern counterparts, established separate institutions for individuals labeled as feeble-minded. This trend represented both the increasing specialization and professionalization within the mental health field and the growing national fear of the threat posed by feeble-minded individuals. The movement to establish feeble-minded institutions was anchored firmly to Progressive era beliefs in the uses of empirical scientific methodology and the efficacy of concerted state action to ameliorate social ills.[12] The rediscovery of Mendelian genetics in 1900 and the implications of Francis Galton's eugenic theories led many mental health professionals to call for permanent segregation of those whom a Georgia physician deemed "human rubbish."[13] "Such colonies are considered necessary by all enlightened countries," concluded the Florida Farm Colony's 1921–1922 Biennial Report, "as it is now well known that a large part of crime, immorality, and destitution is due to this cause."[14] While sometimes couched in humanitarian terms, the movement to establish institutions for the feebleminded clearly reflected a concern for social order.

Floridians involved in the movement to institutionalize feeble-minded individuals did not express this concern for social control in explicit racial terms. The apocalyptic expressions of physicians and superintendents concerning the "menace of the feeble-minded" rarely, if ever, mentioned race. In fact, at the institution's founding in 1921, it was, according to Superintendent Hodges, "expected that these [facilities] will be provided for at a later date in a separate colony, situated on the same tract of land, about one mile distant from the white colony." [15] However, the establishment of rigid racial barriers in the 1890s and 1900s, which left the South as two separate and distinct societies, allowed white Florida state officials to conveniently forget Hodges's expectations. The superintendent of the South Carolina Training School (that state's only institution for the feeble-minded) expressed the belief in racial separation cogently in 1937 when he made the presidential address to the American Association on Mental Deficiency. "Tradition, custom, political determination, as well as other economic and social practices have set apart the colored people from the whites." [16] The policy of racial separation allowed white Floridians, and white southerners in general, to ignore the plight of feeble-minded black individuals. With control enforced by legalized segregation, there appeared little need to further control black deviants by way of institutions for the feeble-minded.

The development of institutions for the feeble-minded was not simply an exercise in social control, however. Humanitarian concern for the "unfortunate" feeble-minded individual, both black and white, also seemed important. Of course, by protecting "undesirables" within an institution, society itself would be protected, according to a North Carolina superintendent, from their "ever-increasing hordes." [17]

In the 1910s, the Southern Sociological Congress, a prime example of formalized Southern humanitarianism, sponsored a forum where progressive southerners could express concern about social problems besetting their region. In a volume of its first-year proceedings in 1912, entitled appropriately *The Call of the New South*, the congress set out its goals for social uplift in the South. It called for "the proper care and treatment . . . of the feeble-minded," as well as "the solving of the race question in a spirit of helpfulness to the negro," but made no mention of the two as interrelated problems. In the eight-year lifespan of the congress, no author noted the special needs of the black feeble-minded, or problems caused particularly by their presence.[18]

Progressive reform leaders in Florida and the rest of the South, therefore, established institutions for the feeble-minded as a means of protection both for and from the individuals they were expected to house. During a time period in which a North Carolina official announced that "society must look upon germ plasm as belonging to society, not solely to the individual who carries it," individual rights were subsumed under society's needs.[19] In Florida, separation of the races appeared paramount among societal needs. This separation carried over into the institutionalization of the feeble-minded.

After the Florida Farm Colony for Feeble-Minded and Epileptic opened its doors to white patients in 1921, plans to house black patients in a segregated facility gradually collapsed. On December 19, 1921, the *Gainesville Sun* reported, "As yet, no funds have been provided for the negro department."[20] Thereafter, no legislature until the 1950s appropriated monies for the anticipated black facilities. Legislators, bureaucrats, and institutional administrators made no mention of the desirability of serving black patients, or of the needs of the black feeble-minded population of the state. In 1945, a Special Survey, authorized by the legislature and Governor Millard Caldwell to investigate conditions at the Farm Colony, concluded with a series of ten recommendations for the facility's improvement, but made no mention of the lack of facilities for black patients nor gave any suggestions for ameliorating this problem.[21]

Florida, then, provides an example of one southern strategy for the treatment, or rather the nontreatment, of feeble-minded blacks. Florida Farm Colony, the state's only public institution for feeble-minded individuals in the first half of the twentieth century, made no provisions at all for black patients. In spite of the earlier plans for a "negro unit" on the grounds of the institution, Superintendent Dr. J. Maxey Dell simply reported in the institution's 1939 annual report that "there are no facilities for the care of colored patients."[22]

This lack of facilities, explicitly stated but codified in neither statute nor administrative regulation, was tested by Florida county and juvenile court judges. Between the years 1929 and 1940, these jurists, authorized under Florida law to implement commitments to the Farm Colony, initiated commitment proceedings for at least twenty-nine blacks to the institution.[23] As a matter of course, superintendents did not accept any of them into Florida Farm Colony. In rejecting an application regarding a black Tampa youth in 1939, Superintendent Dell wrote Tampa's chief probation officer that "we are not in a position to admit any colored cases to the institution."[24] Two years later, Dell succinctly addressed the issue of black admissions for the first time in his official *Biennial Report*: "There are no facilities for the care of colored patients." He offered no further explanation or elaboration.[25]

To Dell and the two previous Florida Farm Colony superintendents, the lack of facilities for black patients was singularly unimportant. There was little or no mention of it in their correspondence, their speeches, or their official reports. When confronted with the issue, as when they denied commitment applications for black patients, they simply stated that their facility didn't accept black patients. They did not feel the need to either justify the ban or question it. This nondiscussion of the admission of African American patients represented a complete victory for the proponents of segregation. To the officials at the Florida Farm Colony, black Floridians simply functioned in another world—a world with which officials had little contact and even less interest.

State statutes authorized county judges to initiate commitment proceedings to state institutions, including Florida Farm Colony, at the behest of family members, school officials, or representative of social service agencies such as county welfare offices or probation departments. Many commitment requests to the institution for white persons concerned individuals involved in petty crimes, immorality, and status offenses. In his 1929 *Biennial Report*, Superintendent Hodges admonished judges that "we cannot agree that the institution should be used for unruly children who are not feeble-minded, however much of a problem they may be in the community."[26]

Hodges's expression of concern did not apply, however, to those African Americans for whom commitment was requested. The majority of those individuals appeared quite low in functional abilities and more a strain on family dynamics and structure than a problem either in school or in the streets. Sociologist Bernard Farber would label these persons "incompetent."[27] These black youths were not, then, delinquents to be committed to the Florida Farm Colony as an alternative to some other form of incarceration or punishment. Rather, institutionalization was sought as either a form of relief for beleaguered families or as a means of removing a child from a difficult or possibly abusive home situation.

A 1937 application regarding a twelve-year-old African American girl from Orange County seems typical. The document reported that the girl could not "feed herself, or sit, or walk, or talk." It also revealed that she was not "troublesome" but "as she grows older, [she] is becoming more and more of a problem to the family. This is particularly trying during the school months as the mother cannot leave her alone while the other children are in school." Replying in coldly bureaucratic terms, Superintendent Dell wrote that "this has been more or less a community problem and I am sorry that we are not able to help you further in regard to same." Dell concluded by stating that "there is no Statewide place for such patients."[28] The Florida Farm Colony provided no follow-up studies for such rejected commitment cases, either black or white, so we have no knowledge of the eventual disposition of the adolescent girl. The "community" that Dell mentions, however, is undoubtedly the black community of Orange County. Reading Dell's answer to the commitment request, one sees the racial bifurcation of the Depression-era South. The African American community would handle their feeble-minded cases, Florida Farm Colony would handle white cases, and the two worlds would not be allowed to intersect.

A year after the Orange County commitment request, a Pinellas County judge sought commitment for an even more distressing case. The City of Clearwater's chief probation officer reported to Dell that "we have in our possession commitment papers for one K. L., colored age 10. The situation is pitiful as well as tragical. We found this child anchored with rope to an iron post in the yard. In some way the family is taking care of her at night. She has never been to school, cannot talk understandingly, and is a pronounced subject for your institution." Again, Dell curtly responded that "we cannot take colored patients here."[29]

The incompetent black individuals who were refused admission to Florida Farm Colony posed no threat to the social order of the state of Florida. Far from functioning as an instrument of social control in these cases, the institution would have served both as a last resort for beleaguered black families strapped with the burdens of a handicapped child and a place of refuge for children abused by parents unable to cope. An application by parents for their ten-year-old boy, initiated through the Hillsborough County Court, exemplified the former rationale. The boy did not appear troublesome, but had "had convulsions every night for four years." The parents, the application continued, "appear tired and can no longer handle the child." Superintendent Dell responded to the application in the manner that Farm Colony superintendents handled all black commitment requests: "We do not accept colored patients at the Colony." [30]

While Florida made no provisions at all for African American feeble-minded individuals at Florida Farm Colony prior to 1953, it did admit a few feeble-minded blacks to the Florida Hospital for the Insane, located in Chattahoochee, which housed patients of both races in segregated wards. Those black feeble-minded individuals admitted to Chattahoochee appeared to be of a higher intellectual level and more likely to be involved in criminal offenses than the individuals for whom commitment to Florida Farm Colony was recommended. [31] Chattahoochee officials, reflecting early-twentieth-century medical and psychological wisdom, opposed the housing of insane and feeble-minded patients in one facility. The 1915–1916 *Biennial Report* of the Florida Hospital for the Insane in Chatahoochee concluded that "we must find a way to remove the feeble-minded individuals from the hospital. They do not respond to treatment in the same way as our other patients." [32] In spite of such professional concerns, however, Florida made no efforts to place black feeble-minded persons in a specialized institution such as the Florida Farm Colony.

During the 1930s, the federal government began to intervene in the previously state-controlled world of care for the feeble-minded. Florida welcomed the presence of funds from Washington, as the Depression-ravaged state budget could not provide for maintaining and improving the facilities at the Farm Colony. The colony erected several new wards and a hospital from 1937 to 1939 under the auspices of funds from the WPA and PWA. [33] Initially at least, the federal dollars did not bring with them desegregation mandates, primarily because Franklin Roosevelt's New Deal coalition depended on the votes of white southern politicians.

The inroads made by federal agencies in the 1930s, however, enabled the national government to play a more prominent role in southern life generally. With federal involvement came the possibility of forced change from the outside. The confining structures of a southern caste society based totally on race began to break down slowly, almost inperceptibly, during the 1930s as the initial stirrings of an activist federal government made small inroads into the legalized system of segregation.[34] The effects of government policy and the liberating rhetoric of World War II quickened the pace of racial change even more. President Truman's 1948 decision to desegregate the armed forces shook the segregated South to its very foundations. U.S. Supreme Court cases in the 1940s and in 1950 gradually dismantled white-only primaries and some forms of segregated higher education.[35]

In this atmosphere of federally directed change, state bureaucrats and Farm Colony officials made the decision to allow African American patients into the institution. Yet, it was a determination reached with little public fanfare. The seeming lack of importance that institutional staff placed on this momentous change masked the conflicts between state officials over how to comply with approaching federal desegregation mandates. On the one hand, the belated admission of a small number of African American patients to separate facilities within the Farm Colony simply verified the commitments of white Floridians to a segregated society in the early 1950s. Conversely, however, the mere fact that African Americans were finally admitted to Florida Farm Colony after thirty-two years of systematic exclusion opened cracks in that caste society that would eventually lead to its demise.

Florida Farm Colony records first mention of the need for facilities for African American patients in the 1949 *Biennial Report* of Superintendent Raymond Philips. Philips, appointed in 1945 as the first nonmedical superintendent of the colony, had worked as the institution's business manager since 1932. A tireless crusader for the facility and an excellent legislative lobbyist, Philips oversaw the Farm Colony's rapid expansion during the late 1940s and 1950s. Philips viewed the admission of African American patients as part of the larger process of institutional expansion and improvement. After making the usual statement in his *Biennial Report* that "there are no facilities for the care of colored patients," Philips reported, "A recommendation has already been made by the State Budget Commission for an appropriation of $200,000 for the establishment of a negro unit at the Farm Colony. This is definitely a step in the right direction, as there are no State facilities for the Negro mentally deficient at this time." [36]

Philips's desire to admit African American patients was influenced by a major survey of Florida's entire mental health programming, undertaken by the U.S. Public Health Services at the request of Governor Fuller Warren. The survey, conducted in the summer of 1949 by Dr. Riley Guthrie, a specialist in mental hygiene, recommended a series of fifteen steps to improve Florida's care of feeble-minded patients. Number 12 on the list was: "Provisions should be made for the care and training of Negroes who are mentally defective or epileptic." [37] The report's findings were disseminated widely throughout the state. The February 1950 issue of the *Newsletter of the Mental Health Society of Southeast Florida* reported, in commenting on the Guthrie Report, "We fail to provide for Negro children who are mental defectives and epileptics. They are chained up at home and Negroes comprise 25 percent of our [total state] population." [38]

Philips's request gained even more credence with the publication of the 1951 *Report of the Florida Children's Commission*. The authors of the annual report, which in previous editions had made no mention of the need for black facilities at the Farm Colony, concluded, "Citizens showed deep concern that Florida made no institutional provision for these [African American] children. We recommend 150 beds for Negro children as a practical first step towards adequate institutional care for Florida's mentally deficient children." [39]

The addition of black units for Florida Farm Colony took place in a spurt of building on the facility grounds, raising the institutional population from approximately five hundred in 1945 to more than 1,200 by 1957. In addition to the anticipated construction of the units for blacks, Philips also lowered the age of admission for patients from six years to birth when nursery facilities were built on the institution's grounds. Philips viewed the addition of black wards as but one piece of the larger expansion plans. "The state is definitely behind in its provision of proper and adequate facilities," he reported in 1951. "Any plan for expansion should most certainly include facilities for negro persons." [40] By 1955 Philips was asking the legislature for $2.4 million in funds to increase the Farm Colony's size to 2,000. Fully behind Philips's ambitious plans, the legislature appropriated all but $200,000 of the request for the expansion program. [41] Florida Farm Colony, soon to be renamed Sunland Training Center, had entered a new phase of its existence.

The Board of Commissioners of State Institutions, the state body overseeing the Farm Colony, voted in its October 2, 1951, meeting to construct "five negro low-grade buildings" at the facility. [42] Philips pushed for this addition as a major part of his ambitious expansion plans. In a September 1951 address to the Gainesville Kiwanis Club, Philips publicly announced plans for an $890,000 building program to include "a negro unit to house about 100 persons, . . . [and] the construction of three more white wards for 120 additional patients." [43] Expanding on these comments in his 1953 *Biennial Report*, Philips stated that the funding for the black wards would include monies for "four ward buildings . . . [to house] approximately 150 colored patients [as well as] two wings to be added to the Hospital and Clinic to provide care for Negroes." Philips added, "Applications for Negroes are now being received for patients to be admitted when the buildings are opened. . . . [They] indicate that the approximately 150 beds already provided will be filled very rapidly." [44]

The black wards provided a new experience for the rapidly expanding institution. Philips needed help in the development of these new facilities, as he had never worked with African American patients before. He turned to the superintendents of similar southern institutions, who since the end of World War II had overseen the admission of black patients into segregated wards of their facilities. In July 1952, Philips wrote to the Board of Commissioners suggesting that "a visit to two or three institutions for negro defectives in the south would be very helpful to me in setting up our program here for our Negro Unit. . . . These visits would probably include institutions in Alabama, Mississippi, and possibly Georgia or South Carolina." The board approved Philips's request and he visited Partlow State School in Alabama, Ellisville State School in Mississippi, and Georgia's Gracewood facility in August and September 1952. [45]

On July 15, 1953, the Negro Unit of Florida Farm Colony admitted its first fifteen patients. Located at the back of the institution's grounds, the unit was a self-contained cluster of four buildings "of brick and concrete construction." Food served in the dining room in each ward was cooked in a central kitchen built exclusively for the "colored" unit. In addition to the initial admissions, Philips had a "waiting list of approximately 80 Negroes at this time." Separate ward space had been reserved for African Americans at the Farm Colony hospital and work had already started on a "small school for the Negroes," to be located next to the black wards. Ten employees, all black, had been hired to work on the new wards, and Philips reported that "more will be added later as the number of Negroe patients is increased." Philips was quite careful in his public pronouncements to tie the addition of the $195,000 African American wards to more general expansion, "an overall capital improvement program . . . [of] $890,000 to improve the institution." [46]

The admission of African American patients to Florida Farm Colony did not take place in a political vacuum. Institutional officials and state bureaucrats were aware of the growing concern about equalization of treatment for blacks. The 1896 U.S. Supreme Court ruling in *Plessy v. Ferguson* had held that segregation was permissible as long as the same general rights, such as riding on a train or receiving an education, were applied to both races. [47] By 1950, however, the decision itself, as well as the doctrine of "separate but equal" that underlay it, was under attack by African American plaintiffs who held that segregation was inherently unequal and should be set aside.

By systematically denying any services to black individuals simply by virtue of their race, state officials and Farm Colony administrators had relied on a policy that was legally untenable by the early 1950s. No lawsuits on behalf of potential black patients were ever filed, but state officials saw the direction the legal winds were blowing. They opened Florida Farm Colony to black patients as a sign of the state's willingness to accommodate racial integration. As the first black patients arrived, Philips remarked that "the addition of Negro facilities to the Farm Colony is another step in the state's plan to provide equal facilities for the two races." [48] In the broader picture of state policy, however, the Farm Colony decision seemed exceedingly insignificant—a small bone thrown to mollify the advocates of integration.

On the major issues of public schools and public accommodations, Florida officials remained steadfast in their support of segregation.[49]

The initial flood of interest in the admission of blacks to the Farm Colony quickly faded. Philips made no mention of the black facilities in his biennial reports except to acknowledge their existence. The minutes of the meetings of the Board of Commissioners overseeing the institution also make little mention of the black wards, except periodically to approve the addition of more buildings for the black facilities.[50] The *Gainesville Sun* made only one mention of the newly opened black units in its articles on the Florida Farm Colony from 1953 to 1957. The residents at the Negro Unit became simply patients at the colony who happened to be black. In a region where race was all-important, the lack of attention paid to it at the colony can best be demonstrated by monthly average attendance figures gathered by institutional staff for statistical purposes. On these sheets, reporting of patients was aggregately broken down by sex only, not by race. Within the confines of Florida Farm Colony, staff considered black patients as feeble-minded first and as members of a racial category second.[51]

With that said, it must be remembered that Florida Farm Colony remained a profoundly segregated institution after the admission of black patients. African American patients attended their own school, swam in their own pool, ate food prepared in separate kitchens, and participated in separate recreational activities. By 1954, when the population of the Negro Unit had increased to 119, the school there had enrolled six pupils, four males and two females. Two years later, the unit population exceeded two hundred and the school population had increased to twenty-six. The black students participated in the same activities as their white counterparts—producing mats, rugs, belts, and tea towels for use and sale, learning simple academic skills such as basic arithmetic and letter recognition, and participating in community activities. Of course, African American students had to confront the fetters of a segregated society outside the gates of the colony. When they participated in a high school homecoming activity, it was that of Lincoln High School, Gainesville's black secondary school. Their Christmas pageants were held for the black patients only, in the small multipurpose room at the black school instead of the main auditorium at the white school.[52] Though a part of the routine at Florida Farm Colony, African American patients remained unseen and separate. The dual burdens of being black and feeble-minded weighed heavily upon the African American patients at Florida Farm Colony.

In the first forty-five years of its existence, Florida Farm Colony had provided almost nothing in the way of care and training for blacks. Only in the last four years did the colony even admit African Americans, and then only in segregated quarters. Living in a state beset by endemic poverty and low social welfare expenditures, black feebleminded individuals and their families suffered more than most. The contours of a strict caste society based on race denied all but the minimum humanitarian care within institutional facilities. Trapped by a system of institutions that either treated them as deviants, trained them for increasingly obsolete occupations, or ignored them, feeble-minded African Americans and their families were left to fend for themselves. A 1926 special bulletin of the North Carolina State Board of Charities and Public Welfare accurately summarized the state of Florida's position during this entire era regarding mentally handicapped blacks. The problem of feeble-mindedness, the report concluded, "is inherently a question for the Negro to solve for himself." [53]

Notes

1. *Gainesville Sun*, December 19, 1921, 3. Feeble-mindedness is a condition roughly analogous to the 1993 category of mental handicap or mental retardation. The definition of feeble-mindedness could be quite vague, allowing for many different interpretations of the handicap, which often led to institutions serving a population of miscellaneous deviants instead of a strictly defined group of feeble-minded individuals. For the effect of this phenomenon on southern institutions for the feeble-minded, see Steven Noll, " 'From Far More Different Angles': Institutions for the Mentally Retarded in the South, 1900–1940" (paper presented at the 1988 Annual Meeting of the Southern Historical Association, Norfolk, Virginia).

2. Dr. J. H. Colson to E. C. Bogue, April 16, 1935, Superintendent's Correspondence, Vault files, Tacachale Community. Sunland Center in Gainesville was renamed Tacachale Community in 1991. It is presently serving a population of approximately five hundred.

3. The terms "feeble-minded," "mentally defective," and "mentally deficient" were used by physicians, mental health professionals, and social

workers to categorize individuals who today would be labeled as mentally handicapped or mentally retarded.

4. *1st Annual Report of the Petersburg State Colony for the Fiscal Year ending June 30, 1939*, 5. The ten southern states are Alabama, Georgia, Florida, Kentucky, Louisiana, Mississippi, North Carolina, South Carolina, Tennessee, and Virginia. These states are designated as southern in Howard Odum's seminal 1936 work *Southern Regions* (Chapel Hill: University of North Carolina Press). The eleven institutions housed 6,110 individuals in 1939. This compared with the 68,103 who resided in the South's twenty public institutions for the mentally ill. (*Patients in Mental Institutions, 1939*, U.S. Department of Commerce, Bureau of the Census, 1943, 12, 252).

5. Shomer Zwelling, *Quest for a Cure: The Public Hospital in Williamsburg, Virginia, 1773–1885* (Williamsburg: Colonial Williamsburg Foundation, 1985), 48, 54; Norman Dain, *Disordered Minds: The First Century of Eastern State Hospital in Williamsburg, Virginia, 1766–1866* (Williamsburg: Colonial Williamsburg Foundation, 1971), 19, 109–113; Clark Cahow, *People, Patients, and Politics: The History of the North Carolina Mental Hospitals, 1848–1950* (New York: Arno Press, 1980), 34; Todd Savitt, *Medicine and Slavery* (Urbana: University of Illinois Press, 1978), 275–79; and Samuel Thielman, "Southern Madness: The Shape of Mental Health Care in the Old South," in *Science and Medicine in the Old South*, ed. Ronald Numbers and Todd Savitt (Baton Rouge: Louisiana State University Press, 1989), 273–74. For the example of Alabama's treatment of black persons labeled insane, see John Hughes, "Labeling and Treating Black Mental Illness in Alabama, 1861–1910," *Journal of Southern History* 58, no. 3 (August 1993): 434–60.

6. Dr. James King Hall to Haskins Hobson, January 31, 1936, James King Hall Papers, Box 20, Folder 234, Southern Historical Collection, Wilson Library, University of North Carolina, Chapel Hill.

7. George Fredrickson, *The Arrogance of Race: Historical Perspectives on Slavery, Racism, and Social Inequality* (Middletown, Conn.: Wesleyan University Press, 1988), 174. See also Joel Williamson, *The Crucible of Race: Black-White Relations in the American South since Emancipation* (New York: Oxford University Press, 1984), passim.

8. Ira Hardy, "Schools for the Feeble-Minded: The State's Best Insurance Policy," speech read before the Southern Medical Association, Jacksonville, Florida, November 14, 1912, 5, North Carolina Collection, Wilson Library, University of North Carolina, Chapel Hill. For other examples of the paternal attitudes toward feeble-minded residents of southern institutions, see C. Banks McNairy, "An Appeal to the Appropriations Committee of 1915 for the North Carolina School for the Feeble-Minded," Raleigh, February 12, 1915, 3, North Carolina Collection; and the *Annual Report of the South Caro-*

lina State Training School for the Feeble-Minded, 1920, 6–7, South Carolina State Archives, Columbia. The report concluded that "the Inmates of this Institution are commonly referred to as 'children' regardless of their ages. This term is used both to enable us to avoid the use of the term 'inmate' and also to serve as a reminder that our charges are entitled to the tactful and affectionate treatment that all young children require."

9. *Laws of Florida* (1919), 2 vols., 1: 231. For more on the founding of the Farm Colony, see Steven Noll, "Care and Control of the Feeble-Minded, 1920–1945," *Florida Historical Quarterly* 69, no. 1 (July 1990): 57–62.

10. Dr. J. H. Hodges, Address to the Florida State Conference for Social Work, April 8, 1922, Miami, 3., P. K. Yonge Library of Florida History, University of Florida, Gainesville.

11. See the works by Gerald Grob, *Mental Institutions in America: Social Policy to 1875* (New York: MacMillan, 1973), *Mental Illness and American Society, 1875–1940* (Princeton, N.J.: Princeton University Press, 1983), and "Abuse in American Mental Hospitals in Historical Perspective: Myth and Reality," *International Journal of Law and Psychiatry* 3 (1980): 295–310, and by Constance McGovern, "The Myth of Social Control and Custodial Oppression: Patterns of Psychiatric Medicine in late Nineteenth Century Institutions," *Journal of Social History* 20 (1986): 3–23, for representative examples of the "humanitarian" side of the dispute. For the social control argument, see David Rothman, *The Discovery of the Asylum: Social Order and Disorder in the New Republic* (Boston: Little, Brown, 1971), *Conscience and Convenience: The Asylum and its Alternatives in Progressive America* (Boston: Little, Brown, 1980), and "The State as Parent: Social Policy in the Progressive Era" in Willard Gaylin, Ira Glasser, Steven Marcus, and David Rothman, *Doing Good: The Limits of Benevolence* (New York: Pantheon, 1981); and Andrew Scull, "Humanitarianism or Control? Some Observations on the Historiography of Anglo-American Psychiatry," in *Social Control and the State*, ed. Stanley Cohen and Andrew Scull (New York: St. Martin's Press, 1983), and *Social Order/Mental Disorder: Anglo-American Psychiatry in Historical Perspective* (Berkeley: University of California Press, 1989). For a voluminous overview of the field, see Ellen Dwyer, "The History of the Asylum in Great Britain and the United States," in *Law and Mental Health: International Perspectives*, ed. David Weisstub, vol. 4 (New York: Pergamon Press, 1988), 110–60.

12. The literature on the Progressive era is incredibly rich. See especially Robert Wiebe, *Search for Order, 1877–1920* (New York: Hill and Wang, 1967), and Daniel Rodgers's suggestive "In Search of Progressivism," in *The Promise of American History: Progress and Prospects*, ed. Stanley Katz and Stanley Kutler (Baltimore: Johns Hopkins University Press, 1982), 113–32. For two excellent case studies of this progressive impulse in action in the South, see

John Ettling, *The Germ of Laziness: Rockefeller Philanthropy and Public Health in the New South* (Cambridge, Mass: Harvard University Press, 1981), and James Jones, *Bad Blood: The Tuskegee Syphilis Experiment* (New York: Free Press, 1981).

13. Dr. W. L. Funkhouser, "Human Rubbish," *Journal of the Medical Association of Georgia* 26, no. 5 (May 1937): 197–99.

14. *2nd Biennial Report of the Superintendent of Florida Farm Colony, 1921–1922*, 16.

15. Dr. J. H. Hodges, Address to the Florida State Conference, 2.

16. Dr. Benjamin Whitten, "Presidential Address to the American Association on Mental Deficiency, May, 1937," *Journal of Psycho-Asthenics*, 42 (1936–37): 36. The Progressive coalition in the South, too loosely organized and composed of too many disparate groups to be called a movement, often simultaneously proposed social and political reforms while establishing a legalized caste system based upon race. See Jack Kirby, *Darkness at the Dawning: Race and Reform in the Progressive South* (Philadelphia: J. B. Lippincott Company, 1972), passim, and J. Morgan Kousser, *The Shaping of Southern Politics: Suffrage Restriction and the Establishment of the One-Party South, 1880–1910* (New Haven: Yale University Press, 1974), passim, for the fullest expression of this. See also Dewey Grantham, *Southern Progressivism: The Reconciliation of Progress and Tradition* (Knoxville: University of Tennessee Press, 1983), 112–59; C. Vann Woodward, *Origins of the New South, 1877–1913* (Baton Rouge: Louisiana State University Press, 1951), 321–95; and George Tindall, *The Emergence of the New South, 1913–1945* (Baton Rouge: Louisiana State University Press, 1967), 1–32.

17. Dr. C. Banks McNairy, "An Appeal to the Appropriations Committee," 1–2, North Carolina Collection, Wilson Library, University of North Carolina, Chapel Hill, and "Cause and Prevention of Feeble-Mindedness," speech read before the Tri-State Medical Association of the Carolinas and Virginia, February 18, 1915, 26, North Carolina Collection. McNairy served as superintendent of North Carolina's School for the Feeble-Minded (renamed Caswell Training School in 1915) from 1914 to 1924.

18. James McCulloch, ed., *The Call of the New South: Addresses Delivered at the Southern Sociological Congress, Nashville, Tennessee, May 7–10, 1912* (Nashville; Southern Sociological Congress, 1912), 8. For more on the congress and its role in southern social change, see *The Call of the New South* and the other five published volumes of congress addresses, as well as E. Charles Chatfield, "The Southern Sociological Congress: Organization of Uplift," *Tennessee Historical Quarterly* 19 (December 1960): 328–47, and "The Southern Sociological Congress: Rationale of Uplift," *Tennessee Historical Quarterly* 20 (March 1961): 51–64; Grantham, *Southern Progressivism*, 374–85; and Woodward, *Origins of the New South*, 423–24.

19. C. Banks McNairy, "Eugenics," speech read at the Onslow County Medical Society, Jacksonville, North Carolina, January 21, 1916, 11, North Carolina Collection, Wilson Library, University of North Carolina, Chapel Hill. For more on the needs-rights dichotomy, see David Rothman's suggestive "The State as Parent: Social Policy in the Progressive Era," in Gaylin et al., *Doing Good*, 69–96.

20. *Gainesville Sun*, December 19, 1921, 3.

21. 1945 Special Survey of Florida Farm Colony, May 5, 1945, chaired by Ellen Whiteside, Superintendents' Files, Whiteside Folder, Vault files, Tacachale Community. The experience appeared similar in North Carolina. In 1936, a massive study of the state's mental health programming recommended sixteen provisions for the improvement of the state's efforts in the area of mental health care. Improved care and treatment of the black feeble-minded population, then housed in overcrowded quarters, often not segregated from insane patients, at the State Hospital of the Black Insane in Goldsboro, was not even mentioned as a recommendation. See *A Study of Mental Health in North Carolina: A Report to the North Carolina Legislature of the Governor's Commission Appointed to Study the Care of the Insane and Mental Defectives* (Ann Arbor, Michigan: Edwards Brothers, 1937), and Nell Battle Lewis, "Detailed Survey Completed of Mental Health Problems," *Raleigh News and Observer*, February 7, 1937, 1.

22. *11th Biennial Report of the Superintendent of Florida Farm Colony, 1939– 1941*, 2.

23. These commitment applications were found in Superintendent's Correspondence, Vault files, Gainesville Sunland Center. Since the files found there were by no means complete, there remains a distinct possibility that more black individuals could have been committed.

24. J. Maxey Dell to Edna Hennessee, October 6, 1939, Superintendent's Correspondence, Vault files, Tacachale Community.

25. *11th Biennial Report of the Superintendent of Florida Farm Colony 1939– 1941*, 6, Vault files, Tacachale Community.

26. *5th Biennial Report of the Superintendent of Florida Farm Colony, 1927– 1929*, 10, Vault files, Tacachale Community. For more on this issue of concern about improper commitments, see Steven Noll, "Care and Control of the Feeble-Minded," 66–69.

27. Bernard Farber, *Mental Retardation: Its Social Context and Social Consequences* (Boston: Houghton Mifflin Company, 1968). Farber dichotomizes the labeling of persons as mentally retarded into two categories: deviant and incompetent. Those labeled deviant are "a threat to established social relations" because of a "motivation . . . antithetical to cultural norms" (23– 24). These persons are usually higher-level retarded individuals, labeled "morons" in the nomenclature of the first forty-five years of the twentieth

century. These persons were placed in the retardation system to protect society. Conversely, those labeled "incompetent" are nonthreatening and "cannot attain the level of conduct necessary" (23) for participation in society. Furthermore, incompetent individuals are unable, not unwilling, to conform to societal norms. These persons, labeled "idiots" in the nomenclature of the early twentieth century, were placed in the retardation system for their own protection. By attempting to handle both types of retardation in one institution, southern reformers failed to aid either group. For more on the deviancy-incompetency argument, see Farber, 23–42 and 260–63.

28. Application form of September 17, 1937; Dell reply of September 25, 1937, Superintendent's Correspondence, Vault files, Tacachale Community.

29. R. L. Turner to Dell, March 4, 1938; Dell reply, March 9, 1938, Superintendent's Correspondence, Vault files, Tacachale Community.

30. Application of February 11, 1938; Dell's reply of February 14, 1938, Superintendent's Correspondence, Vault files, Tacachale Community. Dell's responses appeared typical of the superintendents of the Farm Colony.

31. For two examples of African American feeble-minded patients who eventually were placed in Chattahoochee, see Minutes of the Board of Commissioners of State Institutions, Minute Book Y, December 11, 1956, 475, and Minute Book Z, July 2, 1957, 203, Florida State Archives, Tallahassee. One of these patients was described as "suffering from schizophrenia," the other "adjudged psychotic." The Board of Commissioners consisted of the governor and the elected cabinet members. For more on this unique form of governmental control, see V. O. Key, *Southern Politics in State and Nation* (New York: Vintage Books, 1949), 99–100.

32. *20th Biennial Report of the Florida Hospital for the Insane, 1915–1916*, 7.

33. "Florida Farm Colony," *Gainesville Sun*, June 15, 1937, 7. For more on the beginnings of federal involvement in the workings of state institutions such as Florida Farm Colony, see Peter Tyor and Leland Bell, *Caring for the Retarded in America: A History* (Westport, Conn.: Greenwood Press, 1984), 136–37; and R. C. Scheerenberger, *A History of Mental Retardation* (Baltimore: Paul Brookes Publishing Company, 1983), 197–201.

34. For more on the relationship of the federal government to race relations in the 1930s and 1940s, see Harvard Sitkoff, *A New Deal for Blacks: The Emergence of Civil Rights as a National Issue* (New York, 1978), and "The New Deal and Race Relations," in *Fifty Years Later: The New Deal Evaluated*, ed. Harvard Sitkoff (New York: Knopf, 1985), 93–112; John Kirby, *Black Americans in the Roosevelt Era, Liberalism, and Race* (Knoxville: University of Tennessee Press, 1980); Robert Korstad and Nelson Lichenstein, "Opportunities Found and Lost: Labor, Radicals, and the Early Civil Rights Movement," *Journal of American History* 75 (December 1988): 786–811; and John Modell, Marc Goulden, and Magnusson Sigurdur, "World War II

in the Lives of Black Americans: Some Findings and an Interpretation," *Journal of American History* 76 (December 1989): 838–48.

35. For more on the South and race relations in the late 1940s and early 1950s, see Key, *Southern Politics* (New York: Vintage, 1949); David Goldfield, *Promised Land: The South since 1945* (Arlington Heights, Ill.: Harlan Davidson, 1987); Mcrl Reed, "FEPC and the Federal Agencies in the South," *Journal of Negro History* 65 (Winter 1980): 45– 56; Monroe Billington, "Civil Rights, President Truman, and the South," *Journal of Negro History* 57 (April 1973), 127–139; Numan Bartley, *The Rise of Massive Resistance: Race and Politics in the South during the 1950s* (Baton Rouge: Louisiana State University Press, 1969); and Harvard Sitkoff, "Harry Truman and the Election of 1948: The Coming of the Age of Civil Rights in American Politics," *Journal of Southern History* 37 (November 1971): 597–616.

36. *15th Biennial Report of the Superintendent of Florida Farm Colony, 1947– 1949*, 5, 14. For more on the appointment of Philips as superintendent, see Steven Noll, "Care and Control of the Feeble-Minded," 77–80.

37. *Report on the Florida State Hospital System by the United States Public Health Service*, 2, Superintendent's Files 1950–1955, Guthrie-Corcoran Survey Folder, Vault files, Tacachale Community.

38. *News Bulletin of the Mental Health Society of Southeast Florida* 3, no. 2 (February, 1950): 2, Superintendent's Files 1950–1955, Guthrie-Corcoran Survey Folder, Vault files, Tacachale Community.

39. *Report of the Florida Children's Commission for 1951*, 2, Superintendent's Files 1950–1955, Brochures Folder, Vault files, Tacachale Community.

40. *16th Biennial Report of the Superintendent of Florida Farm Colony, 1949– 1951*, 14. For more on the decision to allow admissions from birth onward, see Raymond Philips to Leah Battle, April 27, 1956, Superintendent's Files, Board of Commissioners correspondence, Vault files, Tacachale Community. Battle was the secretary of the Board of Commissioners.

41. "Farm Colony Funds Allowed," *Gainesville Sun*, May 30, 1955, 1.

42. Minutes of the Board of Commissioners of State Institutions, Minute Book 5, October 2, 1951, 281, and January 3, 1952, Florida State Archives.

43. "Farm Colony to Launch $890,000 Building Program in Near Future," *Gainesville Sun*, September 20, 1951, 1.

44. *17th Biennial Report of the Superintendent of Florida Farm Colony, 1951– 1953*, 6–7.

45. Raymond Philips to Agnes Bremer, July 17, 1952, Superintendent's Files, Board of Commissioners Correspondence, Vault files, Tacachale Community; Minutes of the Board of Commissioners, Minute Book W, July 22, 1952, 110, Florida State Archives. Agnes Bremer was the secretary of the board. See also Bremer to Philips, July 22, 1952, and Philips to Bremer, July 24, 1952.

46. "First Negro Wards to be Opened Wednesday at Florida Farm Colony," *Gainesville Sun*, July 12, 1953, 3.

47. See *Plessy v. Ferguson*, 163 U.S. 537 (1896) for the case that upheld the "separate but equal" doctrine that southern states clung to for over fifty years.

48. Raymond Philips, quoted in "First Negro Wards to be Opened Wednesday," *Gainesville Sun*.

49. For more on Florida's governmental response to desegregation decisions in the mid-1950s, see Steven Lawson, "The Florida Legislative Investigation Committee and the Constitutional Readjustment of Race Relations, 1956–1963," in *An Uncertain Tradition: Constitutionalism and the History of the South*, ed. Kermit Hall and James Ely (Athens: University of Georgia Press, 1989), 296–325; and David Colburn, "Florida's Governors Confront the Brown Decision: A Case Study of the Constitutional Politics of School Desegregation, 1954–1970," ibid., 326–55.

50. "Minutes of the Board of Commissioners," Minute Book W, July 21, 1953, 413; Minute Book X, April 5, 1955, 377; and August 8, 1955, 502, all had reports on the construction of new facilities for the Negro Unit. The August 1955 entry noted board approval for the construction of a school, infirmary, and swimming pool.

51. Superintendent's Files 1950–1955, Average Attendance Folder, Monthly Attendance Figures, 1950–1955, Vault files, Tacachale Community.

52. All information in this paragraph gathered from Superintendent's Files, 1950–1955, Negro School Folder, Vault files, Tacachale Community.

53. "North Carolina's Social Welfare Program for Negroes," *North Carolina State Board of Charities and Public Welfare Special Bulletin no. 8*, 1926, 11.

Groveland
Florida's Little Scottsboro

*Steven F. Lawson, David R. Colburn,
and Darryl Paulson*

THE RESIDENTS of Lake County, Florida, awoke on the morning of July 16, 1949, to a drama that was hauntingly familiar, yet disturbingly different. Word passed quickly through the area of small towns and rural communities that before dawn on this summer Sunday a white woman had been attacked and raped by four black men near Groveland. In the past, such crimes had stirred lynch mobs into acts of vengeance, and this occasion proved no exception. In this instance, bloodthirsty vigilantes did not succeed in rendering summary punishment, but they partially achieved their objectives through lawful means. Although lynching diminished in the post–World War II South, public officials, responding to social and political pressures, accomplished the same goals in a legally sanctioned fashion.

Following the war, black veterans who returned home found the Jim Crow South virtually unchanged. They encountered hostile whites determined to preserve the rigid system of racial oppression. Despite the elimination of the white primary by the U.S. Supreme Court in 1944, southern politicians applied literacy tests, poll taxes, and other devices to keep blacks disfranchised. These official forms of discrimination were reinforced by private acts or threats of violence. In 1946 Senator Theodore Bilbo of Mississippi encouraged his "red blooded" constituents to prevent blacks from voting by paying them a visit "the night before the election." [1] During the first half of 1949, the Southern Regional Council reported 108 cases "in which southern private citizens and public officials attempted to usurp the functions of our legal institutions." [2]

Florida also faced a stiff challenge to its defense of the racial status quo. Led by the state NAACP and local civic groups, black Floridians launched an assault on the edifices of discrimination. After the defeat of the white primary, Harry T. Moore formed the Florida Progressive Voters League to encourage blacks to register. Between 1947 and 1950, the number of blacks enrolled on the suffrage lists swelled from 49,000 to more than 116,000. Moore also served as president of the state conference of NAACP branches, and he initiated judicial action to equalize the salaries of underpaid black school teachers with those of whites. For his activities, he and his wife were fired from their teaching positions in Brevard County.[3] In 1949 Moore turned his attention to the Groveland rape case, an episode that put Florida racial justice on trial before the nation and the world.

Nestled in the center of citrus and lake country in mid-Florida, Groveland became a home for blacks almost immediately after its establishment in 1910. Whites living in nearby Mascotte decided that they did not want blacks in their community, although they did want them sufficiently close at hand to work in the citrus groves. Because citrus tended to be a seasonal occupation, blacks were encouraged to develop small farms to feed their families during the off-season. Many of Groveland's blacks resided in an area called Stuckey's Still, where several owned their own homes. This measure of independence was tolerated, even supported by grove owners, as long as blacks remembered that when it came time to pick the fruit or fertilize the trees, they returned to the groves. This condition of dependency existed for many years, requiring little violence or intimidation to enforce it successfully.[4]

Following World War II, however, a number of young blacks returning home from military service were less acquiescent to this labor system. The threat to racial traditions in the community did not escape the attention of grove owners, who worked closely with county sheriffs to dissuade returning veterans from creating unrest. In 1945 the Workers Defense League, a group closely aligned with the Socialist party, accused the sheriff's office in Lake County of actively supporting peonage in the orange groves. Thus, when Walter Irvin and Samuel Shepherd returned to Groveland from the military and seemed reluctant to work in the citrus industry, Sheriff Willis McCall reportedly told them to remove their uniforms and take their places in the groves where they belonged.[5]

A forty-year-old Lake County native, McCall liked to boast that he had received his education "mostly in the University of Hard Knocks." He had prospered in the dairy business, served as the county inspector of fruit, and built a network of supporters who helped him win the sheriff's post in 1944. Once in office, McCall clashed with labor union organizers and civil rights groups and blamed communists for stirring up trouble among black workers. In 1946 he personally chased a union representative out of the county.[6]

McCall had no use for an "uppity nigger" like Sammy Shepherd, the son of an independent farmer who had become embroiled in a series of altercations with his white neighbors. Since 1943 Sammy's father, Henry Shepherd, had diligently worked his farm, which he had reclaimed from swampland. He had come into periodic conflict with whites who let their cows graze on his property and trample his crops. He put up fences to protect his land, only to have them torn down. The Shepherds belonged to the small group of black families that had raised their standard of living during the war. When the younger Shepherd returned from military service and declined to seek employment with the citrus growers, whites were reported to grumble "that it was time now that somebody put both Henry and Sammy in their places."[7]

Soon afterward Sammy Shepherd and his army buddy, Walter Irvin, found themselves in the midst of a racial maelstrom that neither would be able to escape. Together for two hitches in the military, they had served a prison sentence during their second enlistment for "misappropriation of government property" and subsequently were discharged dishonorably from the army.[8] This trouble behind them, they returned to their homes in Lake County to find that another shared ordeal was just about to begin.

In the early morning hours of July 16, 1949, Irvin and Shepherd, along with two other black men, Charles Greenlee and Ernest Thomas, stood accused of kidnapping and raping Norma Padgett and assaulting her husband, Willie Padgett. He told the police that he and his wife had left a dance and that his car had stalled on the road as he was turning around. Although he said that the four blacks who stopped had initially offered assistance, Padgett claimed that they soon turned on him, beat him, and drove off with his wife. Greenlee, Shepherd, and Irvin were arrested within hours of the incident. For over a week, Thomas eluded a posse led by McCall and three other sheriffs before being shot and killed in the woods of Taylor County, nearly two hundred miles northwest of where the search began.[9]

As news of the rape spread through the town and into Lake County, a caravan of more than two hundred cars, carrying five hundred to six hundred men, descended on Groveland during the evening of July 17. Unable to locate the defendants in the town jail, they drove to the county seat in Tavares. The mob gathered at the jail and demanded the release of the three prisoners. But Sheriff McCall persuaded the mob that the men had been transferred to the state penitentiary, although he had hidden them in the jail. The mob seemed satisfied after Norma Padgett's husband and her father inspected the facility, and McCall promised that justice would be served. "This is a crucial moment that could cause a crisis here and throughout the state," the sheriff admonished the crowd. "Let's let the law handle this calmly."[10]

Unable to get their hands on the accused but still eager to exact retribution, the caravan returned to Groveland, where it set fire to black homes and fired shots into them. Apparently local black families had recognized the impending danger and had departed with the assistance of several white residents. The following day, a mob from Mascotte waylaid cars on the highway outside Groveland in hope of intercepting any local black, but they went home frustrated. Responding to pleas from the NAACP and local black residents, Governor Fuller Warren, an opponent of the Ku Klux Klan, sent in the National Guard. Arriving on Tuesday, July 18, and leaving the following Sunday, the militia gradually restored order, though most black homes had been seriously damaged by this time. The house and other property of Samuel Shepherd's father had been singled out by the mob and virtually destroyed.[11]

Why some white residents assisted blacks while others sought revenge remains uncertain. Perhaps the more prosperous local whites feared that violence against blacks would hurt business. "The Negroes are a vital part of our economy," a Groveland merchant declared. "They spend a great percent of the money in local stores.

They are badly needed by farmers and growers." [12] Though others may have been aware of the value of blacks as customers and laborers, they thought it more important to take action to keep blacks subservient. By resorting to violence and making an example of the accused rapists, whites who resented the economic strides some blacks had made were issuing a warning to "other Negroes [to] stay in line." With racial barriers under attack throughout the South, whites felt extremely anxious and were inclined to preserve their supremacy through violent means if necessary. The presence of many out-of-state license plates among the automobiles transporting the vigilantes around the county demonstrated the widespread concern over perceived threats to white control of race relations. [13]

The image of the black rapist had long provoked the wrath of white mobs. In placing white women on a protected pedestal to keep them out of reach of "black beasts," white males also kept their wives, sisters, and daughters in a separate and unequal sphere. "White women," Jacqueline Dowd Hall has written, "were the forbidden fruit, the untouchable property, the ultimate symbol of white male power." [14] Chivalry, the code of honor that meant paternalistic rather than equal treatment for southern women, guaranteed swift retribution against blacks who were suspected of violating the purity of white womanhood. A Lake County resident explained the motivation of the frenzied mobs that burned black homes: "They had to protect their wives, or they couldn't leave them alone at night." [15]

Though the paternalistic ethos lived on, lynching as a response to rape had declined since the 1930s. This abatement was largely due to the educational campaigns of organizations such as the NAACP and the biracial Association of Southern Women for the Prevention of Lynching, both having active Florida branches. [16] Increasingly, whites expected the judicial process to achieve those ends once gained through private acts of terror. Lake County residents reflected this new emphasis on legal revenge. The female editor of the *Mount Dora Topic* reminded the journal's readers that the honor of the rape victim "will be avenged in a well-conducted court of law, and, if the facts are straight and a guilty verdict is returned—revenge will be accomplished by a more frightening and awful means than a mob has at its command." Another newspaper summed up the more ambiguous sentiments of many people in the area: "We'll wait and see what the law does, and if the law doesn't do right, we'll do it."[17]

Prior to Groveland, the infamous Scottsboro case had shown that "due process of law" in southern courts might operate less savagely than vigilante actions for blacks charged with interracial rape, but it did not ensure them justice. In March 1931, nine young black men, out of work and drifting through the South, allegedly raped two white women aboard a train passing through the small Alabama town of Scottsboro. A white mob assembled shortly after the arrest of the nine youths, but a lynching was averted by the sheriff. Nevertheless, the trial was conducted in a hysterical and highly charged atmosphere, and the defendants were found guilty on very questionable evidence. The Communist party and the NAACP took up the cause of the "Scottsboro Boys," and over a period of twenty years managed to win several landmark opinions from the U.S. Supreme Court and eventually obtain their release from prison.[18]

In May 1950, the last of the Scottsboro defendants walked out of jail, an outcome that seemed to suggest the South had taken a step forward, however shaky. The case also revealed the limits of southern justice, for it had taken two reversals by the Supreme Court, widespread public condemnation of the trials, and considerable self-doubt in Alabama before the defendants escaped the death penalty. If the case had not captured national headlines, eight of the nine men almost certainly would have been executed. Had the South and southern justice, then, truly moved forward with the Scottsboro case? Groveland, Florida's "Little Scottsboro," provided some answers to that question.

Shortly after the charges were filed against the four Groveland defendants on July 17, the president of the Orlando branch of the NAACP telephoned the national office to request legal assistance. Franklin Williams, a young attorney on the Legal Defense Fund staff, answered the phone and said he would fly down the next day. Upon arriving in Orlando, Williams began to hear evidence suggesting that the case was highly suspect. From a meeting with Irvin, Shepherd, and Greenlee he learned that despite the sheriff's announcement that the accused had admitted their guilt, they had been badly beaten by the deputies until they had agreed to confess. Their story was corroborated when an examination completed by Williams several days after their arrest revealed numerous cuts and bruises all over their bodies. The three men said they had been suspended from pipes along the ceiling and cut glass had been scattered on the floor underneath. Whenever they moved, their feet were cut by the glass. They were also beaten with clubs around the chest and head. The journalist Stetson Kennedy claimed that Jefferson Elliott, Governor Warren's special investigator, had told him that it was evident from the wounds and scars on Greenlee, Irvin, and Shepherd "that they had been beaten around the clock." Even so, Irvin had refused to admit his guilt.[19]

Further investigation by Williams disclosed other problems with the prosecution's case. While Irvin and Shepherd were good friends and acquaintances of Thomas, they did not know Greenlee, who had arrived in Groveland from Gainesville only hours before the rape. Thomas apparently had brought Greenlee to town to help him with his bolita (gambling) business. Rumors persisted in the black community that Thomas had pocketed some bolita receipts rather than turn them over to his reputed boss, Henry Singleton, a local black. These charges were never substantiated, but Sheriff McCall regarded Thomas as a troublemaker who needed disciplining.[20]

Perhaps even more disturbing, Williams and many black residents doubted that Norma Padgett had been raped. Only seventeen years old, she and her husband had been married for a brief period of time when she returned to her parents' home because her husband had beaten her. Padgett had been warned by his in-laws not to hit Norma again. On the evening of July 15, Padgett had persuaded his estranged wife to attend a dance with him in an attempt to reconcile their differences. On the way to the event, Padgett bought a bottle of liquor which he and his brother-in-law subsequently consumed. Following the dance, the Padgett couple planned to have dinner near Groveland but changed their minds. Instead, Padgett turned the car around to take his wife home, but what happened after that remains a mystery. Padgett claimed his car had stalled because of a weak battery, and four blacks stopped their car to offer assistance. According to his own testimony, he was assaulted by the men, who then kidnapped and raped his wife. Norma Padgett was next seen early the following morning standing near a restaurant on the outskirts of

Groveland, where she was spotted by the restaurant owner's son. He gave her a ride into town, and he noted that she did not appear unusually concerned or upset and did not mention being raped. Willie Padgett had in the meantime been able to start his car and drive it to a gasoline station in Leesburg, where he told attendant Curtis Hunter that he had been assaulted and his wife kidnapped.[21]

Norma did not claim that she had been raped until she encountered her husband and a deputy sheriff, who were searching for her. Willie took his wife aside, spoke alone with her for several minutes, and then she told her story. Franklin Williams speculated that the Padgetts had fabricated this tale on the spot to protect Willie. He guessed that following the dance, Willie had beaten Norma for refusing to grant him his "matrimonial rights," then implored his wife to claim she had been raped by blacks so that family would not take revenge upon him.[22]

When Norma and Willie Padgett first saw Greenlee, who had been arrested at a gasoline station during the early morning hours for vagrancy, they did not implicate him. In fact, they disagreed whether he was one of the culprits. Willie Padgett did, however, identify Shepherd and Irvin when he accompanied sheriff's deputies to Irvin's home and the home of Shepherd's brother. He also contended that the car owned by Shepherd's brother was the one used in the crime.[23]

The circuit court judge and county attorney quickly assembled a grand jury to hear the charges. In a move calculated to show that the defendants could receive a fair trial, Lake County Attorney Jesse W. Hunter impaneled a black resident on the jury. According to the local newspaper, he was "the first ever to serve on a Lake County Grand Jury." Emotions ran very high in the county, however, and it was not likely that any black in such a position could exercise much independence of judgment. On the day before the grand jury convened, the *Orlando Morning Sentinel*, the largest newspaper in central Florida, ran a front-page cartoon depicting a row of four electric chairs with the headline "The Supreme Penalty" and the caption "No Compromise!" Not surprisingly, the jury ruled quickly and unanimously that there was sufficient basis for indicting the three men.[24]

When the grand jury met, Franklin Williams, who lacked a license to practice in Florida, had yet to find a Florida attorney to defend Shepherd, Irvin, and Greenlee. He had hoped to find a white lawyer from the area to improve their chances of receiving a fair hearing. Williams approached Spessard Holland, Jr., the son of one of Florida's U.S. senators, who had represented some black migrant workers in peonage cases. Though sympathetic, Holland declined, explaining: "My wife is a typical flower of southern womanhood and this is a rape case and I can't take it." [25] Instead, Williams secured the services of Alex Akerman, Jr., of Orlando, who had recently completed a term as the only Republican in the state legislature. Akerman chose his assistants—Joseph L. Price, Jr., and Horace Hill, a black attorney from Daytona Beach—to help with the defense. [26]

A trial date was set for August 29, but Akerman asked for a month's extension because he had just been hired and had not had ample time to prepare a defense. Circuit Judge Truman G. Futch, a native of Lake County, refused his request, contending that Williams had been involved in the case since July. Futch also commented that since Akerman was convinced of his clients' innocence, he must have sufficient evidence to go to trial. Futch did agree, however, to delay the trial for three days. [27]

When the trial opened, Akerman petitioned for a change of venue, arguing that a fair trial in Lake County was impossible because of the negative publicity surrounding the case. But the mayor of Tavares, E. L. Burleigh, and a black insurance agent, F. L. Hampton, testified that race relations in Lake County were "the best in Florida." Akerman also moved to quash the indictments because blacks had been systematically excluded from grand juries in Lake County for twenty-five years, arguing that the one black who had been placed on the grand jury was there "for the sole purpose of creating the impression of compliance with the 14th Amendment." The voting rolls showed 802 blacks in the county, but only one had previously been called to serve on a grand jury. Futch rejected both appeals, ruling that the first motion did not comply with the laws of Florida and that no evidence had been introduced that suggested a fair trial could not be held in Lake County. Futch denied Akerman's second motion, pointing to the presence of a black on the grand jury as a fair and lawful impaneling of this jury. [28]

Testimony began on the third day of the trial with Norma Padgett taking the stand as the state's star witness. She repeated her story as she had reported it to the county attorney's office. After the four kidnapped her, she asserted, they drove her to a small road off the highway and took turns raping her. She then recalled, "They asked me if I wanted them to take me to town, and I told them I'd rather walk." This seemed like a curious question from four blacks, three of whom resided in Groveland, after they had just finished raping a white woman. Charles Greenlee later testified that if he had known at the time that a white woman had been raped he would have left the county immediately. The four had allegedly released Norma in a field, and she swore she hid in the woods until daylight.[29]

Willie Padgett followed his wife to the stand and repeated her testimony. He also declared that the blacks who had overpowered him were driving a 1941 or 1946 Mercury with a prefix number on the license plate that indicated it came from Lake County. As had his wife, he identified the three black defendants and the deceased as the men who had kidnapped and raped Norma. Padgett also stated that they stole his wallet which contained a driver's license and $20.[30]

Besides the Padgetts' testimony, that provided by Deputy Sheriff James L. Yates proved most crucial to the state's case. According to Yates, footprints and tireprints left at the scene of the crime were directly traceable to Irvin and the car owned by Shepherd's brother. The prosecution presented plaster casts that Yates supposedly had made at the crime scene and later matched to Irvin's shoes and the Mercury sedan. When Akerman asked Yates where he learned to make plaster moldings, the deputy replied that he had been doing it for years. A handkerchief that belonged to Norma had also been found by Yates, and according to his testimony the lint on it was similar to that discovered in the rear of the Mercury and on Norma Padgett's dress.[31]

The state rested its case following Yates's testimony. Significantly, it had not introduced any medical evidence to show that Norma had been raped. Nor did it introduce the confessions of Greenlee and Shepherd. County Attorney Jesse Hunter believed that he could win a conviction without the confessions, and that they would damage the state's case on appeal because the defense could produce evidence showing that the defendants had been beaten.[32] At the same time, the defense did not attempt to break down Norma Padgett's story of the rape or introduce medical evidence to refute it. As Akerman recalled, cross-examination "had to he handled delicately—you couldn't have gotten anywhere by roughing her up."[33] Given the inflammatory nature of the rape charge, defense counsel thought it prudent not to risk arousing further sympathy for Norma.

All three men accused of the rape testified on their own behalf. Shepherd and Irvin recounted their trip to Orlando on the evening of the crime and told of their visit to a series of bars. Both testified that they had not seen Norma and Willie Padgett that evening, nor did they know Greenlee. Shepherd's brother testified that he had let Sammy borrow his car and that when the younger Shepherd returned it, he was not nervous nor did he act as if he were trying to hide something.[34] Greenlee admitted that he had been arrested in the early morning hours, just prior to the rape, at a closed gasoline station in Groveland. He said he had left Gainesville because his mother cried constantly over the deaths of his two sisters, who had been run over by a train. Greenlee added that he had not known the Padgetts nor his fellow-defendants.[35]

Despite the defense team's efforts to show that Greenlee could not have been at the scene of the alleged rape when it occurred, and the testimony of all three about their innocence, the jury returned a guilty verdict only ninety minutes after it had been charged by the judge. Irvin and Shepherd were sentenced to death, but the jury recommended mercy for the sixteen-year-old Greenlee, presumably because of his youth. Franklin Williams remarked that the trial had "all the characteristics of a dime store novel . . . a perfect frameup." The *Mount Dora Topic* vigorously disagreed and declared that the "county can well be proud of the conduct of its officers of the law, its prosecutor and its judge from the start to the finish of the Groveland Story."[36]

The defense immediately filed an appeal to the Florida Supreme Court amidst rumors of a federal inquiry. In response to a series of articles written by Ted Poston, a black reporter covering the trial for the *New York Post*, U.S. Attorney General J. Howard McGrath ordered an investigation into charges that the three defendants had been tortured while in custody. A surgeon and a dentist had examined the trio at Raiford State Prison and reported that all showed signs of brutal beatings. The investigation collapsed, however, when U.S. District Attorney Herbert Phillips of Tampa inexplicably refused to call either the surgeon or the dentist. With the case against the sheriff and his deputies resting on the unsupported testimony of the defendants, the federal grand jury dismissed the charges.[37]

In this instance, as well as others, the federal government proved less than helpful. Although President Harry Truman had committed his administration to advancing the cause of civil rights, the Justice Department exercised restraint in prosecuting criminal cases involving racial discrimination. With considerable justification, federal lawyers believed they could not win such litigation before southern white juries, which were not inclined to convict their neighbors for violating black civil rights. The Justice Department might instruct the FBI to investigate thoroughly "whether or not a violation of federal criminal law was committed," but the bureau did not accord these matters a high priority.[38] Its director, J. Edgar Hoover, had little sympathy for the civil rights cause, and he was reluctant to assign the needed manpower to cases with little likelihood of success. Moreover, because the agency depended on the cooperation of local law enforcement officials in investigating what they judged to be their primary concerns, such as bank robberies and other thefts of cash, it was usually cautious in taking action that might upset indigenous racial customs. This approach drew criticism from civil rights groups. The NAACP said it could not understand how the FBI had "maintained a world-wide reputation for great efficiency in the investigation, apprehension, and successful prosecution of the cleverest criminals in history," but was "unable to cope with violent criminal action by bigoted, prejudiced Americans against Negro Americans." [39]

Though federal agencies failed to shed fresh light on the Groveland case, a crusading and unusually progressive Florida newspaper did so. In April 1950, the *St. Petersburg Times* published an investigative series demonstrating that it was physically impossible for Charles Greenlee to have been at the scene of the crime. Indeed, he had been arrested nineteen miles away during the time the assault allegedly occurred. The article also raised a number of questions about the fairness of the trial and the charges against Shepherd and Irvin. In the second of three articles, the reporter, Norman Bunin, observed that all the jurors were aware of the pretrial publicity surrounding the case and had read about the confessions of the defendants. The reporter also painstakingly traced the steps of Irvin and Shepherd during the evening of the rape. They were last seen at Club 436 in Altamonte Springs after midnight, according to two witnesses. Irvin and Shepherd claimed they started for home around 12:30 A.M. and drove directly to Groveland, a trip of nearly forty miles and a considerable distance from the place where the assault was said to have occurred. Both men testified that they never drove near the area of the alleged rape, although, in contrast to Greenlee, they would have had sufficient time to do so. The *Times* did report that on a tape recording provided by Sheriff Willis McCall, Greenlee acknowledged that all four had committed rape. Yet when asked about the confession while in prison, Greenlee charged that McCall had taken him into his office, held a gun to his head, and told him what to say. At various points in the "confession," McCall turned off the recording machine and gave Greenlee instructions on how to proceed.[40]

These revelations had no influence on the Florida Supreme Court, however, when it heard the appeal. The litigation involved only Shepherd and Irvin because their counsel feared that if Greenlee was also granted a new trial, a white jury might sentence him to death this time. Yet on the long shot that Shepherd and Irvin were subsequently acquitted, the attorneys could then seek to reopen Greenlee's case. Akerman based the appeal on five conditions: widespread publicity that prejudiced the case; lack of sufficient time to prepare an adequate defense; cruel and illegal treatment of the prisoners; failure of the state to prove its case; and absence of blacks on the jury. Three months later, the state justices found no reason to overturn the convictions, writing that "all legal rights of the appellants were ably and thoroughly presented in the lower court." Though acknowledging that race relations had been strained in Lake County as a result of the crime, the justices asserted that "our study of the record reflects the view that harmony and good will and friendly relations continuously existed between the white and colored races in all other sections of Lake County." In concluding, the court found that "the inflamed public sentiment was against the crime . . . rather than [the] defendants' race" and that there was no evidence of any intentional discrimination against blacks in the selection of persons for jury duty.[41]

Less than one year later, the U.S. Supreme Court unanimously overturned the convictions of Shepherd and Irvin. In a blistering opinion delivered by Robert Jackson, the justices called the pretrial publicity "one of the best examples of one of the worst menaces to American justice." Jackson found numerous examples of prejudicial influences outside the trial courtroom that warranted a change of venue, including the *Orlando Sentinel* political cartoon picturing the row of four electric chairs and its report of the alleged confessions of the defendants. Noting that neither the county attorney nor the sheriff had ever repudiated the confessions, Jackson observed that prospective jurors all assumed them to be true. He added that such confessions either did not exist or had been "obtained under circumstances which made [them] inadmissible." A majority of the seven justices were also prepared to overturn the verdict because no blacks had been included on the jury. But as Justice Jackson pointed out, even if blacks had been allowed to serve on the jury, the pretrial publicity had prevented the defendants from obtaining a fair hearing, and he did not see "how any Negro on the jury would have dared to cause a disagreement or acquittal." [42]

Lake County officials denounced the Supreme Court's decision, and Sheriff McCall commented that "the mere fact that mercy was recommended for Greenlee is proof that the jury was fair and impartial." Despite the Court's pronouncement, County Attorney Jesse Hunter did not believe that the merits of his case had been weakened, and he was eager to retry it and obtain another conviction. A former schoolteacher, railroad mail clerk, and self-taught lawyer, the seventy-year-old Hunter was a folksy character with a cracker-barrel wit, whose participation in this celebrated legal affair would climax what had been a very popular public career.[43]

In November 1951, while the defense submitted a petition for a new trial site and also sought to disqualify Hunter as prosecuting attorney, Sheriff McCall went to Raiford State Prison to transfer Irvin and Shepherd to Tavares for the pretrial hearing. Transporting both prisoners in his automobile, McCall followed Deputy Yates's patrol car to the county seat. While driving along a back road near his home town of Umatilla, McCall complained to his prisoners that the air in his right front tire was low. He also alleged later that Irvin had asked to relieve himself. As a result, McCall said, he pulled to the side of the road to let Irvin do as he asked, but first instructed Irvin and Shepherd to get out and change the tire, though they remained handcuffed together. When McCall opened the door, he claimed,

Samuel Shepherd and Walter Irvin lie alongside the highway after being shot by Sheriff Willis McCall in November 1951. Irvin recovered from his wounds and accused McCall of deliberately trying to kill them. McCall claimed they had tried to overpower him and he had shot in self-defense. AP World Wide.

Shepherd hit him with a flashlight. Fending off Shepherd's alleged attack, McCall pulled his gun and shot both prisoners, apparently killing them. According to this version, McCall radioed Deputy Sheriff Yates, who went into town after checking with McCall and returned with Hunter and several others. To their surprise, they discovered that, although Shepherd was dead, Irvin was still alive.[44]

Despite two serious bullet wounds, Irvin survived and told his lawyers a substantially different story from McCall's. He claimed under oath that after McCall pulled his car over to the side of the road, he ordered the prisoners from the car and without provocation shot Shepherd and then shot Irvin himself in the upper right chest. Irvin, pretending to be dead, heard McCall mutter, "I got rid of them; killed the sons of bitches." He then called Yates on his car radio and informed him that the two had "tried to jump me and I did a good job." When Yates arrived he turned his flashlight on Irvin, who had opened his eyes. "That son of a bitch is not dead, let's kill him," Yates shouted. When he pulled the trigger, his revolver misfired. He and McCall examined the gun almost nonchalantly in the automobile headlights, apparently exchanged weapons, and Yates turned and shot Irvin in the neck.[45]

If McCall at that point chose to practice vigilante justice, why had he saved the two from a lynch mob earlier? Initially McCall may have felt confident that the accused would be sentenced to death, especially after he had extracted confessions from them. Perhaps he believed that a lynching would tarnish his record. When the U.S. Supreme Court overturned the case, however, McCall probably began to have second thoughts. Having promised the lynch mob and local residents that justice would be done, McCall may have decided on the road to Tavares that the circumstances were convenient for him to take summary action. Mabel Norris Reese, editor of the *Mount Dora Topic* and a strong supporter of McCall prior to the shooting, also claimed that the fruit growers were anxious for the issue to be settled because their black workers were becoming afraid to go to work as the trial approached. McCall may have thought that his action would return the county more quickly to normal.[46]

A coroner's inquest into the death of Shepherd and the wounding of Irvin exonerated McCall, praising him for "acting in the line of duty." The NAACP denounced the verdict and called on Governor Fuller Warren to order the arrest or at least the suspension of McCall. A special investigator appointed by Warren concluded that McCall had not used "maximum precaution" in transporting his prisoners, but he found no evidence of criminal wrongdoing.[47] Accordingly, Judge Truman Futch dismissed the grand jury that had been called after the coroner's inquest. Nevertheless, this inquiry left many questions unresolved. Why had McCall driven the prisoners at night along an out-of-the-way backroad instead of along the main highway? Why did the sheriff transport Irvin and Shepherd alone in his car? Why did McCall have to use deadly force against two men who were handcuffed together? An FBI probe of this shooting revealed no answers to these questions, and Sheriff McCall was never indicted on federal charges.

Despite Judge Futch's decision to clear McCall, for the first time a number of people began to question whether justice was being served. Mabel Norris Reese doubted the sheriff's version of the shooting and began reexamining the evidence in the first trial. She deplored the "black mark etched on the night of November 6 by

Sheriff Willis McCall checks moonshine in Lake County in 1963. McCall was accused of murdering Samuel Shepherd and seriously wounding Walter Irvin while transporting them to trial in the Groveland case. McCall was subsequently removed by Governor Reubin Askew in the early 1970s for brutality against black prisoners in his custody. Courtesy of the *Orlando Sentinel*.

the gun of a man who lost his head."[48] Reese also discovered that Jesse Hunter had developed some misgivings about the case. Before Irvin's retrial, Hunter offered the defendant a life sentence if he would acknowledge his complicity in the rape. Akerman and Thurgood Marshall, the future U.S. Supreme Court justice, who had replaced Franklin Williams as chief counsel, discussed Hunter's offer with Irvin, but he insisted on his innocence and refused to negotiate with the county attorney.[49]

The shooting not only embarrassed some of Lake County's leading citizens but the rest of the United States as well. McCall's brand of justice sparked an international incident at the height of the cold war. Andrei Vishinsky, the chief Soviet delegate to the United Nations, declared that the United States "had a nerve talking about human rights and upbraiding other nations while Negroes were shot down by an officer of law while in custody." Though not unmindful of the lack of freedom in the Soviet Union, the NAACP picked up its line of argument. "Samuel Shepherd is no better off for this American hypocrisy," the organization asserted, "nor are his fifteen million fellow Americans who happen not to be white."[50]

The glare of such unfavorable publicity prompted a shift in the course of the litigation. In December 1951 Judge Futch approved a motion by the defense to remove the location of the trial from Lake County. It was rescheduled for Marion County, a curious choice because the sheriff there had been murdered the previous spring by a young black.[51]

Before the new trial could begin, another act of violence cast a bloody stain on Florida race relations. On Christmas Eve 1951, dynamite blasted the house of Harry T. Moore, the NAACP statewide coordinator, killing him and mortally wounding his wife. Moore had been active in raising funds for the Groveland defendants, and following the shooting of Shepherd and Irvin, he had led a campaign urging Governor Warren to remove McCall from office.[52] The NAACP believed Moore's "death fits into the pattern of terror which has centered around the town of Groveland . . . and advertises to the world that though we preach democracy abroad we cannot practice it at home."[53] Despite a reward offered for the capture of Moore's killers and an FBI investigation, the murderers were never apprehended.[54]

The latest outrage, however, did not keep Irvin from his scheduled court appointment. Recovered enough from his wounds to stand trial on February 13, 1952, Irvin watched as his defense counsel sought a change of venue and introduced the results of an Elmo Roper survey showing that residents of Marion County were prejudiced against the defendant. However, Hunter was able to convince Judge Futch that the public opinion poll had attempted to deceive people who were questioned and therefore was biased and unreliable. Futch also refused to suppress the introduction of Irvin's clothes as evidence, notwithstanding charges by the defense that they had been seized illegally. Mrs. Delilah Irvin, Walter's mother, told Judge Futch that Deputy Yates had said he was coming for "that black Nigger boy's clothes" and later warned her that "there may not be no trial." [55]

The second trial produced a few surprises. The prosecution's case relied heavily on the testimony of the Padgetts and Yates as it had the first time, but the defense added two new witnesses to its presentation. The first, Herman V. Bennett, a former law enforcement official for the federal government, stated that the plaster cast of footprints made by Deputy Yates had not been made while Irvin was wearing the shoes in question. The witness pointed out to the jury that footprints would be concave if made by a person standing on a soft spot, but they would be convex, as those in question were, if made by an empty shoe. Attorney Hunter could not shake the testimony, but he did note that this witness was being paid by the defense counsel. The other key witness for the defense was Lawrence Burtoft, the first person to encounter Norma Padgett walking along the road after the original incident. As he stopped his car to offer assistance, she called "Good morning" and asked if she could get a ride to town. Burtoft stated that she seemed calm and unruffled. As he drove her toward town, Mrs. Padgett told Burtoft that "she had been abducted by four Negroes, and said she could not identify them." He added that "she made no complaint of having been attacked." During the cross-examination, Burtoft declared he had brought this to Hunter's attention during the first trial and had been subpoenaed as a witness, but Hunter had not asked him to testify. Irvin once again testified in his own behalf and maintained his innocence. [56]

Later, during the 1960s, information came to light in another rape case that raised serious doubts about the veracity of Yates's testimony in the 1950s. In circumstances very similar to those of the Groveland case, Lake County deputies had made a plaster molding of a shoe print that Yates insisted had been taken at the scene of the crime. Testimony revealed, however, that the shoe print had been made by Yates in the sheriff's office.[57]

But these revelations were yet to come, and despite the questions raised by the testimony of Bennett and Burtoft, the Marion County jury deliberated only an hour and a half before finding Irvin guilty and recommending a death sentence. The defense immediately filed an appeal, arguing that numerous errors in the trial, especially the unlawful search and seizure of Irvin's clothes, warranted overturning the verdict. The appeal stood pending before the U.S. Supreme Court for a year until January 1954, when the Court declined to rehear it.[58]

With Irvin facing the death penalty in November 1954, his lawyers petitioned Governor Charley Johns for clemency. Some white Floridians also joined the campaign to spare Irvin's life. On its editorial page, the *St. Petersburg Times* noted the doubts that surrounded the conviction of Irvin and declared: "Both compassion and calm judgement argue for his sentence to be changed to life imprisonment."[59] The Reverend Ben Wyland of the United Churches of St. Petersburg agreed, as did Jesse Hunter, the prosecutor who had won the conviction in the first place.[60] Nevertheless, Governor Johns, an outspoken segregationist, denied the petition. The NAACP, however, won a stay from the U.S. Supreme Court just two days before the scheduled execution.

A change in governors finally saved Irvin. As a result of the election in November 1954, LeRoy Collins, a moderate on racial issues, replaced Johns and asked his assistant, Bill Harris, to reexamine the case. Harris found numerous errors in the investigation of the crime. In his report to Collins, Harris emphasized the questionable nature of the plaster cast moldings that Deputy Yates had produced at the first trial. He observed that Yates had testified he did not understand what "integrity of footprints" meant and that several hours had passed before he made a set of the plaster casts. He had also waited several hours before making moldings of the tire tracks. Harris went on to raise questions about the entire inquiry conducted by state and county officials. He noted that no effort was ever made by the state to explain what had happened to Willie Padgett's wallet or

Norma's perfume, which remained missing since the morning of the alleged rape. Unexplainedly, the prosecution had also failed to introduce medical testimony establishing conclusively that a rape had occurred. On the basis of Harris's investigation, Governor Collins commuted Walter Irvin's sentence to life imprisonment, informing the State Pardon Board that Irvin's guilt had not been established "in an absolute and conclusive manner." [61]

Collins's decision was angrily denounced by Lake County officials. Judge Futch was so upset that he ordered a grand jury investigation of the commutation proceedings. Collins refused to participate in the hearing. The jurors' report charged that the governor had mistakenly reached the wrong conclusions, but it exonerated him of malfeasance. Feelings still remained high in the county, however. In February 1956, Collins and his wife took part in a parade in Eustis, Florida, when Norma Padgett, escorted by two of McCall's deputies, approached his car. She yelled at the governor, "You're the one who let out the nigger that raped me. Would you have done that if it had been your wife?" [62]

Norma Padgett was not alone in expressing anger against Collins. Sheriff McCall left no doubt about how he felt, viewing the commutation as a threat to the preservation of law and order. He admonished that in the future "all a negro criminal would need to do would be pick out some innocent helpless white woman as a target to satisfy his ravishing sexual desires, keep his mouth shut, proclaim his innocence and let the NAACP furnish the money and lawyers and beat the rap." [63] Seconding the sheriff's opinion, Herbert S. Phillips predicted the governor's action would produce dire consequences. In his capacity as U.S. district attorney in 1950, Phillips had failed to obtain an indictment from a federal grand jury investigating McCall for beating the Groveland prisoners in his custody. His sympathies apparently rested with the sheriff rather than the defendants. Six years later, in retirement, he called Collin's handling of the case "a victory for the National Association for the Advancement of Colored People [that] is bound to encourage lynchings in rape cases." [64]

These warnings notwithstanding, the Groveland case gradually drifted from public view in the late 1950s, with the accused staying behind bars despite widespread doubt about their guilt. Greenlee was not paroled until 1962, and Irvin remained incarcerated until

1968, when he was paroled by Claude Kirk, Florida's first Republican governor in the twentieth century. After his release, Greenlee left the state permanently, settling in Tennessee. Irvin moved to Miami but returned to Lake County for a visit in 1970 and died there of an apparent heart attack. Meanwhile, Sheriff Willis McCall continued in office despite the deaths of three black prisoners in his jail and numerous charges of corruption and abuse of office against him and his deputies. After Governor Reubin Askew suspended McCall for kicking a black prisoner to death, he resigned in 1973.[65]

Like its predecessor in Scottsboro, Groveland was a "tragedy of the American South." In both instances, alleged rapes of white women by blacks occurred amidst circumstances that raised serious questions about their guilt and about the fairness of the southern judicial system. Despite the intervening war years and the precedent of the Alabama case, the four black Floridians were presumed guilty once a white woman had identified them as culprits. The interval between Scottsboro and Groveland did not diminish the white southern response to allegations of rape. The crime remained an emotionally charged one. Clearly, the accusation of rape by a white woman against a black man carried a special burden that could not be readily dismissed; the protection of southern white womanhood was held to justify racial control. However questionable in specific cases, the word and sexual morality of southern daughters were considered equally pure. The fear of rape and the threat of menacing blacks provided a potent rationale for keeping all blacks subordinate.[66]

Without outside intervention, the situation for the surviving Groveland defendants would have been even worse. The NAACP waged a national fund-raising campaign to conduct the defense and assigned some of its best legal talent to plead the case. Along with the Workers Defense League, it gathered information and testimony and extensively publicized the plight of the defendants. Though unsuccessful in the trial courtroom, the NAACP managed to convince the U.S. Supreme Court to overturn the original verdict. When the second trial failed to change the outcome, the NAACP persuaded the high tribunal to issue a stay of execution. However, the civil rights organization was less successful in getting the executive branch in Washington to act forcefully. In response to NAACP protests, the Justice Department and the FBI investigated the violence against the black prisoners and against Harry T. Moore, but they were unwilling or unable to press charges.

Left on its own, the state of Florida would have quickly electrocuted Irvin and Shepherd. Neither all-white juries nor state supreme court justices hesitated to conclude that the defendants had been proven guilty beyond a reasonable doubt. Similarly, when called upon to judge the actions of Sheriff McCall, a coroner's jury of Lake County residents cleared him of wrongfully killing one prisoner in his custody and seriously wounding another. In the end, only the governor could spare Irvin's life. Convinced that too many questions remained unanswered, LeRoy Collins issued a reprieve. Nevertheless, it had taken appeals to two governors to gain the reprieve and even Collins acted cautiously. In announcing his decision, the governor emphasized that he was not bowing to outside pressure, and considering it politically expedient, he denounced the NAACP's handling of the case.[67]

Like most areas confronting racial conflicts in the postwar South, Lake County intended to preserve white supremacy, legally or otherwise. The old order of lynching may have passed, but as one reporter observed after the second Groveland trial, the "rope and faggot is giving way to the even more deadly and unobtrusive deputations of one or two persons, who do the job with less notoriety and greater impunity." [68] The social changes and ideological battles surrounding World War II and the cold war made little difference to the Lake County officials charged with trying the Groveland case. Attacks by black men upon white women, or even the suspicion of such assaults, could not be tolerated or second-guessed. To do so would pose a challenge to the traditional assumptions governing race relations in the postwar South, assumptions that remained little changed as Florida prosecuted the Groveland case.

Notes

1. The white primary case was *Smith v. Allwright*, 321 U.S. 649; Steven Lawson, *Black Ballots: Voting Rights in the South, 1944–1969* (New York: Columbia University Press, 1976), 100.

2. Reported in "Major Racial Issues at Stake in Trial of Three Florida Negroes," *Christian Science Monitor*, clipping, n.d., Franklin H. Williams

scrapbooks (Philadelphia, in possession of Franklin Williams; hereinafter cited as FHW Scrapbooks). See also Edward L. Ayers, *Vengeance and Justice: Crime and Punishment in the Nineteenth Century American South* (New York: Oxford University Press, 1984).

3. Gloster Current, "Martyr for a Cause," *Crisis* 59 (February 1952): 72–81; Lawson, *Black Ballots*, 134.

4. L. Allen, "Lake County, Florida," Federal Writer's Project, *American Guide*, Orlando, December 12, 1939, 12.

5. Interview with Franklin Williams by David Colburn and Steven Lawson, February 11, 1985, CRG 2 AB, University of Florida Oral History Archives, Florida State Museum, Gainesville (Colburn-Lawson interview with Williams hereinafter cited as Franklin Williams Interview). "Report on Groveland," 1, Box 192, Worker Defense League Files, Archives of Labor, History, and Urban Affairs, Wayne State University (hereinafter cited as WDL Files); James W. Ivy, "Florida's Little Scottsboro: Groveland," *Crisis* 56 (October 1949): 266; Interview with Mabel Norris Reese (Chesley) by Franklin Williams, n.d., copy in possession of the authors.

6. Mabel Norris Reese (Chesley), "Lake County Personalities," *Mount Dora Topic*, July 28, 1949, 1; Dudley Clendenin, "The Legend of Iceman McCall Chills the Air in Lake County," *Floridian*, *St. Petersburg Times*, November 5, 1972, 22; Rowland Watts to Mr. Baskin, September 15, 1949, 1, Box 192, WDL Files.

7. Ivy, "Florida's Little Scottsboro," 266; "Mobile Violence: Motorized Mobs in a Florida County," *New South* 4 (August 1949): 1–2.

8. *Orlando Sentinel-Star*, September 4, 1949, 2.

9. Ibid., July 17, 1949, 1, and July 27, 1949, 1; *Mount Dora Topic*, July 17, 1949, 1; *New York Times*, July 27, 1949, 48; "Mobile Violence," 5.

10. *Miami Herald*, July 18, 1949, 1; July 20, 1949, 1; "Mobile Violence," 2–3; *Pittsburgh Courier*, August 23, 1949, 1.

11. *Orlando Sentinel*, July 18, 1949, 1; July 19, 1949, 1; "Mobile Violence," 3–5; *New York Times*, July 19, 1949, 1; July 20, 1949, 14; July 25, 1949, 30; *Lakeland Ledger*, July 20, 1949, 1; Franklin Williams Interview.

12. "Mobile Violence," 6.

13. Edna B. Kerin, "Another Chance for the Groveland Victims," *Crisis* 58 (May 1951): 319; *New York Times*, July 20, 1949, clipping, FHW Scrapbooks; Ted Poston, "A Good Nigger—But They Ruined Him Too," *New York Post*, September 3, 1949, clipping, FHW Scrapbooks.

14. Jacqueline Dowd Hall, "'The Mind That Burns in Each Body': Women, Rape, and Racial Violence," in *Powers of Desire: The Politics of Sexuality*, ed. Ann Snitow, Christine Stansell, and Sharon Thompson (New York: Monthly Review Press, 1983), 334. The myth of the black rapist was

at least as significant as the actual incidence of interracial rape in justifying lynching. The figures show that from 1882 to 1968, 25 percent of lynchings involved rape or attempted rape. The largest percentage of lynchings, nearly 41 percent, stemmed from homicides. Jacqueline Dowd Hall, *Revolt against Chivalry: Jesse Daniel Ames and the Women's Campaign against Lynching* (New York: Columbia University Press, 1979), 149; Robert L. Zangrando, *The NAACP Crusade against Lynching, 1909–1950* (Philadelphia: Temple University Press, 1980), 8. See Ayers, *Vengeance and Justice.*

15. "Report of Investigation Made in Florida on the Groveland Case," by Hornell Hart, Duke University, School of Religion, and the Reverend Paul Moore, Jr., Grace Episcopal Church, Jersey City, New Jersey, n.d., Box 192-1, WDL Files.

16. Hall, *Revolt Against Chivalry*, 235–36; Zangrando, *The NAACP Crusade against Lynching*, 213–15; James R. McGovern, *Anatomy of a Lynching: The Killing of Claude Neal* (Baton Rouge: Louisiana State University Press, 1982), 138–39. Between 1920 and 1939, there were 1,067 lynchings in contrast to forty-six between 1940 and 1968 (calculated from figures in Zangrando, 6–7).

17. *Orlando Sentinel*, July 17, 1949, 1.

18. Dan T. Carter, *Scottsboro: A Tragedy of the American South* (Baton Rouge: Lousiana State University Press, 1969).

19. Franklin Williams interview; *Chicago Defender*, September 17, 1949, clipping, FHW Scrapbooks; Ivy, "Florida's Little Scottsboro," 267, 285; M. C. Thomas to Watts, May 11, 1951, Box 192-6, WDL Files; article by Stetson Kennedy for *Droit et Liberté*, n.d., typewritten copy, Stetson Kennedy Files, Southern Labor Archives, Georgia State University.

20. M. C. Thomas to Watts, May 11, 1951, Box 192-6, WDL Files; interview with Mabel Norris Reese (Chesley), by Franklin Williams. There was additional speculation that Singleton paid protection money to McCall, that the sheriff wanted to punish Ernest Thomas for pocketing money, and that he led the posse out of his jurisdiction to silence Thomas. No evidence to substantiate these allegations has surfaced.

21. Franklin Williams Interview; *Orlando Sentinel*, July 17, 1949, 1; Ivy, "Florida's Little Scottsboro," 267–68.

22. "Mobile Violence," 3; *St. Petersburg Times*, April 8, 1959, 17; Franklin Williams Interview.

23. *St. Petersburg Times*, April 8, 1950, 17.

24. *Orlando Sentinel*, July 19, 1949, 1; July 21, 1949, 1, 3; *Mount Dora Topic*, July 21, 1949, 1. Thomas had brought Greenlee to Lake County from Alachua and left him at the gasoline station. When local police arrested Greenlee several hours later at the station, they found the gun on him.

25. Franklin Williams Interview; Transcript of Testimony, *State of Florida v. Charles Greenlee, Walter Irvin, and Samuel Shepherd*, Florida Supreme Court, Tallahassee, Florida, 2.

26. Franklin Williams Interview; interview with Alex Akerman by David Colburn, May 31, 1984, CRG 1 A, University of Florida Oral History Archives, Florida State Museum, Gainesville.

27. Franklin Williams Interview; Ivy, "Florida's Little Scottsboro," 268.

28. *Orlando Sentinel*, September 1, 1949, 1; *Mount Dora Topic*, July 29, 1949, 1.

29. *Orlando Sentinel*, September 3, 1949, 1, 2; September 4, 1949, 1, 2; *St. Petersburg Times*, April 7, 1950, 13; April 8, 1950, 17.

30. Transcript of Testimony, Florida Supreme Court, 467–76; *Orlando Sentinel*, September 3, 1949, 1, 2; September 4, 1949, 1.

31. Transcript of Testimony, Florida Supreme Court, 538–41; Bill Harris to LeRoy Collins, n.d., 7–9, 13–14, LeRoy Collins Papers, University of South Florida; *Orlando Sentinel*, September 3, 1949, 2; *Mount Dora Topic*, September 8, 1949, 5.

32. Harris to Collins, 9, Collins Papers.

33. Interview with Alex Akerman by Franklin Williams, 17, FHW Scrapbooks. A Lake County grand jury reviewing the case in 1955 concluded that it would have been impossible for a doctor to furnish clinical proof of rape because Norma Padgett had gone home and "cleaned herself up before the doctor ever saw her." "Presentment of the Grand Jury to Honorable T. G. Futch," 11, Governor T. LeRoy Collins Administrative Correspondence, Box 25, Laf-Leg, 1955– 56, Rg 102, Series 776a, State Archives, Tallahassee.

34. *Mount Dora Topic*, September 8, 1949, 1–2; *Orlando Sentinel*, September 3, 1949, 2; September 4, 1949, 2.

35. *Mount Dora Topic*, September 8, 1949, 1–2, 8; *Orlando Sentinel*, September 4, 1949, 2; Franklin Williams interview.

36. Ivy, "Florida's Little Scottsboro," 268; *Mount Dora Topic*, n.d., clipping, FHW Scrapbooks; *Orlando Sentinel*, September 4, 1949, 1.

37. *New York Post*, September 19, 1950; April 6, 1950; April 7, 1950, clippings, FHW Scrapbooks; Ivy, "Florida's Little Scottsboro," 267; *Orlando Sentinel*, April 19, 1950, 1–2. Poston described a high-speed chase from Tavares to Orlando in which a car he was riding in with another black reporter and the two black attorneys was pursued by a carload of whites.

38. "Florida Shooting," *Crisis* 58 (December 1951): 638.

39. "Resolutions Adopted by Forty-Third Annual Convention of the NAACP at Oklahoma City, Oklahoma, June 28, 1952," *Crisis* 59 (August–September 1952): 448. The criticism of the FBI leveled by the NAACP resulted from numerous instances of postwar violence against blacks.

40. *St. Petersburg Times*, April 7, 1950, 13; April 8, 1950, 17.

41. *Shepherd v. State*, 46 So. 2d. 1950, 880, 884; *Orlando Sentinel*, April 17, 1950, 1.

42. *Shepherd v. Florida*, 341 U.S. 50 (1950), 55. The jury included farmers and businessmen from the county but no women.

43. *Orlando Sentinel*, April 10, 1951, 1, 25; Mabel Norris Reese (Chesley), "Lake County Personalities," *Mount Dora Topic*, September 8, 1949, 1.

44. Sworn statements of Willis McCall and James L. Yates, 59–68, 51–58, Box 53, Lab-Lar, Rg 102, S 235, Administrative File, Governor Fuller Warren Papers, Florida State Archives, Tallahassee; *Orlando Sentinel*, November 7, 1951, 1; November 8, 1951, 9; *Mount Dora Topic*, November 8, 1951, 1.

45. Affidavit of Walter Lee Irvin, 1–5, Box 53, Governor Fuller Warren Administrative Correspondence; *Orlando Sentinel*, November 9, 1951, 1, 11; *Mount Dora Topic*, November 15, 1951, 1.

46. Interview with Mabel Norris Reese (Chesley) by Franklin Williams, 14, FHW Scrapbooks.

47. J. J. Elliott to Fuller Warren, November 21, 1951, Box 53, Lab-Lar, Rg 102, S 235, Governor Warren Administrative File, Warren Papers. Stetson Kennedy, a journalist, charged that Elliott had been a member of the Ku Klux Klan in Georgia. Stetson Kennedy, *I Rode With the Klan* (London: Arco Publishers, 1954), 245–47.

48. *Mount Dora Topic*, November 29, 1951, clipping, FHW Scrapbooks; interview with Mabel Norris Reese (Chesley) by Franklin Williams, 13–15, FHW Scrapbooks, 56.

49. Interview with Alex Akerman by David Colburn.

50. Both statements are quoted in "Answer to Vishinsky," *Crisis* 58 (December 1951): 666–67

51. *Mount Dora Topic*, December 6, 1951, 1, 4; *New York Times*, December 7, 1951, 30.

52. Harry T. Moore to Warren, November 15, 1951, Box 53, Rg 102, 1949–1951, Governor Warren Administrative Correspondence, Warren Papers.

53. "Terror in Florida," *Crisis* 59 (January 1952): 35.

54. The FBI initially conjectured that Moore may have been killed by either the NAACP or the Communist party "for propaganda purposes." Its investigation led the bureau in a more sensible direction to five members of the Ku Klux Klan; but in 1953, when a federal judge threw out the indictments against them on related charges of perjury, the Justice Department decided not to pursue the case. On September 16, 1955, the case was officially closed. This account was reconstructed from files obtained under the Freedom of Information Act by WTSP Channel 10, St. Petersburg–Tampa. The material was inspected at the offices of the station.

55. *Mount Dora Topic*, February 14, 1952, 1, 8. *Orlando Sentinel*, Febru-

ary 12, 1951, 1, 11; February 13, 1951, 1, 13; February 14, 1952, 1, 7. *New York Times*, February 17, 1952, 22.

56. *Orlando Sentinel*, February 13, 1952, 1, 13; February 14, 1952, 1, 7. *New York Times*, February 14, 1952, 28.

57. *Leesburg Commercial*, December 10, 1962, 1; December 21, 1962, 1.

58. *Orlando Sentinel*, February 15, 1952, 1, 2; *New York Times*, February 15, 1952, 42; *Irvin v. State*, 66, So 2d 288 (1953); *Irvin v. Florida*, 346 U.S. 927 (1954).

59. *St. Petersburg Times*, February 21, 1954, 4.

60. Interview with the Reverend Ben F. Wyland by Darryl Paulson, December 8, 1981, St. Petersburg. Interview in possession of the authors.

61. *Crisis* 61 (December 1954): 18; Harris to LeRoy Collins, 7–10, Collins Papers; Lula L. Mullikan to L. C. Chapman, File—Irvin, Walter, Death Warrant, Governor LeRoy Collins Papers, Florida State Archives.

62. Thomas Wagy, *Governor LeRoy Collins of Florida: Spokesman of the New South* (University, Ala.: University Press of Alabama, 1985), 66–68; *Orlando Sentinel*, March 15, 1956, 1; *Tampa Tribune*, May 5, 1956, 1; Presentment of the Grand Jury to Honorable T. G. Futch, 15, Box 29, Laf-Leg, 1955–56, Rg 102, Series Ba, Governor LeRoy Collins Administrative Correspondence, Collins Papers, Florida State Archives.

63. McCall to Herbert S. Phillips, July 8, 1955, Box 5, Herbert S. Phillips Family Papers, University of South Florida, Tampa.

64. *Tampa Tribune*, January 1, 1956, 5; Phillips to Collins, March 23, 1955, Box 5, Phillips Family Papers.

65. Franklin Williams Interview; Clendenin, "The Legacy of Iceman McCall," 23.

66. Hall, *Revolt against Chivalry*, 153.

67. "Florida Governor Errs on NAACP, Lawyer Says," Press Release, December 15, 1955, GOF II, A 229, NAACP Papers, Library of Congress, Washington, D.C.

68. Stetson Kennedy, "Ocala: Old Trials in New Bottles," typescript, Stetson Kennedy Papers, Southern Labor Archives, Georgia State University.

◇ **13**

The Pattern of Race Relations in Miami since the 1920s

Raymond A. Mohl

SEVERAL YEARS AGO, in her provocative book on Miami, writer Joan Didion noted with more than a little sarcasm that it was "a city in which black people and white people viewed each other with some discontent."[1] Few would disagree. But it is also worth remembering that it is only three decades since the walls of legal segregation began to crumble in South Florida. Legalized discrimination is now part of the past, and blacks exert a degree of political influence unknown prior to the civil rights legislation of the 1960s. Nevertheless, interracial and interethnic tensions remain high in late-twentieth-century Miami.

The city's racial and ethnic tension is evident in a variety of contexts. Most blacks, whites, and Hispanics live in racially distinct neighborhoods, a form of de facto residential segregation perpetuating the racial patterns of the past. As in most other large metropolitan areas, the level of black "spatial isolation" in contemporary Miami is quite high. Recent studies have also demonstrated that as a group, blacks in Miami, as elsewhere, remain economically disadvantaged. On most measures of civic and social well-being—schooling, housing, income, occupation, health, crime, government services, and the like—blacks fare poorly compared with whites and with Cubans.[2] Police-community relations have suffered as a result of serious racial violence and rioting in the Miami area in 1968, 1980, 1982, and 1989. Moreover, the massive influx of Cuban newcomers after 1959 has raised questions of fairness and equity among blacks, who tended to resent the government support and favoritism displayed toward the Cuban exiles. Thus, even as the civil rights movement of the 1960s ended the official segregation of the Jim Crow era, the legacy of the past lingers uncomfortably on in the Miami region. "You have in South Florida," as one urban sociologist summed it up early in 1990, "the worst example of black, white, and Hispanic race relations in the country."[3] Little has happened in the Miami area in the past few years that would challenge that judgment.

Ethnic and Racial Diversity

Florida has always had a diverse, multicultural population base. In the 1930s, for instance, researchers on the Florida Writers Project working on ethnic culture and folklore could report that "Florida has a great conglomeration of people hardly equalled anywhere in America." Cuban exiles in the late nineteenth century and in the 1930s, black migrants from Georgia, black immigrants from the Bahamas, Jews from the Northeast, Italians in Tampa, Greeks in Tarpon Springs — all contributed to Florida's diverse cultural pattern even before 1940. In particular, the *Miami Herald* reported in 1939, Miami's black population was "a melting pot of individuals from virtually every island of the Caribbean, the Bahamas, the cotton belt, Washington, D.C., and Harlem."[4]

The new Latin and Caribbean immigration of the past several decades has strengthened those early patterns of cultural, racial, and ethnic diversity. Haitians, Jamaicans, Cubans, Puerto Ricans, Nicaraguans, Colombians, and innumerable other smaller groups of newcomers from the Caribbean basin have revolutionized the demographic structure of South Florida over the past thirty years. The United States historically accommodated and ultimately assimilated (or mostly assimilated) tens of millions of European immigrants in the nineteenth and early twentieth centuries, before the end of open immigration in the 1920s. This "melting pot" model has not worked well in South Florida, however. Immigrant cultural, linguistic, and familial traditions remain deeply entrenched in South Florida's ethnic communities. Exile groups such as Cubans, Nicaraguans, and Haitians, in particular, have retained more than a tenuous relationship with their native lands, and they have resisted assimilating forces. For these peoples, some social scientists say, the immigration process has been one of "adjustment without assimilation." The maintenance of strong ethnic identities has also contributed to powerful interethnic rivalries and conflicts.[5]

Race, as well as ethnicity, has been a powerfully divisive issue in South Florida. Florida has been a "Deep South" state for much of the twentieth century, and blacks who migrated or immigrated to the South Florida area early in the twentieth century encountered Jim Crow in law and in custom.[6] Legal segregation and racial discrimination prevailed in every aspect of life. For South Florida blacks, reality meant residential segregation and substandard housing; it also entailed job discrimination and economic marginality. It often meant that blacks suffered from the white terrorism of the Ku Klux Klan and from brutal treatment at the hands of the local police. It meant that political leaders paid little attention to the needs of black communities, and that government policy-making usually served other groups. This essay explores some of these issues in more detail and discusses the black activism and civil rights efforts that challenged the system of segregation.

Residential Segregation

One legacy of the segregation era has been deeply etched on the urban landscape of South Florida. Residential segregation has achieved a special sort of permanence in the Miami area, stemming partially from the influence of the local real estate industry on the urban land market, and partially as a consequence of the cumulative impact of public policy decisions on racial zoning, annexation, public housing, and highway building. In Miami's earliest years, for instance, blacks were clustered residentially in a confined, inner-city area known at the time as "Colored Town" and now called Overtown. By 1930, most of Miami's black population of approximately 25,000 was crowded into an area of about fifty small blocks covered over mostly with shotgun shacks and slum housing. Racial zoning policies kept blacks confined to Overtown and a few other areas of the city.[7]

Given the nature of race relations in South Florida, shifts in black residential patterns usually were dictated by public policy decisions. By the 1930s, white business leaders were interested in pushing outward the boundaries of the relatively confined downtown business district, at the expense of Miami's black community. New Deal public housing programs during the Depression decade provided the first such opportunity. A New Deal public housing project for blacks named Liberty Square was completed in 1937 on undeveloped land five miles northwest of the central business district. The city's white civic elite saw the availability of federal housing funds for this project as an opportunity to push blacks out of the downtown area and permit downtown business expansion.[8]

Other efforts were under way during the 1930s to achieve the same goal. In 1936, for instance, the Dade County Planning Board proposed a "negro resettlement plan." The idea was to cooperate with the City of Miami "in removing [the] entire Central Negro town" to three "model negro towns" on the distant agricultural fringes west of Miami. A year later, in a speech to the Miami Realty Board, former Coral Gables developer George Merrick proposed "a complete slum clearance effectively removing every negro family from the present city limits." The idea of black removal from the central district died hard. In 1945 Miami civic leaders were still discussing "the creation of a new negro village that would be a model for the entire United States." Although never implemented, slum clearance plans in 1946 called for the removal of Miami blacks from the central area to a distant new housing development west of Liberty City. As late as 1961, the *Miami Herald* was reporting on new plans to eliminate Overtown to facilitate downtown business expansion.[9]

These proposals were never implemented, but New Deal housing agencies such as the Home Owners Loan Corporation and the Federal Housing Administration contributed to changing racial patterns. Through their appraisal policies, both agencies "redlined" Miami's black community and nearby white areas of "transition," thus hastening the physical decay of the inner-city area. Until the 1950s, the Dade County Planning Board permitted the gradual and "controlled" expansion of black residential areas. In actual practice, the Liberty Square housing project became the center of a new and rapidly growing black ghetto now known as Liberty City. A tacit agreement among city and county officials, real estate developers, and some black leaders designated the northwest area of Miami and Dade County for future black settlement.[10]

Aerial view of the Liberty Square housing project, completed in 1937. In the mid-1930s, Miami civic leaders sought to move all blacks outside the Miami city limits. This housing project was conceived as the nucleus of a new and distant black community. White property owners profited from the development of the surrounding land. Courtesy of the Historical Association of Southern Florida, Miami.

Interstate-95 and the Black Community

Liberty City became the nucleus of a new black ghetto, as Miami's white business leaders of the 1930s had anticipated. But their plans to eliminate Overtown—to move all the blacks out of Miami and be-yond the city limits—were still unfulfilled by midcentury. In the late 1950s and early 1960s, the federal interstate highway program pro-vided a new opportunity to tear down the Overtown community and remove the blacks to more distant residential areas on the northwest fringe of the metropolitan area. At the same time, Miami's white civic leadership perceived the new urban interstate as a massive building project that might revitalize the languishing central business district and permit future expansion and redevelopment.

In retrospect, it is clear that the construction of the interstate highway system had an enormous impact in reshaping the spatial order of urban America. The interstates not only linked far-flung cities but also pierced into their commercial centers. In the process, they destroyed wide swaths of built-up urban land, often uprooting entire communities—usually black or working-class ethnic neighborhoods. A general pattern developed of using highway construction to eliminate "blighted" neighborhoods and to redevelop or "reconvert" valuable inner-city land. In most big cities, the forced relocation of blacks and other low-income urbanites intensified the spatial reorganization of residential neighborhoods that had been underway since the end of World War II. This process of residential movement and change underlay the creation of what historian Arnold R. Hirsch has called, in a study of postwar Chicago, the "second ghetto." [11]

The building of Interstate-95 in the Miami area provides a devastating example of the human and social consequences of urban expressway construction. As early as 1956, the Florida State Road Department, in conjunction with local officials and business leaders, routed Interstate-95 directly through Overtown and into downtown Miami. Alternative plans using the FEC Railroad corridor were rejected in order, as the planners stated, to provide "ample room for the future expansion of the central business district in a westerly direction." When the downtown leg of the expressway was completed in the mid-1960s, it ripped through the center of Overtown, wiping out massive amounts of housing as well as Overtown's main business district, the commercial and cultural heart of black Miami. One massive expressway interchange alone (I-95 and I-395) took up twenty square blocks of densely settled land and destroyed the housing of about 10,000 people. Some 40,000 blacks had made Overtown home before the interstate came, but less than 8,000 now remain in what is an urban wasteland dominated by the physical presence of the expressway. By the end of the expressway building era, little remained of Overtown to recall its days as a thriving center of black community life, when it was known as the Harlem of the South.[12]

The Second Ghetto

By the time the Miami expressway system tore through Overtown in the early 1960s, the process of second-ghetto growth had been underway for almost two decades. Liberty City began pushing out its boundaries into nearby white neighborhoods by the mid-1940s, eventually absorbing separate, smaller black communities such as Brownsville, also on Miami's northwest side. Punctuated by white protest marches, Klan bombings, cross burnings, and racial violence, the process of residential turnover was not an easy one. In August 1945, for instance, two black families crossed the "red line" and purchased homes in a white residential area adjacent to Brownsville. The blacks were harassed by county health, zoning, and police officials and eventually jailed for zoning violations. Once blacks were released on bond, the Ku Klux Klan burned a fiery ten-foot cross in their neighborhood—a warning, a black reporter wrote, "to prevent Negroes from expanding their residential section." Three months later, the Klan struck again, burning five crosses in the same neighborhood while armed whites drove through the area in cars and trucks. It was a classic second-ghetto confrontation, as tersely reported in the *Pittsburgh Courier*: "Tension has been mounting in this section . . . for quite some months, as whites started fighting expansion of adjoining Negro sections." In November 1947, the Klan burned not only a cross but also the homes of two black families that had moved near "the dividing line between the two races." According to John A. Diaz, the Miami correspondent of the *Pittsburgh Courier*, these incidents "signalled the beginning of a concerted Ku Klux Klan drive in the neighborhood." The campaign of intimidation and violence continued in 1948, as fiery Klan crosses illuminated night skies in Miami's black districts in May, October, and November of that year.[13]

Racial skirmishing on the frontiers of the ghetto persisted well into the 1950s. The black population of the Miami metropolitan area was increasing rapidly, rising by 31 percent in the 1940s and 111 percent in the 1950s. Hemmed in for decades by race and custom, Miami's blacks how now pushed out of the inner-city ghetto into new housing areas. Numerous white real estate developers directed the process, buying up large tracts for future black housing and suc-

So This Is Miami

So This Is Miami, 1938. Throughout the 1930s, the Miami Police Department often looked the other way when the Ku Klux Klan made an appearance in Miami. This cartoon makes obvious the apparent connection between the Klan and the police. Originally printed in the *Miami Daily News*, May 8, 1938.

cessfully challenging Dade County's racial zoning ordinance in the Florida courts. City and county officials, by contrast, fought to retain the residential color line in South Florida.[14] Similarly, several white neighborhood groups and homeowners associations actively lobbied local government agencies and engaged in protest demonstrations as blacks began to push out of Overtown and Liberty City into nearby areas. Not coincidentally, the Ku Klux Klan experienced a resurgence in the Miami area in the postwar era, as it did throughout the rest of the South.[15]

Second-ghetto tensions flared once more in 1951, when the owners of the Knight Manor apartment complex, a rental property for whites located in Edison Center on the eastern fringes of Liberty

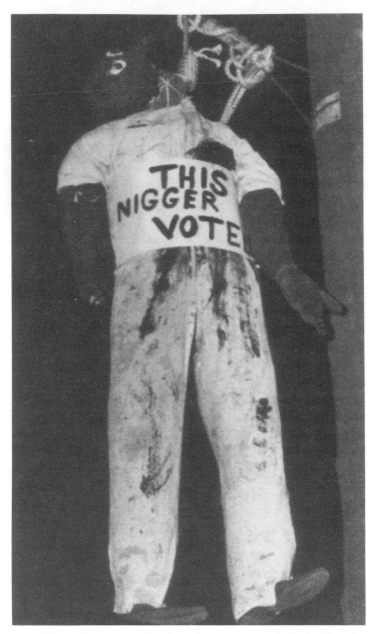

This Nigger Voted, 1939. During the 1939 municipal elections in
Miami, blacks registered to vote in unprecedented numbers. The Ku
Klux Klan sought to discourage the black vote by hanging effigies
such as this one from lampposts in the black community, but to no
avail. Originally printed in *Life*, May 15, 1939.

Ku Klux Klan highway sign, 1946. The Klan was rejuvenated in Miami after 1945, as cross-burnings and Klan parades became commonplace. This sign on the Dixie Highway welcomed visitors to postwar Miami. Courtesy of the Stetson Kennedy Collection.

City, began renting some apartments to blacks. The Dade County Property Owners Association complained to Governor Fuller Warren that "by vacating white tenants and replacing them with colored tenants," the owners were disturbing the peace of "a long established white neighborhood." A local Citizens Action League sprang up "to protect our Southern way of life." Others complained that "the negro area is to be extended into what has always been a white area." The Klan injected itself into the controversy, distributing hate literature and organizing white motorcades through the area. Leaving little to the imagination, the Klan torched giant wooden *K*s around the black apartment section of Knight Manor.[16]

A series of dynamite bombings in late 1951 brought the Knight Manor conflict to a head, as militant whites sought to scare off their new black neighbors. Massive dynamite blasts on September 22, on November 30, and again on December 2 left the black section of the complex, which had been renamed Carver Village, virtually unlivable. Jewish synagogues and schools and a Catholic church in Miami

Ku Klux Klan parade, Miami. Courtesy of the Historical Association of Southern Florida.

were also bombed during this period, suggesting the coordinated work of white hate groups such as the Ku Klux Klan.[17]

Behind the scene, however, other forces were at work in reorganizing the racial characteristics of Miami's residential space. The owners of Knight Manor, John A. Bouvier and Malcolm B. Wiseheart, were well-known Miami slumlords with investments in Overtown, Coconut Grove, Brownsville, and Liberty City. Bouvier was also a member of the Dade County Zoning Board during this period. Through several real estate development companies, notably South Kingsway Corp. and Fiftieth Street Heights, Inc., Bouvier and Wiseheart were actively buying property in transitional areas for black housing. Edison Center whites believed, apparently with good reason, that the movement of blacks into Knight Manor was the opening wedge for designating the entire area for black residency, with the landowners and realtors profiting immensely. In fact, property transfer records in Miami indicate that Bouvier and Wiseheart had purchased a large amount of vacant land in the Edison Center neighborhood. They were well positioned to profit from any racial transition of the area.

Numerous other real estate developers and speculators were engaged in the same process throughout the Miami metropolitan area. As the Carver Village bombings suggest, the efforts of blacks to challenge the residential color line in Miami was a difficult process, punctuated during the 1950s by hostility, racial conflict, and violence. But often managing the process of residential change were real estate people such as Bouvier and Wiseheart.[18]

The controversy over race and space did not end with the 1950s. In the next two decades, a large and still expanding corridor of black residential housing emerged in the northwest quadrant of Dade County, reaching beyond Liberty City to Opa-locka and Carol City. An extensive housing development in the Bunche Park section of Opa-locka, mostly built in the 1950s by white developers Milton H. Davis and Julius Gaines, set the stage for second-ghetto development in Opa-locka in the 1960s and 1970s. Carol City, an overbuilt white residential area begun in 1954, experienced a high rate of recession-induced mortgage foreclosures, "block-busting" by realtors, and pervasive white flight by the 1960s. The *Miami Herald* reported in 1971 that the "next ghetto is Carol City." [19]

The Carol City story typified the rapid racial turnover of northwest Dade County neighborhoods. The concentration of blacks in this second-ghetto area stemmed from the racial zoning and housing decisions of earlier decades. The outflow of black population from Overtown resulting from expressway construction and other urban redevelopment in the 1960s intensified the racial transformation of Miami's residential space. Throughout the period, white real estate developers and slumlords were actively managing the process of residential "transition." The arrival and settlement of about 800,000 Cubans between 1959 and 1980 also shaped the local housing market, effectively limiting the housing choices of blacks displaced from Overtown by redevelopment activities.[20]

In recent years, urban redevelopment policies in South Florida have begun yet again to redefine areas of black residence. In Miami, urban redevelopment continues to chip away at what is left of Overtown, as city, county, and state office buildings, a new sports arena, high-rise and townhouse housing for middle-class professionals, and innumerable parking lots push into the area. Other black communities in Dade County have faced the same redevelopment pressures.

In the black area of Coconut Grove, citizens recently fought off a proposal to build a highway through a historic black residential district. In the only black area of upscale Coral Gables, city commissioners in 1987 proposed a redevelopment plan that would raze and replace multifamily housing with single-family residences, meaning that "some people will have to move out of the area." In 1985 in northwest Dade County, middle-class blacks in the Crestview, Lake Lucerne, and Rolling Oaks Estates subdivisions unsuccessfully fought against the construction of the new Joe Robbie football stadium, which they claimed would destroy their neighborhoods.[21]

Thus, black residential patterns in South Florida continue to shift in response to governmental decision making and land market factors. Usually these changes have reinforced historic patterns of residential segregation throughout the South Florida area. The consequence, as several sociological studies have demonstrated, was that between 1940 and 1960 Miami had the highest degree of residential segregation among more than one hundred large American cities. This was not a racial pattern that happened by accident, but one that reflected the controlled expansion of black residential areas throughout that entire period. Miami's "index of residential segregation" has improved modestly since 1960 compared with other southern cities. Nevertheless, in 1980 and again in 1990, after thirty years of civil rights activism in urban America, Miami still ranked in the high range, compared with other large metropolitan areas, in the extent of black residential segregation.[22]

The city's segregated black ghettos had also become slums. Reports by the Greater Miami Urban League in 1953 and 1954, for example, confirmed what most blacks already knew. Slum housing conditions were pervasive in most Miami-area black communities. Density was extremely high—as much as 1,000 percent higher for some black neighborhoods than for whites generally. Overcrowded apartments, excessive rents, inadequate plumbing, deteriorating buildings, few municipal services, and rampant public health and social problems characterized black Miami in the 1950s. A third Urban League report issued ten years later revealed little improvement in housing and social conditions. Black housing in Miami, according to Urban League researcher James W. Morrison, was twice as crowded and ten times more dilapidated than that of whites in 1960.[23]

Slum housing, 1950. Using dramatic posters such as this one, Miami housing reformers led by Elizabeth Virrick successfully pushed slum-clearance and public-housing ordinances through a local referendum in 1950. Courtesy of the Elizabeth Virrick Papers.

In an effort to address these problems, some Miami area social activists initiated housing reform for blacks as early as the post–World War II period. For instance, in the late 1940s, a black Baptist preacher named Edward T. Graham led the Negro Service Council, the Miami Urban League affiliate at the time, in pushing for federal action for housing and social reform in Miami.[24] Similarly, the bi-racial Coconut Grove Citizens' Committee for Slum Clearance was organized in 1948 under the leadership of local civic activist Elizabeth Virrick. Working with black community leaders, such as the Reverend Theodore Gibson, an Episcopal priest, Virrick launched a vigorous movement against Miami slumlords and for improved housing and social conditions in the black section of Coconut Grove. By the 1950s, Virrick's group expanded its scope of action to Overtown and Liberty City, successfully guiding passage of referenda on public housing and urban renewal issues.[25] But governmental inaction, public inertia, and virulent opposition from the local real estate industry meant that the Virrick housing reform group achieved only minor improvements in a few isolated places. Meanwhile, the slum and the ghetto expanded apace at the end of the segregation era.

Economic Discrimination

Historically, blacks in South Florida have also faced a substantial degree of economic discrimination, particularly in the local job market. Blacks in South Florida had historically been concentrated in unskilled, agricultural, heavy labor, and domestic jobs. A small professional and entrepreneurial group served the black community, but this sector was too small to provide jobs for many blacks. Job discrimination was the order of the day. In the 1920s, Miami had ordinances prohibiting black skilled artisans and tradesmen from working in white neighborhoods. The city of Miami was still enforcing this ordinance in the 1940s. A 1953 Miami Urban League survey of thirty-seven large private firms employing more than 12,000 workers revealed that only one black among those served in a supervisory position, and "possibly" only one—a chef—held a skilled position. Few labor unions in South Florida admitted black laborers or craftsmen.[26]

Job discrimination extended to the public sector, as well. No blacks were hired for the police force until the mid-1940s, when a completely segregated black police unit was created to patrol Overtown; this segregated police unit continued to function into the 1950s. As late as 1953, there were no black firemen in Miami. About 850 blacks worked for the city of Miami in 1953, and about 500 for Dade County, but almost all of these municipal workers were employed in laboring, custodial, and service positions. Blacks composed 16 percent of the Dade County teaching force, but all served in black schools, and job discrimination kept them from promotion within the school system. In the 1940s, the Negro Service Council, which later became the Miami branch of the Urban League, began pushing local businesses and government agencies to hire black workers, but with little success. Racial discrimination in employment remained a deeply ingrained tradition in this part of the Deep South at the end of the segregation era. Indeed, as one scholar has noted, Florida by the mid-1950s "retained nearly all the Jim Crow aspects of the Deep South. . . . Floridians were segregated in schools, churches, public facilities, job opportunities, and almost all other significant ways." [27]

The discriminatory job pattern continued even as the civil rights movement got underway. The Greater Miami Urban League, in its 1962 report, documented the economic disadvantages suffered by Miami area blacks. Inadequate education and racial discrimination in employment condemned most blacks to low-income jobs as un-skilled laborers, service workers, and domestic servants. Black unem-ployment also surpassed that of white Miamians by a considerable margin. Consequently, the median income level for Miami blacks was about half that of whites in 1960.[28]

A separate study by the Florida Council on Human Relations, also published in 1962, painted an equally stark picture of the economic prospects for blacks in South Florida. Despite a few success stories, the council reported that in the Miami area "the great majority of Negroes work as garbage collectors, cooks, kitchen helpers, porters, maids, bellboys, elevator operators, household domestics, dry clean-ing pressers, and helpers in the construction trades." In Broward and Palm Beach counties, blacks were also heavily concentrated in low-wage service, agricultural, and unskilled labor jobs. African Ameri-cans in South Florida seemed permanently lodged at the bottom of the region's economic structure as the civil rights movement began. Moreover, little had changed by the end of the 1960s, when a *Miami*

Herald report noted that job opportunities for Miami blacks were "still severely limited." The *Herald* also suggested that black aspirations exceeded available opportunities in South Florida—a consequence of the civil rights movement that had ominous implications during a decade of intense racial violence.[29]

White Terrorism and Black Response

Residential segregation and job discrimination had become central elements in the pattern of race relations in South Florida by mid-century. Harassment, violence, and terrorism against blacks by such white groups as the military, the Ku Klux Klan, and the Miami Police Department had also become part of the order of the day. During the Spanish-American War of 1898, some of the 7,000 soldiers stationed in Miami "invaded the colored settlement and terrorized the negroes," apparently simply "to keep up the excitement" of wartime. A few years later, in 1908, after police killings of Bahamians in Miami and Key West, a British consular official reported that "it is a common occurrence for negroes to be shot" by police while evading arrest. In Florida, he wrote, "the killing of a man for practically no reason whatever is a common occurrence." [30]

Blacks in South Florida resisted white supremacy and white terrorism in a variety of ways. In 1919, for example, Miami blacks formed the militant Negro Uplift Association to protest routine police invasions of black neighborhoods and to demand better treatment.[31] The black nationalist ideology of Marcus Garvey, in particular, had great appeal in South Florida. By 1921, Garvey's Universal Negro Improvement Association (UNIA) had about 1,000 members in Miami and another 700 in Key West. According to an agent of the Federal Bureau of Investigation in Miami, most of the UNIA members in Miami were Bahamians, who "bitterly resent[ed] the color line as drawn in Florida." A resurgent white racism in Miami threatened racial peace, according to this federal agent, and Miami blacks apparently were arming themselves in defense. Mass meetings sponsored by the UNIA in Miami in 1927 brought eight hundred new members to the organization, and a black reporter for Garvey's *Negro World* noted that "Garveyism is spreading like wild fire down here in Miami." As many as 3,000 blacks gathered at one big UNIA meeting in 1927, reflecting the widespread support for the organization in Miami's black community, but the movement also suffered internal divisions that blunted its effectiveness.[32] Despite black flirtation with Garveyite nationalism in the 1920s, white terrorism continued without any serious interference from, and sometimes with the participation of, the local police.

The ubiquitous pattern of police harassment of blacks in South Florida communities persisted for decades. One recent study has demonstrated that Miami police killed blacks at an extremely high rate during the 1920s. In 1928 Miami's police chief himself was indicted for ordering the 1925 beating and murder of a black hotel worker. Although ultimately acquitted, Chief H. Leslie Quigg was dismissed as chief because he had condoned rampant police brutality. But Quigg's removal brought little change; in fact, Quigg was back as Miami's police chief by the end of the 1930s. In the 1940s, according to one black professional man, the Miami police were "full of intolerance, bigotry, and sadism. . . . These policemen liked to see blood run; they were overly aggressive." Another black leader in Miami reported that "our police protection consisted of a reign of brutality. Beatings and killings by the white police officers were common place." A third black Miamian in the 1940s portrayed white policemen as "trigger happy" — "there was a great deal of promiscuous killing, and they had no respect for Negro life at all."[33] Actor Sidney Poitier, who arrived in Miami from the Bahamas in 1943 as a fifteen-year-old, wrote in his autobiography, *This Life*, "I decided that Miami wasn't so good for me when I began to run into its not so subtle pattern of racism." The Miami police played a powerful role in maintaining the color line through midcentury.[34]

In response to police violence, blacks armed themselves, eventually posing such a potential threat that white policemen were characterized by one black leader as "insecure and afraid" and rarely entered black neighborhoods. By the early 1940s, only two police officers at a time, riding in a patrol car, were assigned to Overtown to provide police protection for a community of about 40,000 people. White police entered the area only when actual crimes had been reported, but they were reluctant to patrol black neighborhoods on a regular basis as they did in white communities — a pattern that had long been commonplace in the urban South. Ultimately, the dangers posed to white officers patrolling black areas led to the creation of an entirely separate black police unit in Miami in 1944.[35]

Although blacks may have exercised some degree of control within their segregated communities, they faced white hostility and terrorism whenever they ventured beyond the color line. Poitier's encounters with police, for instance, all came while he was working or traveling outside the black community. On matters of race relations, the Miami police differed little from the Ku Klux Klan. Both adhered strongly to white supremacy, and both used violence and terrorism to maintain Jim Crow segregation. With about 1,500 members in Miami during the mid-1920s, and with about 30,000 members statewide by the 1930s, the Ku Klux Klan acted with impunity throughout the Depression decade. As one black writer cynically noted of Miami during that period, "The Ku Klux Klan had begun to subsidize the sheet industry." The Klan's Imperial Wizard in the late 1930s and early 1940s, James A. Colescott, devoted considerable attention to organizing activities in Florida. Between 1939 and 1942, for example, the Klan's monthly paper, *The Fiery Cross*, focused on Colescott's speaking tours in Florida and the Klan's membership drives in the Sunshine State. By the early 1940s, two separate KKK klaverns, along with women's auxiliaries, had sprouted in Miami.[36]

The Klan adopted a low profile during World War II, partially because it faced charges of federal tax evasion. But it roared back to life in Miami after 1945. Imperial Wizard Colescott, a veterinarian in Atlanta, retired to Miami after the war. It was no coincidence that the KKK in Miami resurfaced at about the same time. Cross burnings periodically flamed over the next decade as blacks began crossing the color line into new residential areas. By 1946, Miami's John B. Gordon Klan No. 5, named after a Confederate general, welcomed travelers to the city with several huge billboards at the city limits. As was true in Atlanta and other southern cities, the Klan drew membership from the Miami police department, which helps to explain the absence of police during cross burnings and the vigorous police enforcement of the color line.[37]

The Ku Klux Klan remained dangerously active in Florida throughout the 1950s, when segregation was coming under increas-

The dynamited Knight Manor Apartment in Miami, 1951. When blacks began moving into the white apartment complex in 1951, the Klan responded with dynamite attacks on three separate occasions. Courtesy of the Florida State Archives.

ing attack. In 1951, as noted earlier, the Klan organized the bombing of Carver Village, as well as the murder of Harry T. Moore, state NAACP president, who had organized the Florida Progressive Voters League and conducted voter registration drives among blacks in Miami and elsewhere in Florida.[38] By 1952, the Florida Klan's Grand Dragon, Bill Hendrix, announced the formation of the American Confederate Army, a group "sworn to uphold segregation by force." Bombings of schools, churches, and synagogues in Miami, Jacksonville, and other cities occurred as late as 1958. A "Confederate Underground" took credit for the 1958 bombings; its leaflets promised "Regular bombings . . . Negroes and Jews our Specialty."[39] Even more insidiously, the Klan wrapped itself in the mantle of true patriotism and anticommunism during the McCarthy period of the 1950s, tarnishing the NAACP and civil rights groups as dangerously left-wing and un-American. The White Citizens' Council movement also had its advocates in the Miami area, especially as the school integration issue heated up in the mid-1950s. These groups, which claimed 15,000 members in Miami, distributed segregationist and anti-Semitic literature, resisted school integration, and generally stirred racial hatred. For the Klan and those with Klan mentalities, white terrorism and Red-baiting propaganda went hand in hand.[40]

The Political Context

African Americans in South Florida found little solace in the political system. For much of the twentieth century, Florida politicans have held firmly to the color line. Segregation and white supremacy were enforced not just through the terrorism of the Ku Klux Klan but also through the political decision-making process in the state legislature and in city and county governments. Prior to the 1950s, blacks made little political progress in the Miami area. The state poll tax (repealed by the Florida legislature in 1937), the white primary system (outlawed by the U.S. Supreme Court in 1944), and other, later registration restrictions and voting procedures, such as at-large elections, effectively excluded blacks from the political process for many decades.[41]

Miami blacks generally remained politically quiescent during the segregation era, except in some local city elections. In the early 1930s, a few Miami blacks paid poll taxes and sought to vote in Democratic primaries, but they were often harassed by the Klan and turned away from the polls by voting officials. Only a handful regularly voted, as one black Miamian reported to the NAACP, "when conditions are favorable." Miami had a nonpartisan city commission, so the white primary did not apply. As early as 1939, however, with the poll tax gone, Miami blacks began organizing politically and voting regularly in city elections. Sam B. Solomon, who headed Miami's Negro Citizens Service League at the time, spearheaded a voter registration campaign among blacks, eventually registering about 1,500 blacks for the May 1939 city commission primary election. With Solomon and other black leaders pressing the need for better municipal services in the black community, Miami blacks voted in record numbers.[42]

This display of black political activism was not without its costs. On election eve in May 1939, the Ku Klux Klan organized a massive downtown rally, followed by a Klan motorcade through black neighborhoods; some of the seventy-five cars and trucks in the motorcade had thick hangman's nooses dangling menacingly from their windows. The Klan burned twenty-five crosses at one-block intervals in the black district and hung black effigies from lampposts, labeled "This Nigger Voted." Leaflets were distributed with an ominous KKK warning: "Respectable negro citizens are not voting tomorrow. Niggers stay away from the polls." Suggesting the links between the Klan and the Miami police, the *Miami Herald* comented on "the absence of policemen from the scene during the Klan's night parade through the heart of the negro section." Blacks remained undeterred, however, and challenged the Klan with an unprecedented voter turnout.[43]

White supremacists in Florida were alarmed over black political participation. Within a week of the 1939 election, white political leaders sought to add a white primary rule to the Miami city charter and thus prevent blacks from voting.[44] Later in the year, a proposed Miami charter "reform" that would have replaced at-large elections with a district system was defeated, partially because of white fears that at least one of the new districts would have a majority black population. As one writer noted in the *Miami Herald*, under the new district system, "You are sure to have at least one negro councilman and you might have two. Do the people of Miami want that?" Advocates of the charter reform promised to amend the district boundaries so that there would be "absolutely no possibility of a negro ever being elected to the city commission under any circumstances." But it was too late. The injection of the racial issue into the charter-reform debate dictated the outcome, as Miami voters clung to white supremacy by more than a four-to-one margin. These incidents in 1939 set the stage for the racial politics of the next two decades, as Florida politicians persistently sought to deter blacks from voting and to "preserve the purity of the ballot."[45]

With only a few exceptions, Florida's political leaders through the 1960s strongly supported segregation and black political exclusion. Running successfully for the U.S. Senate in 1950, Miami's George Smathers typically blasted a black voter registration drive in Florida as a "dangerous invasion of carpetbaggers" and insinuated that his opponent, Claude Pepper, was a Communist. Smathers successfully ran, one scholar has written, "a nigger- and red-baiting" campaign against Pepper. Florida's twentieth-century governors enthusiastically supported white supremacy, even after the barriers of segregation began falling in the mid-1950s. Only LeRoy Collins, first elected governor in 1954, followed a more moderate path on race relations. During the period from 1954 to 1960, he abandoned his support of segregation and came to advocate a program of racial justice for blacks.[46]

At the local level, county and municipal officials throughout Florida held firmly to the color line during the 1950s. One Dade County legislator, John B. Orr, however, spoke out often against segregation as "repugnant to our great democratic principles" and voted against every segregation measure before the Florida House of Representatives in 1956. But Orr was atypical. The white supremacist views of the Ku Klux Klan retained widespread support in Florida well past midcentury.[47] Some white liberal and leftist groups — the Anti-Defamation League, the American Jewish Congress, the National Conference of Christians and Jews, and the Civil Rights Congress, among others — were actively promoting better race relations in South Florida as early as the late 1940s, but these groups had little impact in the years before the civil rights movement. In fact, left-wing groups such as the Civil Rights Congress were targeted for harassment and eventually driven underground by the Klan, the Miami police, and the FBI. Black voter registration drives in South Florida, promoted by the Greater Miami Urban League, the Congress of Racial Equality, and the NAACP, picked up steam at the end of the 1950s, but as late as 1962, not a single black held elective public office anywhere in the state of Florida.[48]

The Civil Rights Movement

The civil rights era for blacks in Florida began in the mid-1950s. The 1954 U.S. Supreme Court decision outlawing school segregation, of course, was a turning point in race relations in South Florida, as elsewhere. But school desegregation was implemented very slowly in Florida. Dade County voluntarily integrated its schools in 1959 but only in token fashion. After much preliminary study, the Orchard Villa School in Miami admitted four black students when school opened in the fall of 1959, but the neighborhood was already in the midst of rapid racial transition. By the end of the school year in 1960, most of the whites had already moved from the Orchard Villa neighborhood. Liberal critics at the time described as "phony" the school board's public embracement of desegregation. The fact was that deeply imbedded patterns of housing segregation in the Miami area produced a form of de facto school segregation that continued for many decades.[49]

Despite the slow pace of school integration, the barriers of racial segregation in South Florida had begun to fall by the end of the 1950s. Legal challenges by the NAACP, economic pressure by the Urban League, and militant activism by the Congress of Racial Equality (CORE) began to produce results. Local black activists and white liberals, especially Jewish liberals, worked together to challenge the color line. Several Miami Beach hotels and restaurants, generally those owned by Jews, desegregated as early as 1956, when they accommodated 15,000 black delegates to an African Methodist Church convention. Voter registration drives among South Florida blacks, particularly those led by CORE between 1958 and 1964, brought a new sense of empowerment.[50] The civil rights legislation of the mid-1960s speeded the end of Jim Crow, as white politicians began to solicit black votes and a few blacks were elected to city and county commissions and to the state legislature. In Miami, voters sent a black woman, Athalie Range, to the city commission in 1967, and she was succeeded in the 1970s by black activist clergymen Edward T. Graham and Theodore R. Gibson.[51]

Many political and social gains came as the result of persistent black activism. As early as 1945, for instance, Miami blacks led by Edward T. Graham of the Negro Service Council successfully conducted a "wade-in" on Miami Beach, demanding beach access to the Atlantic Ocean for the first time.[52] By the early 1960s, new black wade-ins signaled the demand for integrated beaches. Black activists from the Fort Lauderdale NAACP also conducted wade-ins in 1961, successfully integrating public beaches in Broward County.[53] Black activism brought integration in other areas as well. The Urban League facilitated the integration of the medical staff at Miami's Jackson Memorial Hospital in 1952. The Miami NAACP threatened a bus boycott in 1956, following a successful transit boycott in Tallahassee, and eventually used legal challenges to end the Miami Transit Company's segregated bus system in 1957.[54]

The civil rights movement in South Florida moved to a new level in April 1959, when the Miami affiliate of the Congress of Racial Equality conducted its first lunch-counter sit-ins in downtown "five

After successful bus boycotts in Montgomery, Alabama, and Tallahassee, Florida, the Miami NAACP used legal challenges to force the desegregation of transit in Miami. Here, the Reverend Theodore Gibson of the Miami NAACP sits at the front of the bus after transit service became integrated in 1957. Courtesy of the Historical Association of Southern Florida, Miami.

and dime" stores. CORE targeted Miami for direct action as early as 1958, sending field operatives to the city and conducting "action institutes" in 1959 and 1960. As CORE executive secretary James R. Robinson put it in a letter to a Miami activist, "I have been interested in Miami because it is strategic and yet basically not so intolerant as most cities of the Deep South; it is South of the South and could play an important role from that side." CORE's 1959 Miami sit-ins, or "testings" as they were called, did not produce immediate results, but the power of direct action had been demonstrated. Over the next two years, CORE's nonviolent direct action successfully integrated downtown lunch counters, restaurants, hotels, and theaters.[55] The relative ease of the desegregation process, as compared with that in other southern cities, owed much to behind-the-scene negotiations among business leaders, black representatives such as Gibson and Graham, and state and city officials, particularly Miami Mayor Robert King High. Mayor High and Governor Collins were both heavily involved in negotiating the end of segregated public facilities in South Florida in 1960.[56]

There were other gains, too. A CORE-sponsored economic boycott of local supermarkets that refused to hire blacks ended successfully in 1960. Black activists in the Urban League and the NAACP integrated Dade County beaches, parks, swimming pools, and golf courses by 1960. In Broward County, the Fort Lauderdale NAACP picketed and boycotted supermarkets, department stores, and utility companies to open up employment for blacks. Because of the heavy in-migration of northerners, white resistance to desegregation was weaker in South Florida by the 1960s than elsewhere in the state, but blacks had to march, picket, boycott, demonstrate, litigate, speak out, sit-in, stand-in, kneel-in, wade-in, and use their collective economic and political clout to banish Jim Crow.[57]

Blacks and Hispanics

The civil rights movement thus held out some hope to the South Florida black community by the early 1960s. In the Miami area, however, the civil rights movement coincided with the Cuban Revolution of 1959 and the subsequent exile migration to South Florida. Some have argued, in fact, that the Cuban migration short-circuited the economic, political, and social gains blacks were making elsewhere in the civil rights era. The exile "invasion," as it increasingly came to be called in the 1960s, touched off thirty years of competition and conflict between blacks and Hispanics over jobs, residential space, government services, and political power in the South Florida area.[58]

The subsequent economic and political success of the Cubans contributed to a pervasive sense of powerlessness, resentment, and despair in black Miami. Often penniless on arrival, many Cuban immigrants moved at first into the low-paying service jobs traditionally held by blacks, particularly in tourist hotels and restaurants in Miami and Miami Beach. They also competed with black workers in the garment industry, construction, and other areas of blue-collar employment. In 1963, *Ebony* magazine wrote that "the economic penetration of the refugees is now universal," creating serious social and economic problems for the black community. By the early 1960s, the

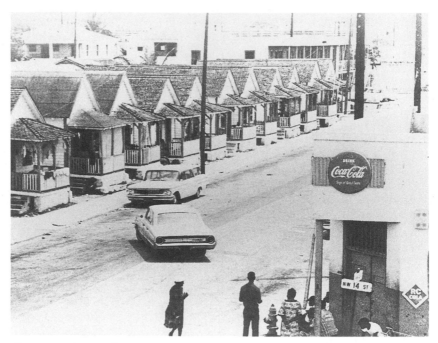

Overtown shotgun houses, ca. 1960. Miami's inner-city community of Overtown was covered with small "shotgun" houses such as these until the urban renewal and highway building of the late 1950s and 1960s ripped the neighborhood apart. From the *Miami Herald*, ca. 1960.

Greater Miami Urban League noted unhappily that blacks were "systematically being pushed out of [jobs] to make room for Cubans." Similarly, the Miami branch of the NAACP protested in 1965 to Governor Haydon Burns over the "economic oppression" created by the Cuban exile migration. Donald W. Jones of the NAACP also complained about job competition to Florida's U.S. Senator George A. Smathers, hinting of "inevitable friction" between Miami blacks and the Cuban newcomers. African Americans in Miami, Jones wrote, were tired of being the "sacrificial lamb," offered up by the government "for the extension of freedom and democracy to refugees from another land." In 1965, a Dade County representative to the Florida legislature warned that the continuing Cuban influx was "creating a powder keg that could blow at any moment." By the end of the 1960s, of course, Miami's black community had exploded in racial

Aerial view of Interstate-95 Downtown Interchange. The construction of the interstate highway system provided a new opportunity to destroy Overtown and force blacks to more distant neighborhoods. This massive I-95 interchange, completed in the mid-1960s, sprawled over twenty square blocks and destroyed the housing of about 10,000 people. Courtesy of the Florida Department of Transportation, Tallahassee.

violence. Close observers attributed Miami's 1968 race riot in part to economic competition with the new Cuban exiles.[59]

During the 1960s and 1970s, as earlier Cubans moved upward economically and professionally, newer exiles from Cuba and elsewhere in Latin America took their places at the bottom end of the Miami economy. Over time, Hispanics replaced blacks in the low-wage service economy where they had formerly predominated. Despite the area's growing economy over three decades, blacks have remained on the economic margins, with poverty-level incomes, high levels of unemployment, and little economic opportunity. "By all social indicators," the U.S. Civil Rights Commission reported in 1982, "blacks have been excluded from the economic mainstream in Miami." Despite the gains of the civil rights era, the commission contended, "generations of explicit and race-based employment discrimination have left a legacy that continues to infect the labor market." [60]

The Cuban exiles have also been energetic entrepreneurs, having a dramatic impact on business activity in the South Florida area. It is now clear that the Cuban exiles created a self-sufficient "enclave economy," one entirely separate from the mainstream white business community and separate as well from the peripheral black minority economy.[61] Some evidence suggests that Cuban entrepreneurial success often came at the expense of black-owned businesses. For example, blacks owned 25 percent of all the gas stations in Dade County in 1960. By 1979, black ownership of service stations had dropped to 9 percent, while Hispanic stations numbered 48 percent of the total. Cuban business formation was aided substantially by almost $50 million in loans from the federal Small Business Administration between 1968 and 1980, while black businesspeople in the Miami area received a miniscule amount by comparison.[62] The emerging Cuban enclave economy absorbed hundreds of thousands of Hispanic newcomers over the years, but did little to advance the economic position of the black community. As writer David Rieff recently put it, "The blacks were frozen out" by the Cubans, who "saw no particular reason to have to assume the burden of America's historical obligation to black people." [63]

Race relations in the South Florida area, particularly in Miami, remain in severe disarray, despite the racial reforms of the 1960s. Black resentment continues to fester over the economic success of the Cubans, their dominance of the job and housing markets, their newly developed political power, and the preferential treatment they have received from government. Other issues such as police harassment and violence, or the perception of police violence, in the ghetto combined to produce racial explosions that have symbolized Miami race relations since 1968. Behind these overt incidents lie thirty years of ethnic and racial competition between South Florida's blacks and their new Hispanic neighbors from the Caribbean basin. The persistent failure of the system to deliver often-promised social and economic improvements—better housing, improved schools, job training, better services—has kept blacks in Miami and elsewhere in South Florida on the edge of rage and despair. When the Miami city commission, dominated by three Hispanic commissioners, snubbed the visiting Nelson Mandela in 1990, few Miami blacks were surprised.[64]

The civil rights movement, especially as it gained strength in the late 1950s, seriously challenged the legal and social bases of the Jim Crow society for the first time, but even the gains of the civil rights movement have been transitory. Blacks now have some political power, but housing and schooling remain mostly segregated. New immigrants to Florida, such as the Cubans and other Hispanics, have been successful economically, while blacks seem confined to menial jobs. Since Miami's first ghetto riot in 1968, black discontent and despair have boiled to the surface on numerous occasions. For much of this century, government policy and decision-making have had a profound impact on the role and position of blacks in South Florida. Activism in the black community has periodically produced positive change, but government at varied levels often has responded more readily to countervailing pressures from land developers, real estate interests, white community organizations, and new immigrant political and economic pressure groups.

As the twentieth century draws to a close, it seems clear that racial change is a slow process. Indeed, the historical record suggests that only persistent black activism or significant shifts in government policy will produce lasting change. The 1992 federal court decision throwing out the Dade County at-large election system will empower blacks as never before in the Miami metropolitan area; the implementation of the new district election system ultimately may produce positive changes at the local level similar to those of the civil rights revolution of the 1960s.[65] Yet few black residents are satisfied with the state of race relations in South Florida today, and much remains to be accomplished before the legacy of racism is completely overcome.

Notes

1. Joan Didion, *Miami* (New York: Simon and Schuster, 1987), 39–40.

2. *Miami Herald*, September 30, 1990. Census tract data from the 1980 and 1990 censuses indicate that levels of residential segregation in Miami have been declining modestly since 1970, but as geographer Thomas D. Boswell has pointed out, "Segregated residential patterns are likely to continue to exist in metropolitan Miami into the future." Thomas D. Boswell, "Hispanic Segregation Patterns in Metropolitan Miami," *Florida Geographer* 24 (1990): 34–66, quotation on p. 62; Thomas D. Boswell, *Ethnic Segregation in Greater Miami, 1980–1990* (Miami: Cuban American National Council, 1992); Douglas S. Massey and Nancy A. Denton, *American Apartheid: Segregation and the Making of the Underclass* (Cambridge, Mass.: Harvard University Press, 1993), 63–66, 86–87.

3. *Miami Herald*, July 26, 1990. See also Marvin Dunn and Alex Stepick, "Blacks in Miami," in *Miami Now: Immigration, Ethnicity, and Social Change*, ed. Guillermo J. Grenier and Alex Stepick (Gainesville: University Press of Florida, 1992), 41–56.

4. Zora Neale Hurston et al., "The Florida Negro: Folklore," typescript in Florida Writers Project Collection, University of South Florida Library, Tampa; *Miami Herald*, May 9, 1939.

5. Raymond A. Mohl, "Immigration through the Port of Miami," in *Forgotten Doors: The Other Ports of Entry to the United States*, ed. M. Mark Stolarik (Philadelphia: Balch Institute Press, 1988), 81–98; Raymond A. Mohl, "Miami: New Immigrant City," in *Searching for the Sunbelt: Historical Perspectives on a Region*, ed. Raymond A. Mohl (Knoxville: University of Tennessee Press, 1990), 149–175.

6. Jerrell H. Shofner, "Custom, Law, and History: The Enduring Influence of Florida's 'Black Code,'" *Florida Historical Quarterly* 57 (January 1977): 277–98.

7. Paul S. George, "Colored Town: Miami's Black Community, 1896–1930," *Florida Historical Quarterly* 56 (April 1978): 432–477.

8. Raymond A. Mohl, "Trouble in Paradise: Race and Housing in Miami during the New Deal Era," *Prologue: Journal of the National Archives* 19

(Spring 1987): 7–21; Paul S. George and Thomas K. Peterson, "Liberty Square, 1933–1937: The Origins and Evolution of a Public Housing Project," *Tequesta: The Journal of the Historical Association of Southern Florida* 49 (1988): 53–68.

9. Dade County Planning Board Minutes, August 27, 1936, in George E. Merrick Papers, Box 2, Historical Association of Southern Florida, Miami; Dade County Planning Council, "Negro Resettlement Plan," 1937, in National Urban League Papers, part 1, series 6, Box 56, Library of Congress, Washington, D.C.; George E. Merrick, *Planning the Greater Miami for Tomorrow* (Miami: Miami Realty Board, 1937), 11; *Miami Herald*, April 5, 1945, May 28, 1961; *Pittsburgh Courier*, July 20, 1946.

10. Mohl, "Trouble in Paradise," 14–20; Warren M. Banner, *An Appraisal of Progress, 1943–1953* (New York: National Urban League, 1953), 20–24; *Miami Herald*, November 1, 1946, May 29, 1947, December 2, 1952.

11. Thomas H. MacDonald, "The Case for Urban Expressways," *American City* 62 (June 1947): 92–93; Thomas MacDonald, "The Interstate System in Urban Areas," May 16, 1950, in Thomas H. MacDonald Papers, U.S. Department of Transportation Library, Washington, D.C.; Mark H. Rose, *Interstate: Express Highway Politics, 1941–1956* (Lawrence: Regents Press of Kansas, 1979), 55–67; Mark H. Rose and Bruce E. Seely, "Getting the Interstate System Built: Road Engineers and the Implementation of Public Policy, 1955–1985," *Journal of Policy History* 2 (Spring 1990): 23–55; Arnold R. Hirsch, *Making the Second Ghetto: Race and Housing in Chicago, 1940–1960* (Cambridge, England: Cambridge University Press, 1983).

12. Miami Planning and Zoning Board, *The Miami Long Range Plan: Report on Tentative Plan for Trafficways* (Miami: City of Miami, 1955); Wilbur Smith and Associates, *A Major Highway Plan for Metropolitan Dade County Florida Prepared for State Road Department and Dade County Commission* (New Haven: Wilbur Smith and Associates, 1956), 33–44; Raymond A. Mohl, "Race and Space in the Modern City: Interstate-95 and the Black Community in Miami," in *Urban Policy in Twentieth-Century America*, ed. Arnold R. Hirsch and Raymond A. Mohl (New Brunswick, N.J.: Rutgers University Press, 1993), 100–158.

13. *Pittsburgh Courier*, August 11, 1945, November 17, 1945, November 15, 1947, November 22, 1947; *Atlanta Daily World*, November 11, 1945, December 1, 1945; "Lynchings and Mob Violence," 1947, typescript, Papers of the Civil Rights Congress, microfilm edition, part 2, reel 17; "Pattern of Violence," *New South* 4 (March 1949): 3–5.

14. Miami Planning Board, *Dwelling Conditions in the Two Principal Blighted Areas: Miami, Florida* (Miami: City of Miami, 1949); Reinhold P. Wolff, *Greater Miami Population and Housing Survey: Real Estate Division* (Coral Gables: University of Miami, 1949); Reinhold P. Wolff and David Gillogly,

Negro Housing in the Miami Area: Effects of the Postwar Housing Boom (Coral Gables: University of Miami, 1951); Harold M. Rose, "Metropolitan Miami's Changing Negro Population, 1950–1960," *Economic Geography* 40 (July 1964): 221–38; and more generally, Raymond A. Mohl, "Making the Second Ghetto in Metropolitan Miami, 1940–1960," *Journal of Urban History* 21 (March 1995). For black population growth in Miami and Dade County during these years, see Raymond A. Mohl, "The Settlement of Blacks in South Florida," in *South Florida: The Winds of Change*, ed. Thomas D. Boswell (Miami: Association of American Geographers, 1991), 112–19. For the legal challenge to racial zoning in Miami, see *Pittsburgh Courier*, December 1, 1945, February 16, 1946, March 2, 1946, March 30, 1946, April 20, 1946, May 11, 1946.

15. On the postwar resurgence of the Ku Klux Klan in Miami and the South generally, see *Pittsburgh Courier*, December 15, 1945, April 6, 1946, May 4, 1946, November 29, 1947, December 6, 1947; *Atlanta Daily World*, December 9, 1945; Harold Preece, "The Klan Declares War," *New Masses* 57 (October 16, 1945), 3–7; Stetson Kennedy, "The Ku Klux Klan: What to Do About It," *The New Republic* 114 (July 1, 1946): 928–30; Carey McWilliams, "The Klan: Post-War Model," *The Nation* 163 (December 14, 1946), 691–94.

16. Ira D. Hawthorne to Fuller Warren, August 28, 1951, September 25, 1951, Box 22, Fuller Warren Papers, Florida State Archives, Tallahassee; Ira D. Hawthorne to Miami City Commission and Dade County Commission, September 10, 1951, Warren Papers, Box 22; Lorine S. Reder to Fuller Warren, August 8, 1951, Warren Papers, Box 21; *Miami Herald*, July 14, 1951; Charles Abrams, *Forbidden Neighbors: A Study of Prejudice in Housing* (New York: Harper, 1955), 120–36; Stetson Kennedy, *The Klan Unmasked* (Boca Raton: Florida Atlantic University Press, 1990), 219–33.

17. *Miami Herald*, July 14, 1951; *Miami Times*, September 29, 1951, December 1, 1951; Stetson Kennedy, "Miami: Anteroom to Facism," *The Nation* 173 (December 22, 1951): 546–47; Joe Alex Morris, "The Truth about the Florida Race Troubles," *Saturday Evening Post*, June 21, 1952, 24–25, 50, 55–58; William S. Fairfield, "Florida: Dynamite Law Replaces Lynch Law," *The Reporter* 7 (August 5, 1952): 31–34, 41; Teresa Lenox, "The Carver Village Controversy," *Tequesta: The Journal of the Historical Association of Southern Florida* 50 (1990): 39–51.

18. Property transfer records show that Bouvier and Wiseheart purchased an extensive tract of land near Knight Manor in 1947. See Deed Books, 1946–48, Book no. 2886, p. 429, in Official Records Library, Office of Dade County Clerk, Miami. For newspaper reportage on Bouvier and Wiseheart, see *Miami News*, March 23, 1947, November 3, 1948, November 28, 1948, November 31, 1948; *Miami Herald*, January 5, 1949, February 3, 1949, February 4, 1949.

19. Wolff and Gillogly, *Negro Housing in the Miami Area*, 4–6, 8, 21; Teresa Lenox, "Opa-locka: From Dream to Ghetto," graduate seminar paper, Florida Atlantic University, 1988; C. E. Wright, "Carol City—A Complete One-Man-Built Florida Town—to House, Serve 40,000," *Municipal South* 2 (March 1955): 20–22; Metro-Dade County, *Carol City Area Study* (Miami: Metro-Dade County Planning Department, 1972); Metro-Dade County, *Population Projections: Race and Hispanic Origin, Dade County, Florida, 1980–2000* (Miami: Metro-Dade County Planning Department, 1987); *Miami Herald*, October 3, 1965, April 2, 1971, March 12, 1989.

20. Clyde C. Wooten, *Psycho-Social Dynamics in Miami* (Coral Gables: Center for Advanced International Studies, University of Miami, 1969), 531–554; Metro-Dade County, *Mobility Patterns in Metropolitan Dade County, 1964–1969* (Miami: Metro-Dade County Planning Department, 1970); Morton D. Winsberg, "Housing Segregation of a Predominantly Middle-Class Population: Residential Patterns Developed by the Cuban Immigration into Miami, 1950–74," *American Journal of Economics and Sociology* 38 (October 1979): 415; *Miami Herald*, November 1, 1982.

21. *Miami Herald*, December 7, 1987, January 17, June 28, 1988; *Miami News*, October 14, 1987.

22. Donald O. Cowgill, "Trends in Residential Segregation of Non-Whites in American Cities, 1940–1950," *American Sociological Review* 21 (February 1956): 43–47; Karl E. Taeuber and Alma F. Taeuber, *Negroes in Cities: Residential Segregation and Neighborhood Change* (Chicago: Aldine Publishing Company, 1965), 39–41; Annemette Sorenson et al., "Indexes of Racial Residential Segregation for 109 Cities in the United States, 1940–1970," *Sociological Focus* 8 (1975): 125–42; Douglas S. Massey and Nancy A. Denton, "Trends in the Residential Segregation of Blacks, Hispanics, and Asians: 1970–1980," *American Sociological Review* 52 (December 1987), 802–25; Douglas S. Massey and Nancy A. Denton, "Suburbanization and Segregation in U.S. Metropolitan Areas," *American Journal of Sociology* 94 (November 1988): 592–626; Massey and Denton, *American Apartheid*, 63–66, 86–87; *Miami Herald*, December 30, 1987.

23. Banner, *An Appraisal of Progress*, 20–42; H. Daniel Lang, *Food, Clothing and Shelter: An Analysis of the Housing Market of the Negro Group in Dade County* (Miami: Greater Miami Urban League, 1954); James W. Morrison, *The Negro in Greater Miami* (Miami: Greater Miami Urban League, 1962), 6–12.

24. Edward T. Graham, "A Brief of Conditions Surrounding the Housing Problem in Miami As It Relates to the Negro," 1947, typescript, National Urban League Papers, part 1, series 3, Box 57, Library of Congress.

25. Marjorie S. Douglas, "Grove Slum Clearance Movement Reviewed," *Voters' Voice* (Coconut Grove Citizens' Committee for Slum Clearance),

February 24, 1949, p. 1; Elizabeth L. Virrick, "Miami Citizens' Committee for Slum Clearance, First Annual Report of the Chairman," January 19, 1953, in National Urban League Papers, part 1, series 6, Box 56, Library of Congress; Elizabeth L. Virrick, "Civic Cooperation in Miami," in *Grass Roots Private Welfare*, ed. Alfred de Grazia (New York: New York University Press), 64–68; Martin Millspaugh and Gurney Breckenfeld, *The Human Side of Urban Renewal* (Baltimore: Fight-Blight, 1958), 121– 55; Mohl, "Race and Space in the Modern City," 119–124; Elizabeth Virrick, interviews with Raymond A. Mohl, October 8, 11, 25, 1986, January 31, 1987, March 28, 1987.

26. Raymond A. Mohl, "Black Immigrants: Bahamians in Early Twentieth-Century Miami," *Florida Historical Quarterly* 65 (January 1987): 271–97; Lorenzo J. Greene and Carter G. Woodson, *The Negro Wage Earner* (Washington, D.C.: Association for the Study of Negro Life and History, 1930), 323; Dade County, District Welfare Board No. 9, Monthly Report on Defense Developments, May-June 1942, in National Urban League Papers, part 1, series 6, Box 56, Library of Congress; Banner, *An Appraisal of Progress*, 11–12.

27. David H. Cohn, "The Development and Efficacy of the Negro Police Precinct and Court of the City of Miami," (M.A. thesis, University of Miami, 1951); *Miami Times*, July 25, 1953; Banner, *An Appraisal of Progress*, 7–9; Helen L. Jacobstein, *The Segregation Factor in the Florida Democratic Gubernatorial Primary of 1956* (Gainesville: University of Florida Press, 1972), 10, 12.

28. Morrison, *The Negro in Greater Miami*, 15–22.

29. "Negro Employment in Miami," *New South* 17 (May 1962): 10; James W. Button, *Blacks and Social Change: Impact of the Civil Rights Movement in Southern Communities* (Princeton: Princeton University Press, 1989), 101; Philip Meyer et al., *Miami Negroes: A Study in Depth* (Miami: Miami Herald, 1968), 4.

30. H. W. Kennard, "Report on Enquiry into the Circumstances of the Death of Robert Hulbert, a British Subject at Miami," March 29, 1908, CO 23/264, Public Record Office, London; Isidor Cohen, *Historical Sketches and Sidelights of Miami, Florida* (Miami: privately printed, 1925), 36–37.

31. *Miami Herald*, June 2, 1919; Arthur Chapman, "History of the Black Police Force and Court in the City of Miami" (D.A. thesis, University of Miami, 1986), 28–29; George, "Colored Town," 441.

32. *The Marcus Garvey and Universal Negro Improvement Association Papers*, ed. Robert A. Hill, vol. 3 (Berkeley: University of California Press, 1984), 513–15; ibid., vol. 6 (1989), 594–95; ibid., vol. 7 (1990), 124, 133–34, 141–42, 166–71; *Negro World*, June 11, 1927, April 7, 1928; Franklin K. Vought, "The UNIA in Miami," seminar paper, University of Miami, 1991; James Nimmo, videotape interview with Gregory Bush, 1987.

33. William Wilbanks, *Murder in Miami: An Analysis of Homicide Patterns and Trends in Dade County (Miami) Florida, 1917-1983* (Lanham, Md.: University Press of America, 1984), 57; "Sunny Florida," *The Crisis* 35 (June 1928), 203-4; *New York Times*, March 3, 27, 1928; Cohn, "Development and Efficacy of the Negro Police Precinct," 73, 84, 90.

34. Sidney Poitier, *This Life* (New York: Ballantine Books, 1980), 42-43.

35. Cohn, "The Development and Efficacy of the Negro Police Precinct," 4, 23-24, 73, 76, 82; Chapman, "The History of the Black Police Force and Court in the City of Miami," 38; Elliott M. Rudwick and August Meier, "Negro Retaliatory Violence in the Twentieth Century," *New Politics* 5 (Winter 1966): 41- 51; Howard N. Rabinowitz, "The Conflict Between Blacks and Police in the Urban South, 1865-1900," *The Historian* 39 (November 1976): 62-76.

36. David Chalmers, "The Ku Klux Klan in the Sunshine State: The 1920s," *Florida Historical Quarterly* 42 (1964): 209-15; George, "Colored Town," 445-47; Bob Hayes, *The Black American Travel Guide* (rev. ed.; San Francisco: Straight Arrow Books, 1973), 197; *The Fiery Cross* 1 (October 1939): 1, 8; 1 (December 1939): 2; 1 (February 1940): 3; 1 (March 1940): 3; 3 (April 1941): 1.

37. On Colescott, see *Philadelphia Afro-American*, April 6, 1946; *Pittsburgh Courier*, April 6, 1946; Preece, "The Klan Declares War," 3-7; Stetson Kennedy, *Southern Exposure* (Garden City, N.Y.: Doubleday, 1946), 173-74, 176-79, 203-4, 209-12; Kennedy, *The Klan Unmasked*, 219- 57; *Negro Year Book, 1941-1946*, ed. Jessie Parkhurst Guzman (Tuskegee, Ala.: Tuskegee Institute, 1947), 218; David M. Chalmers, *Hooded Americanism: The History of the Ku Klux Klan* (New York: Doubleday, 1965), 318-24; Wyn Craig Wade, *The Fiery Cross: The Ku Klux Klan in America* (New York: Simon and Schuster, 1987), 265-66, 271-75.

38. On the Moore murder, see *Miami Times*, December 29, 1951; Stetson Kennedy, "Murder By Bombing," *The Nation* 174 (January 5, 1952): 4; "Bigotry and Bombs in Florida," *Southern Patriot* 10 (January 1952): 1, 4; Gloster B. Current, "Martyr for a Cause," *The Crisis* 59 (February, 1952): 73-81, 133-34; George Breitman, *Jim Crow Murder of Mr. and Mrs. Harry T. Moore* (New York: Pioneer Press, 1952); Hugh D. Price, *The Negro and Southern Politics: A Chapter of Florida History* (New York: New York University Press, 1957), 45, 57, 117-18; James Clark, "The Murder of Harry T. Moore and Ku Klux Klan Violence in Central Florida," unpublished paper, 1992; Carolyn E. Poore, "Striking the First Blow: Harry T. Moore and the Fight for Black Equality in Florida" (M.A. thesis, Florida State University, 1992).

39. For the Confederate Underground and the 1958 bombings, see *Southern Patriot* 10 (November 1952): 4; Nathan Perlmutter, "Bombing in Miami: Anti-Semitism and the Segregationists," *Commentary* 25 (June 1958): 498-

503; *Southern School News* 4 (April 1958): 9; 4 (May 1958): 5; 4 (June 1958): 13.

40. For red-baiting of the NAACP in Florida, see Steven F. Lawson, "The Florida Legislative Investigation Commission and the Constitutional Readjustment of Race Relations, 1956–1963," in *An Uncertain Tradition: Constitutionalism and the History of the South,* ed. Kermit L. Hall and James E. Ely, Jr. (Athens: University of Georgia Press, 1989), 296–325. On the White Citizen's Councils in South Florida, see *Southern School News* 4 (September 1957): 8; 4 (October 1957): 11; 4 (December 1957): 12–13; and, on the movement generally, Harry L. Golden and Julian Scheer, "Klan Without Hoods," *Congress Weekly* (American Jewish Congress) 23 (March 23, 1956): 5–8; and Neil R. McMillen, *The Citizen's Council: Organized Resistance to the Second Reconstruction, 1954–1964* (Urbana: University of Illinois Press, 1971).

41. Price, *The Negro and Southern Politics,* 23, 28; William G. Carleton, "Negro Politics in Florida: Another Middle-Class Revolution in the Making," *South Atlantic Quarterly* 57 (Autumn 1958): 419–32.

42. For Miami voting in the early 1930s, see Charles S. Thompson to NAACP, August 11, 1931, NAACP Papers, Voting Rights Campaign, microfilm edition, part 4, reel 1; Thomas L. Lowrie to William T. Andrews, July 14, 1931, ibid.; Alonzo P. Holly to Walter White, July 13, 1932, ibid. For Sam Solomon's voter registration campaign in 1939, see *Miami Herald,* May 1–3, 1939, May 12, 1939.

43. *Miami Herald,* May 2–3, 1939; "Miami Klan Tries to Scare Negro Vote," *Life,* May 15, 1939, 27; Ralph J. Bunche, *The Political Status of the Negro in the Age of FDR* (Chicago: University of Chicago Press, 1973), 199–200, 307; Price, *The Negro and Southern Politics,* 23.

44. *Miami Herald,* May 11–12, 1939, May 20, 1939.

45. *Ibid.,* October 19–20, 1939, October 23, 1939, November 8, 1939; Price, *The Negro and Southern Politics,* 28.

46. Robert Sherrill, *Gothic Politics in the Deep South: Stars of the New Confederacy* (New York: Grossman, 1968), 150; Morton Sosna, *In Search of the Silent South: Southern Liberals and the Race Issue* (New York: Columbia University Press, 1977), 165; David R. Colburn and Richard K. Scher, *Florida's Gubernatorial Politics in the Twentieth Century* (Tallahassee: Florida State University Press, 1980), 220–36; Tom R. Wagy, *Governor LeRoy Collins of Florida: Spokesman of the New South* (University, Ala.: University of Alabama Press, 1985).

47. Jacobstein, *The Segregation Factor,* 8–12, 73; *Miami News,* July 26, 1956; Wilma Dykeman and James Stokely, *Neither Black Nor White* (New York: Rinehart, 1957), 357–59; William C. Havard and Loren P. Beth, *The Politics of Mis-Representation: Rural-Urban Conflict in the Florida Legislature* (Baton Rouge: Louisiana State University Press, 1962), 30.

48. M. A. F. Ritchie, "A City Works at Human Relations," *New South* 7 (March-April 1952): 1–8; Raymond A. Mohl, "Blacks, Jews, and the Civil Rights Movement in Miami, 1945–1960," unpublished paper, Southern Historical Association, November 1992; Havard and Beth, *The Politics of Misrepresentation*, 29; Matilda ("Bobby") Graff, "The Historic Continuity of the Civil Rights Movement," unpublished manuscript, 1971, in possession of the author; Gerald Horne, *Communist Front? The Civil Rights Congress, 1946–1956* (Rutherford, N.J.: Fairleigh Dickinson University Press, 1988), 190–95.

49. Dade County Schools, "Orchard Villa Survey," November 13, 1958, Dade County Public School Collection, Historical Association of Southern Florida, Miami; *New York Times*, August 16, 1959; Southern Regional Council, "A Background Report on School Desegregation for 1959–60" (1959), 36–37, in LeRoy Collins Papers, University of South Florida Library, Tampa; Shirley Zoloth, clipping scrapbook, 1957–59, in author's possession. Zoloth was a founding member of the Miami chapter of the Congress of Racial Equality in 1958. For Florida generally, see David R. Colburn, "Florida's Governors Confront the *Brown* Decision: A Case of the Constitutional Politics of School Desegregation, 1954–1970," in *An Uncertain Tradition*, ed. Hall and Ely, 326–55.

50. *Jewish Floridian*, February 6, April 24, 1959; *Pittsburgh Courier*, May 12, 1956; August Meier and Elliott Rudwick, *CORE: A Study in the Civil Rights Movement* (New York: Oxford University Press, 1973), 176, 260.

51. Raymond A. Mohl, "Miami: The Ethnic Cauldron," in *Sunbelt Cities: Politics and Growth Since World War II*, ed. Richard M. Bernard and Bradley R. Rice (Austin: University of Texas Press, 1983), 83; James W. Button, "Blacks," in *Florida's Politics and Government*, ed. Manning J. Dauer (Gainesville: University of Florida Press, 1984), 289–90.

52. Edward T. Graham, "Negro Service Council, Progress Report," 1945, in National Urban League Papers, part 1, series 13, Box 16, Library of Congress.

53. Richard V. Kelleher, "The Black Struggle for Political and Civil Rights in Broward County, 1943–1989" (M.A. thesis, Florida Atlantic University, 1990), 60–66.

54. W. C. Pinkston, "Negro Physicians to Practice on Staff of County Hospital in Miami, Florida," news release, February 21, 1952, in National Urban League Papers, part 1, series 5, Box 42, Library of Congress; Charles U. Smith and Lewis M. Killian, *The Tallahassee Bus Protest* (New York: Anti-Defamation League of B'nai B'rith, 1958); *The Civil Rights Movement in Florida and the United States*, ed. Charles U. Smith (Tallahassee: Father and Son Publishing, Inc., 1989); Robert W. Saunders to Gloster B. Current, January 19, 1957, NAACP Papers, group 3, series C, Box 25,

Library of Congress; *Miami News*, June 7, 1956; *Miami Times*, June 16, 1956, November 17, 1956, August 17, 1957.

55. James R. Robinson to Thalia Peters, October 13, 1958, Papers of the Congress of Racial Equality, microfilm reel 19, State Historical Society of Wisconsin, Madison; Gordon R. Carey to James R. Robinson, March 3, 1959, ibid.; Shirley M. Zoloth to James R. Robinson, April 22, April 30, July 14, 1959, ibid.; "Report on Greater Miami Core," July 21, 1959, ibid.; James R. Robinson, *1959 Miami Interracial Action Institute: Summary and Evaluations* (New York: Congress of Racial Equality, 1960); *Miami Herald*, April 30, June 14–15, 1959, March 5, April 12–16, 1960; *Miami News*, June 14, 1959, April 12, 1960; *Miami Times*, July 23, August 6, September 3, 1960; Marvin Rich, "Miami Experiences Racial Stalemate," *The Progressive* 24 (February 1960): 36–37; Jim Peck, *Freedom Ride* (New York: Grove Press, 1962), 51–53; Meier and Rudwick, *CORE*, 90–91; Shirley Zoloth, interviews with Raymond A. Mohl, August 23, 1991, December 14, 1992.

56. Edward T. Graham to Theodore Gibson, August 8, 1960, in LeRoy Collins Papers, Box 33, Florida State Archives, Tallahassee; Governor's Commission on Race Relations, Minutes, April 16, May 14, 1960, ibid.; Faith High Barnebey, *Integrity Is the Issue: Campaign Life with Robert King High* (Miami: E. A. Seemann, 1971), 49–51; Wagy, *Governor LeRoy Collins*, 132–43; LeRoy Collins, "Past Struggles, Present Changes, and the Future Promise for Civil Rights in Florida and the Nation," in *The Civil Rights Movement in Florida*, ed. Smith, 9–28.

57. *Miami Times*, April 19, 1958, November 28, 1959, April 23, May 21, September 3, 17, 1960, April 8, 1961.

58. Raymond A. Mohl, "On the Edge: Blacks and Hispanics in Metropolitan Miami since 1959," *Florida Historical Quarterly* 69 (July 1990): 37–56.

59. Allan Morrison, "Miami's Cuban Refugee Crisis," *Ebony* 18 (June 1963): 96–104; H. Daniel Lang, "Testimony for the Senate Sub-Committee on Cuban Refugees," December 1, 1961, in National Urban League Papers, part 2, series 2, Box 15; Donald W. Jones to Haydon Burns, October 19, 1965, in Haydon Burns Papers, Box 23, Florida State Archives; Ralph R. Poston to Haydon Burns, October 20, 1965, ibid; Donald W. Jones to George A. Smathers, October 13, 1965, George A. Smathers Papers, Box 58, P. K. Yonge Library, University of Florida. On Miami's racial violence of 1968, see *Miami Times*, August 2, 16, 1968; J. Boone and W. Farmar, "Violence in Miami: One More Warning," *New South* 23 (1968): 28–37; National Commission on the Causes and Prevention of Violence, *Miami Report: The Report of the Miami Study Team on Civil Disturbances in Miami, Florida, during the Week of August 5, 1968* (Washington, D.C.: U.S. Government Printing Office, 1969).

60. Haydon Burns to Lyndon B. Johnson, October 5, 1965, Burns Papers,

Box 23; Haydon Burns to Buford Ellington, November 2, 1965, ibid.; T.A.P. Staff to Haydon Burns, Memorandum on "Problems Related to Cuban Refugees in Dade County," October 29, 1965, ibid.; U.S. Commission on Civil Rights, *Confronting Racial Isolation in Miami* (Washington, D.C.: U.S. Government Printing Office, 1982), 18, 124.

61. Harold M. Rose, "Blacks and Cubans in Metropolitan Miami's Changing Economy," *Urban Geography* 10 (1989), 464–86; Kenneth L. Wilson and W. Allen Martin, "Ethnic Enclaves: A Comparison of the Cuban and Black Economies in Miami," *American Journal of Sociology* 88 (July 1982): 135–60.

62. Bruce Porter and Marvin Dunn, *The Miami Riot of 1980: Crossing the Bounds* (Lexington, Mass.: D.C. Heath, 1984), 169, 195–96.

63. David Rieff, *Going to Miami: Exiles, Tourists, and Refugees in the New America* (Boston: Little, Brown, 1987), 172, 174.

64. *Miami Herald*, June 26–29, 1970. On the black tourism and convention boycott movement that followed the Mandela incident, see *Miami Herald*, July 18, August 3, August 8, September 30, December 16, 1990; *Miami Times*, November 14, 1991. A negotiated end to the three-year-old boycott in May 1993 promised better economic opportunities for Miami blacks. See *Miami Herald*, May 13, 1993.

65. *Carrie Meek vs. Metropolitan Dade County, Florida*, 86 U.S. 1820 (1992); *Miami Herald*, August 10, 15, 1992. The new district-based Dade County Commission, elected in April 1993, included four black commissioners out of thirteen, compared with one black commissioner out of nine on the earlier at-large commission. *Miami Herald*, April 23, 1993.

◇ **Contributors**

Jeffrey S. Adler is associate professor of history and a member of the faculty of the Center for Studies in Criminology and Law at the University of Florida.

David R. Colburn is professor of history and associate dean of the College of Liberal Arts and Sciences at the University of Florida.

Robert L. Hall teaches African American studies and history at Northeastern University.

Maxine D. Jones is associate professor of history at the Florida State University.

Patricia L. Kenney is a doctoral candidate at the University of Florida and is completing a community study of African Americans in the urban South from 1865 to 1920.

George Klos is currently pursuing a doctorate in history at the University of Texas at Austin.

June L. Landers is assistant professor of history at Vanderbilt University.

Steven F. Lawson is professor of history and chair of the history department at the University of North Carolina–Greensboro.

Raymond A. Mohl is professor of history at Florida Atlantic University.

Steven Noll is adjunct associate professor of history at the University of Florida, and an adaptive technology teacher for students with mental handicaps in the Alachua County school system.

Darryl Paulson is associate professor of government and coordinator for the College of Arts and Sciences at the St. Petersburg Campus of the University of South Florida.

Larry E. Rivers is professor of history at the Florida Agricultural and Mechanical University.

Daniel L. Schafer is professor of history at the University of North Florida.

anticommunism, 346
Anti-Defamation League, 348
Antietam, 163
Antigua, 81
Anti-lynching bill, 265
Anti-lynching Crusaders Committee, 265
Apalachicola River, 34, 104, 128, 134
Apthorp, Lt. Col. William L., 178
Arango, Juan, 219
Archivo General de Indias (Seville), 6
Arkansas River, 143
Arlington, 178
armed forces: desegregation of, 285
artisans, 52–54, 76
arts, 259–60
Ash, James, 161
Ashanti, 46–47, 52
Askew, Reubin, 319
assimilation, 327–28
Associated Negro Press, 259
Association of Southern Women for the Prevention of Lynching, 302
Atlanta (Georgia), 211
Atlantic Coast Line Railroad, 264
Aucilla, 48–49
"Aunt Venie," 55
Ayers, Edward, 5
Ayllón, Lucas Vásquez de, 19

Bagley, James, 168
Bagley, James, Jr., 168
Bahamas, 96, 120, 133
Bahamians: in Florida, 342, 343
Bailey, William, 107
Bailyn, Bernard, 7, 71
Baker, J. McRobert, 203n. 1
Baker County, 188
Balbentin's saloon (Tampa), 220
Bance Island, 38n. 22, 79, 82–84
Banks, Sophia, 226
Bantu, 44, 49
baptisms, 26, 31, **58, 59**
Baptist Convention, 263
Baptiste (cook), 75
Barbados, 72, 83

Bartram, William, 95
Bascom, William, 7, 43
basket making, 52–54, 76
Bastian, Victorian, 223
Beard, Lt. Col. Oliver, 169–70
Beasville, 245
Beatty, Blanche Armwood, 263, 265–67
Beaufort (South Carolina), 169–70, 175, 177, 189
Beckley, Lt. Alfred, 135
beer dances, 60–61
Bell, Duke, 73
Bell, John R., 129
Bell, William, 221
Bellamy, Abraham, 135
Bellamy, John, 107
Belton, Maj. F. S., 150
Bemrose, John, 142, 147
Benevolent Association of Colored Folks, 198
Benjamin, Stacio, 190
Benjamin, Stephen, 190
Benjamin, William, 191
Bennett, Herman V., 316–17
Berlin, Ira, 7, 10, 44–45
Bethune, Mary McLeod, 12, 240, 264–67
Bethune-Cookman College, 274n. 103
Betsy (nurse), 109
Biassou, Jorge, 32–33
Big Swamp, 129, 142
Bigtree, Camico, 220
Bilbo, Theodore, 298
Bird, Ida, 223
Birts, Lettie, 223
Bissett, Robert, 85
Black Auxiliaries, 32
Black Creek, 120, 175, 178
black militia: activities of, 32–33, 94; members of, 20, 28, 32; place in communities of, 23, 25, 28
blacks: activism of, 348–50; and conflicts with Cuban immigrants, 351–52, 354; friendships of, 189–91; and generational changes, 49–50; health of, 261–62; historiography of,

Carlos IV (Charles IV, King of Spain), 32
Carol City, 337
Carolina (slave), 88
Carr, James, 106–7
Carr, Jane, 107
Carr, William, 114
Carter, Dan, 5, 13
Carter, Mamie, 223
Carver Village apartments, 335, 337, 346, 347. *See also* Knight Manor apartments
Casey, John C., 141
Cass, Lewis, 140, 147
Castillo de San Marcos (St. Augustine), 36n. 7
Castro, Fidel, 14
Caswell Training School for the Feeble-Minded (North Carolina), 278
Catholicism, 28
Cato (slave), 121
cattle, 20, 78, 94, 246
Caty (slave), 138
Cecilton, 96
Central State Hospital (Petersburg), 276
Chaires, Ben, **113**
Chapman, William, 103n. 101
Charles (field hand), 112
Charles (runaway), 49
Charles (sawyer), 96
Charles (slave), 75
Charles Town (Charleston, South Carolina), 22, 72, 76, 78–79, 97; earthquake at, 200
Charlotte Cape (ship), 83
Charlotte Harbor, 134
Charlotte (Peace) River, 129
Charlotte (runaway), 159–60
Charlotte (slave), 116
Chaseville, 178
Chemonie plantation, 109, 111, 116, 117
Chesapeake Bay system, 44
Chesebro farm, 243
Chesley (slave), 110
children: abuse of, 237n. 89; baptism of,

26; freedom for, 29–30; importance of, 90; of interracial unions, 28–29
chivalry, 302
Chloe (slave), 80
Chocote (chief), **136**
churches: African Baptist Church, 52; African Methodist Episcopal church, 56, 349; and Baptist Convention, 263; functions of, 6–7; Shiloh Baptist Church, **59**
cigar industry, 209, **216**, 251, 253. *See also* tobacco industry
Cimarron (boat), 167
Citizens Action League, 335
Citizens' Ticket (coalition), 202
citrus industry, 249–50, 299–300
civil rights, 2, 12, 309, 349–51. *See also* legal system
Civil Rights Act (1964), 14
Civil Rights Congress, 348
Civil War: and Antietam, 163; Confederate forces in, 158, 161, 164–65, 174–75; families during, 161; guerilla activities in, 165–66; and social change, 187; truce during, 165. *See also* abolitionism; Union forces
Claiborne, Thomas, 194, 199
Clara Frye Municipal Negro Hospital (Tampa), 257–58
Clara White Mission, 263
Clark, Alexander, 161
Clark, Lucreaty, 53
Clay County, 159–61
Clearwater, 283
Clinch, Col. Duncan, 144, 147–49
Club 436 (Altamonte Springs), 310
coartacion (right of self-purchase), 18, 21, 29–31
Coconut Grove, 336, 338, 340
Coconut Grove Citizens' Committee for Slum Clearance, 340
Cohen, Mayer, 141
Coi Hadjo (chief), 143, 146
Coleman, Antonio, 28
Colescott, James A., 344, 346
Collins, Juan Bautista, 28

Collins, LeRoy, 317–18, 320, 345, 351

Colored Law and Order League, 198

Colored Medical Protective Health Association, 198

Colored Town (in Miami). *See* Overtown (in Miami)

Colson, J. H., 275

Comfort, Robert F., 194

Communist party, 303

communities: administration of, 23; and agricultural crops, 72; and ceremonies, 32, 60–61; destruction of, 337; establishment of, 1, 3–4, 10, 23–24, 185, 299; and interstate system, 331–32; and redlining, 329; and refugees, 26; social networks in, 187, 189–91, **190**, 197, 227; spatial isolation of, 326, 337–38, 344; and support for mentally handicapped, 283–84. *See also* LaVilla; Overtown (in Miami)

compadrazgo, 23

Conecuh County (Alabama), 45

Confederate forces, 158, 161, 164–65, 174–75

confiscation act (1861), 162

Congo, 43, 53

Congress of Racial Equality (CORE), 348–51

Cook, Samuel, 135

coquina, 20

Coral Gables, 329, 338

CORE. *See* Congress of Racial Equality

Cortés, Hernando, **19**

cotton, 81

crafts, 52–54, 76

Creeks (tribe), 129, 140, 142–46

Creole cultures, 47

Crestview subdivision, 338

Cryer, Andrew, 160

Cryer, Joseph, 160

Cuba: exploration of, 19; immigration from, 14, 326–27, 337, 351–52, 354; resettlement to, 25, 33–34; runaways to, 133; and slave trade, 19, 49; trade with, 134; traditions of, **22**

Cuban Revolution (1959), 351

Cudjo (agent), 141–42, 147

Culekeechowa (Indian), 138

cultures: adaptation of, 45, 63–64; from Africa, 42–44, 49–50, 52–53, 61; creolization of, 47; persistence of, 7, 42–44, 52. *See also* traditions

Cumberland Sound, 47

Dade, Maj. Francis L., 150

Dade County: election system in, 356; integration in, 348, 351; and relocation of blacks, 329, 333, 335–37; and zoning policies, 328–29, 332–33, 336

Dade County Planning Board, 329

Dade County Property Owners Association, 335

Dade County Zoning Board, 336

Dahomey, 43

dance: traditions of, 48, 54–57, 60–61

Darien (Georgia), 133

Daughters of Israel, 198

Dave (slave), 168

David (slave), 109

Davis, Milton H., 337

Deagan, Kathleen, 35

death: beliefs and rituals concerning, 50–52, 61–63

DeBose, E. H., 261–62

Delia (slave), 50–51

Dell, J. Maxey, 281–84

Derrick, Bessie, 245

Derrick, George, 245

desegregation, 285, 346–49

Dexter, Horatio, 131, 138

Diaz, John A., 332

Dickerson, James, 53

Dickerson, Sarah, 222

Dickison, Capt. J. J., 169

Dick (slave), 115

Dick (slave and cook), 76

Dick (slave and fisherman), 90

Dictator (steamer), 178

Didion, Joan, 326

Dieterlen, G., 61

disease: resistance to, 73

Doctor's Lake, 163

federal government: and treatment of feeble-minded, 12, 284–85. *See also* New Deal

Federal Housing Administration, 329

feebleminded. *See* mentally handicapped

Ferguson, Elijah, 216

Ferguson, Leland, 35

Fernández, Juan, **24**

Fernandina, 255; blacks settled in, 178; runaways to, 168–69, 175; Union capture of, 158–59

Fiddler's Flat, **59**

Fiery Cross, The (newspaper), 344

Fiftieth Street Heights, Inc., 336

Finegan, Gen. Joseph, 160, 164–69, 174

Fisher, Bob, 222

Fitzgerald, Capt. J. W., 199

Flemming, David, 164

Florida: abolition of slavery in, 163; British evacuation of, 85, 96–97; ceded to Great Britain, 4, 25, 73; ceded to United States, 33, 128; census of, 130; characteristics of, 3, 129; historiography of, 1–3, 5, 15, 35; legislature of, 177, 202, 348; policies of, 140, 275–76, 279; population of, 3, 5, 51–52, 240–41, **243, 244, 245;** Reconstruction in, 5; retroceded to Spanish, 8, 25; settlement of, 104–5, 128–30; slavery in, 17–18, 48–49; as tourist center, 240. *See also* East Florida; Middle Florida

Florida Agricultural and Mechanical College, 258, 260, 264

Florida Children's Commission, 286

Florida Cigar Company, 251, 253

Florida Constitution (1868), 202

Florida Council on Human Relations, 341

Florida Farm Colony for Epileptic and Feeble-Minded: admission of blacks to, 275, 285–89; discrimination at, 275, 281–83; funding for, 284–87; reports of, 279, 281–82, 285–87, 289; segregation of, 287–90

Florida Institute, 197–98

Florida Land and Lumber Company, 178

Florida Medical, Dental and Pharmaceutical Association, 257

Florida Progressive Voters League, 299, 346

Florida Railway and Navigation Company, 193

Florida State Pardon Board, 318

Florida State Road Department, 331

Florida Supreme Court, 264, 308, 310

Florida Writers Project, 243, 327

Floridian Hotel (Tampa), 247

Floyd, George, 160–61, 178

folk beliefs, 50–51

Forbes, James, 152n. 22

Forbes, John, 91–92

Forester, Affa, 178

Forester, George, 160

Forester, Lewis, 160, 178

Forman, Silas, 178

Fort George, 115

Fort Gibson, 143–44

Fort King, 142

Fort Lauderdale, 349

Fort Mose. See Gracia Real de Santa Teresa de Mose

Fort Myers, 276

Fort Steele, 158

Forum, 212

Foster, Amy, 223

Fraleigh, Mrs. L. A., 248

Francois (butler), 75

Frank (laborer), 159–60

Frank (slave), 90

Frazier, E. Franklin, 60

Fredrickson, George, 278

free blacks: attitudes toward, 34; British treatment of, 25; and Fort Steele construction, 158; as go-betweens, 49; leisure of, 28; occupations of, 26, 28; origins of, 23, 49–51; population statistics on, 20; and Spanish traditions, 18. *See also* Union forces: blacks in

305; investigation of, 308–10, 317–18; newspaper coverage of, 302–3, 308–10, 313, 315, 317; and pretrial publicity, 310–11; reactions to, 301–2; retrial of, 315–17; testimony in, 306–8; verdict in, 308, 318; and vigilantes, 301–2
Guinea, 85
Gullah language, 57–58
gunboats: and refugees, 161–64, 167, 169, 175; resistance to, 166; as route to freedom, 157
Guthrie, Riley, 286
Guthrie Report, 286

Hagen, Alexander, 161
Hagen, Frank, 161
Haiti, 60–61
Halifax River, 78–79
Hall, Bolden, 106, 121
Hall, David, 178, 191
Hall, Gwendolyn, 3, 7, 35, 39n. 34
Hall, Jacqueline Dowd, 302
Hamilton, Fanny, 191
Hamilton, Fred: social network of, **190**, 191
Hamilton County, 246
Hampton, Effie Carrie Mitchell, 255, 267
Hampton, F. L., 306
Hampton, L. R., 257
Hanahan, Henry, 160, 178
Hanger, Kimberly, 35
Hannah (runaway), 120
Hannibal (runaway), 96
Hanson, Daniel Dustin, 177–78
Hansontown, 178
Hardy, Ira, 278
Harford (slave), 75
Harlem Studio (West Palm Beach), 260
Harris, Bill, 317–18
Harris, Carey A., 145
Harris, Donorena, 117, 119
Harrison, Henry, 168
Harry (carpenter), 81
Harry (warrior), 150

Hart, Ambrose B., 63
Hastings, 245
Hately, Col. John C., 165
Havana (Cuba), **22**, 134
Hawkins, Virgil, 264
Hawks, Esther Hill, 175, 177
Hawks, John Milton, 178
Hayes, Arthur Garfield, 264
Haygood, Atticus, 212
head rights system, 20
health care: black professionals in, 255, 257–59; and midwives, 258–59, **259**; and resistance to disease, 73; and root doctors, 50–51; surveys of, 286; and yellow fever epidemic (1745), 73. *See also* mentally handicapped
Helping Hand Day Nursery and Kindergarten, 263
Henderson, John, 226
Hendrix, Bill, 346
Hendry, George, 213
Henry, Rosa Lee, 248, 270n. 36
Henry (soldier), 173
Heriot, Benjamin, 150
Hernández, Joseph, 153n. 46
Herries, Philip, 101n. 58
Herskovits, Melville J., 6–7, 43–44, 57, 60
Hewie (overseer), 81–82, 87
Hicks, Amelia J., 260
Hicks, John, 133
Higginson, Col. Thomas Wentworth, 170–73, 177
High, Robert King, 351
Hill, Horace, 306
Hill, Viola T., 263
Hills, James, 161
Hillsborough County, 211, 243, 255, 259, 284
Hillsborough County Court, 284
Hillsborough County School Board, 255
Hilton Head (South Carolina), 162–63
Hirsch, Arnold R., 5, 14, 331
Hispanics, 3, 14, 326–27, 337, 351–52, 354. *See also* Cuba
Hispaniola, 1, 18, 32

mentally handicapped (*continued*) 79, 281, 284–85; institutionalization of, 279–80, 282–83; segregation of, 275–77, 279–80, 288; surveys on care of, 286; treatment of, 11–12. *See also* institutions for mentally handicapped

Mercy Hospital (St. Petersburg), 258

Merrick, George, 329

Mexico, 34

Miami: charter-reform debate in, 345; conditions in, 355–56; desegregation in, 349–51; diversity in, 13–14, 327; economic development in, 329–32; growth of, 2; Hispanics in, 14, 326–27, 337, 351–52, 354; interstate in, 330–32; killings in, 342; neighborhoods in, 326; ordinances of, 340; police in, 342–44; riots in, 326; second ghetto in, 332–37; segregation in, 338; truck farms near, 243; and urban redevelopment, 331–38, **339**. *See also* Ku Klux Klan; Overtown (in Miami)

Miami Beach: wade-in at, 349

Miami Herald, 327, 329, 337, 341–42, 345

Miami Police Department, **333**, 342

Miami Realty Board, 329

Miami Transit Company, 349

Micanopy (chief), 141, 143–44, 147

Mickens, Alice, 263

Mickler, Jacob, 160

Middle Florida: relations in, 107, 109–11; religion in, 105–7; work patterns in, 111–12, 114–15

Middleton, Benjamin, 190–91

Middleton, Diana, 196

Middleton, Isaac, 191, 196

Middleton, Lymus, 190–91

Middleton, Scipeo, 190

midwives, 258–59, **259**

Mikasukians (Miccosukees), 150

Miller, Robert, 212

Milligan, John D., 45

Milo (slave), 49

Minor, Henry, 112

Minto (slave), 80

missionaries, 49, 62

Mississippi River, 129

Missouri, 163

Mitchell, David, 34

Mohawk (ship), 61

Molly (slave), 115–16

Moncrief, James, 77

Monroe, James, 34

Montgomery, Col. James, 172–73

Montgomery (Alabama), 257

Moore, Harry T., 267, 299, 315, 320, 346

Moore, J. P., 222

Moore, Laura, 222

Morgan, George, **58**

Morris, William, 161

Morrison, James W., 338

mortality rates, 262

mortuary customs, 50–52, 61–63

Mosquito District, 84

Motte, Jacob Rhett, 130, 141

Moultrie, James, 73

Moultrie, John, 73, 85–86, 90–91, 93–94, 96

Moultrie Creek treaty, 129, 134, 147

Mount Dora Topic, 302, 308, 313

Mount Oswald plantation, 79, 81–84, 87, 93, 97

Mount Royal plantation, 74, 95

Moxley, D. N., 106, 111

Mugge's saloon (Tampa), 220, 224

Mugin (slave), 115

Mulberry Grove, 168

Mulcaster, Frederick George, 91

Mullin, Michael, 3, 17–18

Municipal Hospital for Negroes (Tampa), 257

Murat, Achille, 112, 115

Murray, Andrew, 160

Muskogee, State of, 28

NAACP. *See* National Association for the Advancement of Colored People (NAACP)

NAACP Legal Defense Fund. *See* National Association for the Advancement of Colored People: Legal Defense Fund of

day laborers, 192; in domestic ser-
vice, 247–49; lawsuits over, 299; for
midwives, 259; for nurses, 258; in
phosphate industry, 249; of slaves,
26, 90; in tobacco industry, 251; on
truck farms, 243–44
Walker, Jonathan, 121
Walker, Mrs. R. H., 260
Wally (overseer), 115
Wanderer (ship), 49
Warnell Lumber and Veneer Company
No. 17 Laundry, **254**
Warren, Fuller, 286, 301, 304, 313,
315, 335
wars: Indian, 8, 32; Patriot, 28, 34; Red
Stick, 144; Revolutionary, 25, 46, 85,
97; Seminole, 49, 126n. 63, 135, 146;
Spanish-American, 342; World War I,
249, 263; World War II, 285, 299–300,
346. *See also* Civil War
Washington School, **256**
Watkins, Berta Mae, 264
Watson, Leola, 251
Waukeenah plantation, 109
Way, Andrew, 95
Webb, Richard, 215
Welaka, 160
Welaunee plantation, 109
Welfare League (Tampa), 254
Wells, Irene, 248
West Africa: blacks from, 77; names
from, 46–47; spirit possession in, 60;
traditions from, 44–45
West Indies, 78, 85
Westscott, James, 140
White, Eartha, 262–67
White, Joseph, 137
White Citizens' Council movement, 346
Whitehead family, 213
white primary system, 298–99, 347
whites: attitudes of, 278, 302; in domes-
tic service jobs, 249; and fears of rape,
212–14, 224–25; residential areas of,
332–33, 335, 337
Wiet, Juan Bautista, **27**
Wiggins, Job, 38–39nn. 29–30

Wiggins, Nansi, 38–39nn. 29–30
Wildfire (ship), 61
Wilkerson, Judge, 105–6
Wilkinson, John, 94
Williams, Benjamin, 160
Williams, D. E., 255
Williams, Edward, 220
Williams, Franklin, 303–6, 308, 315
Williams, Henry, 161
Williams, James, 161
Williams, John Lee, 141
Williams, William, 220
Williams, Willis, 121
Williamson, Joel, 5
Williams (ship), 61
Will (slave), 75–76
Wilson, Charles, 178
Wilson, Claude Augusta, 106
Winslett, John, 120, 134
Winter (slave), 117
Wirt, Ellen, 112, 114
Wirt, Henry, 110, 116
Wirt, Louis, 116
Wirt, William, 109–10, 114
Wirtland plantation, 107, 109, 112,
115, 116
Wiseheart, Malcolm B., 336–37
Withlacoochee River, 129
Witten, Glasgow, 26
Witten, Judy, 26, 28, 32
Witten, María Rafaela (Polly), 26, 33
Witten, Prince, 26, **27**, 32, 33
women: in agriculture, 243–46, 248–
50; discrimination against, 241; in
domestic service, 194, 246–49; histori
ography of, 12, 240; in Ku Klux Klan,
346; in laundry business, 253, **254**; as
midwives, 258–59; occupations of,
28–29, 194–96, **196**, 241, 260–61, **261**;
in politics, 266–67; in professions,
253–55, 257–60; as reformers, 262–67;
roles of, 240, 255, 266–67; statistics
on, 194–95, **197**; in tobacco industry,
250, 251, **252**, 253; and violence,
221–24; voting rights of, 266
Women's Bureau, 253